Morell Mackenzie

Essays

Morell Mackenzie

Essays

ISBN/EAN: 9783742827241

Manufactured in Europe, USA, Canada, Australia, Japa

Cover: Foto ©Andreas Hilbeck / pixelio.de

Manufactured and distributed by brebook publishing software (www.brebook.com)

Morell Mackenzie

Essays

BY
SIR MORELL MACKENZIE.

"Luceo non uro."

LONDON:
SAMPSON LOW, MARSTON & COMPANY
LIMITED,
St. Dunstan's House,
Fetter Lane, Fleet Street, E.C.
1893.
[*All rights reserved.*]

CONTENTS.

	PAGE
SPECIALISM IN MEDICINE	1
MEDICAL SPECIALISM: A REJOINDER	22
IS MEDICINE A PROGRESSIVE SCIENCE?	36
HEALTH-SEEKING IN TENERIFE AND MADEIRA	49
SPEECH AND SONG:	
PART I.—SPEECH	71
PART II.—SONG	89
THE DREADFUL REVIVAL OF LEPROSY	109
THE REFORM OF THE COLLEGE OF SURGEONS	132
THE EFFECT OF SMOKING ON THE VOICE	159
THE USE AND ABUSE OF HOSPITALS	169
EXERCISE AND TRAINING:	
EXERCISE	194
EXERCISE (*continued*)	202
TRAINING: ITS BEARING ON HEALTH (I.)	214
TRAINING: ITS BEARING ON HEALTH (II.)	227
TRAINING: ITS BEARING ON HEALTH (III.)	236
INFLUENZA	245
THE NEW YACHTING	259
THE RELATION OF GENERAL CULTURE TO PROFESSIONAL SUCCESS	288
SWIMMING	302

SPECIALISM IN MEDICINE.

AMONG so many changes of wider importance, the revolution of opinion which has taken place in regard to specialism in the practice of the healing art is likely to be overlooked. Yet any one who should take the trouble to glance through the medical journals of twenty-five years ago and compare the tone of their remarks on this subject with that of those of the present day could not fail to be struck by the contrast. Then the very name of "specialist" was a bar sinister excluding a man from the more highly coveted hospital appointments and from admission to some of the principal professional societies. The medical press lost no chance of abusing him; his brethren sneered at him in public and slandered him in private. Is it wonderful, then, that even moderate men, brought up in the traditions of old-fashioned medical practice, should have looked askance at specialism as something not quite orthodox, or at least of questionable respectability? This treatment, on the other hand, produced its natural effect on specialists, leading them sometimes into errors of taste and judgment, for which only the excuse of extreme provocation could be pleaded. It is a significant fact that the hostility to specialism not only originated within the medical profession, but has been all along almost entirely confined to that body. Was the cause of this dislike mere irrational conservatism, or, as the doctors said, virtuous indignation at an *opprobrium medicinæ* of a novel kind? Or was it rather, as the profane did not hesitate to affirm, the outcome of an undignified jealousy? Perhaps, as human motives are generally mixed, all these forces were at work. Specialism was a new thing, and the conservative instincts of the College of Physicians were strong against innovation. It may have had a presentiment that the new dispensation would change the order of things and sweep away old landmarks. In the days of periwigs and gold-headed canes it had striven to hold the surgeons, and at a later period the apothecaries, in subjection to its authority; in the same way it now opposed the emancipation of specialists.

Now everything is changed; specialism has taken its place among recognized institutions, the millennium has come upon the medical world, and the wolf lies down with the lamb in the most edifying manner. Notwithstanding all this, the hatred of specialism is suppressed rather than extinct. The change, such as it is, is entirely due to pressure from without; public opinion has, in fact, declared itself with such emphasis on the side of the specialists that the profession has been coerced into sullen acquiescence in the inevitable. The initiated, however, can see sparks of the still smouldering fires in many subtle but unmistakable signs. The latent feeling reveals itself in suggestive shrugs of the shoulders or elevation of the eyebrows at the mention of certain names; sometimes even in sly innuendo or in mild detraction, which is all the more effective because it is couched in a tone rather of sorrow than of anger. Again, there is the almost indecent eagerness with which any error or oversight on the part of a specialist is proclaimed, and the too obvious intent with which it is made the text of a discourse on the uselessness of specialists. It may be pointed out that this form of hostility altogether misses its mark, as it is really an unconscious and consequently all the more cogent testimony to the superior skill of the persons attacked. No one thinks any blunder, however gross, on the part of an ordinary physician worth even a momentary feeling of surprise; and if it were to be argued that because one practitioner has erred doctors are useless, what would become of the profession?

If specialists did not meet a distinct want they would soon be driven off the field. It is idle to inquire whether in this instance the demand created the supply, or *vice versâ*; all that we are concerned with here is the fact that the public voice decisively approves of the existence of specialists. This is convincingly demonstrated as time goes on by the increasing confidence which is placed in their opinion and advice. A striking confirmation of this is afforded by the circumstance, that, when medical men have sickness in their own families they put prejudice aside and invoke the assistance of the despised specialist. In my own province it is my pleasure and privilege to treat a large number of my professional brethren, with whose personal ailments or those of their wives and children I am occupied during a considerable portion of each working day. Many other specialists are doubtless recipients of the like indisputably sincere form of compliment. The growing favour with which specialism is looked on by the public is also fully recognized by young physicians, and still more by successful general practitioners ambitious of emerging into the more rarefied atmosphere of consulting work. The press of competition is so fierce in the present overcrowded state of the medical profession, that, unless a man has some peculiar and decided advantage over the general run of his fellows he stands no chance of coming to the front. Something more is necessary nowadays for success in the higher walks of medicine than mere general ability. Supreme talent will, of course, ultimately find its level, unless kept down by accident or misfortune; but for the average clever man there is little prospect of brilliant success unless he has (or can persuade the world he has) the power of doing some particular thing better than any one else, or at any rate pre-eminently well.

It may not unnaturally be asked why specialism was so vehemently opposed by the medical profession. In the first place it was, as already said, what Americans call a "new departure," and as nearly every page of the history of human progress shows, the pioneers of any onward movement have been exceptionally fortunate if they escaped persecution. Again, there is an innate tendency in human nature to look with suspicion on knowledge or skill which is the possession of a select few. The distrust of doctors as a class, which is still sometimes met with (by no means always among the ignorant), is in itself an illustration of this. Coming, however, to more definite examples of this form of jealousy, we find that it especially pervades limited societies of men, as may be seen in the case of guilds and trades-unions. Among the rules of the latter associations, at any rate in their earlier days, there were many which had for their object the reduction of the skilled artisan to the position of the ordinary labourer; indeed the spirit is the note of a certain form of communism which would lower all men to the same level. The medical Corporations of this country have retained many of their mediæval traditions, and though they have not been able to oppose specialism actively, some of them have by mild ostracism endeavoured to exclude specialists from positions of distinction within their own bodies. It is certain, however, that this natural attitude of mankind towards anything wearing the semblance of monopoly or privilege was, in the case of specialism, deliberately encouraged by a portion of the medical press from motives of enlightened self-interest. When there were twenty thousand general practitioners in England, and only a few hundred specialists, it was obviously in accordance with trade instinct to minister to the prejudices of the greatest number. I am happy to say, however, that there have always been some medical journals which have placed the interests of science above financial prosperity and professional influence, and which, without particularly favouring specialism, have shown an honest independence in the matter. Especially has one important paper, as the organ of a powerful Association, always stood above mere mercantile considerations.

Opposition in the public prints had for good and sufficient reasons to be carried on professedly from a quasi-scientific point of view; there was necessarily more of the argumentative than of the frankly vituperative element in their diatribes on specialism. In private however, where no such reticence was needed, envy, hatred, and all uncharitableness found the freest expression. At the dinner-table, at the medical societies, in the gossip that relieves the aridity of scientific discussion, at all places where doctors most do congregate, specialism and its professors were denounced with a wealth of epithet that the refined controversialists of Billingsgate might have envied.

The Nestors of the profession shook their heads and augured ill of the "promising young men" who were already making larger incomes than they themselves had done at a much later period of their career. It was whispered and even said aloud that specialism was not "respectable."

Now this imputation, it must be allowed, was admirable as a stroke of fence, however a fine moral sense may condemn it. In the breast of the ordinary middle-class John Bull no emotion is stronger than the desire to appear "respectable;" in the heart of the medical body corporate this feeling is intensified almost into a passion. The truth is that in this country at least we are just a little doubtful as to our position in the social scale, and we are naturally therefore somewhat ticklish about the matter. Indeed, from the way in which medical men sometimes talk about the "dignity of the profession," it would almost seem as though that were always the first object to be considered. Some of us need to be occasionally reminded that the profession exists for, and I may add by, the public, not the public for the profession. Touching this subject of respectability, a thoughtful foreigner, who has evidently resided many years in this country, has remarked in a little work which has recently appeared, that in England "professions rise or fall in dignity and repute according as they are or are not connected with the State." Not to mention the army and navy, which actually wear the Queen's livery, the clergy through the episcopal bench hold a high position. The Bar again is in close connection with the Crown through the judges and other high legal officers of State; but the medical profession, though a few individuals have personal relations with royalty, includes within its rank no high functionaries of the realm. Feeling itself therefore to be rather at a disadvantage as compared with its learned sisters, it is anxious to make up for lack of social position by increased respectability. No more poisoned arrow could have been shot against specialism than the allegation that its existence in some way dimmed the lustre of our respectability or lowered the esteem in which the profession is held.

In America, where there is no "leisured class" to look down upon those who labour, the medical faculty is recruited from the best families in the land, and its members accordingly act with an independence quite unknown in this country. Under these circumstances, specialism, instead of meeting with opposition, was received with open arms. I may say that when I was travelling in the United States three years ago,* nothing astonished me more than the universal diffusion of specialism. It would be almost impossible to find a city with ten thousand inhabitants in which there were not at least three or four specialists; whilst in one city, with a population of only one hundred and thirty thousand, I found thirteen specialists exclusively engaged in treating throat diseases. Indeed the practical genius of the American people was never more clearly evinced than in the manner in which it embraced specialism. In England, on the other hand, there are many towns with a population of fifty or sixty or even a hundred thousand persons without a single laryngoscopist. In France also, where class distinction has been to a great extent done away with, and where there are between thirty and forty doctors in the Chamber of Deputies, the medical profession is much more unconstrained, and accordingly it has not been found necessary to bolster up the position of medical practitioners by artificial codes. This being the case, it is natural to find that specialism has spread much more quickly and established itself much more widely in France than in England. In Germany, again, specialism is almost universal; in fact, this is perhaps one of the strongest points in its favour, as it shows how specialism is a natural development in the midst of the highest culture. The examples of Germany and America prove, moreover, that where education is most widely diffused, there specialism finds the kindliest soil to flourish in—a fact which of itself should silence those who do not scruple to hint that it is a mode of trading on human ignorance.

Jealousy of specialism rankles alike in the breast of the "pure" physician and in that of the general practitioner. The former sees his empire slowly but surely passing away, and his place and function in the profession becoming obsolete. I am speaking, of course, of London, where "pure" physic is now

* In 1882.

represented only by two or three eminent men who maintain their position owing to their connection with the Court, and by a very few (and their number grows less year by year) who, as successful clinical teachers, have established a large *clientèle* amongst their former pupils. Many young doctors, highly equipped with degrees and other academical distinctions, start every year on the race for wealth and honour as "pure" physicians, but the force of circumstances drives them sooner or later, avowedly or not, into a speciality. Although attached to general hospitals and posing there as champions of anti-specialism, they become known to the profession and to the public only as men who have paid special attention to some particular disease or group of diseases, from which, it may be added, they in point of fact derive their entire income. It is only natural and human that amongst those veiled specialists are to be found the most virtuous and virulent opponents of specialism "naked and not ashamed." In like manner operating surgeons are often mere specialists in disguise, though, of course, they would protest in a most life-like tone of outraged innocence if they were accused of such a thing. Specialists, however, they are *ex vi termini*, even the most enterprising among them, and the operative speciality at its broadest is after all essentially a narrow one. Many operating surgeons, however, limit their range still further by confining themselves to a single organ or a group of closely interconnected organs.

The general practitioner, on the other hand, is jealous of the specialist, but with less reason. He at least is in no danger of being improved off the face of the earth like the physician; but still he finds his position with regard to the consultant gradually changing, and not perhaps altogether to his own advantage in some ways. The old relations between consultants and general practitioners were of a very pleasant character. Those "calling in" a certain physician were generally former pupils; by meeting their old teacher they were to some extent kept abreast of advancing knowledge, and any oversight on their part in diagnosis or treatment was sure to be very tenderly handled. This relation is still to a considerable extent kept up in the suburbs of London, but patients are beginning to show much more independence than formerly, and insist on consulting whom they please, the opinion sought being often that of a specialist. Not so very long ago the general practitioner looked upon his patient as his private property, and trespassers were warned off with all the terrors of exposure in the pillory of the medical journals. He now feels that his position has lost something of its security, for he knows that if his patient does not rapidly mend, inquiry will be made for the name and address of the greatest authority on the disease in question, to whose care his patient will straightway commit himself. The family doctor thus comes to look on the specialist as a receiver of stolen goods, if not as the actual thief. The latter, on the other hand, is often placed in a difficult position, for if any special treatment is required, it is too likely that the general practitioner will not be competent to carry it out, whilst if the specialist retains the patient under his own immediate care he is open to misconstruction of a kind that is peculiarly galling to an honourable man.

The opposition to specialism in medicine is the more curious because, so far as I know, no ignominy or discredit has ever been supposed to attach to specialists in any other profession. The practice of the law is more highly specialized than that of medicine, yet no objection has ever been raised either on the part of the legal profession or the public to this subdivision of labour; and though no doubt a Chancery barrister thinks himself a little above an Old Bailey practitioner, yet the specialist practising at the Parliamentary bar, or in the Probate, Divorce, Admiralty, or Ecclesiastical Courts, and those confining themselves to Bankruptcy or to Patents, all hold an equally good professional position. Again, surely painters are not despised who, deeming excellence in one thing more worthy of attainment than mediocrity in many, give themselves entirely to one line of work, training their eyes to see and their hands to limn every smallest detail within their chosen range. Has Cooper been jeered at for spending his days in the sole endeavour to paint cattle supremely well? Was Landseer scorned because his brush was wholly given up to the forms and attitudes, the virtues and vanities of our "poor relations"? Does the

Academy close its august portals to those who confine themselves to landscape, or sea, or the human form divine? To take even an extreme instance of specialism, who shall say that Canaletto wasted his powers in the utter devotion of them to the palace walls and watery thoroughfares of Venice? The engineering profession is of comparatively modern growth as regards many departments, yet putting aside military, naval, and civil engineers, there are mechanical, mining, hydraulic, marine, railway, electrical, gas, and sanitary specialists, and this classification is far from being exhaustive. Engineers have to deal with inert matter which can be accurately weighed and measured, not with "vital force," and the uncertain quantities connected with physiological and pathological conditions. It might therefore be thought that so great a multiplication of specialities was in this instance unnecessary, if not actually inconvenient. Experience, however, has proved the contrary. The tendency, indeed, is towards the still further division of each of the great branches of engineering, and this is felt by practical men to be inevitable; so far, indeed, from specialists being ostracized, they are encouraged to perfect their work by limiting its range.

After all, whatever be the result to the medical profession, there can be no doubt that the existence of specialism is a distinct advantage to the public. The laity, which does not concern itself about the internal dissensions of the medical body, and which has never treated even the decencies of orthodox medicine with more than modified respect, was not long in settling the question for itself. Approaching the matter as it did from a mere business point of view, the decision could not be doubtful. It was obvious that a man who gave himself wholly up to doing one thing thoroughly well was more likely to be successful in his aim than persons of wider range but less concentration. When the general opinion on the subject became too clear for even the dullest to misapprehend, medical men found themselves obliged to look at specialism from a different standpoint, and in self-defence to establish a *modus vivendi* with it. The necessity of specialism in medicine may now be said to have been solemnly ratified by the profession at large by the institution of the International Congresses which have been held in recent years. These meetings are almost entirely based on the idea of subdivision of labour which is the great principle underlying specialism, so that they constitute at once a formal recognition and a gigantic concrete example of it. It was not, however, till the Congress of Copenhagen (1884) that the existing specialities were fully represented each in an independent section. The programme of the London Congress (1881) was disfigured by an act of petty jealousy which at one time threatened to create a small schism. Only those behind the scenes know the heart-burnings and intrigues and all the arts of diplomatic finesse that were required to wring even partial recognition from the stage managers of that most successful "show." If the plain unvarnished tale of this storm in a teacup could ever be unfolded to the public, how greatly would the revelation add to the respect in which our noble profession is held!

But it may be asked, What is this "monster of such fearful mien" that has excited such unholy wrath where the Olympian serenity of science should reign undisturbed? Is it, to speak plainly, a system of downright imposture, a "sham" in short, or a super subtle refinement of half-conscious quackery? Or a short cut to fame and fortune without too nice regard to the cleanness of the road? Or, to be more charitable, is it, however honest, a delusion and a snare, an unnecessary overgrowth of our somewhat rankly luxuriant civilization, or at best a necessary evil? Now, it may be as well for me to say here that, in upholding *specialism*, it is no part of my thesis that *specialists* must individually be immaculate, any more than that every one of them must possess the highest skill. There are black sheep in every fold, and a man may make a medical speciality a means of fraud as easily as he can pretend to cure all diseases. Unscrupulous opponents have, no doubt, tried to establish in the public mind an association between specialism and humbug, and they have been careful to guard themselves from retort by declaring that their blows were aimed, not at the thing, but at its abuse. I have no desire to question the good faith of these righteous persons, but, like the bear in the fable, they crush the head of specialism in their eagerness to destroy a fly on its face. They involve the system itself and the just men who honestly practise it in the assault which they profess to direct solely against the sinners who trade on it. I am inclined to think, however, that it is not so much in special fields of practice that charlatanism flourishes most abundantly as in the vaguer and more nebulous region of "pure" physic, where plausible theories are less easy of disproof, and the consequences of treatment can less readily be traced. Hence it is among general physicians rather than among specialists that assumed airs of dignity take the place of the careful investigation of symptoms, and oracular sententiousness does duty for technical skill.

I now proceed to the main argument of my paper, and in discussing the nature of specialism it will be easy to show that in medicine, so far from being an evil, it is a distinct good; and that whilst it is necessary in some branches, it is, under certain conditions, desirable in all. Specialism is simply a recognition of the natural limitation of the powers of the human mind, and a deliberate concentration of a man's best powers on a single object. Thus stated, it would seem to be a mere truism to say that specialism is necessary for work to be effectual; and indeed this is accepted as an axiom in every other department of knowledge. In science and even in literature the mere accumulation of facts is so colossal that no single mind can hold anything but comparatively small fragments of the whole. The encyclopædic erudition of the Scaligers and Casaubons of a bygone age is altogether impossible to modern scholars; a scientific man who nowadays should, like Bacon, "take all learning to be his province" would be in danger of being sent to associate with kindred enthusiasts in Bedlam. Nowhere is the change more evident than in medicine. Physicians of the present day read with a feeling of half-amused wonder the mere list of Boerhaave's writings, which include essays *de omni scibili* in medical and natural science, and marvel at the complex talent of Haller, who embodied in his own single person a fairly complete professorial staff, besides being an accomplished linguist and a poet above mediocrity. Such leviathans of omniscience loom dim and gigantic through the

vista of the past like the megatherium and mastodon of remote
geological periods, and the type is as utterly extinct. In fact
the *Zeitgeist* looks with suspicion on universal learning, and
inclines to believe that the soundness of a man's knowledge
is in the inverse ratio of its extent. Whoso, indeed, is not
a specialist is at once set down as a dilettante. No one
comparing the present race of physicians with those of a time
not so very remote can fail to observe a remarkable dissimilarity,
less from a strictly professional point of view, than from the
difference in their mental equipment. The older physicians were
usually the foremost representatives of the best and widest
culture of their time. At once scholars and men of science,
they commanded respect more by the vastness of their erudition
than, it must be confessed, by the results of their practical
skill. They were often distinguished in literature. Arbuthnot
and Garth could associate with the wits of their day without
any sense of inferiority as regards culture. Our latter-day
doctors have altogether lapsed from the category of scholars;
they are now probably the least learned of the three liberal
professions. Even as men of science we are no longer up
to the level of our predecessors. The branches of knowledge
which were formerly considered as ancillary to medicine are
now on an altogether independent footing, and have even,
in a few instances, renounced their allegiance to their former
mistress. There are now anatomists and physiologists who
have never set foot within the walls of a hospital, whilst,
on the other hand, a knowledge of chemistry is deemed by
many a superfluous accomplishment in a physician.

The development and expansion of medicine and the
cognate sciences during the last half-century have probably
been greater than in all the previous ages of the world's history,
and the mass is every day growing larger and more unwieldy.
Under these circumstances specialism is simply unavoidable,
unless "a little learning" is to become the rule. No one,
I imagine, can seriously maintain the contrary. If, as already
shown, specialism is found necessary in the purely mechanical
arts, *a fortiori* the infinitely more intricate problems of medical
science, dealing as they do with organic matter in its most

complex development, can be thoroughly investigated only by a system of minute subdivision of labour. Take for example the single subject of diseases of the throat. The scientific literature relating to these dates from little more than twenty-five years back, and already it has grown to a bulk that would surfeit the voracity of the most persevering bookworm; and it goes on increasing and multiplying in a manner that makes one long for a Malthus to preach some degree of moderation to its producers. Every week, every day brings me books, pamphlets, articles, lectures, reprints about all sorts of uncomfortable things in *itis* and *osis*, as seen in the throats of Englishmen, Frenchmen, Germans, Italians, Danes, Russians, Americans, and all the other offspring of Babel. A certain proportion of these, no doubt, are of great value, but not a few might be consigned to the waste-paper basket without serious loss to science; all must be read, however, lest some grains of wheat should be thrown away with the chaff. Several periodicals dealing exclusively with diseases of the throat appear with praiseworthy regularity; and there are also societies, associations, etc., founded for the same purpose, each of which, of course, issues its yearly volume of transactions. All this makes up a solid mass of literary material the mere reading of which would fully employ all one man's time; to those who have other engagements the task is simply impossible. Abstracts of the more important papers are humanely furnished from time to time by the journals; but even with this help the burden is a heavy one for the strongest shoulders. This may give some faint idea of the Herculean labour which the specialist who wishes to keep abreast of the progress of knowledge in his own subject from the literary point of view alone has to undergo; and it must be remembered that in medicine reading is, after all, only subsidiary to the practical work by which skill is perfected and experience gathered and extended. Multiply the literary production of this one speciality by fifteen, the number of sections into which the London Medical Congress was divided (and even these do not adequately represent the full degree of specialization which medicine has now reached), and it will be conceded by the most bigoted anti-specialist that not only the natural limitation of each man's capacity but the elementary question of time makes it impossible for the conscientious worker to be other than a specialist.

It is clear that if specialism in knowledge has become the rule in medicine, specialism in practice must follow as a necessary corollary. In dealing with disease two things are requisite, diagnosis and treatment; that is to say, recognition of the nature of the evil, and the selection and right use of remedies to overcome it. I say advisedly "selection and right use," because it is one thing to know what ought to be done, and quite another thing to be able to do it. Now, diagnosis and treatment are just the points in which the healing art has made most progress in modern times, this advance being chiefly owing to the invention of "instruments of precision," whereby parts of the body formerly as inaccessible to our senses during life as the centre of the earth can be accurately explored and subjected to direct treatment. Many of these mechanical aids are of complicated structure, and all of them require much practice before they can be used with ease and accuracy. Now, life being, as Hippocrates said, "short," whilst "art is long," and is daily growing longer, in other words, more difficult to acquire, it is obvious that it is utterly impossible for one man to be equally skilled in all the departments of practical medicine. The mere enumeration of such things as the stethoscope, the ophthalmoscope, the laryngoscope, the microscope, the pleximeter, the cardiograph, the sphygmograph, the spirometer, to say nothing of the various electrical instruments, is sufficient to strike dismay into the most resolute heart. In general practice, no doubt, some of these aids can be and are dispensed with, but in cases which present any special difficulty the proper means of diagnosis must be employed or justice will not have been done to the patient.

The conclusion is absolutely inevitable that from the mere force of circumstances there must be specialists, *i.e.* men who by concentration of effort and larger opportunities of practice have acquired more than ordinary skill in one particular line. The Father of Medicine, himself the model and exemplar of general physicians, and a man of the most philosophic breadth of mind, acknowledged the necessity of specialists in at least one branch of practice requiring more than ordinary skill. In the oath which his disciples had to take before they were admitted to practise there was a clause whereby they bound themselves to leave a certain operation in the hands of those who had acquired special dexterity in its performance. Whilst referring to ancient times, it may not be superfluous to remind the reader that the most scientific of all the nations of antiquity —the Egyptians—had their medical organization based entirely on specialism. "So wisely," says Herodotus, "was medicine managed by them, that no doctor was permitted to practise any but his own peculiar branch. Some were oculists, who only studied diseases of the eye; others attended solely to complaints of the head; others to those of the teeth; some, again, confined themselves to complaints of the intestines, and others to secret and internal maladies." We have unfortunately no evidence, statistical or other, of the practical results of this system. Probably, however, they were as good—that is to say, as indifferent—as those which our modern general hospitals have to show.

The test of actual result is the only sure one in a subject so essentially practical as medicine. A few remarks must, however, be made on certain features of specialism in general which are often made the grounds of condemnation by its antagonists. Those "superior persons" talk of cramping and distortion of the intelligence as likely to result from its being always confined within a narrow range; of impairment of the mental vision as necessarily resulting from too close and too prolonged direction to one object; and even of the mind becoming the prey of its habitual occupation so that its whole outlook is finally coloured thereby. The man, in fact, after riding his hobby to the death, is in turn ridden by it to the disturbance of his mental equilibrium. There is not the slightest doubt that these dangers are far from being imaginary; the various tendencies just indicated have been the sport of satirists since the "wise man" of old who fell into the water whilst absorbed in the study of the stars. Such evil effects, however, are not by any means necessary consequences of exclusive devotion to a single subject. To take the alleged drawbacks seriatim. The "cramping" effect of specialism may easily be exaggerated. If the mind is narrowed thereby, may it not be said that what it loses in breadth it gains in depth? And after all is not this contraction better than the dilution or rather super-saturation of the mind that results from trying to absorb too much. It is a physiological truth that regular exercise strengthens not only the particular set of muscles called into play, but to a certain extent the whole muscular system. In like manner active use of the mental faculties, even if only in one direction, must in some measure tend to invigorate the intellect as a whole. The fact is that in medicine more than in most other branches of science the various parts are bound together in such close interdependence that it is impossible to understand one fact or one order of facts, i.e. know it in all its connotations, without a wide though possibly superficial acquaintance with the whole surrounding body of related facts. For this reason "cramping" of the mind is less likely to result from specialization in medicine than in simpler subjects of study. On the contrary, I maintain that a healthy specialism affords the mental powers the best mode of fruitful exercise. Moreover, it may be the duty of a man to run the risk, such as it is, of "cramping" his mind. Should not one suffer for the good of many? The specialist so amusingly described by Oliver Wendell Holmes, who could not pretend to the title of "entomologist" or even of "coleopterist," but humbly contented himself with the name of "scarabæist," would be sneered at by many self-styled philosophers as narrow; but can it be denied that though stunting their own intellectual stature such single-minded enthusiasts enlarge the boundaries of science? By an excessive use of the microscope the eyesight may be impaired or even destroyed, but who will revile the worker whose personal loss is the general gain? Every profession has its own special bane for the mind, and many industries leave their mark—often a fatal one—on the body. These dangers, however, must be encountered unless the world is to come to a standstill. If the workers suffer in mind or body from their occupation, should they not be regarded as heroes and martyrs rather than as fit objects for contempt or hatred? A specialist whose mind has become cramped from over-devotion to a useful pursuit should be looked upon with the same respect as a veteran who has lost a leg or an arm in fighting the battles of his country.

If cramping may be considered as the first degree of injury caused by specialism, the blindness to everything outside the narrow circle of one's own work may justly be called the second. This mole-like type of specialism is only an exaggeration of the first, and need not be more fully discussed. The third degree, which, again, is only the second pushed to its complete development, is of a more important type than the others, and it may in fact amount to monomania. When a man's intellect is "subdued to what it works in like the dyer's hand," he has reached a stage of mental deterioration in which he is unfit even for the cultivation of his own speciality. In the field of abstract science this surrender of his whole being to his study can lead to nothing worse than eccentricity. The chemist in Balzac's *Recherche de l'Absolu*, who analyzes the tears of his despairing wife, and the pedant who, whilst allowing that Frederick the Great might be a man of some practical ability, gravely doubted whether he could successfully conjugate a verb in $\mu\iota$, are examples of this crystallization of the mind round one object. In the sphere of medical practice, however, such men may be positively mischievous, if not dangerous. Whether it be the "mad doctor" who considers nobody quite *compos mentis*, or the physician who traces every ailment to gout or "liver," and treats it in the light of his theory, or the surgeon who thinks the nose the "hub" of the human microcosm, and therefore the proper object of attack in most diseases, a man possessed by a tyrannous *idée fixe* of any kind is not a safe guide. Or, to take less flagrant instances, by keeping only one particular end in view, the specialist may sometimes be led to over frequent or too prolonged local medication—a course of action which is often attributed to a less worthy motive. In connection with this subject I may perhaps be allowed to say that there is often much misapprehension, not only in the lay mind, but even amongst general practitioners, otherwise intelligent and well informed. Speaking from a not inconsiderable experience in my own particular line, I am disposed to affirm that even among specialists the importance of adequate local treatment is perhaps not always fully appreciated; at any rate, the conviction, if held, is not sufficiently acted upon. It is, however, an undeniable fact that those specialists are the most successful in their treatment who recognize the great principle that, in a large number of chronic diseases, local medication to be effectual must be persevering and gradual, in proportion to the length of time that the morbid process has been going on. Nevertheless this doctrine does not commend itself either to the sufferer, impatient to get well, and expecting to be cured by some physical equivalent to the "Hey presto" formula, nor to the general practitioner, who looks with natural and honest suspicion on any mode of treatment which acts as a derivative of fees from his own pocket. Both are apt to call loudly for more heroic measures; they will have no nonsense! They want something done, and quickly, or the patient will go elsewhere. Now this is not quite fair either to the specialist or to the patient. The belief in remedial agents that shall at once remove conditions which may have been in course of development for years indicates the survival of a barbarous superstition, and is no doubt founded on the ignorant view that every disease is a definite material entity to be cast out like a devil-in-possession by the exorcism of some potent drug. The careful observer, however, soon finds that he gains nothing, but rather loses ground, by too energetic measures, that the real principle of cure is expressed in the words of the poet, *Gutta cavat lapidem non vi sed sæpe cadendo*, and that any attempt to hasten the process is almost sure to end in failure.

In fairly well-balanced minds there is little fear of complete absorption by one subject, especially if a groundwork of broad general culture underlies the speciality. No medical specialist is to be trusted who has not received the best and widest education in medicine and surgery; and they undoubtedly make the best specialists who, either as physicians or surgeons at general hospitals or as family practitioners, have had the largest and most varied preliminary experience. If, under these advantageous circumstances, the change be not made too late in life, all previous work can be brought to a focus on one special point. Specialism of this sort, once fairly looked in the face and stripped of its imaginary horrors, cannot, I feel sure, excite anything but respect in the most conservative breast. However this may be, it is certain that specialism must become more and more developed in proportion to the advance of medical knowledge. We have evidence before our eyes that the process is actually going on. The present divisions are beginning to be still further subdivided. Thus ophthalmic surgery already comprises two if not three different specialities within itself: the purely operative department, the purely optical (more readily intelligible to the popular mind as that which deals with "glasses"), and lastly what may be called the "general practice" of the eye. Obstetric medicine has divided itself into two main branches, namely, that from which it derives its appellation, and that which concerns the diseases peculiar to women. The latter, again, is subdivided into smaller segments. One most justly celebrated man may almost be said to have confined himself to the practice of a single operation, the details and results of which he has been able by this concentration of energy to bring as near perfection as human fallibility permits. Need I say that at the outset of his career professional Podsnaps were as eager to "put down" this benefactor of the human race, as they now are to swell the chorus of praise which the mention of his name everywhere calls forth?

It is easy to foresee that, according to the laws of evolution, the "pure" physician will in time disappear, leaving only the general practitioner and the specialist. The time, indeed, is fast approaching when every physician will have to justify his existence by the possession real or supposed of pre-eminent talent in some one direction. The public is waking up to the fact that the many-sided man is apt to be untrustworthy, at least in the realm of practice. It is not meant to imply that a "good all round man" can ever be useless, but his domain is in the region of family practice. The vast improvement that has taken place in the whole scheme of medical education has made the general practitioner of the present day quite a different person from the "surgeon and apothecary" of the Bob Sawyer period. The level of professional knowledge and skill is in every way much higher than before, especially among the men who have left the schools during the last fifteen or twenty years. This of itself tends to make the consultant who is not a specialist a superfluity. The opinion of a "pure" physician is in fact grounded on a basis of attainments essentially similar in kind to that of the well-informed general practitioner, however it may surpass it in degree. What is wanted, however, in really difficult cases is the assistance of a trained expert, and this can only be supplied by a specialist. The very *raison d'être* of the consultant as such is that he is presumed to have some special skill to which men of less experience cannot attain. With the boundaries of our knowledge widening out in every direction with the rapidity now seen, the conscientious worker will find it hard enough to cultivate adequately even one small corner. The "family doctor" will pursue the even tenor of his way, attending his patients in their progress through most of the seven stages of life, and so getting to know the peculiarities of their constitutions as no specialist ever can. When special need arises special help will be called in, but the specialist can never supplant the general practitioner. The one is simply complementary to the other. Whether we shall ever advance so far in the subdivision of labour as to have no doctors at all but such as are specialists, or whether such a state of things would be desirable, need not be discussed here.

When the worst has been said against specialism, it still remains as a system of work which, if narrow and comparatively humble in its aim, is practically more successful in attaining it than broader and more philosophical methods. The final test of every institution, as of every individual, in these days is the record of actual achievement which it has to show. Judged by the standard of results, whether in the shape of additions to the store of scientific truths or to the armoury of weapons against disease, specialism has nothing to fear. Even its enemies must admit that it is to it that the vast strides which the art of healing has taken in late years are mainly due, and there can be no doubt that medicine can only continue to advance by a process of specialization becoming more and more minute. In the eyes of *idéologues* whose breadth of view rather impairs the keenness of their vision of things close at hand, the specialist no doubt may appear a somewhat unheroic figure beside his larger-minded brethren. Practical men, however, consider less the intrinsic nobility of the work than the efficiency with which it is done. It has been shown that in the present stage of development of medical science the pretence of universal attainment is mere trifling. The question, in short, between the specialist and the general physician is a simple one : By which is the largest measure of relief given to the patients under his care ? The answer cannot, I think, be doubtful ; indeed it has been given with no uncertain sound by the sufferers themselves. Not that I would be thought to disparage for a moment wide culture and philosophical largeness of view ; in medicine as in other things these rare and admirable qualities have their place. That place, however, is the professor's chair rather than the patient's bedside. The ambition of the general physician is no doubt high and noble, though his effect is too often small ; the specialist may justly claim that his object, if less ambitious, is more definite and attainable.

> "This low man seeks a little thing to do,
>   *Sees it and does it:*
> That high man with a great thing to pursue
>   Dies ere he knows it."

MEDICAL SPECIALISM : A REJOINDER.*

THE general physician, whose inevitable disappearance in the struggle for existence I lately foretold, has found a champion in Dr. H. B. Donkin, who has made my essay the pretext for unburdening his soul to the public of sentiments with which he had already edified an appreciative audience of first year's students. Although I cannot lay claim to Dr. Donkin's dialectical skill, I nevertheless feel it incumbent on me to endeavour to expose some of his many fallacies. The gist of my former article was that, owing to the development and expansion of the medical sciences during the last half century, specialism has now become a necessity. I then proceeded to show that, as a matter of fact, it had already gained ground to such an extent that although a few "pure" physicians still survive, the type is irrevocably doomed. I further pointed out that the bulk of those who wear the badge of "pure" physic are in reality "veiled specialists," who live by one kind of disease whilst professing to treat all. In addition to this, I tried to explain a phenomenon which has perplexed many persons, viz. the attempted suppression within the medical

* The preceding essay, which appeared in the pages of the *Fortnightly Review*, in June, 1885, was responded to in the same periodical the following month, by Dr. H. B. Donkin. To that " A Rejoinder " was written at once, and was published in the August number. As the "Rejoinder" recapitulates the leading points of the first essay, and then trenchantly attacks and traverses very fully Dr. Donkin's statements, it is not necessary here to do more than call attention to it as the *raison d'être* of this article. The controversy was playfully alluded to in the pages of *Punch*, on August 15th, 1885.

profession of a system which can be seen to work well for the welfare of mankind, and which is accepted as natural and useful in every other calling. My opponent has not attempted to traverse any of the essential points in my argument, but has spent his force entirely on side issues when he has not been tilting at mere windmills. Thus he endeavours to show that the "pure" physician is not yet quite extinct, and states that there are still a large number, though they have not obtained "pecuniary success." Of course there may be hundreds of Harveys and Sydenhams, of Brodies and Jenners, but if they remain mute and inglorious they are practically non-existent. It will certainly be many years before the "pure" physician disappears as completely as the lamented dodo; it is even possible that, like the Lithuanian auroch and the American bison, he may still be preserved for a long period under artificial conditions favourable to his maintenance. Again, he defends the "veiled specialist" on the curious ground that he does not "deliberately" choose his speciality, but has it thrust upon him. If, however, as is often the case, he "deliberately" encourages the misapprehension on the part of the public whilst drawing the veil still more closely round him in the sight of the profession, I fail to see wherein he is superior to the specialist who makes no pretence to be other than he is.

According to Dr. Donkin, my argument proceeds on the two lines of invective, and a free use of "misleading analogy." The former he returns in kind, and he has failed to show that the latter are in any way "misleading." The complaint of "imputation of motives" would be pathetic did it not so irresistibly remind one of Gracchus denouncing sedition. For years, as I have already shown, specialism and its votaries have been hooted and brayed at. When, however, one of the proscribed party dares to reply in language perhaps not strictly complimentary, a cry of surprise and pain is heard. Perhaps the specialist ought rather to turn the other check to the smiter, and lick the foot that kicks him :—

> "Fair sir, you spit on me on Wednesday last,
> You spurned me such a day; another time
> You called me dog, and for these courtesies"

let me reverently kiss the hem of your garment! Dr. Donkin
takes the Royal College of Physicians in an especial manner
under his protection, and waxes fiercely indignant at my supposed disparagement of that learned body. But what is my
offence? I alluded to the College only in a casual manner as
opposing specialism, as it has done several other things, in
which it has played the part of Mrs. Partington in her historic
contest with the Atlantic. I should be the last person to say
a word against that estimable institution. It has a library
kept almost as jealously closed against intruders as a seraglio;
it does its work as a second-rate licensing board with fair
efficiency; and it discharges the delicate duties of a Mrs.
Grundy to the higher ranks of the profession with a "leniency"
of which Dr. Donkin speaks with an unction almost suggestive
of personal gratitude. But is it intended to imply that human
passions and weaknesses have no part in the dignified conclaves
of the Areopagus of Pall Mall East? Surely one has heard of
favouritism and caprice in the election of Fellows? of jealousy
and malice in the exclusion of men too eminent for that level
of decorous mediocrity which is the characteristic feature of
this as of more famous academies? To say thus much is, after
all, only to assert that the College of Physicians is an assembly
made up of merely human units. A graver charge is the
accusation that I have made an attack on general practitioners.
This is simply inaccurate, as no one who has read my article
needs to be told. On the contrary, I showed that the rank and
file of the profession are now so well educated as to be able to
dispense with any assistance but that of specialists, and that,
owing to the "levelling up" of the general practitioner not
less than to the development of specialism, the general physician
has become a superfluity. Wherein, it may be asked, does the
physician who is not a specialist differ from the well-trained
general practitioner? Both have received precisely the same
professional education. When they emerged from the chrysalis
condition of students they were still, so far as acquirements
went, on a footing of perfect equality in the measure of their
respective abilities. On comparing them ten years later it
would have been found that, whilst the general practitioner

had the wider experience, the physician had a deeper theoretical knowledge on some points, though his memory of others had grown hazy; in fact that, will he nill he, he was drifting towards a more or less pronounced specialization. It is obvious that, as in each case these tendencies must persist and indeed increase, the only truly "all round" adviser must be the general practitioner who continues to see and treat disease in all its forms, his sphere of activity embracing the whole area of physical suffering, and the panorama of each individual life unfolding itself before his eyes. Between highly-educated universal healers on the one hand, therefore, and specialist experts on the other, there is no room left for the physician, who is now nothing better than a mutilated general practitioner. I certainly did show historically that when an entirely new method of practice came into vogue the general practitioner opposed it, but in adopting this attitude he was merely fighting *pro domo suâ*. I yield to none in my admiration for the general practitioner. I know him to be, as a rule, less moved by mercenary considerations than any other class of medical men; in him the virtues which the gratitude of humanity is wont to ascribe to our profession shine with the brightest lustre; and he is probably the most useful member of the community at large. But he too is human, and his actions must occasionally "smell of mortality."

Dr. Donkin complains that I offer no definition of specialism, whilst later on he endeavours to prove that my definition is a bad one. It is kind of him to help me to a better, but I cannot adopt his amendment. "Concentration of one's powers on a single organ" is, on Dr. Donkin's own showing, not often possible; but a man may usefully take a "region" or a group of closely inter-connected organs as the "object" of his special study. A few other subjects of trifling importance will presently be referred to, but I will now proceed to the writer's main proposition. He asserts that specialism is not a benefit to the public—(*a*) Because it leads to a multitude of counsellors, who are not only unnecessary but expensive; (*b*) Because it is difficult to ascertain who is the right specialist to consult until a correct diagnosis has been made, when the use of a specialist becomes *ipso facto* unnecessary ; and, lastly, (*e*) Because it is clear to all who know anything of clinical medicine and pathology that the men who pay exclusive attention to special organs of the body are not those who are best qualified to investigate or treat even the diseases that are assumed to belong to those special organs. This is a very pretty quarrel as it stands, as Sir Lucius would say, and it is rather disappointing to find that my opponent has made so little of his own case. Dr. Donkin is as sparing in proof as he is copious and confident in assertion. He seems to think that his statements are self-evident propositions needing no demonstration ; at any rate he vouchsafes none. He has drawn a picture of a patient suffering from rheumatism complicated with various local affections, whose bed is surrounded by a number of specialists, each provided with his instrument of investigation. But I fail to see why all these specialists should attend at the same time. The fact is that in any given case in which various local complications arise, the intelligent general practitioner of the present day does, as occasion arises, call in the specialist whom he thinks most likely to be helpful. Whether one "pure" physician is called in consultation frequently or different specialists are employed from time to time, I do not see that there would be much difference as regards expense ; indeed, the cost of special advice would probably be much less, as the disease would have a better chance of running a favourable course, and complications would be guarded against which would otherwise prolong the illness and largely increase the cost.

As regards Dr. Donkin's second objection, it may be remarked that the patient is either under the care of a general practitioner who can guide him to a proper selection, or he chooses a specialist for himself. In the former case no mistake is likely to be made, whilst in the latter it rarely occurs. A person with loss of voice is scarcely likely to go to a skin doctor, if he is getting blind he does not consult an aurist, and if deaf he does not expect to be cured by an orthopædist. To pretend, however, that the *diagnosis* once satisfactorily made, there is no further use for the specialist is opposed to everyday experience. It is precisely in *treatment* that the specialist's superiority is most conspicuous. Dr. Donkin's third argument, that specialists are not the persons best qualified to deal with even those diseases which come within their own chosen province, is a statement so paradoxical in itself, that some slight elucidation was surely required. Dr. Donkin, however, is wise in his generation, and gives his opinion without his reasons. To the public who have the most vital interest in coming to a right decision in the matter, a demonstration of the superiority of specialism seems, as a patient of mine expressed it, like an argument to prove that A is the first letter in the alphabet. Dr. Donkin, however, denies the competence of the lay judgment on this subject, and sneers at my calling the "public voice" to bear witness on my behalf. It never does any society or corporation much harm to let in a little daylight from the outside on their proceedings, and it is to be noted that I invoked the testimony of the enlightened public, including medical men as well as outsiders, on one definite point as to which they are, in my opinion, pre-eminently fitted to decide, viz. the *results* of treatment. No one, of course, would think of attaching much importance to even the most cultured lay opinion on technical details or questions of scientific speculation, but in the domain of practical result there can be no more competent tribunal.

As to my analogies, Dr. Donkin has not shown that they are inapplicable. Even if law and engineering were not strictly comparable to medicine from a scientific point of view, it is surely a somewhat remarkable fact that whilst specialism has bred such bitter passions in one of these professions, it should be regarded with tolerance and even favour in the other two. But I maintain that my adversary is altogether wrong in fact as well as in spirit. There is a natural connection between all branches of the law in fundamental points, such as procedure, the construction of statutes, and the rules of evidence. Again, it may be allowed that the specialist barrister is retained by the "expert attorney;" but who directs the client to the latter, who often confines himself to a highly specialized line of practice? As for the connection between the various branches of scientific engineering being nothing more than a "verbal tic," Dr. Donkin will, if he inquires, find the notion scouted by every properly educated member of that profession, who will tell him that all the many branches of their science rest on a common basis of mechanical and physical truths.

Dr. Donkin does not disdain to repeat the usual twaddle that specialism must be dangerous because it is impossible to treat the body as a machine in which the component parts can be studied and dealt with piecemeal apart from their connection with the rest. "The body is an organism, not a mechanism," etc. Most true; but who denies it? Certainly not enlightened specialists. Surely it is time that "purists" should clear their minds of this cant, for it is nothing else. I must again refer my opponent to my former article in which great stress is laid on the necessity for a professional education of the widest and most thorough kind as an indispensable preliminary to specialization. I insisted, moreover, on the desirability of this training being followed and completed by the largest and most varied experience in miscellaneous practice. Such disadvantages as are fairly chargeable to specialism have already been fully set forth by me in my former article, in which I also indicated the antidote, or rather the prophylactic. On the other hand, this constant talk of the organic unity of the body and the interdependence of its various parts, though no doubt perfectly true in a certain sense, is, as Dr. Donkin would say, "well calculated to produce a pseudological effect on the minds of whose who mistake words for things." It sounds well, and appeals to that considerable class of semi-cultured persons who profess always to walk in the light of a large philosophy, carrying as it were an electric illuminator into places where the humble rushlight of common sense would guide them better. Granting, as every one must of course do, the intimate connection between the different organs and parts of the human body, does it follow that specialism in practice is either dangerous or in any way reprehensible? The body is often said to have an analogy with a state in which all the organs and parts are under the sway of a supreme ruler—the brain. It would be more exact to compare it to a union of states in which the federal laws prevail in general on foreign matters, whilst the more important home affairs enjoy the benefit of state rights. The affectation of studying every gripe and every pimple on the broadest principles of transcendental pathology is fraught with dangers greater than any that can be proved against specialism even when most narrow. The least drawback of this sham philosophy is that it is so often absurdly ineffectual, its failures being all the more glaring by reason of the airs of superiority which accompany them. Indeed many general physicians practise a *laissez faire* policy as a formal system, conveniently leaving everything to the *vis medicatrix*, and pocketing fees for looking on at the working of morbid processes without any attempt at interference. It would perhaps show a "deplorable spirit" on my part to suggest that the contempt which many medical philosophers profess for local remedies may sometimes arise from inability to apply them, just as scepticism about the effect of drugs is often found associated with a certain want of familiarity with the Pharmacopœia.

Dr. Donkin affirms "that almost all the greatest advancements in medical knowledge have come from our general hospitals." If this be the case, I should like to know to what general hospital we owe the introduction of Peruvian bark, or antimony, or iodine, or cocaine? Was vaccination discovered in a general hospital? Was any one of the splendid series of experiments of Pasteur, which have raised Jenner's great idea from an isolated empirical fact to the dignity of a scientific law, performed within the walls of a general hospital? Medical treatment has made no greater step of late years than in the management of fevers: was the work of Stewart, Jenner, or Murchison done in general hospitals? Did Hansen detect the parasite of leprosy, or Koch that of tubercle, in a general hospital? Are the triumphs of ovariotomy and abdominal section to be reckoned among "the great advancements" which have come from general hospitals? Take diseases of the eye, ear, throat, and skin, will Dr. Donkin kindly name *one* improvement in the diagnosis or treatment of any of these that has come from a general physician or surgeon? The fact is, that a general hospital is about the last place from which one would naturally expect any striking innovation to come. Such institutions are, from the conditions of their existence, schools of routine, and the natural homes of medical "idols of the cave." Originality on the part of a physician or surgeon is looked upon with suspicion by his colleagues, and the scientific Icarus too often finds his wings melt in the fierce heat of unfriendly and not altogether disinterested criticism. Dr. Donkin may possibly remember a recent case in which a physician to a general hospital, who was labouring with honest endeavour to determine the action of a drug, was traduced in the lay press by a colleague who did not dare to sign his name.

My adversary twits specialists with overlooking disease in other organs, even when it is a manifestation of the same disorder which they are treating in the part to which they professedly devote themselves. He is good enough, again, to take the throat as an example, and points out that in cases of "advanced consumption," whilst the throat is being "vainly and perhaps harmfully treated for an indefinite time," the real cause of the disease in the lungs has "totally escaped detection." Dr. Donkin is possibly not aware, on the other hand, that in a large number of cases of pulmonary disease, the lung affection becomes quiescent whilst the patient is carried off by "throat consumption," perhaps one of the most painful of all diseases. In such cases we too often find "pure physicians" ordering medicaments which are absolutely ineffectual or dangerously destructive, whilst the remedies of the specialist will at once relieve the sufferings and nearly always prolong the life of the unfortunate patient. It would be foolish to deny that mistakes such as Dr. Donkin describes are sometimes made, for specialists are no more exempt from carelessness or ignorance than general physicians. Such errors on the part of specialists, however, far from being of common occurrence, are relatively rare, and in any case they are due not to any faultiness inherent in the system, but entirely to the deficiencies of the individual.

If specialism tends to make a man narrow, on the other hand universalism has the worse effect of making him too broad for practical usefulness. A habit is engendered of treating the body as a whole *independently* of its various members—an error opposite in character to that imputed to specialism, and entailing consequences immensely more disastrous in practice. Fanatical specialists may possibly be found who treat all affections by local remedies alone, but they are quite alone, the knowledge necessary to avoid so flagrant an error being the common property of the medical profession. To think that any one can be a really good specialist without a thorough knowledge of the broad foundations of medicine, is as absurd as to suppose that a man could settle "the doctrine of the enclitic *De*," or unravel the subtleties of the Latin subjunctive without knowing the general principles of grammar. On the other hand, general physicians who treat all complaints "constitutionally" are frequently to be met with. The harm done in the latter case is very serious, for the neglect of local measures is irremediable, when destruction of important parts or narrowing of vital passages has taken place. How often is "general debility" made accountable for symptoms for which a well-defined local cause could easily be found by those who know where and how to seek for it? How many local sins has "rheumatism" been made to answer for? and "gout," that refuge of the destitute diagnostician? As for those universal scapegoats, the "stomach" and the "liver," the local symptoms which these organs are credited with the power of producing are as the sands on the sea-shore. "Nerves," also—the modern synonym for the obsolete "spleen" and the still more *rococo* "vapours"—stand many a puzzled pundit in good stead when pressed for an explanation of sensations and symptoms. If Dr. Donkin will allow me to refer to the province in which I am most at home, I could mention numerous instances within my own knowledge, in which disease in the larynx, figuratively speaking "gross as a mountain, open, palpable," had been attributed either to the fancy of the patient or to causes existing only in the equally vain imagination of the physician. Thus, loss of voice caused by the presence of a growth on one or other of the vocal cords has in some cases been attributed to "cold," in others to "debility," in others, again, to "hysteria." One particular instance is within my recollection of a lady who had been treated for loss of voice during five years by several physicians of the widest knowledge, whose remedies were of as little avail as the Mumbo Jumbo of a Zulu medicine-man. It would be difficult to say how much suffering is caused by the dog-in-the-manger attitude of "purists" towards specialists. Not long ago one of the most prominent of "the great clinical physicians and pathologists," of whom, as we learn from Dr. Donkin, the "English profession is justly proud," on being consulted in a case of severe and widespread ulceration of the throat, urged on the patient the necessity of taking food. On being asked, however, how swallowing was to be accomplished, he took refuge in general principles, which doubtless proved consolatory to the starving patient. After a few days of suffering which no attempt was made to relieve, a specialist was called in, who by local medication speedily effected a cure. In another case of which I have personal knowledge, a patient who had been treated by most of the luminaries of the College of Physicians, for organic disease of the brain, in a moment of happy inspiration sought the advice of an oculist, who cured him at once and permanently by fitting him with an appropriate pair of spectacles. In this case special knowledge restored a life to comfort and usefulness which "wide" knowledge had very nearly utterly wrecked. Again, most medical men are familiar with cases in which disease of such concrete objectivity as tumours in the substance of the brain and spinal cord, had been treated by "clinicians and pathologists" of great repute as hysteria and epilepsy. When to all this is added the fact that special methods of examination often reveal the presence of grave general disease long before the eye which is lighted only by "wide knowledge" perceives anything at all ominous of evil, I apprehend that enough has been said to establish the superiority in the realm of medical practice, of knowledge which, however "narrow," is exact.

My critic appears to fancy that I have made a fatal admission in allowing that a specialist may induce the world to credit him with more skill or talent than he actually possesses. By what complex process of "pseudo-logical" reasoning does he bring himself to believe that the admission of a proposition so absolutely axiomatic in its nature can be damaging to anybody? The statement is surely applicable to others than specialists, at least of the operative order, as pretence or want of skill on the part of the latter is almost certain to be detected as soon as they are compelled to come to the sticking-place. The mere physician, however, may conceal his inefficiency beneath the cloak of mysterious profundity, or drown inquiry in a torrent of fatuous verbosity, without risk of having his words subjected to the immediate test of hard fact. In general physic a man may be an impostor to the end of a long life without being found out. Swift detection and exposure, however, await the specialist who merely trades on a reputation without solid basis.

Dr. Donkin brackets together "clinical teachers and pathologists," forgetting the fact that specialism has prevailed so far even in the stronghold of "pure" physic as to have made such a combination preposterous. The professed pathologist, it need hardly be said, is as much a specialist nowadays as the professed physiologist,'and there is as little connection between clinical teaching and pathology as there is between geography and pure mathematics.

My antagonist has such an enviable superabundance of energy that in the very whirlwind of his passion against me he can strike a passing blow at the ancient Egyptians and modern Americans. The former, we are told, walked in "ways that were dark" so far as medicine was concerned, whilst the latter have the avidity of the Athenians for every new thing. Unless Dr. Donkin has been favoured with special and exclusive information about the medical knowledge of the Egyptians, I do not see how he can speak of it with such confident contempt. Who can tell how much clinical insight and therapeutical skill they really possessed? The sneer about their "vain treatment of symptoms" is quite in the key of the medical pseudo-philosopher. Can Dr. Donkin himself in most cases of disease that come before him treat anything but symptoms? If the Egyptians treated symptoms successfully, I maintain that whatever their knowledge may have been their practice was more efficient than that of modern medicine, even of the

D

"widest" range. As for our trans-Atlantic relations, I am surprised to find that the rapid spread of specialism amongst them is attributed to a mere love of novelty and a sordid desire for gain. Dr. Donkin must surely be aware that there is scarcely a department of surgery or medicine that has not been enriched by the research and originality of American practitioners. Indeed their disregard for dogma combined with their highly inventive faculty has, perhaps, done more towards the cure of disease than all the learning of European philosophers.

I suppose I must take some notice of my opponent's insinuation—as impertinent in tone as it is barbarous in expression—that specialists, and especially throat specialists, are exposed to the temptation of "fabulating" disease. But granting that the power of seeing regions beyond the ken of the patient must act as an incentive to deception, can it be said that the general physician is altogether exempt from the temptation to "fabulate" all sorts of morbid conditions, dealing as he usually does, with parts not only invisible but often beyond the sufferer's power of accurate localization? Moreover, if a laryngologist should yield to the temptation, has the patient no means of having his statement checked? Are there no other shepherds in Arcadia?—no brethren of the mirror to whom "all his faults observed, set in a note-book, learned and conned by rote" are a source of pure and lofty gratification? The knowledge that his diagnosis may at any time be submitted to the revision of a jealous rival whose interest as well as inclination it is to catch him tripping, must greatly help the throat specialist in repressing any temptation to "fabulate." The general physician has no such direct check upon his inventive faculty; where all is a matter of more or less probable conjecture, a man has only to uphold his opinion with an air of sufficient conviction, and some plausible sophistry, to have it accepted and acted on.

Putting aside the amenities which Dr. Donkin has introduced, the question between us is not whether specialism in the abstract is superior to broad general knowledge, but whether at the present stage of scientific progress anything else than specialism more or less limited in its range be possible in consulting practice. The subject is not merely of academical interest; it is one of the utmost importance for the public, for science, and for the medical profession itself. I put the public first because it cannot be too strongly urged or too often repeated, that specialism in the sphere of medical practice must be judged primarily if not solely by its results to suffering humanity. Any ill effect, real or supposed, which it may have on the mental constitution of the practitioner, or on the organization of the profession is an altogether secondary consideration. *Salus populi suprema lex est.* Much might be written on the decline and fall of "pure" physic, but it is useless to pursue the subject. On the other hand, specialism being a movement founded on the true principle of progress, and in harmony with the general "stream of tendency" in these days, will gain strength and volume as it advances, sweeping away in its victorious current all the rubbish of pedantic prejudice and malicious bigotry that formerly defiled its waters and hindered their flow.

IS MEDICINE A PROGRESSIVE SCIENCE?

THE art of killing has made vast strides since primeval men fought with the thigh bones of their deceased relations, and in these days of torpedoes and Gatling guns no one will deny that it continues to develop with a rapidity which must be highly comforting to Malthusian economists. The art of healing, on the other hand, has certainly not progressed to a proportionate extent, and scoffers may even be found who maintain that it has not advanced a single step since the time of Hippocrates. Pessimistic views of this kind are not uncommon among clever people, who are enlightened enough to see the shortcomings of medical science, without having sufficient knowledge to appreciate either the difficulties in the way or the manner in which they are met. The opposite tendency is, however, more fashionable at present, and the ever-widening area of conquest achieved by science in the dark realm of disease is the theme of constant jubilation in the lecture-room and the press. Without any wish to damp honest enthusiasm it may be hinted that such rejoicings are often somewhat premature. *Te Deums* are sung for victories which prove to be altogether hollow or even of the Pyrrhic sort, and the enemy supposed for an instant to be crushed is found carrying on the war as fiercely as ever. Remedies vaunted as of sovereign virtue against a particular ailment have on further trial to be discarded as useless; modes of treatment which yield the most brilliant results in the hands of Dr. Diagnosticus fail utterly with the patients of Professor Agnosticus. Systems and theories follow each other like the waves of the sea, and leave but little trace on the rock-bound coast of the unknown, against which human intelligence has shattered itself in vain for thousands of years. The question, therefore, Is Medicine a progressive science? is not so idle as might at first sight appear. At any rate a sober discussion of the matter may be refreshing to some minds in the midst of the shouts of triumph which rend the air at every half-discovery that is announced.

A point which meets us at the outset is whether Medicine is, strictly speaking, a science at all. Although the elementary principles of physiology are as certain as any other scientific truths, the practical application of them in the investigation and treatment of disease can hardly ever possess more than a higher or lower degree of probability. The diagnosis of a case of organic disease of the heart, for example, cannot during the patient's life be treated as a verity of the same order as the circulation of the blood. The final test of a science is the possibility of *predicting* the phenomena belonging to its domain. The astronomer foretells the time of an eclipse to the fraction of a second. The physiologist prophecies with certainty that if the spinal cord be severed about its middle, the lower part of the body will be paralysed. But the physician can never know beforehand the precise effect which a drug will produce in a given case, or whether a particular complication will occur in the course of a familiar fever. It is no doubt perfectly true that, as the candidate in the *Malade Imaginaire* puts it, *opium facit dormire*, but in a small percentage of cases it has precisely the opposite effect. We know that arsenic and belladonna are poisons, but deadly doses of both have often been taken with impunity, and the most experienced toxicologist could not say with certainty how little would suffice to destroy life in an individual case. The science of medicine may almost be said to be limited to the class of truths which adorned the mind of the "natural philosopher" commended by Touchstone. We know that "the property of rain is to wet, and of fire to burn," and we are sure that if a man's heart stops, or if he ceases to breathe, he dies; outside the narrow circle of such fundamental truths, we are in a region of mere probability. It can hardly therefore be wondered at that Laplace should have demurred to the admission of physicians among the scientific members of the Institute, or that our own Royal Society should so seldom open its doors to medical practitioners as such. Nor is there much likelihood that medicine will ever take rank among the exact sciences. The problems of life are too complex to be solved by physical methods, and all other means of investigation from their very nature offer only more or less close approximation to accuracy of result.

With all its inevitable limitations, however, medicine has progressed, and continues to progress, slowly perhaps, and too often wandering from the right path, occasionally even losing ground. By far the greater part of such progress as has been made, has been achieved within comparatively recent times. A hundred years ago the question, Is Medicine a progressive science? might have been answered in the negative without much absurdity. Such advances as had then been made had been mostly of an isolated and fortuitous nature; a few brilliant discoveries had been stumbled on, but the science was pretty much where Harvey had left it more than a century before, whilst the practice was little better than that of Celsus or Galen. Let us take a glance at the state of things which then prevailed. The recognition of diseases of the heart and lungs was to the last degree conjectural, whilst as regards other internal organs it was the merest guesswork. Fevers and other disorders, which are as distinct in their character and course as a horse from a cow, were classed together and treated in an indiscriminately drastic manner, just as at the same period the law hanged with Draconian impartiality for murder and for sheep stealing. Tumours were arranged in a few haphazard groups, as motley in their composition as the various sections of the "great Liberal party." If a man was unlucky enough to fall into the hands of the surgeons, he had to bear cold steel and hot iron with what fortitude he could; death under the knife from sheer pain was not unfrequent, and operations that might have saved life were refused from dread of the agony with which they were accompanied. Compound fracture of a limb entailed the loss of it almost as a necessary consequence, and sufferers from calculus could only obtain relief by one of the most dreadful cutting operations in surgery. Doctors saw no harm in ministering to ladies "in the straw," as it was elegantly termed, immediately after leaving the dissecting-room or the dead-house, and thousands of women must have perished from this cause alone. Ignorance of the laws of hygiene made hospitals and jails little better than pest-houses. The mortality from preventible diseases, such as small-pox, typhus, enteric fever, and all the ghastly progeny of dirt and foul air, defies all computation. Lunatics were chained and beaten like wild beasts, and their affliction was exposed to the jeers of unfeeling men and the leers of shameless women.

There is still, no doubt, a vast amount of suffering and disease amongst us, but it would be folly to deny that the difference between the past and the present is immense. The stethoscope has made it as easy to detect a damaged heart or an inefficient lung as a broken leg. The ophthalmoscope enables us to explore the innermost recesses of the eye, whilst with the laryngoscope we can have ocular proof of the condition of the wind-pipe. The microscope enlightens us as to the true nature of growths, and such timely information often makes it possible to check their development. Anæsthetics have robbed surgery of all its cruelty and half its danger; they have moreover extended its sphere of action, for operations are now frequently performed which formerly could not have been attempted. The introduction of the antiseptic method has largely increased the proportion of recoveries after severe wounds and mutilations, and has also done much to insure the safety of the lying-in chamber. The necessity of cutting for stone is now obviated by measures which involve neither pain nor serious risk, and there can be little doubt that the operation will in the course of the next fifty years become obsolete in civilized countries. Small-pox is no longer the standing menace to beauty that it once was, whilst it is scarcely taken into account as a possible danger to life by ordinary people. Typhoid fever still claims many victims, though it is being gradually driven off the field by an enlightened hygiene; typhus is almost unknown except in the lowest and most

squalid haunts of poverty. Madness is now treated as a bodily
disease, not as a curse of God or spite of the devil, the result
being a large proportion of recoveries, and infinitely less
suffering among the incurable. A like improvement is seen
in other branches of the medical art. The loathsome
compounds—invented, one might suppose, by a council of
ghouls and scavengers—which used to be ordered, no longer vex
the palates or upheave the stomachs of unfortunate patients ;
the active principle of the most important remedies has been
separated, so that the agent can be administered in a purer
and more efficient form, whilst the physiological action of the
drug is determined by experiment and is taken as the index
of its therapeutic value. Less physic is given, but it is
prescribed with a clearer purpose. Better still, more attention
is paid to diet and the hygienic surroundings of the patient,
and, above all, Nature is less encumbered with the officious help
of a blind ally who insists on aiding her with a zeal that
is not according to knowledge. The truth has at last been
borne in on the medical mind that many diseases run a certain
definite course on which no medicine has any effect for good,
though it may have for evil, and that accordingly a policy of
masterly inactivity is the wisest in such cases. The physical
changes wrought by disease and the morbid processes which
give rise to them are now to a certain extent accurately known,
and this field of inquiry promises to be increasingly fruitful
of solid result. Some scattered rays of light, too, are beginning
to pierce the shroud of darkness which formerly made the origin
of disease a more impenetrable mystery than the source of the
Nile. This marks one of the greatest advances in the history
of medicine, and its practical importance is obviously incalculable. The cause clearly known, the effect can often be
removed, or, better still, prevented. Specific fevers may possibly
be banished from among men, and even those fell scourges,
consumption and cancer, may in course of time be stamped out.
One disease after another is traced to the action of organisms
infinitesimal in size, but having an almost inconceivable power
of self-multiplication. From leprosy to a cold in the head, the
"conqueror worm" is credited with the generation of almost

every form of disorder; where it has not yet been found, it is suspected. In a word, the sign Bacillus is in the ascendant in the medical firmament.

Fascinating, however, as the theory of the parasitic origin of disease undoubtedly is, it is clear that it does not altogether solve the problem. Granting the existence, *e.g.*, of a distinct species of bacillus in the lungs of consumptive patients, and granting that the bacillus is the cause of the disease, the question still remains, What is the *causa causans* of the invading organism itself? Whence does it come, and how did it get there? This may recall to profane minds the famous riddle which once baffled a royal intellect, How the apple got into the dumpling? but it is a question which must be answered, for the presence of the bacillus may obviously be the consequence of the disease instead of its cause. It cannot be too strongly insisted on that inquiries into etiology must not stop at the discovery of a minute organism in the affected tissues.

Hygiene is in great measure of modern growth, and one has only to compare our condition as regards wholesomeness of dwellings, drainage, water supply and personal cleanliness, with that of our great-grandfathers, to recognize a vast and wonderful change for the better. It was not so much indifference, perhaps, as sheer ignorance which made people formerly such Gallios respecting these things. The sounder views which begin to prevail at the present day are the most striking proof that medicine has made real progress. It may, however, be hoped that we are as yet only in the twilight that pervades the dawn. Already the death-rate has been sensibly lowered in England and some other countries, and insurance statistics show that the average span of human life has been materially lengthened. It may be said that this is the result of better means of prevention rather than of improved methods of cure; but surely medicine may claim as her own the triumphs of hygiene which is her offspring? As the science of medicine perfects itself it tends necessarily towards its own annihilation. When everything can be prevented there will be nothing left to cure. Medicine will then, like Alexander, have to sheathe its sword for want of fresh worlds to conquer; it will cease to exist, or become transformed into a religion of the body preached by properly qualified ministers, or into a code of health promulgated and enforced by the State. Death or suffering from disease will then be unknown; life will be cut short only by violence, or will quietly collapse with "a general flavour of mild decay" when its natural lease is out.

When this Utopian state of things has been arrived at, one cannot help wondering (though the matter hardly concerns us) what is to follow. The mere struggle for food must lead to wholesale slaughter compared with which even Biblical massacres will seem paltry, or ultra-Spartan modes of repressing exuberance of population will have to be adopted.

In the meantime medicine still lives, and may I be allowed to say, flourishes. Nor does there seem to be any immediate prospect of its becoming obsolete or superfluous in the world. Doctors have still to do battle with disease, and the Priesthood of Health is as yet embodied only in the persons of Inspectors of Nuisances. It has been shown that the art of healing has made very decided progress, but the more interesting question remains, Will it continue to advance? Blessed as our state undoubtedly is, compared with that in which our forerunners had their being, the most fervid optimist must allow that there is yet much room for improvement. The Sphinx of disease still propounds many riddles fraught with destruction to such as cannot solve them, and no Œdipus comes to the rescue. Many ills are still our heritage which have been handed down from one generation to another as long as there is any record of man in the world, whilst new ailments are developed in the feverish atmosphere of our modern life. Nevertheless it is impossible for any competent observer to deny that medicine moves onwards almost from day to day. The path of progress lies in the continual expansion of surgery at the expense of pure physic; in other words, the domain of what the French more correctly call *pathologie externe* is by degrees annexing and absorbing that of *pathologie interne*, and to a proportionate extent substituting proof for conjecture. Not much more than ten years ago a surgeon of the highest eminence gave public expression to his belief that operative surgery had then reached its greatest possible degree of perfection, and yet even within that short time a considerable tract of the waste land of medicine has been reclaimed and brought under surgical cultivation. The lung, the stomach, the kidney, and even the brain have been successfully invaded by the knife, and some portions of the body can now be *seen* which not very long ago were as invisible during life as the *divinae particula aeräi* itself. A word of caution, however, may not be out of place respecting these signs of progress. It is questionable whether the mere demonstration of the fact, that the human frame can be wounded or mutilated in a particular way without causing the death of the patient, is anything more than a barren triumph. Again, increased facility in detecting disease which we are powerless to relieve may not seem to ordinary minds a very solid gain. On the other hand, it must be remembered that when a malady is *sure* to kill its victim if allowed to run its course unchecked, an operation which saves even one life in a million cannot justly be condemned as useless. Furthermore, as the accurate identification of the mischief is an absolutely essential condition of successful treatment, any help towards this is to be welcomed as a step in advance, however far removed it may seem to be from the sphere of practical usefulness.

It is impossible to deny that there are great difficulties in the way of medical progress, probably more than in that of any other branch of human inquiry. The question, Is engineering a progressive science? for instance, would strike every one as palpably absurd. Yet it will hardly be contended that the amount and quality of intellect brought to bear on the problems of medicine, are in any way inferior to that which so successfully copes with those of mechanical science. The truth is that medicine does not progress so much as other sciences, simply because it has to do with matters infinitely more complex and abstruse than any of them. The properties of living matter cannot be thoroughly investigated without destroying the very principle, the secret of whose working it is that we wish to discover; vital energy cannot be weighed or analyzed.

Dissection of the dead body shows nothing more than the structure of the machine, and that imperfectly; experiments on one kind of living animal cannot be taken as conclusive in the case of another.

The inherent difficulties of the subject are increased by popular prejudice and ignorance, which throw obstacles in the way of even such slight means of investigation as we have. Furthermore, there is room for improvement in the inquirer himself. Medicine is by the vast majority of its professors taken up solely as a means of livelihood, and the pursuit of truth for its own sake in the present arrangement of things requires first of all the possession of independent means. Virtue is its own reward in the practice of medicine, more, perhaps, than in any other sphere of labour. Hence those who are most fitted to do work that would make all mankind their debtors have too often no material on which to exercise their powers, whilst those who have the largest opportunities for observation have not time to make full use of them. Moreover, original work does not *pay*, and the reputation of being a discoverer is often disadvantageous to the practitioner. The publication of Harvey's immortal *Exercitatio de Motu Cordis* was immediately followed by the loss of most of his patients. For this incompatibility between research and practice I can see no remedy, unless a way can be found of freeing the physician from his dependence on patients without lessening the salutary stimulus to exertion. If the State were to undertake the medical guardianship of its subjects, and doctors were to be Government officials, paid not by individuals but out of the public purse, on a scale strictly commensurate with their activity and success, the sick would probably be just as well cared for as at present, and their attendants would have a position of greater freedom, and at the same time of greater dignity. Promotion in the service would be strictly according to merit as estimated by the medical body itself, and special encouragement would be given to original investigation. It appears to me that this plan would have all the advantages claimed for the endowment of research without its drawbacks. Abstract science would thus be at once self-supporting and less apt to lose touch of the immediate needs of suffering humanity. At the same time, the great work of progress could be powerfully assisted by the State in other ways. It might be enacted, that, a careful and complete autopsy of all dead bodies without distinction should be made by thoroughly qualified officers expressly appointed for the purpose, that full records of such examinations should be kept, and should be issued to members of the medical profession at frequent intervals. This plan would, there can be little doubt, make medicine advance more in a few years than it has done since the days, when it was the custom for those who had recovered from any illness, to hang a record of the means of cure in the temple of Æsculapius for the benefit of fellow-sufferers. I scarcely dare do more than hint at another source of knowledge, which the flabby sentimentalism of this humanitarian age would probably recoil from with a shudder. Yet, as long as capital punishment continues to be enforced, society might surely be allowed to get some benefit from the criminal who has outraged its laws beyond merely purging itself of his presence. Of course, it would be a cardinal principle that not the slightest bodily pain should be inflicted, and things might easily be managed so that even mental suffering should be spared to the condemned man. In fact, the dread penalty of the law might be exacted in a way at once less unpleasant to the victim than at present, and infinitely more advantageous to mankind. Gabriel Fallopius, who was professor of anatomy at Padua in the sixteenth century, tells us that the Grand Duke of Tuscany from time to time gave orders that a criminal should be handed over to him "*quem nostro modo interficimus et eum anatomizamus;*" and, even as I write, the experiment of innoculating a man with leprosy as an alternative to the gallows has been tried in the Hawaian Islands. It may be said that this would degrade medicine, and make its professors more hateful than common hangmen. If carried out, however, by State functionaries, and with all due safeguards against abuse, the execution would be transfigured into the likeness of a solemn sacrifice on the altar of science.

Even with such limited means as we have at command,

however, there is every reason to believe that medicine will continue to make progress. A more philosophical spirit governs the mind and directs the efforts of its practitioners. There is less bigotry and scientific sectarianism than in days not long gone by; the art of healing is now eclectic in the best sense, and does not scruple to borrow useful hints from any source, however heretical. Like Molière, the medicine of to-day "prend son bien où il le trouve." Its aim, too, is more definite and individual than it used to be. We think less of framing systems which are, as it were, the algebraical formulæ of disease, and more of working out to a correct solution the particular problem before us. Hence the tendency to specialization, both in research and in practice, which is one of the most powerful elements in the progress which medicine is making.

The enlightened humility of intellect which prefers patient interrogation of nature to the formation of brilliant theories; the careful assay of all facts in the crucible of experiment, and the use of the comparative method whereby the diseases of other animals, and even of plants, are made to throw light on those of man, combine to make up a tone of thought in the medical world which is full of promise for the future. Another feature of scientific research in the present day is what may be called the *bandwork* which modern facilities for rapid communication have made possible. Results of inquiry thus easily become known through the whole civilized world, and can at once be tested by a number of independent investigators. In this way error is strangled at its birth, or at any rate before it has had time to do much harm, whilst truth is likely to be more quickly accepted. Pregnant hints run less risk of being left slumbering in the Limbo of neglect till they are forgotten. The numerous organs, also, which exist for the purpose of collecting and systematizing the records of what has been attempted and accomplished, and presenting a summary of results month by month, and year by year, assist community of effort by showing each individual what his fellow-workers in the same field are doing. This prevents much waste of time and intellectual energy, which can be more profitably applied

IS MEDICINE A PROGRESSIVE SCIENCE? 47

in other directions. Much is justly expected from the Collective Investigation which has within the last few years been set on foot. The scheme is still in its infancy, and is only directed to one or two common disorders, but it is so clearly a step in the right direction that it cannot fail to expand itself so as to embrace the whole field of diseases.

It does not seem rash, therefore, to anticipate that medicine will in the future progress at once more rapidly and more surely than it has done in the past. The present condition of the science, the precision of our diagnosis, the abundance and efficacy of the therapeutical resources at our disposal, our knowledge of the cause and power of forecasting the issue in many diseases, would appear miraculous to Hippocrates or Galen, and wonderful to Harvey or even Edward Jenner. How far the art of healing will progress is a question which lies beyond my scope. There are certain limits which it can never hope to overpass, but within these bounds it will continue to advance indefinitely. Much of the traditional obloquy with which medicine is still sometimes assailed is founded on a misconception of its true aim and function. More is asked of it than of any other art or science. Prolongation of life beyond the patriarchal term ; the extirpation of all disease ; the immediate cure of all injuries ; and the abolition of pain are among the modest demands made on medicine ; and all this is to be done by the wave of a magician's wand, so to speak, without any regard for the inexorable laws of nature. People have long ceased to sneer at chemists for their inability to transmute base metal into gold, and engineers would not be expected to move Ireland, say, to the North Pole ; but doctors are still reviled because they cannot enable a glutton to outrage all the laws of digestion with impunity, or *create* anew an organ destroyed by disease.

Medicine has the threefold function of curing, preventing, and alleviating human suffering. As regards the first, we have made comparatively little headway ; but if we do not cure more, we, at any rate, kill less, and that of itself is a good deal. I confess I do not share Professor Huxley's expectation, that a remedy for nearly all forms of disease

will sooner or later be found in drugs. This hope seems
to me not only baseless in itself, but likely to prove a will-
o'-the-wisp to investigators. Means of prevention should be
sought for rather than specific antidotes, which have seldom
been discovered except by accident, and which often fail in the
time of need. Much progress has already been made in the
prevention of disease, and it cannot be doubted that in this
direction lies the way for medicine to follow if it is to be truly
progressive. Apart, however, from either cure or prevention,
there is a vast field for the power of medicine to display itself.
The art must not be judged solely, or perhaps chiefly, by crude
statistics of recoveries and deaths. Even if it be conceded
that the former are largely the work of nature, the veriest
sceptic who has ever been ill himself or witnessed sickness in
others, must confess that the physician can allay pain, ward
off danger, soothe apprehension, and infuse hope. Even when
the issue is fatal, is it to be counted as nothing that death,
although victorious, has been disarmed of its sting of physical
anguish? It may be boldly asserted that if medicine never
wrested a single life from an untimely grave, it would still
deserve supremely well of humanity for its power of relieving
pain. In nothing is the progressive character of the healing
art more conspicuous than in the constant additions which are
made to our means of dealing with troublesome symptoms,
which, even if they do not threaten life, make it miserable and
perhaps useless. If it be the destiny of mankind to have disease
always going about among them, seeking whom it may devour,
it is still much that more and better safeguards should be found
against it, that its ravages should be lessened, and that our life
into which, brief as it is, such an amount of suffering may be
compressed, should be rendered less and less subject to pain,
and freer from bodily discomfort. On this ground alone medicine
may well take its stand as a progressive science.

HEALTH-SEEKING IN TENERIFE AND MADEIRA.

THE Canary Islands have long been famous in travellers' tales for the balminess of their air and the beauty of their scenery, but until a very few years ago, the majority of Englishmen looked upon them much as the Romans of Virgil's day regarded the *penitus toto divisos orbe Britannos*. Only a few adventurous spirits had carried their search for sunshine so far out of the beaten track ; to the average invalid Tenerife was as much outside the sphere of practical health-seeking as Timbuctoo. Nor can this be wondered at, when the difficulties of access and the total absence of suitable accommodation are borne in mind ; moreover the virtues of the climate were practically little known even to physicians, and few people care to make themselves the subject of experiment in such a matter. Now that the Canaries are being extensively advertised as a land flowing with the elixir of life, where disease drops from the sufferer almost as soon as his feet touch its sacred soil, the pendulum, as usually happens, seems likely to swing too far the other way. Exaggerated expectation will too surely breed disappointment, and the rising tide of popularity may, in its inevitable ebb, leave the new health resort in lower water than it was before. This would be a pity, for the natural advantages of the islands are certainly very great, and, indeed, in some cases of disease altogether unrivalled. My object in this paper is to give the results of my personal observations of Tenerife during a short visit made in the spring of the year 1889. I may claim to be an impartial witness, for I went there with no other object in view than to seek for rest and change of scene, and my ideas of the climate and hygienic possibilities of the island were so vague that my mind was free from bias of any kind on the subject. As very few European physicians have visited the Canaries, the impressions which I formed there may have some interest for invalids and lovers of sunlight generally, who are on the outlook for some new haven of refuge for the winter.

Tenerife is the largest of the group of "seven sisters" which form the Canary Islands; it measures about sixty miles in length by thirty in breadth at the widest part. To most people it is probably known chiefly, if not solely, for the famous "Peak" which rises more than twelve thousand feet from the sea level, and is visible from fifty to a hundred miles around. The island was not so very long ago of some commercial importance, and did a large trade in Canary wine and in cochineal. The oidium ruined the one and the introduction of aniline dyes the other, and the Tenerifeans are now fain to fall back on their climate as a staple product, embodying "the potentiality of growing rich beyond the dreams of avarice." In former days Tenerife supplied European apothecaries with Guanche mummies and "dragon's blood" (the juice of the dragon tree, *Dracœna Draco*), which served as ingredients of mystic potency in their horrible concoctions; people are now awaking to the fact that in its air the island possesses a natural medicine which has more than all the supposed virtues of these charms.

Santa Cruz, the capital of Tenerife, is easily reached from Plymouth in five days. The town is beautifully situated, with a background of conical mountains and flanked by steep red cliffs which reminded me of some of the Norwegian fjords. As most visitors use Santa Cruz simply as a landing-place, and at once hurry on to Orotava, its value as a health resort is scarcely so much appreciated as it deserves to be. It is warmer and therefore more relaxing than Orotava, where the trade wind from the north-east makes itself more or less felt every day; but for that very reason it suits some patients better. Dr. Douglas, a former patient of mine, has established a sanatorium at Salamanca, about a mile from Santa Cruz. He has a fine house and a charming flower-garden, in which his patients looked very comfortable as they sat in the shade. One gentleman, who had tried Orotava without much success, had found the air of Santa Cruz very beneficial. I was informed that Mr. Camachio, the proprietor of the principal hotel at Santa Cruz, intends to build another at Salamanca, which will be expressly fitted up for the reception of invalids, for whom there is at present no proper accommodation in the capital itself. From Santa Cruz I proceeded to Orotava, on the north side of the island. The distance is only twenty-five miles, but it takes six hours to cover it, as the ascent for the first five miles is very steep. On the crest of this slope, at a height of two thousand feet above the sea, is Laguna, the ancient capital of Tenerife. It is situated on a plateau surrounded by hills, and has the advantage—almost unique in the island of Tenerife—of having comparatively level ground around it for some distance. Within easy reach of it are the charming forests of Agua Garcia and Mercedes and the Anaga hills. The town itself, though interesting to a stranger for its historical associations and the quaint architecture of its buildings, is one of the dreariest places in the world. It has such a deserted appearance that one might almost take it for a city of the dead; it reminds one of Defoe's description of London after the Great Plague. Its climate, however, in the summer and autumn is deliciously cool, and hence it is the favourite residence during the hot weather, not only of the well-to-do inhabitants of Santa Cruz, but of many people from Orotava. In winter, however, it is often cold and wet, so that, as Mrs. Stone says in her excellent work,* "If any one should be tired of the perpetual sunshine of Orotava, and longs for rains and murky skies such as England possesses, he can obtain a semblance of them by going to Laguna in the winter months." The severity of this remark, however, may have been partly due to the particularly bad weather which the author experienced on the occasion of her winter visit.

From Laguna to Orotava the road winds down a gentle

* "Tenerife and its Six Satellites."

declivity for twenty miles. The valley of Orotava, though it has been greatly praised, did not strike me as particularly beautiful. Humboldt described it as the loveliest valley in the world. Perhaps, as Mr. Edwardes * has suggested, the very extravagance of the praise that has been lavished on it prepares the mind for something so transcendently beautiful that no mere earthly landscape could come up to the expectations that have been excited. It must be remembered also that Humboldt was a young man, and was just starting on his travels when he saw Orotava, and he described his impressions long afterwards, when probably distance of time and indistinctness of memory lent enchantment to the view. Even the most ardent champion of the Fortunate Islands must allow that the country lacks the greenness of Madeira, and the "finish" of the Riviera, and has a general appearance of not being well kept. As in most volcanic districts in the south, the fig, the cactus, and the vine flourish, but the latter is not now extensively cultivated in the valley of Orotava. The aloe is largely used for making hedges, but it does not seem to blossom nearly so freely as in the south of France and in Italy. The cliffs and lower hills are covered with a small shrubby euphorbia, whilst higher up the magnificent *Euphorbia canariensis* with its candelabra-like branches, often attaining a height of twenty feet, is very abundant. The valley itself has something of the form of an amphitheatre sloping down to the sea. There are two towns of Orotava, the Puerto or port, and La Villa or old town. The former is only fifty feet above the sea-level, while La Villa is nearly a thousand feet higher, though only two miles and a half from Puerto. Dotted about the valley of Orotava there are some twenty or thirty villas at various elevations between Puerto and La Villa; these are let to foreigners, mostly Englishmen. Both Puerto and La Villa are depressing places at first; the streets are grass-grown and deserted like those of Laguna, and one would be glad to have even one small wave of that "full tide of human existence" which delighted Johnson in Fleet Street. This desolate appearance of Tenerifean streets is chiefly due to the almost total absence of vehicular traffic; one soon

* "Rides and Studies in the Canary Islands," p. 25.

becomes accustomed to the quiet of the towns, however, and even ceases after a time to notice it. For many invalids, too, the very stillness has a soothing effect, which no doubt plays some part in the general beneficial effect of the change.

Orotava is almost the only place in Tenerife where there is any hotel accommodation for invalids, and even there it is still far from adequate. The place has suffered indirectly from the exuberant enthusiasm of Mr. Ernest Hart, to whose opinion, after his visit in the spring of 1887, great weight was rightly attached. He described the climate, the scenery, the products, vegetable and human, and the arrangements for the reception of invalids, with such tropical luxuriance of epithet, that the island was invaded the following winter by crowds of sufferers, real and imaginary, with their friends and attendants. The result was that the hotel accommodation proved utterly insufficient, the arrangements were unsatisfactory, and considerable discomfort was caused. The next winter, accordingly, there was a marked falling off in the number of invalids who visited Tenerife. Very few of those who had experienced the miseries of life in an overcrowded hotel went back the following winter. On the other hand, those who had been fortunate enough to get villas for themselves almost without exception returned, or remained through the summer on the island. It was the want of proper accommodation, therefore, and not dissatisfaction with the climate, which caused the diminution in the number of visitors. That there was disappointment with the climate in some cases, however, is undeniable, and this is only what was to be expected. The exaggerated reports of the health-giving properties of Tenerife led people to expect miracles; when the inevitable disenchantment followed, the blame of the failure was, of course, laid on the climate. On this subject I shall have something to say further on. A third cause for the diminished influx of visitors to Orotava last winter was a false report that was circulated as to the presence of yellow fever at Santa Cruz. This was naturally taken by most people to mean the capital of Tenerife; there had not, however, been any cases of yellow fever there, but one or two had been imported into Santa Cruz in the Island of Palma.

The Tenerifeans have not failed to profit by the lesson of last winter. The science of hotel management has been carefully studied, and nothing could be more satisfactory than the arrangements now made at Orotava for the comfort of guests. On this point the testimony of the English people whom I met was practically unanimous, and from my own experience I can conscientiously add my voice to the rest.

The "Grand Hotel and Sanatorium" of Orotava is situated at Puerto, some fifty feet above the level of the sea. It was originally a private house built in the Cuban style by a gentleman who made his fortune in Cuba some years ago. It was opened as a hotel on the 1st of September, 1886, but before that date Mrs. Stone had pointed out the advantages of its situation, which gives ample opportunity for gentle exercise in its vicinity. Part of the house is retained by the widow of the former owner, Doña Antonia Dehesa, for her own use, leaving only about twenty bedrooms for visitors. In addition to the main building there is a kind of annexe in the garden of the hotel; this is called the Pavilion, and contains three bedrooms and a sitting-room. From the back of the house projects two long wings, open on one side, and connected together at the farther end by a broad verandah on both sides. This verandah separates the *patio* from the garden. The former is gay with rose-trees, New Zealand flax, and subtropical plants; there is also a magnificent Bougainvillea whose purple flowers cover the billiard-room and spread over one side of the house, whilst on the open verandah there is a splendid creeping Bignonia covered with rich yellowish-brown clusters of flowers. In the garden on the north side of the verandah, the hybiscus, together with the orange, citron, pomegranate, and a number of splendid date palms flourish with the richest luxuriance. The verandah is shaded at one end by some glorious specimens of the Laurus Indica, or royal bay, which here attains the size of a well-grown forest tree. The other side of the verandah opens on to a large basin of artificial water, in which some fine swans with numbers of goldfish live very happily together. It was with a certain sense of "disillusion," however, that I learned that the swans had been supplied to order by the "Universal Provider."

There is, of course, a crumpled leaf in this bed of roses. Señora Dehesa has a passion for domestic pets, and Mrs. Stone describes the house and verandah, when she saw the place, as full of birds of all kinds, while the *patio* was a miniature "wilderness of monkeys." These have disappeared, or, at any rate, I did not see them; but there is still a multitude of bantam cocks and hens together with a large variety of pigeons about the place, which their humane mistress tends with the most loving care before the visitors are about. It is graceful and idyllic, no doubt, but as a matter of prosaic detail the crowing of the cocks is a serious nuisance to invalids and light sleepers. I heard several complaints of broken rest due to this preventible cause. Moreover, the presence of large numbers of poultry so close to the hotel no doubt increases the plague of fleas which swarm everywhere in the Canaries, and seem to have a special predilection for visitors in whom, I suppose, they find "pastures new," more to their taste than their native pabulum.

Another slight drawback, so far as invalids are concerned, is that the verandah is open to the north-east trade wind which, as already said, blows constantly in this region. This wind is not really cold like those sometimes felt in the Riviera, and to people in robust health it is delightfully refreshing. For delicate persons, however, it is a little too strong, and while I was at Orotava I came across one or two invalids who had caught cold owing to this cause, and I have no doubt many others suffer, though perhaps unconsciously, from its effects. This inconvenience might easily be remedied by partly closing the north side of the verandah with glass, an arrangement which would give invalids the advantage of the sun without exposure to the wind.

The Grand Hotel also includes three other establishments which, though separate in themselves, are in organic relation with the central one just described. These (Fonda Marqués, Casa Zamora, and Casa Buenavista) between them can accommodate a hundred guests, so that the total number which can be housed by the Sanatorium is about a hundred and twenty. A new hotel which is being built at Orotava by the same company is now rapidly approaching completion. It will contain accommodation for nearly two hundred visitors, and great efforts are being made to make it comfortable for invalids. It is situated at a level of three hundred feet above the sea, and among other advantages there will be a beautiful verandah absolutely sheltered from the north-east wind, but exposed to the warm rays of the sun. Although this establishment will have advantages of its own, it is to be hoped that the present one will not be given up, for it is certainly rather warmer than the new building will be. Another hotel under different management is, I understand, about to be built at Orotava; it will be most healthily situated at La Paz, on a pleasant site at about the same elevation above the sea as the one just mentioned, but rather farther from the town. It will accommodate about one hundred and fifty visitors. This establishment will not, however, be available till the winter of 1890. Next autumn a boarding-house will also be opened under the management of a Swiss who has lived in England for many years. The several private villas already described can be taken for longer or shorter periods at fair rates. It is clear from all this that the Tenerifeans are determined that the future of their island as a health resort and playground shall not be compromised by the want of accommodation for visitors.

I found Orotava so comfortable that I stayed there most of the time I was at Tenerife, and did not explore the island to any great extent. In my rambles, however, I paid a visit to a place called Icod de los Vinos, which was once the centre of a flourishing wine trade, but which has now fallen on evil days, commercially speaking. It is about twenty miles to the west of Puerto, and stands at a height of some seven hundred feet above the sea. It is beautifully situated on the northern slope of the Peak, but though it has been called one of the "pearls" of Tenerife, its attractions seemed to me to be sufficiently summed up in the words of Justice Shallow, "Marry, good air." I had intended to visit the Grand Canary, but, as I have said, I found my Capua at Orotava, so far as the wandering instinct was concerned. I met a number of travellers, however, who had come on to Orotava from Las Palmas, the capital of Gran

Canaria. The accommodation there is scanty and very inferior to that at Orotava. No hotels have at present been built on high ground, the new hotel which is in process of construction being situated like its predecessor, the oldest in the Canary Islands, on the sandy shore which stretches along the coast. As a consequence of this there is a great deal of dust, which is very trying to invalids. The interior of the island has not been developed nearly so much as Tenerife, and as far as I am aware there are no comfortable villas in the higher parts of the island, so that the invalid is practically confined to the sea-level. The climate of the Grand Canary is, however, rather drier than that of Tenerife, and I have therefore no doubt that it suits some persons better.

The natives of Tenerife struck me as particularly fine specimens of the human race. The men are strong, well-grown, and healthy-looking, and many of the women are very beautiful; but those of the lower class, owing to their being so much occupied in field labour, become old and worn in appearance at a comparatively early age; while the ladies, from want of exercise, soon lose their slimness of figure. Dark eyes and complexions prevail, but a trace of the extinct Guanches is often seen in light-coloured eyes and ruddy hair. The peasantry wear a light cotton jacket and short trousers, but each man has a thick Witney blanket, which is worn as a cloak when the weather is wet or cold. Everybody smokes—urchins of five or six seeming to find as much relish in their cigarettes as their fathers. The outdoor life which is led in these privileged regions makes this apparently excessive indulgence in tobacco harmless. Tobacco is grown in Tenerife, and still more extensively in the Grand Canary, and this might easily be developed into an important industry; but it is not encouraged by the Spanish Government, lest the importation of a cheap tobacco from the Canaries should injure the monopoly in the peninsula. Potatoes grow in such abundance that their exportation to England would be a profitable industry. New potatoes could be sent to Covent Garden in time for Christmas. The soil is so fertile that three crops can be raised in the year without manure. Vines could also no doubt be again cultivated on a large scale, but the wine of the Canaries—whatever may have been its reputation in past days—is now neither agreeable to the palate nor comforting to the stomach. I was informed by a native that the two great advantages of Tenerife are its freedom from marshes and from poisonous snakes. Whilst fully admitting the importance of these negative features, the island has other and better titles to fame as a health-resort—as I shall now proceed to show.

With regard to the climate of Tenerife as a whole, there are three great points which can hardly fail to strike every one who stays in the island for any length of time. These are: (1) the relative *uniformity of temperature*, not only throughout the different parts of the day, but through the various seasons of the year; (2) the *dryness* of the air; and (3) the *variety* of climates within a comparatively small area.

In point of mildness Tenerife compares favourably, not only with all European health resorts, but with Madeira, the mean annual temperature being between 66° and 67° F. in the former, and 63° F. in the latter. At Puerto de Orotava, which faces the sea to the north at an elevation of fifty feet, and which is protected by mountains on the other sides, the mean annual temperature is about 68°; it ranges from 62° in January and February to 76° in July, the extreme difference between winter and summer being therefore not more than fourteen degrees. At Nice the corresponding difference is nearly thirty degrees, whilst even at Algiers it is between twenty-three and twenty-four. The mean temperature during the five months of November, December, January, February and March is between 63° and 64°, the mean range between maximum and minimum being about eleven degrees. This degree of variation is maintained with remarkable steadiness throughout the year, the average temperature in spring being 64°, in summer nearly 71°, in autumn between 69° and 70°, and in winter a little over 60°. The average range of temperature throughout the year therefore does not exceed from ten to eleven degrees. From some careful records of meteorological changes at Puerto de Orotava, for which I am indebted to Dr. Perez, it appears that in January of the present year the mean temperature at 9 a.m. was 61·2, at 2 p.m. 62·7, and at 9 p.m. 57·9; in February the corresponding means were 60·1, 62·5, and 53·5; in March 64·3, 66, and 59·7; and in April, from the 1st to the 25th inclusive, 64·5, 68·2, and 56·5. Careful observations made by Mr. Borham, which that gentleman has with great courtesy placed at my disposal, show that at his villa San Antonio, above Port Orotava, and 346 feet above the sea-level, the mean temperature in November (1888) was at 9 a.m. 66·3, and at 9 p.m. 63·1; in December the corresponding figures were 60·8 and 59·2; in January (1889) 58·9 and 56·4; in February 60·6 and 56·6, and in March 61·8 and 59·4, giving a mean variation between the morning and the evening of 2·8. In November the absolute lowest temperature in the shade was 54·9, in December 51·8, in January 51, in February 50, and in March 49·1; but the mean minimum was for November 59·3, for December 55·4, for January 53, for February 52·7, and for March 54·1. The climate is always better before Christmas than it is afterwards, November and December being perfect. In the early months of the year the weather usually becomes a little unsettled. As a proof of the mildness of the season last December, I may mention that the visitors were able to sit with perfect comfort in the verandah of the Grand Hotel, which, as already remarked, is open on both sides, after a late dinner on Christmas Day. At Villa de Orotava the mean annual temperature is between 66° and 67°, at Santa Cruz between 70° and 71°, and at Laguna about 62°. The wonderful equability of the temperature is largely due to the fact that on most days, just as the sun's rays threaten to make themselves oppressively felt, the trade wind furnishes a refreshing breeze from the north-east to temper their heat. This wind blows every day, but rarely with violence except sometimes in March. In summer and part of the autumn it is scarcely strong enough to shake the withered leaves from the trees. The canopy of cloud that hangs about the hills during the greater part of the day also affords protection. The barometric pressure is also extraordinarily uniform, and violent atmospheric disturbances are almost unknown. Dr.

Grabham of Madeira, however, informs me that he found the land breeze blowing at the rate of four miles an hour at Orotava in February, 1887, showing great terrestrial radiation and rapid cooling. It is important to note that there is hardly any difference in the temperature between the open air and the inside of the house.

No fires or other means of generating artificial warmth are used by the natives, but there are occasionally days on which English people would enjoy a small fire—especially in the evening. It need scarcely be pointed out that delicate persons feel chilly at a temperature which is pleasant and invigorating to the healthy, the slight difference between the sunshine of day and the shade of evening being disagreeably felt by invalids. Both the new hotels will be provided with fireplaces in the public rooms and in many of the sitting-rooms.

The dryness of the atmosphere is not less remarkable than the mildness and equability of the temperature. The mean relative humidity of the air at Port Orotava from November to April was ascertained by Dr. Hjalmar Öhrvall, of Upsala, to be 65·3 at 8 a.m., 60·1 at 2 p.m., and 69·1 at 9 p.m., giving a mean of 64·9 (saturation being expressed as 100). The average rainfall is about 13 inches, and the average number of rainy days in the year, taking the mean of ten years, is only 51. During the winter of 1883-4, a season of extraordinary and almost unparalleled wetness at Tenerife, there were seventy-eight rainy days, but the average number in ordinary winters is only 41. In January of the year of my visit rain (counting every drizzle) fell on fourteen days, the rainfall for the whole month being 2·39 inches; in February it rained on ten days, the amount for the month being 1·57 inches; in March the corresponding numbers were eight days and 1·15 inches; and from April 1 to 25, rain fell on nine days, the amount being ·55 inch.* The air is, as a rule, so dry that a piece of paper can be exposed all night without losing its crispness.

* Mr. Borham's tables, which have already been referred to, are here appended. The figures, which, it is needless to say, are absolutely trustworthy, give, as it were, a summary of the climate of Tenerife during the past winter, which was considered exceptionally cold. Indeed, a lady

HEALTH-SEEKING IN TENERIFE AND MADEIRA. 61

The chief advantage, however, of Tenerife as a health resort is the facility for frequent change of air and scene which it offers within a very small area. In this I think Tenerife stands alone among the Canaries, and is not equalled by Madeira. Custom cannot stale the infinite variety of climate which this *multum in parvo* of an island contains within the narrow circle of its own shores. If the Valley of Orotava is too relaxing, there is Laguna only a few hours' drive away, which is as bracing as Eastbourne, without its east winds ; if Puerto is not warm enough, there is Santa Cruz with the air of who had lived in the island for twenty-three years told me she had never experienced such a winter.

SAN ANTONIO, PORT OROTAVA (346 feet above mean sea-level).

		November, 1888.	December, 1888.	January, 1889.	February, 1889.	March, 1889.
Means.						
Barometer corrected	9 A.M.	30·206	30·190	30·275	30·241	30·175
	9 P.M.	30·195	30·198	30·256	30·248	30·199
Dry bulb	9 A.M.	66·3	60·8	58·0	60·6	61·8
	9 P.M.	63·1	59·2	56·4	56·6	59·4
Wet bulb	9 A.M.	61·3	58·4	54·8	55·3	57·3
	9 P.M.	59·8	57·1	53·6	53·7	56·0
Dew point	9 A.M.	57·1	56·4	51·2	50·8	53·5
	9 P.M.	57·0	55·4	50·3	50·9	53·2
Vapour tension	9 A.M.	0·480	0·459	0·378	0·373	0·412
	9 P.M.	0·469	0·440	0·369	0·376	0·410
Cloud	9 A.M.	4·8	5·1	5·0	5·0	5·4
	9 P.M.	4·5	5·9	5·5	5·0	6·0
Relative humidity, mean of	9 A.M. 3 P.M. 9 P.M.	75·0	84·0	76·0	74·0	77·0
Rain.	Total	0·513	3·994	2·203	1·430	1·174
	Average	0·064	0·234	0·157	0·143	0·147
Maximum in shade		69·8	65·6	62·7	64·2	64·5
Minimum ,,		59·3	55·4	53·0	52·7	54·1
Maximum on grass		138·5	130·5	135·8	138·7	—
Minimum ,,		55·5	52·7	50·1	47·3	47·6
Sunshine		3h. 48m.	3h. 13m.	3h. 27m.	5h. 16m.	4h. 48m.
Extremes.						
Barometer	Highest	30·396	30·474	30·579	30·556	30·368
	Lowest	30·091	29·726	29·972	29·554	29·879
Shade temp.	Highest	73·8	69·4	65·5	75·5	69·2
	Lowest	54·9	51·8	51·0	50·0	49·1
Solar radiation, max.		152·8	142·9	154·8	149·3	—
Terrestrial radiation, min.		51·0	49·4	47·5	39·9	40·3
Greatest daily rain		0·170	0·860	0·720	0·520	0·722
Rainy days		8·0	17·0	14·0	10·0	8·0
Quantity above or below ten years' average		−1·220	+1·867	+·195	−1·090	−·913

a hothouse tempered by sea breezes. One may say the various climates rise tier on tier as you go upwards from the sea; with each thousand feet of elevation we pass into a different climatological stratum, the air of course becoming colder and more bracing as we go up. These different zones are pretty clearly marked out by the varying type of vegetation. Near the sea, palms, bananas, oleanders, etc., flourish with subtropical luxuriance; from one to two thousand feet above this, gorse and broom, chestnut and apple trees predominate; then comes the region of laurels; then the heaths with the Canarian pines; lastly, a barren waste of rock covered with lava and pumice.

Orotava itself may almost be said to have two different climates, that of La Villa and its neighbourhood being more bracing than that of Puerto. It is a very dull place. La Villa is even duller than Puerto, and at present there is no English hotel in the old town; but, as already stated, private villas may be procured at various elevations above the sea, and in them invalids can be very comfortable. This is unquestionably the best plan if it is possible to carry it out; unfortunately Tenerife has comparatively few of the *quintas* (or *sitios*, as they are called in the Canaries) which exist in such numbers in Madeira. Then there is Laguna, standing nearly two thousand feet above the sea-level, with a mean temperature of 58·3° F. in winter, and 68·4° F. in summer. It is undoubtedly a healthy and bracing place, although it has almost a monopoly of such clouds and mists as ever darken the sky of the Fortunate Islands.

The real mountain resort in the island, however, is Vilaflor, or, as it was formerly called, Chasna. This is the health resort *par excellence* of the natives of Tenerife. It is on the south side of the island, 4,500 feet above the level of the sea, with pine trees covering the hills above it up to a height of 6,000 feet. It is sheltered by the Canadas and the Peak from the north and north-east wind. It boasts a spring of mineral waters which have a high local reputation in disorders of the digestive organs, almost the only form of disease which is endemic in the Canaries. Here phthisis is said to be unknown, and the rate of mortality from all the ills that flesh is heir to is one of the lowest in the world. Under these circumstances it is not surprising to find an enthusiastic physician of La Villa (Dr. Zerolo, " Orotava-Vilaflor : Estaciones Sanitarias de Tenerife," p. 24) claiming for Vilaflor the title of " the first mountain station in the whole universe " !

The other islands of the Canary group are within easy reach, and the excellent inter-insular service of steamers readily enables even invalids to obtain change of air. Las Palmas in the Grand Canary has a singularly bright winter climate owing to the distance of the central heights. The island of Palma is much more wooded than the Grand Canary, and its climate is Atlantic in character. Gomera, another of the islands, is a little paradise which has hitherto been almost entirely neglected.

From this brief sketch it will be seen that in point of climate Tenerife may not unfairly be described as an epitome of all other health resorts, just as its famous botanical garden is a microcosm of the vegetation of the whole earth. There are excellent roads (*carreteras*) over a considerable part of the island, so that all the principal climatic centres, if I may call them so, are readily enough accessible.

One slight drawback connected with the climate of Tenerife must be mentioned, and that is the presence of mosquitos. Though they are neither so numerous nor so ferocious as in many other places, they are a thorn in the flesh of visitors nearly everywhere where the elevation is low. At Santa Cruz they are so abundant that all beds are provided with curtains. Dr. Zerolo indignantly denies that there are any (to speak of) at La Villa ; but whilst I was at Puerto one gentleman told me that he saw a few, and another that he had killed ten before getting into bed. The new establishment, owing to its being at a higher level above the sea than the present " grand " hotel, will probably be free from this nuisance.

The main features of the climate of Madeira are much the same as those of Tenerife, or, to speak more strictly, of Orotava. The mean annual temperature of Madeira is, however, four or five degrees lower ; but, on the other hand, the daily range of variation is on the average about two degrees less. The climate of Madeira is therefore still more equable than that of Tenerife. It is not so dry, the average number of days on which rain falls * being about 70, and the annual rainfall 28 or 29. The relative humidity of the atmosphere is from 76 to 79. The sky is more overcast as a rule than in the Canaries, there being a certain amount of cloudiness nearly every day. The two climates during the last winter underwent a certain amount of change in different directions, the Canary Islands having had less sunshine than they generally have, and the weather in Madeira having been abnormally bright. Dr. Grabham greatly prefers the normal cloudiness, and he has observed that certain acute diseases were more prevalent last winter when the sun played on the island without restraint. The vegetation is similar in type in Madeira and Tenerife, though in the latter island it is rather more African in character. The former has the same advantages as Tenerife as regards residence at different heights, except that in the Portuguese island there are no hotels at an elevation of two thousand feet.

Funchal is situated near the coast, but the best hotels and *quintas* are built on the crests of the hills which form the spurs of loftier mountains further in the interior. When the weather becomes too hot in the neighbourhood of Funchal patients can go higher up either to the villas on the Palheiro road, or to those below the level of the Mount, over which a Scotch mist not unfrequently rests. Those who wish for a still higher elevation and can afford to hire a villa may spend the summer in Comachio, which is more than 2,000 feet above the sea; there they will find a delicious English summer climate with apple and pear trees growing abundantly. For those who prefer the sea, Santa Cruz at the east end of the island, and in the summer months Santa Anna on the north side, will be found very pleasant. Personally, in spite of all the dithyrambs of Mr. Hart and the guide-book writers, I prefer the scenery of Madeira to that of the Canaries. There is a want of trees and, generally, of natural beauty in these islands which makes them much less agreeable to the eye than Madeira. On the other hand, Tenerife has greatly the

* In these statistics the smallest drizzle is counted.

advantage of Madeira in point of roads. There is nothing in the latter island corresponding to the *carretera*. The roads are so steep that ordinary carriages with horses can hardly be used without considerable risk, and the pace is necessarily very slow. The bullock sleighs (or *carros*, as they are called in the island) travel quickly and safely up and down the hills, whilst the hammock affords a very pleasant mode of conveyance. This useful institution has lately been introduced into Tenerife, but the Spaniards have not yet mastered the art of carrying without shaking.

Dr. Grabham, the well-known physician of Madeira, considers that the absence of carriages is an advantage rather than a drawback, as invalids frequently catch cold when out driving, but it is certainly a great inconvenience to other people. Madeira has a great advantage over Tenerife as regards villas, which may be hired by invalids for their sole use; while there are about a hundred and fifty of these near Funchal, there are only some twenty in the Orotava valley. Again, there are six hotels at Madeira, and there will soon be a seventh; they are situated at different levels, and therefore adapted to different cases. There is decidedly more comfort and general convenience in Madeira than in the Canaries, not the least important element in the visitor's happiness in the former, being the excellent Portuguese servants who have been trained to English ways from generation to generation for a hundred years. On the other hand, the expense of living is much higher in Madeira than in Tenerife. All ports in the Canary Islands are free, and English goods can be readily introduced. Both Madeira and the Canaries are now almost equally accessible. Tenerife can be reached in five days from Plymouth, but as the steamers now only travel at the rate of about ten knots an hour, I believe the voyage could easily be reduced to three days. Those who object to a long sea passage can go by Spain, Portugal, and Madeira.

It only remains for me to speak of the various complaints for which these climates are suitable, and of the kind of cases to which each of them is, in my own opinion, more particularly beneficial. With reference to the latter point, however, it

must be borne in mind that it is impossible to say with
certainty what climate will best suit any given case. It is
the same with medicines; the *idiosyncrasy* of the patient may
cause a drug, like opium or quinine, to have little or no effect,
or one altogether different from that which is desired. A
climate which acts like a charm on one person may not benefit
another in what seems to be precisely the same condition.
One can only lay down general rules, which are subject to
modification by the circumstances of the case. Lung disease,
of course, occupies the foreground in all questions of climatic
treatment, and with respect to that I do not know that there
is much to choose between Madeira and Tenerife. Both seem
to be equally beneficial with precisely the same limitations. No
climate can cure a patient in an advanced stage of phthisis,
whose lungs are riddled with cavities and whose vital power
is exhausted by hectic. No patient should ever be sent
abroad who is obliged to keep his bed. The whole benefit
of a new climate consists in its making an open-air life
possible. Doctors, however, are often unjustly blamed for
sending hopeless cases to a health resort when the blame rests
altogether with the patient, who thinks, if he can only reach
some place of which he has heard or read, he will get well.
Some years ago I saw an American gentleman, evidently in
a dying state, who had set his heart on going to Davos, and
would not be turned from his purpose. He reached his
destination, but only to die the day after his arrival. When
the disease is in an early stage, or when there is only some
"delicacy" of the lungs, a stay at either Madeira or the
Canaries for some length of time will in all probability ward
off the danger, and perhaps permanently cure the patient.
In such cases there is no other place that can be compared
to these; and many persons, who would beyond all doubt
have died long ago had they stayed at home, have been
saved by residence in the Canary Islands or Madeira for
three or four years or for longer periods. Several English
people have permanently taken up their abode in each of
them, and the fiend of "tubercle" seems to have been completely exorcized. This happy effect is not due, as is some-

times absurdly stated, to the fact that the pure "balsamic," "antiseptic" air kills the minute organisms which are now believed to be concerned in the causation of the disease, but is the result of the general strengthening of the system, which restores to the tissues sufficient vitality to resist the microbes. This building up anew of the constitution is effected by increased use of the lungs, and the only way to secure that is by exercise in the open air. The exercise must, of course, be carefully adapted to the patient's power of endurance. Young invalids often err in this way, by wasting their strength under the impression that they acquire stamina thereby. I found, for instance, that some of the patients who had spent the winter at Orotava had climbed the Canadas (a large extinct crater halfway up the Peak), taken long rides, made distant excursions across the island, and even played at tilting. I know several cases in which a serious relapse occurred in consequence of such imprudence. A quiet stroll or sitting in the sun will do good where violent exercise would be simply baneful.

A word of caution is necessary as to the risk involved in the case of a person suffering from advanced disease who goes on a journey, like that to the Canaries, of five days from Plymouth or seven from London in a steamer. The sea-sickness, semi-starvation, and general knocking about may easily rouse the smouldering volcano of chronic disease into activity. Many patients would derive much benefit from the Riviera whom it would not be safe to send to the Canary Islands or to Madeira.

Whilst at Tenerife I saw a good many cases of lung disease in consultation with Dr. George Perez, son of a well-known physician at Orotava, and himself a graduate of the University of London. In most of them there was considerable destruction of tissue in one or both lungs. In all but three of these cases, the reparative process was very remarkable, and in two of these exceptions great improvement had taken place, but the patients had lost ground again owing to the effects of their own imprudence, or from accidentally taking cold. As all patients coming to Tenerife and leaving it have to pass through Santa

Cruz, I thought that a favourable place for making inquiries as to the condition of the visitors at the time of their departure for England. The worst that could be said by a person who had had ample opportunities of seeing every patient who embarked, and who was by no means disposed to be over-friendly to Orotava, was that eight or nine persons had been carried on board.

Orotava with its sunny climate seemed to me to be particularly suitable for cases of consumption still in what is called the "first stage." It is also likely to be beneficial to those in the second stage, especially when there is profuse secretion. When there is constant high temperature, especially if there is a tendency to the spitting of blood, Madeira should be selected. Persons in the third stage of consumption should be restrained from going to either of these places or anywhere else; for them emphatically "There's no place like home." Tenerife is also beneficial in cases of bronchitis, when there is much secretion; for "dry" bronchitis Madeira is better. One of these health resorts may, with great advantage, be made to supplement the other according to the variations in the patient's condition, or to the development of different phases of his disease. Dr. Grabham tells me he has for years made use of the Canaries as a change from Madeira in cases of chronic disease, chiefly phthisis, when there is general failure of the vital powers, depression, and loss of appetite. The change is almost invariably most beneficial for a time. If the disease appears to be entering on an inflammatory phase, the sufferer should be sent to Madeira till the febrile symptoms subside. I entirely agree with Dr. Grabham that the slow process of recovery from phthisis may be powerfully aided by this alternation of Madeira with the Canaries. Asthmatic patients as a rule do well at Madeira if an elevation of 300 feet is selected; but most cases, if simple in character, find more relief in the Canaries. This disease, however, is so capricious in all its relations that it is quite impossible to say which place will suit any individual case. I saw one child who was cured of asthma after three or four years' residence at Orotava, and one or two other cases in which improvement had taken place. There is no doubt that in certain varieties of kidney disease much benefit is derived from residence either in the Canaries or Madeira, more particularly the latter. This is not yet, I think, sufficiently realized by English physicians. In cases of convalescence after acute or exhausting illness, especially where protection from chill and sudden changes of temperature is desirable, both Madeira and Tenerife can be recommended. Madeira is for this reason likely to be especially useful in convalescence from scarlet fever.

In addition to what may be termed their peculiar function as health resorts, both Madeira and the Canary Islands have, I think, a great future before them as places of rest where overworked professional men, jaded politicians, and persons suffering from nervous breakdown can recruit their wasted energy. As a playground the Canaries leave little to be desired. Excursions adapted to every organization can be comfortably made. Excellent Andalusian horses are to be had; and, here and there, there is soft ground where healthy persons may enjoy a good canter. There is also a small breed of native horses admirably adapted for climbing up the bridle roads. Comfortable carriages are also to be found both at Orotava and Santa Cruz. Of the restorative power of Tenerife I can speak from experience. I arrived there completely broken down by a winter of unusually hard work, and at the end of a fortnight I was in perfect health.

For invalids the best time to go to the Canaries is about the middle, or, better still, towards the end of October. English people arriving before that time are apt to find the climate oppressive. They can remain at Orotava till June, or if they go first to La Villa and afterwards to Laguna the whole year can be spent most comfortably (as far as climate is concerned) in the island. For those merely suffering from exhaustion or over-tension of the nervous system, I think the spring is the best time. A trip to the Canaries makes an admirable Easter holiday; there are Guanche mummies and undecipherable inscriptions for antiquaries, quaint rites and ceremonies for the curious, and air and sunlight, sea and mountain for everybody.

In conclusion, a word or two may be said on the general subject of climate with reference to its influence on disease. It is a great mistake for a patient to think that he can go to a place which has the reputation of being beneficial to his complaint, and simply absorb health from the atmosphere without any effort on his own part. As Sir James Clark said many years ago, " The air, or climate, is often regarded by the patient as possessing some specific quality, by virtue of which it directly cures his disease. This erroneous view of the matter not unfrequently proves the bane of the invalid by leading him, in the fulness of his confidence in climate, to neglect other circumstances as essential to his recovery as that in which all his hopes are fixed." Climate, in fact, only helps those who help themselves. A visit to a health resort must not be looked upon as an excuse for neglecting necessary precautions or relaxing salutary rules, but rather as an occasion for still more careful living. Not the least beneficial part of the climatic treatment is the enforced freedom from social temptations which at home would lead to imprudent exposure, excitement, and fatigue. Climate, in fact, cannot cure any disease ; it only removes one of the exciting causes of the mischief, and so far leaves Nature a fair field for the exercise of her healing influence.

SPEECH AND SONG.

Part I.—Speech.

In dealing with the two great forms of vocal utterance, it will be most convenient to take them in their historical, or at any rate their logical, order. Whatever "native woodnotes wild" our hypothetical half-human ancestor may have "warbled" by way of love-ditties before he taught himself to speak, there is no doubt that singing as an *art* is a later development than articulate speech, without which, indeed, song would be like a body without a soul. I will, therefore, treat of speech first; and it will clear the ground if I begin with a definition. Physiologically, speech is the power of modifying vocal sound by breaking it up into distinct elements, and moulding it, if I may say so, into different forms. *Speech*, in this sense, is the universal faculty of which the various *languages* by means of which men hold converse with each other are the particular manifestations. Speech is the abstract genus, language the concrete species.

I am happy to say it does not fall within the scope of my present purpose to discuss the origin of language, a mysterious problem, on which the human brain has exercised itself so much and to so little purpose, that some years ago, I believe, the French Academy declined to receive any further communications on the subject. The origin of the *voice* is a different matter. The vocal function is primarily a means of expression. I see no reason for disagreeing with Darwin, when he says that " the primeval use and means of development of the voice" was as an instrument of sexual attraction. The progenitors of man, both male and female, are supposed to have made every effort to charm each other by vocal melody, or what they considered to be such, and by constant practice with that object the vocal organs became developed. Darwin seems inclined to believe that, as women have sweeter voices than men, they were the first to acquire musical powers in order to attract the other sex—by which, I suppose, he means that the feminine voice owes its greater sweetness to more persevering culture for purposes of flirtation. I do not know whether the ladies of the present day will own this soft impeachment, or whether they will be flattered by the suggestion that their remote ancestresses lived in a perpetual Leap Year of courtship. Other emotions, however, besides the master passion of love had to be expressed; joy, anger, fear, and pain, had all to find utterance, and the nervous centres excited by these various stimuli threw the whole muscular system into violent contractions, which in the case of the muscles moving the chest and the vocal cords naturally produced sound—that is to say, voice. These movements, at first accidental and purposeless, in time became inseparably associated with the emotional state giving rise to them, so as to coincide with it, and thus serve as an index or expression thereof. From this to the voluntary emission of vocal sounds is an easy step, and it is probable enough that the character of those sounds was primarily due to the "imitation and modification of different natural sounds, the voices of other animals and man's own instinctive cries." *

The mechanism of the voice is extremely simple in its general principles, though highly complex in its details. Fortunately a knowledge of the latter is not required for the comprehension of the main facts relative to the production of the voice, and I shall not further allude to them here. Vocal sound is produced solely in the larynx, an elementary fact which must be thoroughly grasped, as many absurd notions are current even among people who should know better, such as that the voice may be produced at the back of the nose, in

* "Descent of Man," 2nd ed., 1882, p. 87.

the stomach and elsewhere. The larynx is a musical instrument of very complex structure, partaking both of the reed and the string type, the former, however, distinctly predominating. It is essentially a small chamber with cartilaginous walls, which is divided into an upper and a lower compartment by a sort of sliding floor, or double valve, formed by the two vocal cords. In breathing this valve opens, its two lateral halves gliding wide apart from each other, so as to allow a broad column of air to pass through; in speaking or singing, on the other hand, the valve is closed, but for a narrow rift along its middle. Through this small chink the air escaping from the lungs is forced out gradually in a thin stream, which is compressed, so to speak, between the edges of the cords, that form the opening, technically called the "glottis," through which it passes. The arrangement is typical of the economical workmanship of Nature. The widest possible entrance is prepared for the air which is taken into the lungs, as the freest ventilation of their whole mucous surface is necessary. When the air has been fully utilized for that purpose, it is, if need be, put to a new use on its way out for the production of voice, and in that case it is carefully husbanded and allowed to escape in severely regulated measure, every particle of it being made to render its exact equivalent in force to work the vocal mill-wheel. When the air is driven from the lungs up the windpipe it strikes against the under surface of the floor or double valve formed by the vocal cords, which are firmly stretched to receive the shock, forces them apart to a greater or less extent, and, in rushing out between them, throws them into vibration. The vibration of the vocal cords makes the column of air itself vibrate, and the vibration is communicated to the air in the upper part of the throat, the nose, and mouth, from which finally it issues as *sound*. The vocal cords are the "reeds" of the vocal instrument, and as, owing to the extraordinary number and intricate arrangement of their muscular fibres, they can change their length and shape and thickness in an almost infinite variety of ways, they are equal in effect to many different reeds. If the vocal cords cannot move so as to bring their edges almost into contact, or if there is any substance between them which prevents them from coming together, the voice is destroyed; if there is anything (such as a growth) in or on one of them, its vibration is more or less checked, and hoarseness is the consequence. The primary sound generated in the larynx is modified by the shape, size, and density of the parts through which the vibrating column of air has to pass before it issues from the "barrier of the teeth." These "resonators" include the part of the larynx above the vocal cords, with the little sounding board, the epiglottis, covering it; the upper part of the throat or pharynx, the nasal passages with certain echoing caves in the bones of the skull which communicate therewith; and the mouth, with the soft palate and uvula, tongue, cheeks, teeth, and lips. It is to these resonators, as well as to the size and shape of the larynx itself—and those parts, like the features of the face, are never exactly similar in any two individuals—that the distinctive quality, or *timbre*, of the voice is due.

Timbre is the physiognomy of the voice by which the speaker can be recognized even when unseen. Just as the face may be lit up with joy, darkened with sorrow, or distorted with passion, so may the voice be altered by strong mental emotion. This is due to the influence of the mind on the nervous system, which controls every part of the body; if it be stimulated, increased action will be excited; if disordered by shock, feeble irregular movements will be produced, the limbs will shake, and the voice tremble. From the effect of peculiarities of physical conformation on the voice it will be readily understood that *timbre* may be, in some degree, a national or racial peculiarity. There are also certain physical types which correspond to particular *timbres* of the voice. I have noticed this particularly in persons of like complexion even when different in race. Thus, a certain sharp metallic clearness of articulation is often found in individuals of ruddy complexion, light yellow hair, and hard blue eyes, whilst rich mellow tones, with a tendency to *portamento* in ordinary speech, are often associated with black hair and florid face. A remarkable point is that the same voice may be altogether different in *timbre* in singing from what it is in speaking.

The difference is probably due to the fact that in singing the resonators are, instinctively, or as the result of training, managed in a more artistically effective manner than in ordinary speech.

Speech differs from song as walking does from dancing; speech may be called the prose, song the poetry of vocal sound. Mr. Herbert Spencer has defined song as "emotional speech," but this term might with greater justice be used to designate the hystero-epileptic oratory which threatens to become acclimatized in this sober island, or even to the exchange of amenities between two angry cabmen. It would be more accurate to call song "musical speech," using the word "musical" in its strict sense as signifying sound with definite variations of tone and regularity of time. But, just as there may be "songs without words," so there may be speech without voice, as in whispering. Sound, as we have already seen, is produced in the larynx, but articulation, or the transformation of meaningless sound into speech, is performed in the mouth; in speaking, therefore, the two parts work together, the larynx sending out a stream of sound, and the mouth, by means of the tongue, checks, palate, teeth, and lips, breaking it up into variously formed jets or words. In other words, the larynx supplies the raw material of sound which the mouth manufactures into speech. Time, which is an essential element of song, is altogether disregarded in speech, whilst the intervals of tone are so irregular as to defy notation, and are filled up with a number of intermediate sounds instead of being sharply defined. The voice glides about at its own sweet will in speaking, obeying no rule whatever, whilst in song it springs or drops from one tone to the next over strictly measured gaps. In singing, short syllables are lengthened out and cease in fact to be short, and—except in certain kinds of dramatic singing and in recitative—the accent naturally falls on the vowels and not on the consonants. In speaking, only the lower third of the voice is employed as a rule, whilst in singing the greatest effect is generally produced, except in the case of contraltos and basses, by the use of the upper and middle notes. In speech the range of tone, even in the most excitable persons, hardly ever exceeds half an octave; in singing the average compass is two octaves. Singing tends to preserve purity of language, the rules which govern the utterance of every note also affecting the articulate element combined with it, and keeping the words cast in fixed forms— a stereotype of sound, if I may venture the metaphor. Speech, on the other hand, like handwriting, is always changing. As Max Müller says : "A struggle for life is constantly going on amongst the words and grammatical forms in each language. The better, the shorter, the easier forms are constantly gaining the upper hand, and they owe their success to their own inherent virtue." * Thus speech not only tends to split language into dialects, but each dialect is being continually, though imperceptibly, modified, not only in construction but in pronunciation. The pronunciation of an Englishman of Chaucer's day would be unintelligible to us, whilst that of one of Shakespeare's contemporaries would be as strange to our ears as the accent of an Aberdeen fishwife is to the average Cockney. If the speaking voice has a distinctly sing-song character—that is to say, if it proceeds by musical intervals— the result is as grotesque as it would be to talk in blank verse, or, as Sir Toby Belch says, "to go to church in a galliard and come home in a coranto." On the other hand, the speaking voice becomes most sympathetic in its quality when it approaches the singing voice, the musical character, however, being concealed by the variety of its inflections. It is important that in speaking a musical note should never be recognized; the effect is as unpleasant to our ears as an accidental hexameter in a sentence of prose was to the ancients.

Wide as the difference is between speech and song, the great gulf fixed between them is partly filled up by intermediate modes of using the voice which partake of the nature of both. Thus there is the measured utterance of declamation, which may be so rhythmical in time and varied in tone as to be almost song. On the other hand, the *recitativo* of the opera approaches speech. Various intermediate forms between speech

* *Nature*, January 6, 1870.

and song may be heard in the ordinary speech of certain races, notably in Italians, Welshmen, and the inhabitants of certain parts of Scotland and England. The Puritans, as is well known, uttered their formal and affected diction in a peculiar nasal tone; and the term "cant," though properly belonging to their sing-song delivery, came to be applied to the sentiments expressed by it. Many of the ancient orators, to judge from the description left us by Cicero and Quintilian, would seem to have *sung* their speeches, the style of declamation being, in fact, expressly termed *cantus obscurior*. As they generally spoke in the open air, and to vast audiences, this artificial mode of delivery may have been necessary in order to make the voice reach further than if they had spoken in a more natural way. C. Gracchus used to have a musician behind him while he spoke, to give him the *note* from time to time with a musical instrument called a *tonarion*. A similar plan might, with much advantage to the "general ear," be adopted by certain modern orators, the *crescendo* of whose enthusiasm expresses itself in increasing intensity of shrillness.

Those who have not given much attention to the subject are apt to think of speaking, as Dogberry did of reading and writing, that it "comes by nature"—that it is, in fact, an instinctive act, which no more needs cultivation for its right performance than eating or sleeping. This is a great mistake. Speaking, even of that slipshod kind which is mostly used in ordinary conversation, is an *art*, and as such has to be *learned*, often with much labour. The complicated muscular actions, the nice nervous adjustments, the combination of these into one harmonious effort directed to a particular end, and, finally, the mastery of all these movements till they can be produced automatically without a direct and continuous exercise of willpower, form a complex process which takes years to learn, and which, by many, is even then very imperfectly acquired. Good speaking is a higher development of the art, which bears the same relation to speech as ordinarily heard, that the horsemanship of an Archer or a Cannon bears to the performance of a costermonger's boy on the paternal donkey.

A man who speaks well not only makes himself intelligible

to his hearers without difficulty to them, but with a minimum of effort on his own part. If the voice is properly used the throat hardly ever suffers, but wrong production is a fertile source of discomfort and even disease in that region. It should be clearly understood that public speaking, in addition to its intellectual aspects, is a physical performance which requires " wind " and " muscle " and the perfect management of one's bodily resources, like any other athletic feat. To attempt to speak in public without previous training is like trying to climb the Matterhorn without preparation, and is just as certain to end in failure if not disaster.

It is hardly an exaggeration to say that the training of the voice should begin almost in the cradle. I do not, of course, mean that a baby should be taught to squall according to rule, or that the prattle of children should be made a laborious task. But I wish to insist on the importance of surrounding the child, as soon as it begins to lisp, with persons who speak well. "All languages," as old Roger Ascham says, "both learned and mother tongues, are begotten and gotten solely by imitation. For as ye use to hear so ye learn to speak ; if you hear no other ye speak not yourself ; and whom ye only hear of them ye only learn." Quintilian says : " Before all . . . let the nurses speak properly. The boy will hear them first, and will try to shape his words by imitating them." This applies chiefly to pronunciation and the correct use of words ; but much might also be done for the right management of the voice if every child could grow up among people who speak well. I should be disposed to make it an essential point in the selection of a nurse or governess that she should have a good voice as well as a refined accent.

In antiquity the training of an orator was almost as elaborate an affair as the training of a racehorse is with us. Not only the voice, but the whole man, physical, intellectual, and moral, was carefully prepared, with conscientious minuteness of detail, for the great business of life, the making of speeches. In this system of education the development of the voice naturally held a large place, and the *phonascus*, or voice driller, was an indispensable accessory, not only of every school of oratory, but of many formed orators. Of the methods of the *phonascus* we know little, but we find hints in some of the classical writers that, like certain of his professional brethren in more recent days, he was not disinclined to magnify his office. Seneca, in one of his letters, warns his friend against living, vocally speaking, in subjection to his *phonascus*, and implies that he might as well keep another artist to superintend his walking. In our own day the *phonascus* still survives in public life, though perhaps more as a luxury than an acknowledged necessity. A celebrated novelist, dramatic author, and orator, who passed over to the great majority many years ago, used always to put himself under the guidance of a vocal mentor before delivering a speech. Every tone, every pose, and every gesture was carefully prepared and industriously practised, under the direction of Mr. Frederick Webster, brother of the celebrated comedian, Benjamin Webster. That the elaborate training of the ancients was eminently successful is shown by the powers of endurance which it is clear they must have possessed. They habitually spoke for five or six hours, and even longer, and, in order to appreciate their staying power, it must be remembered that they spoke in the open air, amidst all the tumult of the forum, which was capable of holding 80,000 people, and with an amount and vigour of action of which the gesticulations of an Italian preacher are but a pale reflex. Long-windedness was at one time cultivated as a fine art by Roman orators, when they had to plead before a judge whom they supposed to be in favour of the other side. These prototypes of our modern obstructionists were aptly termed *moratores*, or delayers, because they postponed as far as possible the passing of the sentence. The abuse finally reached such a height that a law had to be passed limiting the length of pleadings in public cases to the running out of one clepsydra. It is impossible to say exactly what period of time this was equivalent to, as the water-clocks of the Romans were of different sizes, and the rapidity of flow must have varied under different circumstances; from twenty minutes to half an hour may, however, be taken as roughly representing the average length of a speech under this strict system of "closure." Much as I admire the eloquence of our own House of Commons, I do not think the business of the country would suffer if a similar "statute of limitations" were introduced into its debates.

If the Romans carried the culture of the speaking voice to a pedantic extreme, we, on the other hand, undoubtedly neglect it too much. It is not that we speak less, but that we have less appreciation than the ancients had of oratory as a fine art; and we are therefore more tolerant of mumbling utterance and slovenly delivery. Many an inarticulate speaker who, in these days, hums and haws through an hour or two of dreary platitudes, would have been hooted down in five minutes by a Greek or Roman audience. The comparative decay of orators in modern times is due to the diffusion of cheap literature; the function of the public speaker has been to a great extent made obsolete by the daily newspapers. Information and arguments on political matters, which had formerly to be supplied by word of mouth from the rostrums, are now served up, spiced to each reader's taste, by innumerable "able editors." But though the necessity for what I may call professional orators no longer exists, a large part of the business of the State in a free country must still be carried on or controlled by talk, and the living voice must always have a power of stirring and swaying popular sentiment—the collective feeling of large masses of men, which is something more than the sum of their individual feelings—far beyond the reach of the pen. John Bright's exquisite purity of style would have made him a most effective writer; but would his great speeches, if cut up into leading articles, have stirred the national heart as did his burning words, thrown red-hot among a living mass of enthusiastic hearers? Again, newspapers have not yet taken the place of the highly fee'd orators of the Bar, nor of the edifying eloquence of the pulpit, to say nothing of Mansion House and Exeter Hall meetings, and the inevitable post-prandial speechifying without which the British Constitution could not, I suppose, hold together long. On the whole, I think we use the voice in public even more than the ancients, and there is, therefore, all the more reason for its being properly trained. Good speaking is nowadays important, not only from the artistic, but from the business point of view; and, even for "practical men," it it cannot be a waste of time to acquire so valuable a faculty. These arguments may perhaps seem superfluous, as the proposition they are intended to support is self-evident. I lay stress on them, however, because I am convinced that the necessity of training the speaking voice is very imperfectly appreciated by most people.

It is not within my province to discuss the technical details of voice training. I will only say that every system of vocal instruction should aim at strengthening the power of the voice, increasing its compass, and purifying its tone, and, above all, at giving the speaker perfect control over it, even in the very whirlwind of oratorical passion. It would be well if every school in the land had a master of elocution attached to it, and if the art of delivery were taught to every boy as part of the regular course of education. As long as it is only an "accomplishment," a luxury, there will always be a certain contempt for it among English schoolboys. In the excellent system of education which Rabelais sketched out, the development of the voice is expressly mentioned as part of Gargantua's athletic training. In the middle of a detailed description of his swimming and climbing exercises and practice in the use of weapons of all kinds, we are told that "pour s'exercer le thorax et poulmons crioit comme tous les diables. Je l'ouy une fois appellant Eudemon depuis la porte Sainct Victor jusques à Montmartre. Stentor n'eut onques telle voix à la bataille de Troye." There is a hint for schoolmasters of the present day. The "young barbarians" under their charge might by degrees be made to look on strength and beauty of voice, and skill in using it, as an *athletic* distinction; this would at once ennoble tne subject in their eyes, and make elocution a matter of keen competition. "Throwing the voice" might become a recognized "event" in their sports, like throwing the cricket ball, and Brown major of Harrow might win deathless fame by "beating the record" of Smith minor of Eton.

As part of the general vocal training which I think desirable, I should be disposed to urge that *all* children and young people should learn to sing as far as their natural capacity will allow. Even those with little or no musical endowment will thus learn to use their voices better in speaking. I may say here, though it is rather anticipating, that, if I think it desirable for speakers to learn to sing, I consider it still more necessary that singers should learn to speak. Too many of those who soar aloft on the wings of song despise the *musa pedestris* of speech, and take no trouble to acquire what they look upon as an inferior and possibly superfluous accomplishment—with what result is known to cultivated listeners, whose ears have been tortured by the uncouth distortions and mutilations to which singers often subject the words they have to utter.

Of the management of the voice I cannot say much here. The chief thing is that the speaker should make himself distinctly heard by the whole of the audience, and to this end art serves better than loudness. A weak voice, properly managed, will carry farther than a powerful organ worked by sheer brute force. Mr. Bright's use of his voice always gave one the impression of a large reserve of power. There seemed to be no effort in his delivery, even when speaking to a mighty concourse of people, and yet his voice was

> "To the last verge of the vast audience sent,
> And played with each wild passion as it went."

One element of success in this matter is, no doubt, the art of compelling an audience to listen. As Montaigne, in his quaint old French says: "La parole est moitié à celuy qui parle, moitié à celuy qui l'escoute; celuy cy se doibt préparer à la recevoir, selon le bransle qu'elle prend: comme entre ceulx qui jouent à la paulme, celuy qui soubstient se desmarche et s'appreste, selon qu'il veoid remuer celuy qui luy jecte le coup et selon la forme du coup." Every speaker should know the exact limits of his own vocal powers, and he must be careful never to go beyond them, for the sake of his hearers no less than his own. He must learn to judge instinctively of distance, so as to throw his voice to the farthest part of his audience. A speaker, and, I may say, a singer also, should not hear his own voice too loudly. Artistes and orators are often very much disappointed, and think their voice is not travelling well when they themselves do not hear it very distinctly. The fact is that when the speaker does not hear his voice it proves that it reaches to a distant part of the room, and that there is very little rebound. Here I may remark that we never hear our voices as other people hear them. Our own voices are conveyed to the auditory nerve, not only through the outside air, but more directly from the inside, through the Eustachian tube, as well as through the muscles and bones of the mouth and head; the singer not only hears his own voice from a different quarter, as we may say, but he hears besides the contraction of his own muscles. The fact is well illustrated by the phonograph: a listener can recognize other people's voices, but if he speaks into the phonograph, and afterwards reproduces his own voice, it does not sound at all like itself to him, because he does not hear it in the manner he is accustomed to, and because he hears it stripped of the various accompanying sounds which are usually associated with it to his ear.

The acoustic peculiarities of the place in which he has to speak must, if possible, be carefully studied beforehand by the orator. Public buildings, however, vary so greatly in their size and construction, that it is impossible to lay down any general rules for the guidance of speakers in this matter. Each hall, church, court, and theatre has its own acoustic character, which can be learned only by experience; the voice must be, as it were, *tuned* to it. It is well if this experience can be gained by the orator before he faces his audience, but he must remember that trying his voice in an empty room, is an altogether different thing from actually using it in the same place packed with a solid mass of wheezing, coughing, and perspiring humanity. Handel is said to have comforted himself when one of his oratorios had been performed to empty benches, by the reflection that "it made ze moosic shound all ze better," but this consolation is denied to the orator. There are some buildings which are so utterly bad from the acoustic point of view that even experienced speakers are little better off than novices. The House of Lords has, or used to have, an unenviable reputation in this respect. A story is told of the late Lord Lyttelton, that, after exhausting his voice in vain efforts to make his brother peers hear a motion which he wished to propose, he in despair wrote it down and asked the clerk at the table to read it out. That functionary, however, was quite unable to decipher the writing, and Lord Lyttelton complained that he was cut off from communication with his fellows. Science has not always been successful in coping with the acoustic difficulty. In 1848 it was so difficult for speakers to make themselves heard in the French Chamber, that a committee, consisting of the leading scientific luminaries of the day—such as Arago, Babinet, Dumas (the chemist, not the author of "The Three Musketeers"), Becquerel, Chevreul (the centenarian who died the other day), Pouillet, Regnault, and Duhamel—was appointed to study the case and suggest a remedy. After numerous experiments they hit on a contrivance, designed on the most scientific principles, which was to make the orator's voice ring like a clarion to the farthest benches. The last state of the speaker, however, was worse than the first; he felt as if his voice was stifled under a huge nightcap, and the highly scientific sound-reflector had to be discarded as a failure. Indeed, modern public buildings are so often defective in this respect that I am not surprised to find M. Ch. Garnier, who designed the Grand Opéra in Paris, exclaiming dolefully: "The science of theatrical acoustics is still in its infancy, and the result in any given case is uncertain." So impressed is he with the shortcomings of modern architecture as regards the conveyance of sound, that he frankly confesses that, in the construction of the Opera House, he "had no guide, adopted no principle, based his design on no theory;" he simply left the acoustic properties of the building to *chance*. The result has not been altogether satisfactory, though it has been no worse than in many other buildings where the architect did his best to make the acoustic conditions perfect. One of the most remarkable buildings from the acoustic point of view that I have ever seen is the beehive-shaped Temple in Salt Lake City. It holds from 12,000 to 14,000 people, and one can literally hear a pin fall. When I was in the Temple, with some other travellers, in 1882, the functionary corresponding to the verger of ordinary churches stood at the farthest end and dropped a pin into his hat. The sound of its fall was most distinctly audible to all present. The scratching of the pin against the side of the hat was also plainly heard across the whole breadth of the building. The Temple was designed by Brigham Young, who professed to have been directly inspired by the Almighty in the matter, as he knew nothing of acoustics. The resonance of the building is so loud that branches of trees have to be suspended from the ceiling in several places in order to diminish it. It is likely enough that Brigham Young's inspiration had a not very recondite and purely terrestrial source, for his Beehive is only a slight modification of the whispering gallery in St. Paul's. The bad acoustic properties of buildings may be remedied by what doctors call "palliative treatment." Charles Dickens' experience as a public reader made him a man of ready resource in meeting such difficulties. On one occasion, when he was going to lecture at Leeds, Mr. Edmund Yates, who had spoken in the same hall the evening before, sent him word that the acoustic conditions of the place were very bad. Dickens at once telegraphed instructions that curtains should be hung round the walls at the back of the gallery; by this means he was able to make himself more easily heard.

The speaker should take the greatest care of his voice, which is the instrument both of his usefulness and of his fame; but, of course, it is not always easy for him to do so. Still he should, if possible, make it a rule not to speak when his voice is hoarse or fatigued, and, when he has a great oratorical effort to make, he should reserve himself for it. Tobacco, alcohol, and fiery condiments of all kinds are best avoided by those who have to speak much, or at least they should be used in strict moderation. I feel bound to warn speakers addicted to the "herb nicotian" against cigarettes. Like tippling, the effect of cigarette smoking is cumulative, and the slight but constant absorption of tobacco juice and smoke makes the practice far more noxious in the long run than any other form of smoking. Our forefathers, who used regularly to end their evenings under the table, seem to have suffered little of the well-known effects of alcohol on the nerves, while the modern tippler, who is never intoxicated, is a being whose whole nervous system may be said to be in a state of chronic inflammation. In like manner cigarette smokers (those at least who inhale the smoke, and do not merely puff it "from the lips outwards," as Carlyle would say) are often in a state of chronic narcotic poisoning. The old jest about the slowness of the poison may seem applicable here, but though the process may be slow, there can be little doubt that it is sure. Even if it does not kill the body, it too often kills or greatly impairs the victim's working efficiency and usefulness in life. The local effects of cigarettes in the mouth must also be taken into account by those whose work lies in the direction of public speech. The white spots on the tongue and inside of the cheeks, known as "smoker's patches," are believed by some doctors with special experience to be more common in devotees of the cigarette than in other smokers; this unhealthy condition of the mouth may not only make speaking troublesome, or even painful, but it is now proved to be a predisposing cause of cancer. All fiery or pungent foods, condiments, or drinks tend to cause congestion of the throat, and if this condition becomes chronic it may lead to impairment, if not complete loss, of voice. The supposed miraculous virtues of the mysterious possets and draughts on which some orators pin their faith, exist mainly in the imagination of those who use them; at best they do nothing more than lubricate the joints of the vocal machine so as to make it work more smoothly. This is just as well done by means of a glass of plain water. In France water sweetened with sugar is the grand vocal elixir of political orators. As Madame de Girardin said, somewhat unkindly: "Many things can be dispensed with in the Tribune. Talent, wit, conviction, ideas, even memory, can be dispensed with, but not *eau sucrée*." Stimulants may give a sort of "Dutch courage" to the orator, and may carry him successfully through a vocal effort in which indisposition or nervousness might otherwise have caused him to fail, but the immediate good which they do is dearly purchased by the thickening and roughening of the mucous surface of the throat to which they ultimately give rise.

Before leaving the subject of the speaking voice, a word or

two may be said on what is more a matter of curious speculation than of practical interest. Is the human voice growing in power and beauty, or is it tending to decay? Certain physiologists assure us that the retina has acquired the power of distinguishing colours by degrees, and that the process will probably continue, so that our descendants will by-and-by evolve the power of seeing colours now quite unknown to us. On the other hand, it is undeniable that civilization, so far from increasing the keenness of our sight, threatens to make spectacles universally necessary. There can be no doubt that the voice has developed greatly since our "half-human ancestors" wooed each other in the primeval forests, and it is conceivable that it may in time to come acquire the power of producing musical effects at present undreamt of. It is also probable enough that as the voice gains in sweetness it may lose in power, the latter quality being more required in barbarous than in highly civilized conditions. On the other hand, we are taller and of larger chest-girth than our predecessors even of a not very remote date; it is reasonable, therefore, to suppose that the average lungs and larynx are bigger nowadays, and the air blast from the lungs stronger. This would appear to justify us in believing that the voice is stronger than it was even two or three centuries ago. There are, however, no facts that I know of to prove it.

Of the *ethnology* of the voice little or nothing is certainly known. Almost the only facts I know of coming under this head are—(1) the superior sonorousness of the Italian voice, and (2) the want of resonance in the voices of some Australian aborigines, which is supposed to be due to the extreme smallness of the hollow spaces in the skull which serve as resonance chambers. Yet there is an infinite diversity in the voices of different nations, arising from difference of physical conformation, habit of speech, climate, etc. It is to our climate that Milton attributed the fact, which strikes all foreigners, that English people speak with the mouth half shut. "For we Englishmen," he says, "being far northerly, do not open our mouths in the cold air wide enough to grace a southern tongue, but are observed by all other nations to speak exceeding close and inward ; so that to smatter Latin with an English mouth is as ill a hearing as law French." Then look at our American cousins, in whom it is not the mouth but the nose that is the "peccant part"—is it climate or variation of structure that has wrought the change in their original English speech? or is it simply a twang inherited from their Puritan ancestors, who took their "cant" with them to the New World? Americans, including even so refined a scholar as Mr. Lowell, boast that they alone keep the true tradition of English speech, but I cannot believe that our forefathers, "in the spacious times of great Elizabeth," spoke in the accents of Hosea Biglow.

The difficulty, or rather impossibility, of studying the variations of the voice under culture has been due to the want of any means of permanently recording its tones. Now, however, that the phonograph has emerged from the condition of a scientific toy, comparative *phonology* may, perhaps, take its place among the sciences. Besides this and other results, Mr. Edison's wonderful instrument will preserve the fame of orators, actors, and singers—hitherto the most evanescent kind of glory, as it had to be taken altogether on trust—in a form as concrete as a picture or a poem. The little revolving cylinders will reproduce "the sound of a voice that is still," and will enable us to have "the little voice set lisping once again" years after our darling has been laid in an untimely grave. There seems to be something almost uncanny in the power of thus permanently enshrining the most fleeting part of man, and re-awakening at will the living accents of one who, being dead, yet speaketh to the bodily ear.

SPEECH AND SONG.

Part II.—Song.

HAVING dealt with the voice in its everyday garb of speech, it now remains for me to speak of it as it is when transfigured in song. The organ is the same in both cases, but in song it is used strictly as a musical instrument—one, too, of far more complex structure than any fashioned by the hand of man. The mechanism of voice has already been described, but, for the sake of clearness, it may be well to recall the three essential elements in its production : 1, the air blast, or motive power ; 2, the vibrating reed, or tone-producing apparatus ; 3, the sounding-board, or reinforcing cavities. These, to parody a well-worn physiological metaphor, are the three legs of the tripod of voice ; defect in, or mismanagement of, any one of them is fatal to the musical efficiency of the vocal instrument. The air supplied by the lungs is moulded into sound by the innumerable nimble little fingers of the muscles which move the vocal cords. These fingers—which prosaic anatomists call *fibres*,—besides being almost countless in number, are arranged in so intricate a manner that every one who dissects them finds out something new, which, it is needless to say, is forthwith given to the world as an important discovery. It is probable that no amount of macerating or teazing out with pincers will ever bring us to "finality" in this matter ; nor do I think it would profit us much as regards our knowledge of the physiology of the voice if the last tiny fibrilla of muscle were run to earth.

The mind can form no clearer notions of the infinitely little than of the infinitely great, and the microscopic movements of these tiny strips of contractile tissue would be no more *real* to us than the figures which express the rapidity of light and the vast stretches of astronomical time and distance. Moreover, no two persons have their laryngeal muscles arranged in precisely the same manner, a circumstance which of itself goes a considerable way towards explaining the almost infinite variety of human voices. The wonderful diversity of expression in faces which structurally, as we may say, are almost identical, is due to minute differences in the arrangement of the little muscles which move the skin. The same thing holds good of the larynx. In addition to this there are more appreciable differences, such as we see in the other parts of the body. The larynx itself is as various in size and shape as the nose ; and this is still more the case with the other parts concerned in the production of the voice. The most laborious anatomical Gradgrind would shrink appalled from the attempt to measure the capacity and trace the shape of the various resonance chambers —chest, throat, mouth, and nose, with the many intricate little passages and cave-like spaces communicating with the latter— yet the slightest difference in the form, size, or material structure of any of these parts must have its effect in modifying the voice to some extent.

It is a curious fact that singers, who are often rather unwilling to believe that the voice is formed solely in the larynx, are yet generally surprised to be told that the true nature of the voice cannot be certainly determined by examination of that organ. From what has been said as to the extraordinary number of the component parts of the vocal machine, it will be evident that it would be almost as rash to pronounce on the nature of the voice from the appearance of the larynx as it would be to take the shape of the nose as an index of moral character. It can only be said in a general way that, other things (notably, the resonance chambers) being equal, one expects a large, roomy larynx, with thick, powerful cords, to yield a deep, massive voice, and a small organ, with slender cords, to send forth a shrill, high-pitched voice. These two types represent the male and female voice respectively; that of the child belongs to the latter category. It must be understood that the difference in size between the largest larynx and the smallest is, after all, very trifling in itself. For instance, the vocal cords in women are but a fraction of an inch shorter than in men, and the other dimensions vary in much the same proportion. A like difference prevails throughout the resonant apparatus, the reinforcing chambers being larger in men, and their walls (which are built up of bone, gristle, and muscle) denser and more solid.

The voice varies in compass no less than in quality. A priori long vocal cords should indicate great range of tone, but so much depends on the management of these vibrating reeds that comparatively little significance can be attached to mere length. The average compass of the singing voice is from two to three octaves, the latter limit being seldom exceeded. The artistic effect produced with this small stock of available notes is as wonderful in its way as the marvellous results that can be got out of the twenty-six letters of the alphabet. In singing up the scale, the vocalist feels that at a certain point he has to alter his method of production in order to reach the higher notes. This point marks the break between the so-called "chest" and "head" registers, or what I may call the lower and upper stories of the voice.

The subject of the registers has been much debated by the learned, and still more perhaps by the unlearned; it is the "Eastern question" of vocal physiology. Quite a considerable literature has gathered round it; philosophers have lost their tempers and musicians have shown a plentiful lack of harmony in discussing it. The inherent difficulties of the subject have been increased by the fantastic terminology which has come down to us from a pre-scientific age, and by the erroneous observations of incompetent persons. I can touch only very lightly on the subject here, but those who may wish for a full exposition of my views on the matter may be referred to a little work which I published some years ago, and which has been already translated into eight languages.* It may be asked,

* "Hygiene of the Vocal Organs." Macmillan & Co. Sixth edition. 1883.

What is a register? The best definition I can offer is that it is a series of tones of like quality produced by a particular adjustment of the vocal cords to receive the air-blast from the lungs. The question is what the "particular adjustment" is in each case. The first step towards clearing up the subject is to discard the terms "chest" and "head" voice, which are meaningless and often misleading. Whatever number of registers there may be, and however they may be produced, it is certain that the change of mechanism takes place only in the larynx. I have suggested that the terms "long reed" and "short reed" register should be used to designate the two fundamental divisions of the human voice. In the former, usually called "chest voice," the vocal cords vibrate in their whole length, and the sounds are reinforced largely by the cavity of the chest, the walls of which can be felt to vibrate strongly when this register is used. In the latter, "head voice," or falsetto, only a part of the cord vibrates, and the sound is reinforced by the upper resonators, mouth, bony cavities of the skull, etc. It is this which has given rise to the absurd statements of singers that they could *feel* their head notes coming from the back of the nose, the forehead, etc. In the "long reed" register the pitch is raised by increasing tension of the vibrating element; in the "short reed" register by gradual shortening of it. This is effected by a curious process, which can be distinctly seen in the living throat with the laryngoscope. The two cords are forced against each other at their hinder part with such force as to stop each other's movement. While the notes of the chest register issue from the natural aperture of the larynx, the head notes come through an artificially diminished orifice, the chink becoming gradually smaller till there is nothing left to vibrate, when the limit of the voice is reached. The two registers generally overlap for a greater or less extent, a few notes about the middle of the voice being capable of being sung in either. Some voices have no break in their entire compass, the same mechanism being used throughout; but this is very rare. It was the constant aim of the famous old Italian singing masters to *unite* the two natural registers so perfectly that no break should be perceptible.

Till a comparatively recent date the generally received explanation of the registers was that, while in the delivery of chest notes the whole substance of the vocal cord vibrated, in the "head" voice only its thin inner margin did so; in both cases the entire *length* of the cord was supposed to vibrate. The shortening of the vibrating reed, however, by the mutual "stopping" process mentioned above, is not a theory, but a *fact* which can be seen. I am inclined to believe, however, that under certain circumstances the two processes of shortening and marginal vibration may be combined. This may possibly be the true mechanism of the falsetto voice, as to which there has been so much dispute. It is clear that the term has been used by different persons in different senses, and much of the confusion which exists on the subject is, in my opinion, due to this cause. By most of the old Italian writers, the term falsetto is used as synonymous with "head voice"; by others it is employed to denote that kind of voice "whereby a man going beyond the upper limit of his natural voice counterfeits that of a woman" (Rousseau, "Dictionnaire de Musique"). A similar difference of opinion exists as to the beauty of falsetto, some speaking rapturously of its flutelike softness, others reviling it as "the most disagreeable of all *timbres* of the human voice" (Rousseau, ibid.). I venture with all humility to submit that "falsetto" and "head voice" should not be used interchangeably. The "long reed" and "short reed" registers are used alike by the two sexes, the greater part of the male voice, however, belonging to the former, and the greater part of the female to the latter. The term "falsetto" should be reserved for the artificial method of delivery, by which the limited "short reed" register in men is forced upwards beyond its natural compass. In this mode of production the air is blown up from the lungs so gently that it has not sufficient power to throw the whole thickness of the vocal cord into vibration. This accounts for the soft, "flute-like" tones which are characteristic of the falsetto voice.

To sum up the mechanism of the registers, there is first the "long reed" or "chest" register, in which the cords vibrate in their whole length and thickness; then the "short reed" or "head" register, in which the vibrating reed is gradually shortened; lastly, the falsetto, which belongs to men alone, and is formed by the vibration of the margins only of the shortened reeds. Pitch rises in the long reed register owing to increasing tension of the cords accompanied by increasing rapidity of vibration; when the cord cannot be made more tense, the device of shortening the reed is brought into play. In the upper register not only is the aperture between the cords ("glottis") diminished to the smallest possible size, but the whole upper orifice of the larynx is compressed from side to side, so as to leave only a very narrow chink for the voice to pass through. In the lower register, on the other hand, the larynx is wide open, and the vibrating air rushes forth in a full broad stream of sound.

Many singing-masters, not content with the great natural divisions of the voice which have just been indicated, insist that there are five different registers, each with a distinct mechanism of its own. I am not a *maestro*, and therefore I am willing to admit that, artistically speaking, there *ought* to be five registers, or, in fact, any number of them that may be thought desirable. But if that is a necessity of art, it is not a necessity of Nature, which does all that is required by the simple process which has been described. The differences of mechanism on which the singing-masters profess to base their division are mostly of so subtle a nature as to be almost invisible to the eye, and sometimes even hardly appreciable by the ordinary intellect. I think, however, there is a way of reconciling their views with mine, diametrically opposed as they at first sight seem to be. As a physiologist, I speak solely of the tone of a note, that is to say, of its place in the musical scale, and I say, That note is delivered by the long reed or short reed adjustment, as the case may be; as musicians, on the other hand, the *maestri*, speaking of the quality as well as the tone, say, That note ought to be delivered in such and such a way to make it artistically beautiful. In the one case, in short, the voice is considered purely as it is produced in the larynx; in the other, as it is delivered by a well-trained singer managing his resonance apparatus to the best advantage.

Now, for this result many things are needed besides the correct adjustment of the vocal cords. The supply of breath must be regulated to a nicety, and the position of the tongue, soft palate, cheeks, and lips must be precisely that which is best for the utterance of each particular note. There are rules founded on experience which govern all these things; these rules are expressed in terms of subjective sensations, which are scientifically absurd, but, at the same time, may be practically useful, as indicating the feelings that should accompany the right performance of the manœuvre required. It is on all this complicated mechanism that the five registers of the singing masters are based; the more or less fanciful changes in the larynx, to which they attribute the slight, but artistically vital, differences in production which their trained ear enables them to appreciate, have in reality but little share in the result. The difference between artistic and inartistic production of the voice depends far more on the management of the resonators than on the adjustment of the vocal cords.

This point will be better understood if it is borne in mind that, as Helmholtz has shown, every musical sound is "compounded of many simples;" that is to say, the fundamental tone is reinforced by a number of secondary sounds or "harmonics" which accompany, and as it were echo, it in a higher key, the whole being blended into one sensation to the ear. Then, again, it is well known that every resonance cavity has what may be called an "elective affinity" for one particular note, to the vibrations of which it responds sympathetically, like a lover's heart answering that of his beloved. As the crude note issues from the larynx, the mouth, tongue, and soft palate mould themselves by the most delicately adapted movements into every conceivable variety of shape, clothing the raw bones of sound with body and living richness of tone. Each of the various resonance chambers re-echoes its corresponding tone, so that a single well-delivered note is in reality a full choir of harmonious sounds.

It has further been proved that each vowel has its own special pitch, and hence it cannot be sounded in perfection on any other. The different vowels, in fact, are produced by modifications in the length and shape of the cavity of the mouth, and the note of each one of them is that to which such a resonance chamber naturally responds. It follows from this that, in order to get the best effect from the vocal instrument, there should be the most perfect possible adaptation of the various vowels to the notes on which they are to be sung. Sounds like *o* and *ou* (*oo*) are best rendered in the lower notes of the voice; *a* and *i* (*ee*) in the upper. It is difficult, indeed almost impossible, to sing the latter vowels on deep notes. The marriage of music to immortal verse cannot be perfect unless the various affinities of the vowel sounds are carefully respected by the composer.

From what has been said it will, I think, be evident that no one, however happily gifted in point of voice, can use his endowment to the best advantage without careful training. Every note requires for its artistic production, not only a particular adjustment of the larynx, but a special arrangement of the resonators and suitable management of the breath, all the complicated movements involved in these various proceedings having to be performed automatically and with the most exact precision, and the whole being combined into one instantaneous act. M. Jourdain's master was not such a fool as he is made to appear, when he insisted on the mechanism of utterance being clearly understood. When this has been acquired the singer is still only like a child that has learned to stand; walking, running, and dancing, in other words the junction of the separate notes into the "linkèd sweetness" of an air, the graces and ornaments of vocalization, and the secret of sympathetic expression have yet to be acquired. There is an unfortunate tendency at the present day to be satisfied with a very inadequate amount of training, and I cannot help thinking that this is partly due to an imperfect appreciation of its necessity. Years are ungrudgingly given to acquiring a mastery of the piano or violin, and it is recognized that to excel with either of these instruments seven or eight hours of laborious practice every day are necessary. Yet many seem to fancy that the voice can be trained in a few months. How preposterous such a notion is must be evident to any one who takes the trouble to think about the matter. In the case of the violin or piano the instrument is perfect from the outset, and the student has only to learn to play it; the singer, on the other hand, has to develop—in some cases almost to create— his instrument, and then to master the *technique* of it. The human larynx is, as already said, a musical instrument of the most complicated kind, for its two reeds are susceptible of almost infinite modification in size, shape, manner of vibration, etc. A distinguished surgeon not long ago edified the public by a calculation of the number of muscular movements executed by a young lady while performing a simple piece on the piano; it would be hopelessly impossible to count the movements of the muscles which work the vocal cords.

The details of vocal training I must leave to the singing-masters; I can only touch on one or two points which lie more or less within my own province. In the first place, the vocal organs must be strengthened and developed by exercise. The excellent maxim, "Memoria excolendo augetur," which we learned from the Latin grammar, is equally true of muscle, and a singer's thyro-arytænoidei should be in as good condition as a pugilist's biceps. Such modes of life as are good for the general health will also help to improve the voice by expanding the chest and keeping all the organs at their maximum of efficiency. In order to "know the stops" of the vocal instrument, so as to be able to "command it to any utterance of harmony," training must be directed to each of the three factors of voice. The art of so governing the breath that not a particle of it shall escape without giving up its mechanical equivalent of sound must first of all be acquired. The vocal cords must use the breath as Jacob did the angel with whom he wrestled; they must not suffer it to depart till it has blessed them. The first thing the singer has to do is to learn to breathe; he must fill his lungs without gasping, and empty them quickly or slowly, gently or with violence, according to his needs. Much has been written on this matter with which I need not perplex the reader. The problem is how the lungs can be replenished most advantageously for the purposes of the singer. The chest is expanded by pulling up the ribs, and by pushing down the diaphragm, or muscular partition which separates the chest from the abdomen. In violent inspiratory effort the collar-bone may be forcibly drawn up by the muscles attached to it, but this mechanism is seldom brought into play except in the dire struggle for breath when suffocation is impending. It is a curious fact that men breathe differently from women, the former using the abdominal method—that is, pushing down the diaphragm—and the latter doing most of the work with their upper ribs. One reason of this difference is that the fair sex insist on fixing their lower ribs, to which the diaphragm is attached, with stays, which make free movement of that muscle impossible. Doctors have fulminated against tight-lacing for the last three centuries,[*] but to as little purpose as the Archbishop thundered against the Jackdaw of Rheims. Fashion must be obeyed whatever its victims may have to suffer. It is right to state, however, that stays not long ago found a champion in no less a person than the Professor of Pathology in the University of Cambridge. Professor Roy caused a little mild scandal at a recent meeting of the British Association, by urging that the use of stays might have certain advantages. If the Archbishop of Canterbury had stood up in Convocation and denied the efficacy of baptism, he could not have shocked his hearers more than Dr. Roy did by such a profession of heresy. The scientific ladies, who resemble the Greek statues in the looseness of their waists if in nothing else, groaned over this backsliding in high places, and their more frivolous sisters rejoiced. A Defender of the Faith, however, opportunely appeared in the person of Dr.

---

[*] Stays are generally said to have been introduced by Catherine de Medicis, who may be supposed to have had a natural genius for the invention of instruments of torture. They were, however, in use long before her time. I have in my possession a drawing made for me in 1884 by Mr. Lewis Wingfield from a MS. in the British Museum of the date 1043. It is figured by Strutt, who calls it "A Droll Devil." Mr. Wingfield more aptly terms it the "Fiend of Fashion." It represents a figure fantastically dressed in what, I suppose, was the height of fashion of the day. Its special interest in connection with the present subject is that it wears a pair of stays, laced up in front, and of sufficient constrictive power to please a modern *mondaine*.

Garson, who at once put the question to the touch by measurements made on a number of ladies and gentlemen then present. These showed that the vital capacity (which is measured by the quantity of air that can be expelled from the lungs after the deepest possible inspiration) was considerably greater in the men than in the women, and that while in the former there was a constant diminution in the vital capacity in every period of ten years after the age of thirty, in the latter it actually increased after fifty, a time of life at which the majority of ladies begin to think more of comfort than of restraining the exuberance of their "figure." The truth appears to be, however, that the slight pressure exercised by stays does not matter in the case of ladies who are not called upon to use their voices professionally, and who do not care to excel as amateurs. In the ordinary work of life stays do not cause any inconvenience, and it is only when they are absurdly tight that they do serious harm to the internal organs. In the case of the *artiste* it is quite otherwise; here anything which in the smallest degree diminishes the vital capacity seriously handicaps the singer.

Although the abdominal mode of breathing may be the *natural* method of inspiration, there can, I think, be no doubt that in singing it is not the most effective. On this point the empirical traditions of singing-masters were abandoned some years ago in favour of what was supposed to be the teaching of science, and now singers are often taught to breathe by pushing down the diaphragm and protruding the stomach. Anatomists are, however, beginning to see that the Italian masters were right in insisting that the diaphragm should be fixed, and the abdomen flat in inspiration; in this method there is great expansion of the lower ribs, and the increase in the capacity of the chest takes place chiefly in this direction. In this form of breathing there is far more control over expiration than when the diaphragm is displaced; the act can be regulated absolutely by the will to suit the requirements of the vocalist. Abdominal inspiration is apt, on the other hand, to be followed by jerky expiration, a defect which is fatal to artistic delivery and most fatiguing to the singer.

The training of the other parts of the vocal machinery, the vibrating element and the resonant apparatus, lies altogether outside my province. What I may call the "fingering" of the vocal cords and the "tuning" of the resonators can be acquired only by constant practice under a good teacher. There is no such thing as a self-taught singer. Constant imitation of the best models and the watchful discipline of an experienced instructor constitute the real secret of the old Italian schools of singing, which gave such splendid results. Tosi insisted that the pupil should never sing at all except in the presence of a master. It is important that the very best teacher that can be found should be chosen; it is a false economy to trust a young voice to an inferior man on the ground of cheapness. To masters I venture to hint that they should strive to train their pupils according to the traditions of the golden age of song before the laryngoscope was invented.

I have only to add that the ear should be not less carefully trained than the vocal organs. An old Scotch minister used to tell his flock that the conscience should be kept "as white as the breast o' a clean sark." The ear is the conscience of the voice, and its purity should be not less jealously guarded. Many singers of the finest vocal endowment fail from a defect of ear; their condition is like that of a colour-blind painter. Passing indisposition may sometimes vitiate the ear as well as the temper; the artist should on no account attempt to sing under such circumstances.

Two questions in connection with the training of the voice still remain to be discussed — viz. when it should be commenced, and whether it should be interrupted during the so-called "cracking" period. With regard to the first of these questions, I am strongly of opinion that training can hardly be begun too early. Of course, the kind and amount of practice that are necessary in the adult would be monstrous in a young child, but there is no reason why, even at the age of six or seven, the right method of voice production should not be taught. Singing, like every other art, is chiefly learned by *imitation*, and it seems a pity to lose the advantage of those precious early years when that faculty is most highly developed.

There is no fear of injuring the larynx or straining the voice by elementary instruction of this kind; on the contrary, it is habitual faulty vocalization which is pernicious. The sooner the right way of using the voice is taught the more easy will it be to guard against the contraction of bad habits, which can only be corrected at a later period with infinite trouble. Many of the finest voices have been trained almost from the cradle, so to speak. I need only mention Mesdames Adelina Patti, Christine Nilsson, Jenny Lind, and Albani; but there are numbers of other queens of song who owe great part of their success to the same cause.

As for the other point, I am still an obstinate dissenter from the "orthodox" teaching of singing-masters on the subject. I have already more than once expressed my belief that there is no reason why training, *within certain limits and under strict supervision by a competent person*, should not be carried on when the voice is in the transition stage of its development from childhood to adolescence. The stock argument, invariably advanced to prove the necessity of suspending the education of the voice till it has passed through the "breaking" period, is that, as the parts are undergoing active changes, they therefore require complete rest. This would equally apply to the limbs, and, in some degree, also to the brain. Yet I am not aware that it has ever been proposed to forbid growing lads from exercising their bodies, even in games involving considerable muscular violence, or to interrupt the education of the mental powers till the brain has become fully formed. Over-pressure there may be, no doubt, in voice-training as in other kinds of instruction. All voices are not capable of bearing the same amount of training. Each case must be dealt with according to what doctors call the particular "indications" that may arise. My thesis holds good only as a general rule, to which there may be many individual exceptions. A judicious teacher will, however, have no difficulty in deciding as to the best course to adopt in any given instance.

After the voice has been developed to its utmost capacity, the next thing is to keep it in perfect condition. How is this to be done? As Danton said that the three things needed to insure success were "De l'audace, de l'audace, et encore de l'audace," I say the three things necessary to keep the things in good order are Practice, Practice, and again Practice. A singer who lets his voice lie idle is pretty sure to lose some of his upper notes, his breathing-power falls below its highest standard, and the larynx becomes less supple and less obedient to his will. Another vital point is never, if possible, to use the voice when it is not at its best. The slightest cold deadens to some extent the vibrations of the cords, and the resonators are also thrown out of tune by dryness or excessive moisture of their lining membranes. Bodily weakness or indisposition is reflected in the voice; the cords do not come firmly together, and their tension is insufficient for perfect purity, much less richness, of tone. A most essential element in the care of the voice is attention to the general health. This is very apt to be neglected by singers, who have rather a tendency, as a class, to lead the life of hot-house plants, living in rooms from which fresh air is shut out almost as if it were a pestilence, and taking little or no physical exercise. It is right, no doubt, that a singer should shield his precious instrument from harm as carefully as a violinist protects his Straduarius or Amati, but exaggerated precaution may defeat its object. Even the most dainty of light tenors cannot live wrapped up in cotton wool, and the delicacy engendered by the unhealthy conditions of life which have been referred to makes the slightest exposure to cold or fog almost deadly to his artificially enervated throat. A singer who wishes to keep himself in good voice should rise, if not exactly with his brother minstrel, the lark, at least pretty early, say, before eight in the morning. Tosi says that the best hour for practice is the first of the sun; but this, I fear, is a "counsel of perfection" beyond the virtue of this unheroic age. The singer should take plenty of exercise in the open air, and should harden his constitution by leading, as far as possible, a healthy outdoor life. Nothing gives richness and volume to the voice like vigorous health; an experienced ear can often tell a man's physical condition by the full, generous "ring" of his tones, both in singing and speaking.

There is even more superstition among singers than among speakers, as to what is "good for the voice." A formidable list of things which were supposed by the ancients to be injurious is given by Pliny; it includes such a variety of animal and vegetable substances that one wonders how unfortunate vocalists could have found life worth living under such ultra-Spartan conditions. Our modern *artistes* tend to err rather in the opposite direction, to judge from their extraordinarily comprehensive views as to what is "good" for the voice. Every species of drink from champagne to hot water, and almost every recognized article of food, including that particularly British institution, cold roast beef, has its devotees. I have no manner of doubt that every one of these things is really beneficial, not from any occult virtue that there is in them, but because the solids give strength, while the liquids moisten and lubricate the throat. That is the whole secret of the cordials and elixirs in which many vocalists place their trust.

A useful example of the proper care of the voice is to be found in a very unexpected quarter. The Emperor Nero, as is well known, believed himself to be a great artist, a notion of which those about were not likely to disabuse him. His dying words, "Qualis artifex pereo!" show that he had at least one feature of the artistic temperament. He sought fame by many paths, in poetry, fiddling, driving, and other branches of the fine arts, to say nothing of his scientific experiments on the bodies of his nearest relations. The imperial *virtuoso* was particularly vain of his voice, which I can well imagine to have been soft and sweet, qualities which often enough accompany a cruel nature. He was proportionately careful of so precious a possession. His system is worth quoting. In addition to such general measures as attending to his liver, and abstaining from such fruits and other food as he fancied to be injurious to his voice, we are told that at night he used to lie on his back with a small plate of lead on his stomach. This was probably for the purpose of checking the tendency to abdominal breathing, which has already been referred to as the less perfect way in respiration for singers. In order to spare his voice all unnecessary fatigue, he gave up haranguing his troops, and ceased even to address the Senate. As in later times there were keepers of the King's conscience, Nero gave his voice into the keeping of a *phonascus*. He spoke only in the presence of this vocal director, whose duty it was to warn him when his tones became too loud, or when he seemed to be in danger of straining his voice. To the same functionary was entrusted the formidable duty of checking the emperor's eloquence when it became too impetuous; this he did by covering the imperial orator's mouth with a napkin. It must have needed no small measure of courage to apply this effectual method of " closure " to the arch-tyrant of history when intoxicated with the exuberance of his own vocalization.

While laying stress on the necessity of proper cultivation in order to make the singer capable of giving the greatest pleasure to his hearers with the least amount of fatigue to himself, I venture to add that many singers who are admirably trained have rather a tendency to " o'erstep the modesty of nature " in their delivery. It was said of Flaubert's Salammbô, that it might be Carthaginian, but it was not human; in the same way I am disposed to say of certain highly " artistic " vocal displays which one is sometimes condemned to hear, that it may be song but it assuredly is not music. When listening to such tremendous performances, I often find myself echoing the words of poor Christopher Sly: " 'Tis a very excellent piece of work, madam lady; would 'twere done!" An old Italian writer, himself both a singer and a teacher, most truly says: " *E vaglia 'l vero, dove parla la passione i trilli e i passaggi devon tacere* "— leaving the soul to be moved solely by the beauty of expression. It was this quality of sympathetic expression that made the singing of Tom Moore, who had no " voice " in the technical sense, more moving than that of renowned artists. In an altogether different line, Mr. George Grossmith contrives by the exquisite clearness of his modulation to add considerably to the gaiety of nations with a very limited stock of notes.

One of the most remarkable things relating to song at the present day is the scarcity of really fine voices. It will not, I suppose, be seriously argued that the human voice is degenerating, and never were the inducements to cultivate it more abundant or more powerful. Yet, if we are to believe many competent authorities, never were first-rate voices so rare as at the present time. The complaint is not altogether new, and is, in part at least, nothing more than the inevitable moan of the *laudator temporis acti* over the decadence of things in general. Rossini at the zenith of his fame complained that there were so few good voices, and quite at the beginning of last century we find Tosi speaking of his own period as one of decay. Mancini also (1774) says that vocal art had then fallen very low, a circumstance which he attributes to singers "having forgotten the old systems and the sound practice of the ancient schools." Still, modern writers on singing are agreed that there is a dearth of really beautiful voices at the present time, and, as this is one of the very few points on which these contentious persons are agreed, there can be little doubt of the truth of the fact to which they bear witness. Good tenors are especially rare, even among Italians, the chosen people of song. There are no tenors now who can be compared with Mario or Rubini; indeed, one gathers from Mr. Sims Reeves's reminiscences, published not long ago, that the world is at present blest with only one really first-rate tenor. Mr. Reeves leaves his readers in no doubt as to the identity of this Triton among contemporaneous minnows of song. We have no basso that can stand beside Lablache. Except Madame Patti, whose glorious voice is now too seldom heard, and Madame Christine Nilsson, who, to the regret of all lovers of song, has quitted the lyric stage, Madame Albani and Madame Sembrich are almost the sole inheritors of the renown of the great *prime donne* of old. It is not only in compass and quality that our latter-day voices are inferior to those of preceding generations, but in endurance. Catalani's magnificent voice remained unimpaired up to extreme old age, and Farinelli's only died with him. Matteucci, when past his eightieth year, used to sing in church every Sunday *per mera devozione*, and such was the freshness and flexibility of his voice that those who could not see him took it to be that of a young man in the flower of his age. Indeed, this was not very uncommon in singers trained according to the best traditions of the old Italian school, which seems to have possessed the secret of perpetual youth as far as the voice was concerned.

Now, to what can our poverty in voices of the highest class be due? I believe to a combination of three different causes: first, inadequacy of training; secondly, the want of good teachers; and, thirdly, the gradual rise of the concert pitch which has taken place in recent years. Insufficient training arises from the breathless haste to "succeed" which is a characteristic of this feverish age. Voices are quickly run up by contract, and as swiftly fall into decay. The preference for supposed "royal roads" over the hard-beaten path that has led former singers to fame is another error which has worked almost as much mischief in song as it has in scholarship. A vocalist nowadays thinks that a year in England and a second year in Italy is all that is needed to equip him for a brilliant artistic career. In "the brave days of old" singers never deemed their vocal education complete until they had given six or seven years to the ceaseless study of their art.

The want of good teachers is closely connected with the inadequacy of modern training, for it is evident that a man who has not himself had the patience or the industry to master his art cannot be a satisfactory guide to others. Show and superficial brilliancy of execution are aimed at rather than solidity and thoroughness; more attention is paid to vocal *tours de force* than to artistic ornament. The firm basis of experience has been abandoned for fantastic methods of teaching which are useless when they are not positively harmful. I would earnestly advise all those who profess to impart the divine art of song, like Prospero, to "drown their books," and study the production of the voice as an art, and not as a branch of Chinese metaphysics.

That the high concert pitch now generally used, especially

in this country, throws an unnatural strain on even the finest voices, is a fact as to which most authorities are agreed. In the classical period of music A (second space, treble clef) represented from 415 to 429 vibrations; this pitch suited the human voice admirably. The desire to get increasingly brilliant effects from the orchestra forced the pitch higher and higher, till so much confusion prevailed that, in 1859, a French Commission fixed the standard pitch at 435 vibrations. This is called the normal diapason, and is now generally used on the Continent; but England, with her customary insular independence, has not conformed to the general rule in this matter, and the pitch has in this country actually risen to 458 vibrations. This result is largely due to the extraordinary impulse given to orchestral music by the genius of Costa, who, so long as he could get brilliant effects from his instruments, cared little for the consequences which the rise of pitch entailed on the voice. But it will be said, Since it is all a matter of convention, why cannot the pitch be lowered? I believe the chief obstacle is the expense which this would involve through the necessity of altering instruments. It has been estimated that it would cost £80,000 to alter those of the military bands alone, and politicians probably think that these are hardly the times to ask for money for such an object.

But worse even than the undue height of the pitch is the difference between this country and the rest of the civilized world which has just been referred to. Herr Joachim complains that he is obliged to begin screwing up his violin eight weeks before he comes to England, in order that the instrument may not be injured by a sudden change. It is not so easy, however, for the singer to prepare *his* delicately strung instrument in the same way, and the result is necessarily great strain to the vocal cords and throat generally. The high pitch used in England leads to the production of very disagreeable shrieking; notes are delivered which are in no sense artistically beautiful, and which only "split the ears of the groundlings." Nearly all singers are in favour of lowering the pitch. The sole exceptions are, I believe, the contraltos, whom a high pitch does not affect so much as it does others. I know of one justly celebrated contralto who produces an extraordinary effect by her low E. If the pitch were altered this vocal feat would no longer be so wonderful, and it is natural, therefore, that this lady should wish the present state of things to continue.

Perhaps, after all, the supposed scarcity of good voices may be more apparent than real. It is possible that it is not only the pitch but the standard of vocal excellence that has risen. We know how the general level of literary style has risen, and, in particular, how the art of melodious versification has been popularized, if I may use the expression, so that every cheap magazine, and even the poets' corner of provincial newspapers, contains copies of verses which would have earned considerable reputation for the authors a hundred and fifty years ago. It is immensely more difficult now to make a name by writing. May not something of the same kind be the case as regards singing? I fear we must not lay that flattering unction to our souls. Great singers are rarer nowadays than in former times, because voice-training is almost a lost art. The remedy lies, as has been said, in a return to methods consecrated by glorious tradition, and fruitful of results which, as experience has abundantly proved, cannot be attained by shorter or easier ways.

THE DREADFUL REVIVAL OF LEPROSY.

In order to explain what may at first sight appear to be an intrusion into a region altogether foreign to my line of professional work, I may perhaps be allowed to say that from a very early period of my career I have taken a particular interest into leprosy. Next to the skin, the throat is the part most often attacked by the worst form of the disease; and for this reason I have sought every opportunity of seeing it at close quarters. At the risk of falling into the "autobiographical" vein so deprecated by Mr. Balfour, I may add that I have made special investigations on leprosy in most of its European haunts, and also in Madeira; I may therefore claim the right to speak of it with some amount of personal knowledge. My attention was first directed to the subject nearly thirty years ago, when I was studying diseases of the skin under the celebrated Hebra at Vienna. In his wards I saw several cases of leprosy, which I understood came from the "Danubian Principalities" of those days. In 1880 I examined a number of lepers in the Hospital de San Lazaro at Seville, in 1881 I saw several cases in the lazaretto at Funchal, and in 1884 I made extensive investigations in Norway, at Molde and Bergen, where I had the advantage of the assistance of Dr. Danielssen and Dr. Armauer Hansen, whose names are familiar as household words to the medical profession throughout the world in connection with leprosy. In Danielssen, who has watched the course of the disease among several generations of his countrymen, the doctrine of heredity finds its most uncompromising champion; in his son-in-law Hansen, the discoverer of the *bacillus lepræ*, contagion has naturally enough one of its most thoroughgoing supporters. One could hardly be in a better position for hearing both sides of this most important question than between those two distinguished men. In 1888 I saw a few cases in Italy, in the Civil Hospital at San Remo.* I have also had a few opportunities during the last twenty-five years of examining cases of leprosy here in London, in my own practice and that of others.

In this country most people, I imagine, were till lately in blissful ignorance of the fact that leprosy still walks the earth in all its original hideousness. Vague notions, derived partly from the Bible and partly from casual references in historical works, made up the sum of popular knowledge on the subject, and to the "general reader" leprosy was but a name, an extinct *deinotherium* of the palæontology of disease. Very few English doctors were better informed. The disease was either not referred to at all, or was dealt with in the most perfunctory way in lectures and text-books of medicine. As Dr. Munro, whose writings on leprosy have done so much to diffuse a knowledge of the disease among medical men, points out, students a very few years ago might have gone out to fulfil their mission of healing in various parts of the world without knowing that such a disease as leprosy was to be met with. Their first introduction to it was often when its existence was forced on them as a strange and disconcerting phenomenon in actual practice.

Space will not permit me to trace the early history of leprosy in ancient times, nor even to chronicle its course in Europe in the dark ages. My regret at being obliged to leave

---

* Invalids visiting this charming health resort need not be afraid of coming in contact with lepers. The few unfortunate victims of the disease are kept under close supervision in the Civil Hospital, which is situated on a high rock, and is separated even from the old town to which the building is adjacent. The part of San Remo which is frequented by those seeking health or sunshine in that delightful spot is as free from lepers as Brighton or Eastbourne.

out some historical details which might prove interesting is
lessened by the fact that an excellent summary of the researches
of Hirsch,* Munro,† and others, was published in 1884, in
the *Nineteenth Century Review*, by Miss Agnes Lambert.

Judging from the long intervals of time which often elapsed
without any mention of the disease, and the frequent notices
of it by writers at particular periods, it would appear that
between the twelfth and the fifteenth centuries the disease
underwent considerable vicissitudes, becoming at times more
prevalent and then again being much less common. These
changes probably corresponded with alternating periods of want
and prosperity, the disease becoming general when the vitality
of the nation was lowered by long wars, pestilences, and famine.
The extraordinary spread of the disease at the time of the
Crusades led to the belief that it had again been imported into
Europe from the East, and Voltaire characteristically says
that this was the only permanent result achieved by these
expeditions. There is, however, abundant proof that even
if leprosy was reimported, it had really never left Europe. In
the early part of the sixteenth century the scourge suddenly
began to abate, and in a relatively short time it became nearly
extinct in most of the countries of Europe.

There are, however, a few strongholds from which leprosy
has never been driven. Spain supplies many centres of
infection, but it is impossible to obtain exact statistics on
the subject. We have, however, the testimony of Dr. Roman
Viscarro to the fact that "from time immemorial lepers swarm
in Spain, especially in the provinces of Asturias, Tarragona,
Valencia and Castellon."‡ Dr. John Webster, who visited the
leper hospital at Granada about thirty years ago, found it
tenanted by fifty-three inmates. He was informed that in
1851 the number of lepers in nine provinces of Spain was 284;
this was probably far below the real number, as the natural

---

* "Handbook of Geographical and Historical Pathology." By Dr.
August Hirsch. Translated from the second German edition by Charles
Creighton, M.D."
† *Edinburgh Medical Journal*, vols. xxii., xxiii., xxiv., xxv.
‡ *El Siglo Medico.* Oct. 21, 1883.

tendency of lepers and their friends to hide their affliction is in Spain intensified by religious superstition, and the supineness of the authorities must lead to perfunctoriness in the difficult task of collecting statistics on the subject. Dr. Webster was informed that leprosy was believed to be spreading in Spain at the time of his visit. At Seville, in 1880, I found thirty-nine sufferers in the Hospital de San Lazaro. During the five years 1875–80, the total number of lepers admitted was eighty-four, the greatest number in any year having been twenty-one (1879–80). Seville itself supplied the largest contingent; then came Cadiz, Huelva, Almeria, Badajoz and Pontevedra. The figures, however, give an altogether inadequate idea of the prevalence of leprosy in these districts. As a high authority says, "in addition to the sufferers from these provinces who enter the hospital, there are many others who remain at home with their families, some maintained by them, others dependent on public charity; and probably only those seek shelter in the hospital who are destitute of all resource."* The late Dr. Jelly† showed how extraordinarily prevalent leprosy is in the district known as La Marina, which takes in the sea-board of the two provinces of Valentia and Alicante; and he also brought forward proofs of the spread of the disease in the south of Spain in recent years.

Portugal has more lepers than any other European country, except Norway: but want of space prevents my showing its distribution. In Italy leprosy is met with on the Genoese Riviera; it was also found till quite recently at Comacchio, in the Ferrara marshes. In Sicily the disease has been steadily spreading for the last thirty or forty years. In annexing Nice, France took over with it a considerable number of Italian lepers belonging to Le Turbie and neighbouring places, but the disease is now almost extinct in these localities. Small foci of leprosy still exist in Thessaly and Macedonia; the affection is not rare in some of the Ægean islands, e.g. Samos, Rhodes,

* Dr. Ph. Hauser, "Estudios Medico-Sociales de Sevilla," p. 319. Madrid, 1884.
† *Brit. Med. Journ.*, July 23, 1887.

Chios, and Mitylene, and it is extraordinarily prevalent in Crete. It is spreading to an alarming degree in Russia, especially in the Baltic Provinces, and it has lately been found necessary to establish a special hospital at Riga. In St. Petersburg cases are occasionally, though very rarely, met with; at least half of them are imported from outlying provinces. "Sporadic" cases are said to occur in some parts of Hungary and Roumania. In Sweden, where the disease was extremely prevalent up to the beginning of the present century, it seems now to have almost died out. Norway is unquestionably the most considerable leprosy centre in Europe at the present day, but the disease is curiously limited to particular regions, such as the districts round Bergen, Molde, and Trondhjem.

In almost every other quarter of the globe leprosy is rife at present, and wherever it exists it seems to be slowly, but surely, extending its ravages. It is impossible to estimate even approximately the total number of lepers now dying by inches throughout the world, but it is certain that they must be counted by millions. It cannot be comforting to the pride of England, "the august mother of nations," to reflect that a very large proportion of these wretched sufferers is to be found among her own subjects.

That leprosy has spread considerably in recent times there can be no manner of doubt. Within the last fifty years the seeds of the disease have been sown in several districts where it was previously unknown, and already the accursed crop has begun to show itself. As has been shown by Dr. Munro,[*] the seeds of leprosy take something like half a century to mature, and there is every prospect that unless the natural evolution of the scourge can in some way be prevented, a terrible harvest will be reaped before many years are past. To say nothing of the notorious case of the Sandwich Islands, where leprosy, imported about the year 1850, either by whaling ships manned by sailors from leprous regions, or by Chinese immigrants, has since made such fearful progress, we have the case of Australia, where it has been carried by the Chinese, and of America,

[*] Loc. cit.

where several distant centres of infection have appeared within living memory. Thus there is California, where it was imported by the "Heathen Chinee;" some of the North-Western States, where it was brought from Norway by Scandinavian emigrants; and Salt Lake City, to which it was conveyed by Mormon converts from the Sandwich Islands.* In Louisiana, where last century leprosy prevailed so extensively that a hospital for it was founded in 1785, it again showed itself in 1866, in a woman whose father was a native of the South of France. From this fresh centre the disease has spread to such an extent that Dr. Blanc recently saw forty-two cases in New Orleans alone. The disease also appeared in Oregon among the Chinese, but was promptly checked, and in South Carolina a limited outbreak occurred between 1847 and 1882. Sixteen cases were reported, the first victims being Jews belonging to families which had emigrated to the United States early in the century; several of the rest were Jews, but there were also some native Americans, and at least one Irishman among them.

In France the disease is also extending, as we learn from a communication made to the Académie de Médecine of Paris on the 14th of October, 1887, by Dr. Besnier, the distinguished physician of the Hôpital St.-Louis. This authority stated that, since France had extended her colonial possessions, French soldiers, sailors, traders, and missionaries have fallen victims to leprosy in large numbers.

In the United Kingdom we have at present no leprosy of home growth, but we are probably never without a few cases amongst those who have lived for some time in countries where the disease is common. From an unofficial return, recently published in one of the medical journals, it appears that in the early part of the present year there were several patients in London suffering from leprosy. There is, or was quite lately, a boy in a large public school in whom there are the strongest grounds for suspecting the existence of leprosy in the early stage: the disease is supposed to have been communicated by

* This fact was communicated to the New York Academy of Medicine by Dr. P. A. Morrow, on the 6th of June, 1889.

vaccination in the West Indies. It is beyond question also that there are many other cases in this country at the present moment which are carefully concealed from the knowledge of every one but the medical adviser. Nearly every skin specialist must be able to attest this fact.

But the most striking extension of the disease has been witnessed in the Sandwich Islands. Here Dr. W. Hillebrand saw the first case—the first spark of the conflagration—in 1853, " in a thinly-populated district of Oahu, about twenty miles from Honolulu, in a small village near the sea." * The disease, however, was not officially recognized till 1859. At that time "only a few cases became known, but with every subsequent year the leprous patients presenting themselves at the public dispensary increased in number, until during 1864 and 1865 it was considered of quite ordinary occurrence that lepers should apply for relief."† A census taken by the Hawaiian Government about that time gave the number of *known* lepers, suffering from the tubercular form of the disease, as 230 out of a population of 67,000. In 1866 the segregation settlement at Molokai was opened, and since that time more than 3,000 cases have been received there. The last report of the Hawaiian Board of Health gave the total number of lepers in the settlement on the 1st of April, 1888, as 749 ; but Dr. Prince A. Morrow, of New York, who visited Molokai in the early part of 1889, puts the present number at nearly 1,100.

In the West Indies the disease has been steadily extending its ravages for many years back. Thus at Trinidad, where in 1805 the three first victims could still be pointed out, an investigation ordered by Governor Woodford in 1813 revealed seventy-three lepers in a total population of about 32,000. Two years later there were seventy-seven.‡ The evil was unfortunately not considered of sufficient magnitude to need

---

* Letter quoted by C. N. Macnamara, "Leprosy a Communicable Disease," 2nd ed., p. 61. London, 1889.

† Ibid.

‡ For the information above given relative to Trinidad, I am indebted to the work already cited, " La Lèpre est Contagieuse," p. 264, et seq. Trinidad, 1879.

State interference. Ten years later, however, a half-hearted attempt at segregation was made, but in 1840 it was found that the number of sufferers had so much increased that a proposal to establish a settlement on a little island a few miles off had to be abandoned, because it was too small to hold them. In 1878 the number of lepers was officially stated to be 860 in a population of 120,000. These figures have an eloquence of their own which requires no comment from me to emphasize the startling truth which they convey—namely, that at Trinidad in the years between 1813 and 1878 leprosy increased nearly four times as rapidly as the population! We shall see presently to what cause it was undoubtedly attributable.

In British Guiana the increase of leprosy in recent years has been not less remarkable. In 1858 an asylum for lepers was established at the mouth of the Mahaica Creek. "On the 31st of December, 1859, there were only 105 inmates at the asylum. In 1869 they had increased to 300, and the place could hold no more. Increased space was provided, and in 1889 we find from the official reports that over 500 were dealt with. Around this leper asylum, outside its boundaries, there are large numbers of lepers not included in these returns.* Dr. Hillis, the best living authority on the subject, informs me that the increase of leprosy in British Guiana during the past ten years has been very great, although during that period the general sanitary condition of the colony has improved. He estimates that at the present time there must be more than a thousand lepers in British Guiana, a number equal to 1 in 250 of the whole population. Considering the very high death-rate of the disease—16 per cent. annually—it is clear that it is spreading with great rapidity.

When New Zealand was first taken possession of by the English, a peculiar form of leprosy akin to the anæsthetic form was found to exist. Dr. John Myles, of Taranaki, who recently paid a visit to this country, informed me that the disease is most common in a zone of about twenty-five miles round Lake Taupo. The whites, it appears, do not become leprous, except

* John D. Hillis, F.R.C.S.I., late Medical Superintendent of the Leper Asylum, British Guiana. *Timehri*, June, 1889: pp. 77, 78.

the "Pakeha Maoris," as the whites are called who live much with the Maoris or intermarry with them. No system of restraint exists now, but when the Maoris possessed the country they killed those who became leprous. Fear of contracting the disease prevented them indulging their cannibal propensities in relation to the poor lepers. It has been noticed in recent years that there has been considerable increase in the amount of leprosy, though it is still principally confined to the neighbourhood of Lake Taupo.

In India, the last official report gives 135,000 as the number of lepers, but Mr. E. Clifford says * that there can be little doubt that they already exceed 250,000, and that their numbers are still growing. In Canada it has recently been discovered that the cases in the lazaretto at Tracadie do not comprise all the lepers in New Brunswick, and a considerable number of other cases are believed to exist, especially among the French residents in the northern part of the province.† At the Cape, though it was recently denied officially that leprosy is increasing, a strong impression prevails that the disease is extending. The same may be said of our Australian colonies; and the statement to that effect made by the Prince of Wales at the first meeting of the committee of the "Father Damien Memorial Fund" at Marlborough House has not, so far as I know, been called in question. Such a state of things may well cause anxiety, not only to those responsible for the welfare of our colonies, but to all lovers of humanity.

The facts above set forth represent an unspeakable amount of suffering to many races whose destinies we have taken into our keeping, but besides this they indicate a possible danger to ourselves. Leprosy has before now overrun Europe and invaded England, without respecting the "silver streak" which keeps off other enemies; and it is perfectly conceivable that, under certain circumstances, it might do so again. It is well known that, in recent years, our countrymen whose lot is cast in places where the disease is indigenous have ceased to show

* "Father Damien," p. 153. London: Macmillan & Co. 1889.
† *British Medical Journal*, August 3, 1889.

the immunity from its attacks which was once thought to be their privilege. Can all this misery be prevented? I do not hesitate to answer, Yes. It may be doubtful whether the disease can be stamped out, but it is certain that its advance can be checked, and that its ravages can be confined within comparatively narrow limits. How is this to be done? Only in one of two ways—by eliminating the cause of the disease, or by preventing its transmission.

The former of these methods is unfortunately impossible, for we are at present entirely in the dark as to the cause of leprosy. The subject has for centuries been a favourite playground for the "scientific imagination," and, as Cicero said of the philosophers, there is no absurdity which has not found defenders among the various scientific pundits who have wrestled with the problem. Climate, soil, and race have each been tried and found wanting, for the disease exists in every kind of climate and on every variety of soil, and no race is exempt from it, although certainly some divisions of the great human family appear to be more open to its attacks than others. Almost since the dawn of medical speculation food has been regarded by many as the *fons et origo mali*, and there has been a remarkable "stream of tendency" towards fixing on fish as the particular esculent at fault. As far back as the days of Aretæus, the eating of fish and milk at the same meal was reputed to be an infallible cause of leprosy; the old proverb of Provence, "Le poisson fait devenir ladre," represented a popular belief which has for centuries been almost universally prevalent in European haunts of leprosy; and even at the present day, when the theory has completely "deliquesced" under the solvent action of what Magendie called *le fait brut*, a distinguished surgeon still tenderly hugs his old *mumpsimus*, and sees putrid fish * at the bottom of every case of leprosy, though the patient may have never had a chance of eating fish of any kind. The "exquisite reason" appears to be that, if the

---

* Raymond ("Histoire de l'Éléphantiasis," p. 23. Lausanne, 1767) tells us that in the South of France it was not putridity, but the opposite condition, that was dreaded. "Les gens du pays attribuent la cause occasionnelle du mal . . . à l'usage du poisson mangé *trop frais*."

leper himself did not, some of his ancestors may have done so. It is, in fact, a case of original dietetic sin, fish being the pathological apple

> "whose mortal taste
> Brought death into the world, and all our woe."

It is interesting, however, to observe that the Maoris in New Zealand attribute the peculiar form of leprosy from which they suffer to eating a small carp which exist in large numbers in a diseased state in the lake of Taupo. White of Selborne attributed the disappearance of leprosy from this country to "improved agriculture and an abundant supply of fresh food and vegetables." Beyond all question good food is an essential factor in the preservation of health, but it does not follow that bad food is the cause of leprosy. The same may be said as to hygienic conditions. Malaria may conceivably predispose to leprosy, as to other diseases, by weakening the constitution— or, as modern pathological *illuminati* phrase it, "lessening the resistance of the tissues to the attacks of microbes "—but there is nothing to show that it has any more direct effect. The gratuitous "primary dyscrasia" of Danielssen and Boeck; the less mysterious but not less gratuitous "defect in development of certain elements in the skin" of Vandyke Carter; the "absence of potash in the blood" of Hjaltelin (of Iceland), and the "absence of salt in the food" of Munro, are all very pretty theories as they stand, but they are rather to be admired than adopted. At present the bacillus holds the field; but that "fearful wild fowl" must be known in all its ten "categories" before our acquaintance with it is likely to prove of practical service. Especially one would wish to know *whence* it comes. At the present time there is a tendency to trace disease germs to our "poor relations;" but animals can hardly be held accountable for the manufacture of leprosy, as it is very doubtful whether they are themselves susceptible of it. It would be curious, however, if after all the bacillus of leprosy should be traced to fish; I am not aware that it has ever been looked for in them, or that any attempts have been made to inoculate them with the disease.

If, however, the origin of leprosy is still one of the great unanswered riddles of the universe, there is not the same mystery as to the mode of its transmission. The evidence in favour of contagion is to my mind quite overwhelming. The contagiousness of the disease was never doubted till it had nearly died out; men ceased to believe in contagion when they no longer saw daily instances of it. The whole system of medical police by which leprosy was finally driven out of Europe was based on the notion that it was contagious, and no measures not based on that principle have ever had the slightest effect in checking its ravages. The alarming spread of this loathsome pest in recent years is in my opinion due to the fact that for some time the opposite doctrine gained the ascendency, and held captive the minds of men. For this pernicious error, and for all the disastrous consequences that have flowed and continue to flow from it, the Royal College of Physicians of London is chiefly responsible.

Though the miserable story is too well known to those who are interested in the subject of leprosy, it may be well briefly to recall the facts. In 1862, some alarm being felt as to the spread of leprosy in Barbadoes, the Colonial Office requested the College of Physicians to draw up a series of questions relative to the nature, causes, and prevalence of the disease. A form containing these questions was circulated throughout the colonies, and upwards of 250 replies were received from medical men in different parts of the world, exclusive of those from Her Majesty's Consuls and of communications from the Governors of British colonies. The mass of information thus obtained was then submitted to the College, which undertook, apparently with a lightness of heart worthy of M. Émile Ollivier, "to collate, digest, and report upon" it.

A committee was chosen by the College to discharge this important public duty, but there is every reason to believe that only two of the physicians on the committee had the smallest practical acquaintance with leprosy. One of them, the late Dr. Owen Rees, had met with one remarkable case, and another, Dr. Gavin Milroy, paid a hurried visit to

Demerara, where he was egregiously hoaxed even by dull-witted lepers.*

The mental condition of the other members of the committee must have been *tabulæ rasæ* of ideal blankness on everything connected with leprosy. One can only marvel at the sublime self-confidence with which such a body—seeing as it did with only one eye, and that, as will presently be shown, a dim or distorted one—undertook to guide the footsteps of Government over ground so difficult even for the clear-sighted. The result of their labours was the "Report on Leprosy" published in 1867, an ill-starred document which has probably done more to propagate the disease than any other single agency since the Crusades. In that report the *Patres Conscripti* of English medicine expressed the following opinion, each individual sentence and clause of which is absolutely and demonstrably erroneous:—

"The all but unanimous conviction of the most experienced observers in different parts of the world is quite opposed to the belief that leprosy is contagious or communicable by proximity or contact with the diseased. The evidence derived from the experience of the attendants in leper asylums is especially conclusive on this point.

"The few instances that have been reported in a contrary sense either rest on imperfect observation, or they are recorded with so little attention to the necessary details as not to affect the above conclusion.

"That leprosy is rarely, if ever, transmissible [in married

* A striking instance, related by Dr. Hillis (*Timehri*, June, 1889: p. 79), will suffice: "One man stated to Dr. Gavin Milroy when he was in Demerara, at the penal settlement, that he believed his leprosy arose from the salt diet the prisoners are accustomed to, whereas in fact his wife had suffered from leprosy previous to his being sentenced to penal servitude, and a child of this same man and woman died at the leper hospital at Mahaica." But what must always discredit Dr. Milroy's judgment is the incredulity with which he received Dr. Hillebrand's account of the outbreak of leprosy in the Sandwich Islands: the subsequent course of events is a terrible commentary on the inability to appreciate facts "gross as a mountain, open, palpable," which inspired the unlucky manifesto of 1867.

life], when one of the parties has no tendency whatever to the disease, is the opinion of the great majority of the respondents who have had the largest opportunities of observation."*

If this deliverance had been merely a theoretical opinion promulgated by the College of Physicians for the edification of the few medical men in this country who concern themselves with its utterances, no one would have had any right to complain. But in this case the decision that leprosy was not contagious led at once to practical consequences of the most far-reaching importance. The measures devised by humane and enlightened statesmen for the mitigation of the scourge were abandoned; the leper-houses throughout Her Majesty's dominions were thrown open, each discharging its measure of pollution into the stream of healthy life near it; and a general relaxation of sanitary discipline with regard to leprosy supervened.† It may

* "Report on Leprosy by the Royal College of Physicians, prepared for Her Majesty's Secretary of State for the Colonies," p. lxix. London, 1867.

† As evidence of this I need only cite two instances, not more flagrant than hundreds of others, but which happen to be the first that come to hand. Dr. Munro says (*Edin. Med. Journ.*, vol. xxv. p. 424): "It is sad to think that in any colony of England a leper should be allowed to *keep a school*, as I have seen to my horror in St. Kitts. In misgoverned Crete such things might be, but done in an English colony, with the tacit sanction of the Government, instructed by the *Royal College of Physicians* of London as to the non-contagious nature of the disease, the latter acting on utterly worthless *negative* evidence—so done, such an affair is a disgrace to humanity!" Again, take the following plain unvarnished tale from Dr. Hillis (*Timehri*, June, 1889: p. 80): "A respectable young lad became leprous through, as I believe, playing with a boy who had leprosy, and who lived further down the street. When seen he was in an advanced stage of tubercular leprosy, covered with sores, and he was sent home and treated by the late Sir Erasmus Wilson, and the family left the house. I subsequently learnt that another family shortly took over the same house without its having undergone any purification or disinfecting, and it must be remembered the boy had been confined for months to one room and was covered with these sores. Had he died of some endemic disease considered contagious, but questionably so, how much money would have been spent on painting, papering, etc., by the authorities! But in the case mentioned no such steps were considered necessary. I am not finding fault with disinfection as carried on in Georgetown—far from it; it is merely contended that, owing to the opinions that the

without much exaggeration be said that if leprosy slew its thousands before, it has slain its tens of thousands within the confines of the British Empire since 1867. Even outside the limits of Her Majesty's sway the evil effect of this decision has been felt, for the authority of an institution which was supposed to be the concrete embodiment of medical science in this country necessarily had great weight on the minds of some foreign practitioners. That this unfortunate "Report on Leprosy" did not do still more harm is only due to the fact that the dangerous doctrine which it was intended to enforce was not universally acted upon; the practical common sense of mankind in many places where leprosy has its home refusing to be led astray by theoretical opinion. Of course I do not blame those responsible for the "Report" for not having known better; they acted according to their lights, and it can hardly be imputed to them as a crime that these "lights" proved *ignes fatui* to those who looked to them for guidance. What they cannot, however, be readily absolved from is the having undertaken to decide a question with which they were quite incompetent to deal.

But if the judges were incompetent, it is no less certain that many of the witnesses were untrustworthy. The answers received to the questions in the circular afford ample proof that many of the respondents knew little and cared less about the disease. The truth is that the mystery still surrounding leprosy is in great measure due to the want of careful study by a sufficiently large number of observers. The subject is so repulsive that it has been, and still is to some extent, "segregated" by medical men from their mental purview as a pariah among diseases. But whilst positive evidence of contagion of the most striking kind is contained in the very "Report"[*]

Executive have to guide them" (*i.e.* the "Report" of the Royal College of Physicians), "they would not be justified under the present rulings on the subject in going to any expense under the Public Health Ordinance, as leprosy is not considered a contagious disease."

[*] I need only cite the evidence of Drs. Goding and Stevenson of Barbadoes ("Report," p. 32), Dr. Aquart of Grenada (ibid., p. 36), Drs. Manget, Reed, Pollard, Duffey, Carney, and Van Holst of British Guiana (ibid., pp. 45, 46), the Proto-Medico of Corfu (ibid., p. 67), Drs. Regnaud

which denies its existence, the College, forgetting the cardinal principle that even one well-attested fact outweighs any amount of negative statements, seems to have settled the matter by the simple expedient of counting rather than weighing the opinions submitted to them. One is reminded of the story of the Frenchman accused of stealing a horse, who, when the judge said, "Three witnesses saw you do it," promptly replied, "Ah, sir! three thousand could easily be found who did not see me."

Let us now consider the conclusions of the "Report" somewhat more closely. The first statement, that "the all but unanimous conviction of the most experienced observers in different parts of the world is quite opposed to the belief that leprosy is contagious or communicable by proximity or contact with the diseased," is to-day exactly the reverse of the truth. For this revolution in opinion we are indebted chiefly to the "Report" itself. The enormous increase of leprosy consequent on the free trade in the disease which followed the appearance of that document opened the eyes even of fanatical non-contagionists. It is a fact of the greatest significance that almost without an exception the men who know most of leprosy, who have lived in the midst of it, are those who believe most firmly in its contagiousness. This is true not only of medical men, but of the missionaries and others who tend the unfortunate sufferers. Such a consensus of opinion is not to be lightly set aside. "Securus judicat orbis terrarum;" the instinct of mankind has more than once been right in the domain of medicine, when science was at fault.

It was not long before the theoretical conclusions enunciated with such self-satisfied optimism by the framers of the "Report" were rudely shaken by the stern logic of facts. The tide of leprosy, as if in mockery of these medical Canutes, rose ever higher; proofs of the contagious character of the disease were forthcoming on all sides;[*] and it became only too evident

and Bolton of Mauritius (ibid., p. 86), the Civil Commissioner of Seychelles (ibid., p. 90), and Mr. Macnamara, then of Mozufferpore (ibid., p. 141).

[*] In 1869 Drognat-Landré supported the contagionist doctrine in a powerful work ("De la Contagion seule Cause de la Lèpre"). In 1878

that in seeking counsel from the College of Physicians the Government had placed its trust in a hopelessly futile oracle.

The "pity of it" seems all the greater when it is remembered that the medical profession in the British Empire could at that time have furnished plenty of distinguished men who had given much attention to leprosy, and had seen it in its worst haunts. A thoroughly competent tribunal of experts could have been formed, from whom a report of permanent value might have been obtained.

Proceeding to the next point—viz. that "the evidence derived from the experience of the attendants in leper asylums is especially conclusive on this point" (non-contagion)—I may remark that, granting for a moment that negative evidence on a matter of this kind is worth anything at all, the argument proves far too much. Exactly the same thing may be said of the attendants in Lock hospitals. The same argument was used to controvert Koch's view as to the contagiousness of consumption, but was rightly held to have no weight. It is not true, however, that attendants on lepers are never attacked. The College might profitably have recalled the historical problem

---

the "conqueror worm" which carries the infection was discovered by Hansen. In 1874 Dr. Vandyke Carter, whose investigations in nearly every part of the world where leprosy is found entitle him to rank as the foremost living authority on the disease, was driven by the facts which he himself had collected to "find salvation" in the contagionist fold. A few years later the *coup de grace* was given to the "Report" by Dr. W. Munro, formerly medical officer of St. Kitt's in the West Indies, in a series of papers (*Edin. Med. Journ.*, vols. xxii., xxiii., xxiv., xxv.) which form a storehouse of facts from which every subsequent writer has freely drawn. I need only mention two other works which have been several times referred to in the course of this article, and in both of which the same conclusion is enforced—Frère Etienne's little book ("La Lèpre est Contagieuse," Trinidad, 1879) and the magnificent monograph of Mr. J. D. Hillis ("Leprosy in British Guiana," London, 1881). In 1884 Miss Agnes Lambert published an excellent article (already referred to) in the *Nineteenth Century* (August and September, 1884). In 1887 Dr. Besnier brought additional proofs of the contagiousness of leprosy before the Académie de Médecine in Paris, while in this country Archdeacon Wright sounded the alarm as to its increasing prevalence throughout the world (*Times*, Nov. 8, 1887).

submitted to the Royal Society by Charles the Second before building an argument on an imaginary foundation. Its own "Report" contains several instances in which persons who had the care of lepers contracted the disease. The most striking of these is the case of Dr. Robertson, medical superintendent of the Curieuse leper establishment, Seychelles,* but there are others equally remarkable.† Several cases of the same kind have also been recorded by Hansen,‡ and Father Étienne.§ One of those mentioned by the latter observer is that of Dr. Goldard, a young French physician, who, in order to demonstrate in his own person the non-contagiousness of leprosy, went to Palestine and took up his abode in a lazar-house. The poor fellow fell a victim to his scientific enthusiasm, and died of leprosy in a few years. Other cases are reported from South America.‖ But what need is there of the laborious collection of such facts when there is the grand object-lesson of Father Damien's life and death before the whole world? Dr. Hoffmann, the medical officer of Molokai, has recently fallen a victim to his devotion, and it is said, though I know not with what truth, that one of Damien's colleagues is now also a leper. In addition to all this we have the crushing fact that, out of sixty-six *kokuas*, or helpers, on the island in 1888, twenty-three were known to have contracted the disease, while in eleven more its existence was suspected. I have taken some trouble to show that the supposed immunity of attendants is a pure myth, for it is really the corner-stone of the vast edifice of error erected by the College of Physicians in 1867.

The argument from married life has just as little foundation. Several illustrations of contagion between husband and wife are given in the "Report" itself, and others are brought

* "Report on Leprosy," p. 90.

† See replies by Drs. Goding and Stevenson, p. 32; Dr. Mantell, p. 41; Mr. N. C. Macnamara, ibid.; Mohamed Naeem, p. 177; and Surgeon-Major J. Rose, p. 199.

‡ *British and Foreign Medico-Chirurgical Review*, April, 1875.

§ "La Lèpre est Contagieuse," p. 122 et seq.

‖ *Boletin de Medicina del Cauca*, No. 1, p. 13 (Dr. Tenorio), and p. 16 (Dr. Escobar).

forward by Frère Étienne * and Hillis. The former relates the case of a Venezuelan lady whose husband died of leprosy. Six years afterwards she herself became a leper. One of Hillis's cases is particularly instructive. A shopkeeper whose business often took him to the asylum became leprous. For ten years his wife remained free from the complaint. The case was well known, and Dr. Hillis was frequently asked to explain how it was, if leprosy was contagious, that she had escaped so long. In the course of time, however, she became an undoubted leper.† The moral of this striking case is that contagion would be more often noticed if suspected persons could be kept sufficiently long under observation. In precisely the same way the case of Keanu, the Hawaiian convict inoculated by Dr. Arning on the 5th of November, 1885, used to be cited as a proof that the disease could not be transmitted in that way. The poison took its own time, however, and the man is now an undoubted leper.

But leaving all other questions out of consideration, the crucial question remains : If leprosy is not contagious, how is it that it spreads ? Granting that heredity plays a certain part in its transmission, the sudden outbreak of the disease in races previously altogether free from it can hardly be explained by ancestral proclivity. The College of Physicians had before their eyes the great fact of the invasion of the virgin soil of Hawaii by leprosy, but, like their prototypes in "Tristram Shandy," "they concerned themselves not with facts—they reasoned." We may supposed them to have argued that, as leprosy is not contagious, therefore it cannot spread from one nation to another. All evidence to the contrary was dismissed as impertinent. Sterne must have foreseen these learned Thebans when he described the disputations of the Strasburg doctors : "'It happens otherwise,' replied the opponents. 'It ought not,' said they."

Nothing which the College of Physicians may do in the future can wipe out the effects of their "Report," or the incalculable misery which it has caused. When the public mind

* Op. cit., p. 95.
† *British Medical Journal*, Nov. 5, 1887.

at last was aroused on the subject, just twenty years after the issue of the first "Report," a second one appeared (July 15, 1887), in which it is admitted that there is a case for inquiry! I venture to suggest that, by way of making some reparation for the past, they should send some of the men of light and leading among them to see for themselves what leprosy is, and to study it, not vicariously through the eyes of others, but face to face in its native haunts. What is wanted is that the full light of modern medical science should be thrown on the dark places where the monster lurks. If some of the eminent scientific men who were invited to join the Marlborough House Committee could study leprosy in its home, great results might be obtained. If an experienced pathologist like Sir James Paget could spend some time in India, important facts as to the nature of leprosy might be discovered ; or if a distinguished physician like Sir Andrew Clark could have five years at Molokai, he might perhaps slay the Sphinx of leprosy, or at any rate evolve a system of diet calculated to be of service to those subjected to the contagion of that dire disease. To send out from time to time a young doctor on a scientific *Wanderjahr* among the lepers, as proposed by the Marlborough House Committee, seems to me mere trifling. Is it likely that a fledgling just escaped from the academic nest should "come, see, and conquer" where Danielssen and Boeck, Vandyke Carter, Hansen, Munro, Arning and Hillis have failed?

Another plan which might lead to some discovery of real importance would be the offer of a prize sufficiently large to tempt men of the highest eminence to compete. Mr. Macnamara suggests* that the Damien Memorial Fund should offer "a prize of £500, open to all comers, for the best essay and original research regarding the bacillus lepræ." This is a step in the right direction, but it is not enough. M. Pasteur received something like £20,000 for his discoveries in the silkworm disease. If he could only be induced to grapple with the leprosy problem, there might be a chance of a "protective virus" being discovered which should make people exposed to the contagion of leprosy invulnerable to its attack.

* "Leprosy a Communicable Disease," 2nd ed., p. 4. London, 1889.

In the meantime the only way of coping with leprosy is to deal with it as a thing dangerous to mankind. It would be criminal to allow the scourge free play because academic pedantry is not satisfied as to the exact mode of its transmission. No half measures will suffice: *écrasez l'infâme*, in a new sense, must be the motto of those entrusted with the task. Our forefathers did not allow themselves to be disturbed by "philosophic doubt," but stamped out the pest by a system of "Thorough" which Strafford might have envied. The sick must be kept strictly apart from the healthy, and all suspicious cases should be detained in quarantine and jealously watched. For this purpose special medical inspectors should be appointed, each with a defined district under his constant personal supervision. I should not be disposed to insist on the separation of married couples; lepers are not prolific, and hereditary contamination has now been shown to be almost a *quantité négligeable*.* There is, of course, the risk of contagion; but if husbands or wives are willing to encounter it, I do not see why they should be prevented. We have the testimony of Father Damien to the good effect of allowing married people to remain together.† There must always be a certain amount of hardship in segregation, but if lunatics can be made comfortable and even happy in confinement, so may lepers. A vast amount of nonsense has been talked about the horrors of segregation; if there is any discomfort beyond the separation from friends and the suffering caused by the disease, it is either due to neglect on the part of the authorities, or to want of funds. The lepers I saw in Norway were, with the exception of those in the very last stages of the disease, clean, cheerful and busy—the men in the workshops, the women at domestic work, and the children in their classes. The last was certainly

* Dr. Armauer Hansen, who recently visited the Norwegian lepers in Wisconsin, Minnesota, and Dacota, found that the offspring of 160 lepers who had emigrated to America had remained free to the third generation (*Archiv für Dermatologie*, 1889, Heft iii.). Again, there is the fact that, although during eighteen years 2,864 persons were consigned to Kalawao (Molokai), only twenty-six children were born during that period, and of these only *two* have become leprous.

† E. Clifford, "Father Damien," p. 82.

a painful sight, but the little patients themselves were not at all gloomy. Those I saw at Seville were less cheerful, but that may have been due to the quasi-monastic atmosphere which surrounded them. Dr. Webster, however, says * that the lepers whom he saw at Grenada were quite a "merry family," dancing, twanging the guitar with their crooked stumps of fingers, and warbling ditties with such remnants of voices as were left them. Frère Étienne's testimony as to Trinidad is not less striking,† and Mr. Clifford tells us that even at Molokai there is little sign of unhappiness.

Apart altogether from the *salus populi*, which must ever be the supreme law in such matters, there can be no doubt that segregation, if properly carried out, is the best thing for the sufferers themselves. If I had the misfortune to be a leper myself, I should prefer to be where one touch of nature makes the whole world kin, though it were only by fellowship in suffering, to being an object of horror to all around me. Medicine, though it cannot cure, can do much to mitigate the incidental miseries of leprosy, and nowhere can treatment be so well applied or the necessary nursing so intelligently carried out as in places where special experience has engendered special skill. Sanitary arrangements must be of the highest attainable perfection, as the concourse of foul smells in leper-houses is especially apt to breed disease, not only among the inmates but among those in charge of them. The food must be abundant and nutritious, and plenty of occupation should be provided for such as can work. Nor should amusements be neglected. It was by attention to all these things that Father Damien was able to humanize the poor outcasts for whom he gave his life ; by these means he transformed a sink of moral as well as physical corruption into a peaceful and happy community.

---

* *Medico-Chirurgical Transactions*, vol. xliii., 1860, p. 29.

† Op. cit., pp. 254, 255. "La tristesse n'est pas du tout, comme je l'ai lu plus d'une fois, un effet inévitable de la maladie. Je puis bien attester qu'il n'y a pas au monde école ou collège *plus gai, plus bruyant*, où l'on joue et babille plus, qu'à Cocorite. Tout est oublié; certainement on n'est pas un lépreux, on est un pensionnaire ; et la reine est bien honorée d'héberger de tels persounages."

There is no reason why this memorable example should not bear fruit wherever lepers are to be found. There is no lack of self-sacrificing men whose hearts are filled by the enthusiasm of humanity; what the Catholic Church beautifully calls the "devout female sex" will always be ready wherever nurses are needed; and of doctors we shall never fall short when there is such a field for scientific discovery. The only thing wanting is money. The stamping out of the most grievous disease which flesh is heir to will no doubt be an expensive undertaking; but is this great and wealthy country to count the cost when poor States like Norway and Hawaii are lavishing their scanty treasure in furthering the good work?

It is to be feared that the wave of philanthropic sentiment which, under the combined influences of pity, fear, and fashion, rose so high a short time ago, is already subsiding. De Quincy gauged the English character correctly when he said that, so far from being phlegmatic, we are the most excitable people on earth; unhappily our excitement, which is so easily fanned into a blaze, burns itself out all the more quickly. As Macaulay observed, our virtue goes to sleep for several years after one of our periodical outbreaks of morality. Let not the same be said of our philanthropy! It will be deplorable, and indeed disgraceful, if our desire to do something to check the advance of leprosy is allowed to die out with the "scare" which engendered it.

THE REFORM OF THE COLLEGE OF SURGEONS.

VISITORS to that legal "Grove of Academe," Lincoln's Inn Fields, can hardly fail to have observed a large building with a sort of shabby-genteel pretension to architectural style which stands on the south side of the square. This, as a Latin inscription on the front informs the passer-by, whose recollections of "Propria quæ Maribus" are not yet too remote, is the Royal College of Surgeons of England, a learned body chiefly known to the public as the custodian of the great museum collected by John Hunter and purchased after his death by the nation. To the bulk of the medical profession in this country the College is familiar as the Inquisition Chamber of their youthful days, where the tortures of "paper" and *vivâ voce* were undergone and the mystic rites of "pass" or "pluck" administered. The College of Surgeons gives the licence to practise, or what Molière calls "virtutem et puissanciam . . . . taillandi coupandi et occidendi impune per totam terram," or at any rate to that very considerable portion of it over which the Union Jack waves. It probably examines three-fourths of the medical students in Great Britain, and perhaps not less than five-sixths of those in England. In recent years, after the necessary diploma had been secured, few doctors in active practice ever gave themselves the least concern about the College or its affairs, and certainly the Council of that institution never troubled itself about them. Occasionally indeed some convicted criminal or particularly blatant quack was struck off the rolls in deference to public opinion ; but there was no active help or even encouragement in the resistance to official tyranny, the struggle for the redress of legitimate grievances, or the battle against unqualified practice which make up so great a part of the professional difficulties of a very large class of medical men. In fact, the rulers of the College hardly recognized its members as forming any part of the body politic ; rights and privileges were not for these but for their betters. In this spirit the College has been governed since the beginning of the present century, and though serious protests against both the system and its practical results were made sixty years ago, the efforts of the reformers were unsuccessful, and it was not till quite recently that the general body of members of the College endeavoured again to vindicate their right to a voice in the management of its affairs.

The editor of a well-known magazine once said to me that there are only two subjects which really interest the British public, viz. religion and politics. It is especially difficult to get the general community to trouble themselves about the affairs of corporations, whether they be city companies, a Royal Academy, or medical colleges. Medical politics are particularly uninteresting even to doctors outside official circles ; to the general public naturally they are a sealed book. If now and again some faint echoes of the revolt of Members of the College of Surgeons against the governing body of that institution have reached the public ear through the din of more momentous conflicts, the matter is probably dismissed with a shrug as only "another squabble among the doctors." I hope, however, to show that the question of the proper management of the College of Surgeons concerns not only its own members, but perhaps to a still greater degree the community at large. The demand for reform is not merely, as the governing body no doubt would like the public to believe, the wail of a few surgical Peris standing at the gate of the dingy paradise in Lincoln's Inn Fields, and gazing with longing eyes into the radiant council-room which they may not enter ; nor is it echoed only by a few busybodies seeking a cheap advertisement. It is in reality a part of a great wave of professional opinion which is slowly but surely rising and gathering force to sweep away the rottenness of constitution, the inertness, inefficiency, evil traditions, and scandalous abuses of all kinds, owing to which our medical corporations, instead of aiding, have seriously obstructed the course of scientific progress. It is not merely a movement to enable persons who are not now represented on the Council of the College of Surgeons to share in the honours and emoluments within its gift ; nor is it simply an agitation for the enfranchisement of the down-trodden Members. These objects are only means to great ends—the furthering the art of healing by the proper employment of the vast resources which the College has at its disposal, the promotion of the common weal by the improvement of medical education, the maintenance of a high standard of knowledge and practical skill in those wishing to enter the medical profession, and the general raising of the intellectual and social level of those who practise it. All this concerns not only the individual members of the public, but the State itself very closely, for the more medical science advances and the more efficient doctors become, the more will human suffering be relieved and the ravages of preventible disease be checked. The whole question will soon be brought before Parliament, and, as it is most important that the real points at issue should be clearly apprehended, it is necessary to glance at the history of the corporation, to describe its present constitution, and to indicate the changes which it is sought to effect.

The Royal College of Surgeons of England is the representative and the lineal descendant of two ancient guilds, the "Barber Surgeons" and the "Fellowship of Surgeons," both of which were in existence about the beginning of the fourteenth century, and possibly at a still earlier date. In 1461 the members of the former of these associations, the "Freemen of the Mystery of the Barbers of the City of London using the Faculty of Surgery," were formally incorporated as a company—"one body and one perpetual fellowship or community," by letters patent of February 24th, 1 Edward IV. In 1540 the two societies were amalgamated by an act of Parliament (32 Henry VIII. c. 42) under the style and title of the "Mystery and Commonalty of the Barbers and Surgeons of London." A large picture of Holbein which is preserved in the Barbers' Company Hall in Monkwell Street, represents Bluff King Hal in the act of delivering the charter to Thomas Vicary, his sergeant chirurgeon, who, with fourteen of his brethren, is kneeling before the monarch. Prominent in the group, and apparently taking precedence of all except Vicary himself, who was the first master of the new company, are his Majesty's barbers, Nicholas Sympson and Edmund Harman.

By the Act of 1540 the union between the surgeons and the elegant fraternity of specialists for the hair was finally consummated. Although at that period surgeons ranked in social scale with "common" bakers, brewers, and scriveners,[*] from a study of the Act it appears that the union between the surgeons and the shavers was rather a mechanical mixture than a chemical combination. The difference between the two crafts is clearly recognized in the Act itself, and no member seems to have been allowed to practise what for convenience may be called both branches of the profession.

The union was not a happy one, and as the surgeons improved in social status they seem to have been more and more anxious to sever themselves from their incongruous yokefellows. In 1684 they petitioned the King to be incorporated as an independent body, but the barbers were by no means equally desirous for divorce, and their voice prevailed. In 1744 a final effort was successfully made by the surgeons, and they managed to get an Act passed on May 2, 1745, by which the "artistic" section of the "mystery" was definitively cut adrift, and a purely surgical corporation instituted under the name of "The Masters, Governors, and Commonalty of the

[*] They are so classed in an Act of Parliament passed in 1530 (22 Henry VIII.). The low position of surgeons in the social hierarchy in the middle ages was of course due to the feudal notion that all manual work was degrading.

Art and Science of Surgery," though they were commonly known after this date as the "Company of Surgeons." In the Act under which the new Company was established the commonalty was to "enjoy the same liberties, privileges, and franchises as by any former Acts and Letters Patent given, granted, or confirmed."* Notwithstanding its imposing title and its freedom from the old degrading associations, the days of the new corporation were not many in the land, nor was its career particularly brilliant. After much mismanagement and irregularities of various kinds, it came to an end by a deliberate violation of its own Act of Incorporation, which required that no Court should be held unless the Master and the two Governors, or any two of them, should be present. Now, it happened that shortly before the meeting of the Court of Assistants, held on July 7, 1796, one of the Governors had died, whilst the other, John Wyatt by name, was living in Warwickshire, blind and paralyzed. Great efforts were made to have the poor old man brought up to London, and tradition says he was dragged for a considerable part of the way in a post-chaise; but in spite of all he did not arrive in time, and notwithstanding the absence of both the Governors, the Court was held on July 7th—an illegal proceeding, by which the Company was declared to have infringed the Act of Incorporation, and, so to speak, snuffed itself out. In the following year an attempt was made by eleven members of the governing body to induce Parliament to grant an Act of Indemnity, and thus to restore the Corporation under the name of a College to more active conditions of life. The Bill, which was ingeniously drawn so as to give almost absolute power to the governing body, had very nearly been smuggled through Parliament before the members of the Corporation were aware of what was going on; but on learning the state of affairs they at once petitioned against the Bill. These eleven Assistants might have attained their ends, owing to their unedifying official record not being generally known; but, as Johnson said of some plausible rogue, they were undone "as soon as their character came up with them." Lord Thurlow championed the cause of

* Mr. Tweedy, in *The Lancet*, March 23, 1889.

the Members in the House of Lords, and the Bill, which had been on the point of being read a third time, was thrown out without a division.* So scandalous were the disclosures which had been made, and so strong had the opposition become, that the Court of Assistants never again summoned up courage to apply to Parliament.

The ingenious idea of obtaining by Charter new privileges which had been refused by the House of Lords occurred to one of the Assistants; and the amiable monarch, who could not have had any idea of the selfish designs of the Assistants, granted a Charter which practically deprived the Members of all vestige of their rights. It was thus that in March, 1800, after a good deal of intrigue, the governing body of the old Company of Surgeons obtained a new Charter, in the preamble of which it is said, "Whereas we are informed that the old Company hath been and now is dissolved," etc., etc. It is contended that this recital is incorrect, and that the Charter of George III. had no power to override an Act of Parliament which has never been repealed. It is evident, moreover, that during the years 1796 to 1800 the old Company of Surgeons must have existed as a legal *nominis umbra*, as they continued to admit persons under letters testimonial, and on December 13, 1799—that is, four months before the Charter of 1800— by a unanimous vote accepted the guardianship of Hunter's Museum. The new Company was intituled "The Royal College of Surgeons in London," and the surviving Assistants of the old Company were to form the nucleus of the new Corporation. To the Royal College were confirmed " all the liberties and privileges by any Act or Letters Patent granted or confirmed to or otherwise belonging to the previously existing body." It seems obvious, as the Members contend, that a Royal Charter could not take away any of the privileges which had been granted to Members by the Act of Parliament of 1745, and as that Act had not deprived the Commonalty of their rights, the ancient privileges of the Members still belong to them *de jure* even if they have lapsed *de facto*. Persons in a position to be well acquainted with all the circumstances of

* "Parliamentary Register of the House of Lords." London, 1797.

the case have not hesitated to say that this Charter of 1800 was obtained by "misrepresentation and fraud,"* and that the Crown was deliberately misled in the matter. It contained several of the provisions which had excited most opposition on the part of the Members, and which as a matter of fact had caused the rejection of the Bill by Parliament. The petition against this measure stated that the "ancient privileges of the Members as such would be annihilated, and their right of meeting in general court would be taken away." The Court of Assistants was to choose the Master, the Governors, and the Examiners, and to fill up vacancies as they arose in their own ranks. In short, the oligarchical form of government into which the old company had gradually degenerated was fully recognized and confirmed by this Charter, and beyond the fact that it is necessarily implied that the Assistants must be chosen from among the Members, no voice in the management of the corporate affairs is given to the Members. The only crumb of comfort which they could find in the document was that their "ancient 'privileges" are nowhere expressly annulled therein. They are simply passed over as of none account.

From those who had nothing, however, even the little that they seemed to have was before very long taken away. By a Charter granted in 1843, a "new class of members . . . to be called Fellows" was created, from among whom alone the members of the Council were in future to be chosen. The Fellows were to be a higher academical order, and were to win their spurs by passing a special examination a good deal more searching than the one required for the ordinary Membership. The Members thus lost the only real "privilege" left them, to wit, their eligibility to the governing body.

By the Charter of 1843 the constitution of the College was practically fixed in its present form. The Commonalty consists of Fellows who must have attained the age of twenty-five years and passed certain special examinations, and Members who must have completed their twenty-first year and passed examinations of a lower, but still qualifying standard. The Fellows alone are eligible for appointment to the governing

* *Lancet*, vol. i., 1843, No. 44, p. 125.

THE REFORM OF THE COLLEGE OF SURGEONS. 139

body or Council, which consists of twenty-four Fellows, inclusive of a President and two Vice-Presidents, who are elected by the Council from its own body. Three members of the Council retire annually, and therefore the members of the Council, as a rule, hold office for the long period of eight years. The Fellows alone constitute the electoral body. Until last year, the Fellows could vote only in person, so that election to the governing body was practically in the hands of those residing in London. By a Charter obtained in 1888, however, voting by means of voting papers is allowed under certain restrictions. The Council can make bye-laws, which must, however, receive the approval of the Crown under the hand of one of the Secretaries of State or the sanction of Parliament; it appoints Examiners, holds the property of the College in trust, and has the absolute control of its funds. Fellows who vote, as a rule, belong, or are ambitious to belong, to the same class as those who monopolize the offices and honours of the College. The result is that the College is practically in the hands of metropolitan hospital surgeons, with a very slight infusion of provincial men belonging to the same class. The vast majority of the members of the College, on the other hand, are general practitioners whose professional interests and necessities are altogether different from those of hospital surgeons. The governing body is therefore out of sympathy and out of touch with the great bulk of the governed, an unsatisfactory state of things which materially lessens the usefulness of the College, and must, if allowed to continue, end in bringing the institution a second time to ruin and disgrace.

Having shown by historical references that the present College of Surgeons is the lineal descendant and heir of the old Barber Surgeons' Company, it would appear unnecessary to pursue this line any further; but the culminating argument is to be found in the fact that the present Council have administered the same trust funds as were originally bequeathed to the Barber Surgeons' Company and, by the Act of 1745, specially granted to the Company of Surgeons. Thus the sum of £510, originally vested in the united companies of the Barbers and Surgeons, and given to them by Edward Arris for the institution of lectures on the muscles, together with an annuity of £16 bequeathed to the united companies by John Gale, for one anatomy lecture, were accordingly "vested in and deemed the sole property, estate, and effects of the Company and Corporation of Surgeons established and incorporated by this Act." Now, the Council of the present College of Surgeons appoints an Arris and Gale lecturer every year, and pays him with money derived from these trusts, the right to administer which comes to it only as being the legal representative of the old Company in which they were vested. But it holds these trusts under the Act of 1745, as they have never been transferred to it by any subsequent Act. Our point, therefore, is that having inherited the property of the old Company, the College must also have inherited its liabilities—in other words, the duty of allowing its Commonalty (to quote the Act of 1745) "to enjoy the same liberties, privileges, and franchises as by any former Acts and Letters Patent given and confirmed."

I have endeavoured to prove by historical evidence * and legal argument that the Members of the College of Surgeons have been most unfairly deprived of their ancient rights, but such pleadings, I fully admit, may have little weight with the general public. I willingly concede that, if the College, in spite of its vicious constitution, had discharged, and was still discharging its functions in a manner calculated to advance the profession and thus to benefit the public, there would be less substantial grounds for appealing to Parliament; and apart from constitutional history and points of law, I prefer to base the claim of the Members to be masters in their own house on the broad grounds of common justice and public expediency. I am quite willing to give up the laborious fishings for charters and statutes in what Carlyle would call "foul Lethean quagmires"—indeed, the argument based on the

---

* Those who wish to pursue these investigations are referred to the excellent summary contained in Mr. Ernest Hart's speech delivered at the deputation of members to the Privy Council (*British Medical Journal*, Nov. 19, 1887). This statement was, I believe, based on an elaborate historico-legal inquiry carried out by the eminent counsel, Mr. B. F. C. Costelloe.

ancient guilds may seem to many like an attempt to vitalize the fossil remains of the ichthyosaurus.

I have already sufficiently dwelt on the absurdity of the existing arrangement under which the Members who form the backbone of the medical profession in England have to leave the government of the College in the hands of a few surgical Brahmins, who treat them as though they belonged to a lower caste, and seem to dread their admission to the Council chamber as something unclean that would defile them. It is somewhat surprising, however, that the high priests of respectability show no unwillingness to meet these pariahs when invited by them to consultations! The unnatural relations between the Council and the Members could never have continued to exist if the Members had possessed an elective power; and, indeed, it might have been thought likely that the whole body of Fellows, and not merely an enlightened few, would have interfered on behalf of their weaker brethren. Mr. Erichsen, formerly a distinguished President of the College, goes so far as to assert * that men of science are scarcely to be found in the ranks of the Members of the College, and he appeals to the Fellowship of the Royal Society as a test. He implies that Fellows of the College have frequently obtained this, the blue ribbon of science, but that Members have rarely gained the distinction. A writer in the *Lancet*,† whose identity was thinly disguised under the pseudonym of "Historicus," has, however, completely demolished this argument, showing that, whilst there were at that time only eight Fellows of the College (by examination) who were Fellows of the Royal Society, there were no fewer than thirty-one Members of the College, besides fourteen who were Fellows of the College only by election, and therefore must rank as Members so far as examination is concerned. It would, indeed, be easy to show that there are many men among the despised Members who are fully the equals of any of the governing body even in surgery, while in all branches of medical science outside that particular speciality they are immensely their superiors.

* *The Member, the Fellow, and the Franchise.* London, H. K. Lewis, 1886.
† December 11, 1886.

The object for which the Royal College of Surgeons was established is indicated in the Charter of 1800 in the following terms : "And whereas it is of great consequence to the commonweal of the kingdom that the art and science of Surgery should be duly promoted. And whereas it appears to us that the establishment of a College of Surgeons will be expedient for the due promotion and encouragement of the study and practice of the said art and science, now we, of our special grace," etc., etc. Now, how has the College fulfilled its mission ? It has assuredly not promoted the study of surgery as it might have done by the teaching given within its walls, nor has it sufficiently encouraged students to resort either to its library or to its museum for purposes of self-instruction. There are, indeed, nominally professors of surgery and pathology and comparative anatomy and physiology, who each deliver *three* lectures in the course of the year, whilst other lectures on special subjects are given under certain trust funds. Excellent as these discourses are, however, they can scarcely be described as an adequate provision for "the due promotion and encouragement of the study and practice of the art and science of surgery." It is noteworthy how little of its own money the College spends on teaching : last year the amount expended under the head of "lectures" is given as £107 2s., while the expenditure of money derived from trust funds was £253. The prizes given by the College are also the proceeds of legacies ; it does not offer any "encouragement" from its own pocket. It has never done anything to encourage physiological or pathological research—departments of science closely connected, one might have thought, with the promotion of surgery ; and it has only lately set about aiding in the establishment of a pathological laboratory after nearly every medical school in the kingdom has organized one. Under the head of what are grandiloquently called "expenses for scientific purposes" last year the total expenditure was £3,126 11s. 10d., the bulk of this sum consisting of salaries and wages to officials and servants in the museum ; of the "promotion" or "encouragement" of research of any kind I see no trace in these accounts ! The Examiners, on the other hand, shared close upon £9,000 among them. The library of the College was actually founded against the wishes of those who obtained the Charter of 1800, one of the conditions insisted on by the opponents being that a library should be part of the new institution. It was more than a quarter of a century, however, before any real effort was made to carry this laudable project into execution, and then, as usual in the history of the College, only on pressure being applied from without. These facts suffice to show how the College of Surgeons, which is the richest medical corporation in the world, fulfils its function of promoting and encouraging the study and practice of surgery. The plain truth is that, instead of being in any sense a college or school of surgery, it is little more than a huge shop for the sale of surgical licences.

It is, however, in its capacity of Cerberus at the gate leading into the medical profession that the College is most interesting to the public. The nation has a right to expect that at least this humble necessary function shall be discharged with all possible efficiency. What are the facts of the case? The College has done nothing for the improvement of medical education; on the contrary, it has sometimes shown itself so obstructive to reform as almost to justify a suspicion that it did not wish its members to become well enough educated to throw off the yoke and insist on the restoration of their rights. By a system of cunningly devised bye-laws it succeeded in closing the private schools of anatomy which flourished in London in the early part of the century, and in preventing provincial teachers from preparing students.* The governing body thus obtained a practical monopoly of hospital appointments† and lectureships, greatly to the detriment of medical education.

The *Lancet* in its early days did much good work in reforming some of the worst hospital abuses, and in fact it made its

---

* These restrictions have now been removed, but for a long time they acted both injuriously and unfairly.

† It will scarcely be believed that the degree of Master of Surgery of the University of London does not qualify for an appointment for the post of surgeon at the general hospitals of London.

position by its successful efforts in this direction; but, though it made vigorous attempts to cleanse the Augean stables of Lincoln's Inn Fields, the *cloaca maxima* of the College proved too severe a task even for Mr. Wakley. Many serious defects still require to be remedied. It will hardly be believed that until the year 1868 the College granted diplomas to practise without requiring from candidates the slightest evidence of any knowledge of medicine; though it is notorious that medical cases make up the bulk of what is called general practice. It was only in deference to the remonstrances of the General Medical Council that Examiners in medicine were appointed, but the examinations were little better than a farce. Even then no means were taken to discover whether a candidate had any acquaintance with the obstetrical art, which forms so important a part of the medical practitioner's duties, and it was not till 1881 that, alarmed by a significant hint from the Royal Commission, they took steps to remedy the omission. But even in the province of surgery, on which the very existence of the College is based, its shortcomings are only too apparent. It will scarcely be believed that it does not even now require candidates for Membership to prove their capacity to perform operations. The Medical Council in 1881–82 * commented most unfavourably on the manner in which candidates' knowledge of practical surgery was tested, but the examination does not seem to have been improved since then to any considerable extent. I am informed by recent examinees that the candidates now mark out lines on the living body with coloured chalk, etc., and afterwards make certain flourishes with wooden knives! This is hardly less absurd than it would be to test the marksmanship of riflemen with pea-shooters. It would appear that the Council is by no means anxious that the Members should become good operators, for at present nearly all operations in London, and many of those occurring in the country, fall into the hands of the Council of the College or their friends the hospital surgeons. It must not be forgotten, however, that there are many persons residing

* The inspectors specially recommended in 1882 that "steps should be taken to test the candidates by actual operations on the dead body."

THE REFORM OF THE COLLEGE OF SURGEONS.

in the rural districts who cannot afford to summon surgeons from London, and hence general practitioners are not unfrequently compelled to use the knife. Again, the surgeons connected with the great slate quarries, coal mines, and many other industries are generally Members of the College, who, as was just shown, have not undergone any examination as to their skill in operative surgery. These gentlemen have to acquire dexterity at the expense of patients, instead of learning it on the dead subject, and I know of several cases in which lamentable accidents have occurred through this want of early training.

With regard to other existing abuses there is, first, the uncontrolled management of vast sums of money by the twenty-four gentlemen who form the governing body. How considerable these are may be gathered from the last balance-sheet published by the College. During the year from Midsummer Day, 1888, to the corresponding date in 1889, the total receipts amounted to £28,476 17s. 3d. Of this sum £20,587 14s. was received in examination fees, £7,057 8s. 9d. came from house property and investments, £558 6s. 11d. from fees paid by office-bearers at election and other miscellaneous sources, and £273 7s. 7d. from trust funds. The gravest doubts are entertained by many Members of the College as to the wisdom which has been shown by the authorities in the expenditure of their large income; and the considerable sums which have been lavished on the construction of new buildings are regarded by many as a piece of wasteful extravagance. Another abuse is that these gentlemen have the distribution of the College loaves and fishes entirely in their hands, and they naturally reserve a large proportion of them for their own consumption. As these Examinerships are now worth between £500 and £600 * a year, and Councillors receive a fee of a guinea every time they attend a meeting of the Council, it is obvious that the lines of a Councillor Examiner are cast in fairly pleasant

* The amount varies in different years, but owing to the increasing number of students there has been a steady rise in the yearly payments to Examiners in the last decennium.

places. One is not surprised to hear, therefore, that some of the fortunate Examiners are loth to relinquish the sweets of office, and get their term protracted in defiance of express regulations to the contrary. The Examiners are elected for five years, and frequently for a second term of the same duration; but a resolution was proposed at the Council on August 19, 1866, and confirmed on October 11th of the same year, that no one who has been twice elected an Examiner should be elected a third time. Notwithstanding this, Sir William Savory remained on the Court of Examiners for fourteen years, during which period he received the sum of £5,361 12s. However excellent an Examiner Sir William Savory may have been, it seems undesirable that one individual should carry off so large a share of the emoluments of office. The plan of keeping the Examinerships "in the family" is an abuse of a very bad kind; it encourages jobbery and tends to lower the standard of examination by placing the examiners beyond the reach of censure or even supervision. It further prevents the formation of an independent Council, for those who are looking for Examinerships dare not express opinions contrary to those of the leaders on the Council. In all properly constituted corporations the members of the governing body are disqualified from being elected to lucrative offices in their own gift. The members of the Senate of the University of London cannot become candidates for Examinerships, and it "is a customary rule in corporations, and even in the vestries, that offices of emolument cannot be distributed by the members among each other."* The system of having paid Examiners who are themselves directors of the institution was years ago felt to be a very crying evil, even by some of the Councillors themselves, and in 1870 Mr. Quain moved a resolution "that no less than four members of the Court of Examiners should be Fellows who are not, and have not been, members of Council." This was passed some time afterwards on the seconding of Sir William Fergusson; but in spite of this rule, in 1884, every member of the Court of Examiners was on the

* Letter from "Lincoln's Inn," *British Medical Journal*, October 29, 1887.

Council, and at the present moment there are no less than six Councillor Examiners. When it was pointed out to the Lord President * that the resolution of the Council had not been carried out, the excuse was that some resolutions were "operative," whilst some others were "inoperative," or, in other words, that the resolution of one Council could be treated as a dead letter by another Council. It is needless to observe that the self-denying ordinance of Mr. Quain and Sir W. Fergusson remained a dead letter, and that no attempt had been made to secure its becoming "operative" by getting it inserted in the recent Charter.

With respect to the distribution of offices and dignities, one of the abuses which is loudly complained of is the manner in which the President of the College is elected. In the earlier times a Warden or Master, chosen by the suffrages of his brother freemen, might feel a legitimate pride in receiving such a mark of honour; but the office is now kept strictly within the charmed circle of the twenty-four who till quite recently undertook the part in regular rotation. In consequence of this the office has become so degraded that it has lost all importance, and as often as not it is filled by a nobody of whom no one outside the profession has ever heard. The President may confer dignity on the office, as in the case of the present eminent incumbent; but this is scarcely as it should be, and if the election of the President were in the hands of the whole Corporation, it would add immensely to the dignity and the prestige of the office. If the President were thus elected it would at any rate be impossible for the temple of surgical science to have a high priest, as has lately been the case, whose eloquence littered the ground with dropped aspirates, "thick as autumnal leaves that strew the brooks in Vallombrosa."

To show the urgent need for reform it should be stated that although the nominal governing body comprises twenty-four members there is an "inner circle" which is the effective managing agency. This consists of the President with a

* The remarks made by Mr. Tweedy at the first meeting of Fellows and Members will be found in *British Medical Journal*, March 29, 1884.

"power behind the throne," in the shape of an official who, if the nominal head of the College is not strong, is the wire-puller who works the whole machinery of government. This is the Secretary, who is not himself a medical practitioner. Nothing better shows the profound distrust with which the governing body regards the Commonalty than the fact that at one time there was a regulation rendering Members of the College ineligible for the office of secretary. Whether this regulation still exists or not, its spirit still survives. The governing body prefers a secretary free from any community of feeling with the members, and whose interests, politically speaking, are opposed to theirs. A friend of mine who is behind the scenes expresses the true "inwardness" of the present *régime* by the following equation—

$$\text{Secretary} + \text{President} = \text{College.}$$

According to another equally well-informed authority, the mode of procedure, say in choosing Examiners, is as follows:— Unless the President has a *protégé* of his own the Secretary generally selects some person known to be inoffensive, that is to say, one belonging to the class of men that are (figuratively speaking) fat and such as sleep o' nights, like those Cæsar wished to have about him. In these quiet but calculating breasts lies no inconvenient reforming zeal. The President and Secretary having agreed upon a candidate, the Vice-Presidents are next "nobbled," and these in turn subject other members of Council who can be trusted to the same process. The matter is thus settled without any fuss, and when the balloting takes place the unanimity of the vote is wonderful. It is impossible adequately to discuss the subject of the reform of the College of Surgeons within the limits of a magazine article, and I have been obliged to omit many points that have great weight with members of the medical profession because they are too technical to be made intelligible to general readers, without long and wearisome explanation. I think I have said enough, however, to show that the reforming party has a very strong case, and that in fighting for their own rights, they are fighting the battle of the public.

Nothing but a thorough reform of the whole constitution of the College will suffice. As things are at present, the retirement in rotation of members of the Council is so arranged that it takes eight years to change the *personnel* of that body. Evil communications corrupt good manners, and under such a system the most ardent reformer is almost sure to "become subdued to that he works in like the dyer's hand," after such prolonged exposure. Mr. Rivington suggested in 1870 that the cycle of complete regeneration should be reduced to four years, and when a representative Government * has been established it will certainly be necessary that the electors should have the power of directing the policy of the College by eliminating, if necessary, obstructive Councillors.

Having shown that earlier associations of surgeons were representative bodies in which every individual exercised his rights as an elector, having exposed the process by which those rights were lost, and having described the abuses which have arisen in consequence of the gradual decay of a once vigorous institution,† it remains to call attention to the present situation, and to point out the steps that are being taken to remedy the most pressing evils. Since 1885 a solemn farce has been enacted by calling an annual meeting of Fellows and Members, a ridiculous parody of the old "moot," when the freemen of the guild elected their officers. But whilst they affect to preserve the outward form of the great constitutional right of meeting, it need scarcely be said that they keep the substance for themselves. Like the lawyer in the fable, they devour the oyster and hand the shell to their dupes. The meetings are summoned by the President, but the Council make a point of taking no part in the proceedings. They sit apart like the gods of Lucretius, "holding no form of creed but contemplating all," and listen with courteous, if occasionally somewhat somnolent, placidity to the debating-society excercitations in

* The arguments in favour of the representation of the Members of the College on the Council, and replies to Mr. Erichsen's contentions, are set forth at length in Mr. Rivington's work on the "Medical Profession," pp. 927, 938.

† See Green's "Short History of the English People," sec. iv.

which the Fellows and Members are permitted to indulge. There may be a good deal of sound and fury in these harangues, but to the Council they signify nothing. Indeed, the peaceful tendencies of the new President were shown by the introduction of tea and coffee at the last meeting, and under the soothing influence of these conditions the ceremony went off like a family tea-party. It must, however, be admitted, that the governing body has to some extent mended its manners towards the inferior beings under its sway. The serene Olympian indifference with which the Council lets the heathen rage and the people imagine vain things around their feet, is a distinct improvement on the open contempt with which it formerly treated its despised subjects.

It is a fact, incredible as it may sound to the ears of this levelling generation, that in the early years of the present century Members were only admitted into the College buildings—their own house, be it remembered—by the back door in Portugal Street, then a "filthy street," crowded with butchers' and costermongers' carts.* In 1824, when a large audience was waiting in the College theatre to hear the Hunterian Oration, Sir William Blizzard suddenly ordered the Members present to take off their hats. The command, which was given in the tone of an angry schoolmaster, was received with laughter, and the pompous official had to comfort his outraged dignity as best he could with the assurance that the audacious rebels were Quakers.† In 1831 an effort was made by the late Mr. Wakley, the proprietor and first editor of the *Lancet*, to recover the right of holding a meeting in the lecture-room of the College of Surgeons. The doors were advertised by the authorities to open at three o'clock, the lecturer not commencing till four. The object of the meeting was very harmless and indeed praiseworthy : it was to get up a memorial to the

---

* "Memorials of J. F. South," p. 71.

† One of the gentlemen, a Mr. William Pollard, as a matter of fact, actually belonged to the Society of Friends. The story is told in a different way in the charming "Memorials of J. F. South" (p. 77), but I have given it as I heard it from the late Dr. Billing, who died a few years ago at a very advanced age.

Admiralty, to induce that body to rescind a recent regulation under which naval surgeons were not allowed to attend the levées of his Majesty. It would seem likely that such a meeting would have been acquiesced in by the authorities, but instead of this, the distinguished reformer who headed the movement was, under the authority of the President, seized by several "Bow-street runners," and expelled with an amount of brutality which even in those days excited astonishment. Indeed, had not Mr. Wakley been a man of great power and some agility, there is no doubt that he would have been murdered on that occasion, for one of the "runners" aimed a blow at his head with a heavy metal staff whilst he was lying prostrate on the ground.* The attempt of Mr. Wakley to revive the ancient rights of the Members to assemble in their own house was, to use the words of Sir Leicester Dedlock, looked upon by the Council as the "opening of floodgates, and the uprooting of distinctions;" and an elaborate bye-law was at once passed (sect. xvii.—Meetings of Fellows and Members), by which it was ordained that any Fellow or Member attempting to take part in "any debate or discussion whatsoever ... at any meeting convened by the President or Council for the delivery of lectures or orations either before or after the same shall have commenced or terminated ... shall forfeit all his rights and privileges as a Fellow or a Member." It will scarcely be believed that this infamous bye-law was acted on in the year 1889, and that several highly respectable members of the profession were threatened with expulsion from the College for endeavouring to assert their rights.

The origin of the present agitation for reform in the constitution of the College of Surgeons is, in my opinion, directly traceable to the immense "betterment" in the intellectual and social condition of medical practitioners, which has been brought about in recent years by the higher standard of general

---

* *Lancet*, 1830-31, p. 796. The authorities at the College of Surgeons had obtained the "runners" from Bow Street, owing to the magistrate being under the impression that a large meeting would take place at the College, and that a number of pickpockets were expected to be present!

education which has been enforced in recent years. Enlightenment has naturally been followed by awakening, and the medical "masses" have now become keenly alive to the injustice and absurdity of a system of class government which was formerly more or less blindly accepted as in harmony with the eternal fitness of things. Errors and shortcomings and other signs of human infirmity in the powers that be are more clearly seen; abuses are more speedily detected and less meekly tolerated. In short, the Members of the College of Surgeons have had it borne in upon them, that, to use the words of one who was himself for several years a member of the governing body, "it is an anomaly that a great institution like this, consisting of, at the very least, thirteen thousand perfectly educated and well-qualified men, should be entirely at the mercy of twenty-four of their number." *

The right of the Fellows and Members to meet in the College for the purpose of discussing collegiate interests was first definitely recognized on March 24, 1870, when a general meeting of the College was called to consider the position of the institution as regards proposed medical legislation. The meeting was convened by the President and Council, in accordance with a requisition signed for the most part by provincial Fellows and Members. The reception of these gentlemen by the President was "childlike and bland;" he smilingly informed them that the Council "gladly and unanimously acceded to their wishes that they should meet in the College." But it subsequently transpired that the pleasant old gentleman who at that time acted as President had an ace up his sleeve, for the day before the meeting he had caused the College beadle to be sworn in as a special constable "to prevent felonies and disorders." † Notwithstanding the unanimity and gladness shown by the Council at meeting the Members in 1870, they

* Mr. Timothy Holmes, in his speech as one of the members of a deputation from the Association of Fellows of the Royal College of Surgeons to the Lord President of the Council, November 11, 1887.—*Brit. Med. Journ.*, Nov. 12, 1887.

† See a letter from Colonel Henderson, then Chief Commissioner of Police, to Mr. Christopher Heath.—*Lancet*, vol. i., 1870, p. 638.

THE REFORM OF THE COLLEGE OF SURGEONS. 153

made no further efforts to dwell together in brotherly unity till 1884. The immediate cause which led to another conference was a proposal emanating from the Council that application should be made to the Crown for a new charter embodying certain alterations in the bye-laws. The most important of these were that the amount of the yearly value of property in land or rents permitted to be held by the College should be raised, and that, in accordance with the repeated demands of the medical press, and of a memorial signed by four hundred Fellows, the mode of election to the Council should be by voting papers as well as in person. Many Members of the Council would have obtained these alterations with the knowledge of the Fellows and Members of the College, but on the motion of Mr. Erichsen, a Member of the Council, it was decided to submit the suggested alterations in the charters to a general meeting of the Fellows and Members. This meeting was held on March 24, 1884, and at it Mr. Paul Swain, a very distinguished Fellow practising at Plymouth, moved four resolutions of an extremely moderate character, but all tending in the direction of reform. Three of these were negatived by the Council, only one being accepted, and that one in such a form that it was practically useless. In fact the Council, like Marshal MacMahon, seemed to say, " J'y suis, j'y reste." This attitude of uncompromising resistance to demands in themselves moderate and equitable, and made in no turbulent or aggressive spirit, led to the formation of two associations, one of Fellows and the other of Members, with the object of effecting a reform of the constitution of the College. The associations have ever since actively pursued the end in view, and they have already done something towards its accomplishment.

The great difficulty in the way of effecting reform of the College has hitherto lain in the supineness and indifference of the great bulk of its Commonalty. Their attitude has been like that of the political Gallios known in America as Mugwumps; they have been willing to let who would attend to the business of the Corporation, so long as they were relieved of all trouble. In his "Physiology of the Medical Student," Albert

Smith describes that interesting personage as not caring after he
had "passed" if the hospital which he had "walked" was burned
down the next day. I do not think I am wrong in saying that
there is a like absence of sickly sentiment with regard to the
College in the breasts of many of its members. Nevertheless,
in spite of the great *vis inertiæ* to be overcome, the associations
of Fellows and Members have aroused the feelings of the
medical profession at large, and this in its turn will, it is hoped,
exercise a powerful influence in Parliament. The action of the
Members' Association is especially likely to attract the attention
of the public, who cannot have forgotten the scandalous way in
which some members of this society were treated by the
Council of the College on February 28th, 1889. After exhausting every effort at conciliation, and after having invited
the President to call a general meeting without effect, the
Association of Members, acting on legal advice, and having
given due notice to the Council, convened a meeting to be held
at the College. I have described the similar demonstration
which took place sixty years previously, on which occasion the
Members gained an entrance to the College, and I have set
forth the ruffianly way in which their leader was subsequently
expelled. In the more recent affair the President showed
greater strategical skill. The precincts of the College were
treated like a proclaimed district in Ireland, and a powerful
body of police was drawn up in the courtyard. The practitioners, however, did not attempt to blow up the gates with
dynamite, or carry the palings by assault. On the contrary,
they retired with dignity to the Venetian Chamber of the
Holborn Restaurant, as their ancestors had marched under
similar circumstances to the Crown and Anchor in the Strand
more than half a century previously. It need scarcely be said
that on both occasions the Members recorded their grave dissatisfaction with the attempts of the President and Council to
deprive them of their rights. But the matter did not end here.
In February, 1890, the Council gave notice to the secretaries of
the Members' Association, the supposed ringleaders of the meeting, that, in accordance with bye-law Section 17, they would be
deprived of their Membership and would thus lose their right

of practice—a sentence which would practically deprive them of the means of earning their livelihood.

With regard to the legal aspect of the Members' claim to hold meetings in the building paid for with their own money, and to have something to say as to the making of the laws by which they are governed, there is in my opinion great force in an argument urged by Mr. John Tweedy * at the deputation of the Association of Fellows to the Lord President of the Council. Mr. Tweedy pointed out that in the Charter the Fellows and Members are called "the body corporate and politic." In the declaration which every Member has to sign on his admission to Membership, he binds himself whilst a Member of the College to observe the bye-laws thereof. But, as has been said, these bye-laws may be altered, rescinded, or added to without the knowledge or consent of the "body corporate and politic," and even against their express wishes; so that, as Mr. Tweedy well says, of two parties to a solemn contract, one is at liberty to alter the terms at pleasure, while the other is bound by it without having any power of approving or disapproving. Such an arrangement can only be described as absolutely contrary to every principle of equity. It is almost as if in subscribing to the Thirty-nine Articles, one bound oneself to accept all others that theological imagination might at any time devise.

What is it, it may be asked, that the reforming party wants? Its aims are clearly expressed in the draft of the Bill which will soon be introduced into the House of Lords by Lord Dunraven. The principal features are: That the Council of the College shall be elected by voting papers by the Fellows and such Members of the College as are of ten years' standing.† That the Fellows and Members shall be entitled to meet at reasonable times within the College, and that resolutions passed by a

* Deputation of the Association of Fellows to the Privy Council, 1887. Published in supplement to the *British Medical Journal*, November 12, 1887.

† In the most recent draft of the proposed Bill the Members are not necessarily compelled to wait ten years before they can acquire the right to vote, but the Council is to have the power to effect this end by providing a bye-law. This appears to be a distinction without a difference, as the Council is not likely to shorten the period of probation.

majority of two-thirds of a meeting consisting of at least 300 Members concerning the bye-laws or the expenditure of the College shall be binding on the Council. That the iniquitous penal bye-law (sect. xvii.), which has hitherto prevented Members meeting, shall be rescinded. That six Members of the College of twenty years' standing may sit on the Council after being duly elected. Finally, that the manner of election of Examiners shall be amended, and the term of office of the members of the Council shortened. There is much in this Bill which is good; but a more liberal scheme is really required. The fact that only three members of the Council retire annually makes it impossible for any constituency to seriously change the character of the Council, except after a lapse of several years.

In obtaining a new Constitution it is of the greatest importance that the Examiners should be prohibited from sitting on the Council, and, indeed, no member of the Council should be allowed to become an Examiner until he has ceased to act on the Council for a period of at least five years. Again, considering that the share of the income of the College provided by the Members is nine times as great as that contributed by the Fellows,* it appears to me that the Members are making a mistake in asking that only six of their body may sit on the Council, whilst the remaining eighteen seats will be occupied by Fellows. Perhaps what strikes one most in the proposed bill is the extreme modesty of the Members in estimating their own capacity to vote for Councillors, and the long term of self-imposed probation they consider they must undergo before any of their persecuted race could sit by the side of the august autocrats of the Council table. The Member, under the proposed plan, must wait ten years before he is worthy to become an elector, and he must prove by another ten years of toil and long-enduring patience that he is fit to enter into the glorious company of the elect. Although the workman and small tradesman, the clerk and the

* In 1889, according to the balance sheet set out in the Calendar of the College, Members contributed £18,347 14s. as against £1,914 10s. paid by its Fellows.

THE REFORM OF THE COLLEGE OF SURGEONS. 157

artisan, are considered qualified to vote on the most momentous public questions of the day without any term of probation, a Member of the College of Surgeons, according to the proposed new Act, would require ten years to educate himself as regards the intricacies of his corporation before he would be able to give a vote to the person he would like to represent him on the governing body of the College! This is all the more remarkable, when his very education as a medical man would give him the kind of information which it is desirable an elector should possess. The affairs of great corporations, such as banks, railways, gas companies, and insurance offices are certainly more intricate than those of the College of Surgeons; but I am not aware that any company exists in which a shareholder is obliged to wait several years after purchasing stock before he can become sufficiently educated to take part in electing directors. It is to be hoped, therefore, when the modest Bill which the Association of Members of the College of Surgeons have requested Lord Dunraven to introduce into the House of Lords comes up for discussion that its provisions will be greatly enlarged, so that the Commonalty may be properly represented, as they were in the old days of the guilds.

Even in the suggestion which I have made there is nothing of a revolutionary nature, nothing smacking of Nihilism or anarchism or tending in the remotest degree to upset that glorious ark of our political covenant, the British constitution.*
The purpose in view is simply to restore the Members to the

* When the Bill, by which the governing body of the old Company of Surgeons sought to have itself reconstituted as a College, was before the House of Lords in 1797, its principal supporter was the Bishop of Rochester, who said " he thought that he perceived an equalizing spirit at the bottom of the opposition to this Bill. He thought Democracy a monster that ought to be unkenneled from its lurking-places and hunted down wherever it could be found. It was a monster which in these times ought to be extinguished in the birth." The Right Reverend Father in God had probably not recovered from the shock of the French Revolution; indeed, the disturbance of his mind is seen in the "nice derangement of his epitaphs." Yet even this defender of the divine right of governing bodies was obliged to confess himself "unfriendly to the idea of investing twenty-one members with an absolute dominion over the property of the whole corporation."

position from which they have been unjustly deposed, and to place the College on a more representative basis. As now constituted the governing body represents nothing but itself; that is to say, it is elected by a mere fraction even of the small minority who possess the franchise.*

It is easy to forecast the issue of the struggle which is now perhaps only beginning. However long it may last, whatever checks or reverses we may have to encounter, the weakest must in the end go to the wall. We are many thousand to a mere handful, and the flowing tide is with us. The oligarchical system has been tried and found wanting, and it must now give place to something better. Reform is in the air, and if the Council of the College of Surgeons is wise in its generation it will yield with the best grace it can to the inevitable.

* In 1887, the Councillor returned at the head of the poll received only 205 votes, and the gentleman whose name stood lowest on the list of those elected had only 101. The Council, therefore, altogether did not represent more than a fifth part of its very limited constituency, and a man was raised to a position which gave him power to manage the affairs of about 17,000 educated men by the votes of 100 among them!

THE EFFECT OF SMOKING ON THE VOICE.

In these days of aggressive sanitation, tobacco, like nearly every other gift of God to man, has been denounced by well-meaning fanatics as the cause of numberless ills both to soul and body. I am inclined to think that to this indiscriminating anathema the practice of smoking owes, at least in some measure, its present all but universal diffusion. A French *dévote* is reported to have said of some innocent pleasure that it would be perfect if it were sinful. In the same spirit, no doubt, the "average sensual man" feels that indulgences in themselves almost indifferent gain additional relish from the fact that they are regarded as wrong by the "unco' guid," or by truculent sanitarians as hurtful. The gospel of health is an excellent thing, but, like the world, it is perhaps a trifle too much with us, and the relentless zeal of its preachers wearies men of ordinary mould as the just Aristides bored the Athenians. I say this out of no irreverence towards Sir Edwin Chadwick, Dr. B. W. Richardson, and the other apostles of hygiene, whom I honour on this side idolatry as much as any, but because it seems to me that they are apt to forget that physical well-being is not the sole end of existence. I wish it to be understood that, though a doctor, I do not consider it to be my function to stand at the feast of life and, like poor Sancho's physician, condemn everything on the table. I am not a member of the Anti-Tobacco League, nor do I believe that all those who seek solace from the "herb nicotian"—

> "Go mad and beat their wives,
> Plunge, after shocking lives,
> Razors and carving knives
> Into their gizzards."

On the contrary, I am teleologist enough to think that as tobacco is supplied to us naturally from the bounteous bosom of Mother Earth it is meant to be used, and if used in the right way it is often helpful rather than injurious. I have no sympathy with the fanatics, from the Royal author of the famous "Counterblast" downwards, who would deprive poor humanity of one of the few pleasures which tend to make our way of life, in however small a degree, less desolate than it otherwise would be.

Having now, as I hope, gained the confidence of devotees of the "weed" by this profession of faith, I can speak of the effect of smoking on the vocal organs without being suspected of prejudice.

In dealing with the voice, we may concentrate our attention on the singing voice and the marvellous organ which produces it, with its delicate tissues, its highly complex nervous apparatus, and its accurate muscular adjustments; or we may speak of the voice as used in ordinary speech, in which, though there is less question of artistic effect, the mechanism is still extraordinarily complicated and not only the larynx and throat are used, but the tongue, cheeks, and lips are brought into more active play than they are in singing. Speaking concerns the whole human family, while singing belongs to a comparatively small though highly privileged fraction thereof. Tobacco affects both the speaking and the singing voice, though of course its influence is much more noticeable in song, where the physical processes are more elaborate and where anything that interferes with the smoothness and sweetness of tone is as conspicuous as spots on the sun. The singing voice therefore affords the most delicate test whereby the effect of external agencies, so slight that in speech their influence would be unnoticed, can be accurately gauged. I shall, therefore, first consider the effect of tobacco smoke on the singing voice, and it may be well to ask at the outset, Has it any effect at all? Does the utterance of the smoker bewray him, as the husky tones of those who love to look on the wine when it is red often proclaim their infirmity?

That the voice is affected by tobacco is proved by the testimony of singers on the one hand and by the experience of physicians on the other. A very large acquaintance with vocalists of all grades, extending now over a longer period of years than I care to think of, enables me to say that while a few consider their voice as improved, the vast majority think it is more or less injured by smoking. I attach far more importance to the testimony of the latter than to that of the former, as singers have frequently the most eccentric notions of what is "good for the voice." As stout, mustard, and melted tallow candles have each been vaunted by distinguished artistes as vocal elixirs of sovereign efficacy, it is not surprising that tobacco should also have its adherents. The example of Mario, who smoked incessantly, is often cited as a proof of the utility, or at any rate the harmlessness, of the practice. It is obvious, however, that an exceptional singer is so by virtue of possessing an exceptional throat, and no rule for general use can be safely founded on such an instance. Balzac used to say of great men who were victims of the tender passion, that there was no knowing how much greater they might have been if they had been free from that weakness. In the same way we may say of Mario, How much finer might even *his* voice have been without his eternal cigar! It might at least have lasted longer than it did. Nearly all singers who have not been accustomed to the use of tobacco feel, when first they take to smoking, that it makes the throat dry and uncomfortable, and the voice thick, husky, and tremulous, or in some undefined way mars the perfection of their execution. Medical men who have eyes for such things can often see the baleful effects of immoderate smoking writ large on nearly every part of the mucous membrane of the throat. Such, however, is the power possessed by the human organization of adapting itself to injurious influences, that in many persons, just as the stomach becomes tolerant of tobacco, the tissues of the throat become accustomed to the irritating effect of the hot and acrid fumes. Nevertheless, when such impressions cease to be perceptible, the effect on the mucous membrane may continue to be hurtful, and I have no doubt that a sensitiveness to the effects of cold, or as it is called, "a catarrhal tendency," is frequently kept up even by the moderate use of tobacco. It is often the abuse of tobacco that is at the bottom of chronic congestion or other slight deviations from the normal condition of the throat, which are put down to other causes. But besides that, I have not the least doubt that smoking may be injurious to the voice, even when it leaves no visible marks of its action, by impairing the precision of muscular movement necessary for perfect production.

The effect of tobacco on the body is both general and local; that is to say, it acts on the nervous centres and on the heart as well as on the parts with which the smoke or the juice comes immediately in contact. The general effect does not concern us here, except in so far as the larynx may be affected thereby. It usually finds expression in what is vaguely called "nervousness;" the pulse becomes flurried and the muscles more or less relaxed and unsteady. This is why smoking is so strictly forbidden to men training for athletic feats. So marked is the effect of tobacco in relaxing the whole muscular system that before the days of chloroform it was employed in surgical operations in which it was necessary that the muscles should be perfectly limp. It will be readily understood that, under the influence of a drug possessing these properties, the exquisitely delicate adjustments of the various parts of the complicated vocal machinery are to some extent disordered, and the voice, if not quite "like sweet bells jangled, out of tune and harsh," loses something of its richness and brilliancy. Something analogous to what takes place in the eye as the result of the abuse of tobacco occurs in the larynx, or rather in the part of the brain which governs the movements of that organ. Oculists are familiar with "Tobacco Amblyopia"—that is, *dimness* of sight due to what may be called, figuratively, *blurring* of the retina by tobacco smoke. "Tobacco Amblyphonia" would be an equally appropriate name for the corresponding *dulness* of voice caused by excessive smoking. It must be understood that I speak here solely of singers; the effects which have been mentioned would be scarcely, if at all, noticeable in the speaking voice.

When the nicotine does not injure the nervous system the smoke may still irritate the lining membrane of the throat and windpipe. Any one who has been in a Highland cottage must be painfully familiar with the effect of the " peat reek " on the eyes. As the mucous membrane lining the larynx is even more sensitive than that covering the organ of vision, the effect of blasts of hot smoke passing over it may be imagined. Unfortunately, it is possible to harden this delicate membrane to these rough experiences! but in losing its sensitiveness it also loses a good deal of its smoothness and elasticity.

The evil effects wrought by tobacco on the larynx consist generally in patches of congestion affecting the upper part of the organ and occasionally the vocal cords themselves. In addition to this, in severe cases the cords show a certain sluggishness of movement, which of course makes the tone dull, harsh, and uncertain. A marked feature in these cases is dryness of the mucous membrane, a physical condition which deprives the voice of all brilliancy. In a given case it would be impossible by mere ocular inspection to feel certain that these signs of disease arose from smoking; but in the case of young men not thoroughly habituated, I have repeatedly seen conditions brought on by a few days' smoking which have disappeared altogether when the patient has abstained.

In the upper portion of the throat the parts most exposed to the action of hot smoke are the uvula and the soft palate, or little curtain which screens off the mouth from the back of the throat; and it is there, accordingly, that the effects are most marked. Patches of redness, enlargement of the tiny blood-vessels, swelling of the uvula, crops of little blisters which break and give rise to small but painful ulcers, and finally a rough, gritty, almost warty and discoloured condition of what was once a beautiful, smooth, pink surface—these are the chief features of the picture too often presented by the smoker's palate. Dryness is here also a very characteristic feature of chronic nicotism. Everywhere in the throat the natural secretion which should lubricate the parts is dried up, or thickened to a glutinous material which clogs instead of oiling the wheels of the vocal machine.

The tongue often suffers severely from the effects of tobacco. Small excoriations, blisters, chronic superficial inflammation, and white patches sometimes of almost horny consistency are formed on the surface of the organ; and a permanently unhealthy condition is induced which in those predisposed to cancer is apt, under the influence of advancing age, or as the result of the prolonged vocal irritation, to lead to the development of that disease. The same observation applies to the superficial ulceration which affects the sides of the root of the tongue. In this situation there are a number of delicate projections, or so-called "papillæ," the exquisitely fine points of which readily become inflamed when exposed to irritation. It is in this situation that cancer of the tongue is exceedingly apt to commence; but whether this terrible disease actually originates from mere irritation, or whether it must first be in the system and is only brought to a focus, so to 'speak, by local irritation, has not yet been determined. Even if the latter hypothesis, however, be correct, the disease must be often brought on by smoking many years before it would otherwise develop, and it occurs in a situation where its symptoms are peculiarly distressing.

More rarely, smoking causes chronic inflammation of the lips, which sometimes gives rise to cracks which are always very troublesome and not infrequently end in deadly disease. In several of the morbid conditions which I have described it is obvious that the changes of structure are more important than the loss of vocal function, and indeed in many cases serious disease may be present whilst the voice is but little affected.

It need hardly be said that the conditions of the throat and other parts of the vocal instrument which I have here sketched are not the work of a few months, or of moderate smoking; they are the result of years of excessive indulgence. There is, of course, every shade of degree in the susceptibility of different in lividuals, and much also depends on the kind of tobacco used, and on the manner of smoking. Persons whose skin and mucous membrane are naturally irritable are more easily affected than others; and those of strongly marked rheumatic or gouty tendencies are especially likely to suffer.

The speaking voice does not generally become seriously affected as the result of smoking, except in the case of those who have to make professional use of the voice. I have noticed such effects occasionally in the case of military men, and more rarely amongst the clergy, who have generally the good sense to give up the habit of smoking when they find it injurious. They are certainly, however, most common amongst actors. In members of the dramatic profession there is often a great strain on both the throat and the nervous system, especially in learning and rehearsing new parts; and it is at such times that actors often exceed the bounds of moderation in smoking, which is had recourse to as a sedative to their overtaxed cerebral and nervous energies. It is easy to drift into excess under such circumstances, all the more that the throat is then in what may be called "a condition of least resistance." The result is that most of the leading actors in London suffer from a relaxed condition of the upper part of the throat, brought on entirely, I believe, by smoking. As a high standard of excellence can only be maintained in the dramatic profession under a sparing use of alcohol, tobacco must be looked upon as the sole cause of the evil. I may add, moreover, that whilst actors suffer very much from congestion and relaxation of the pharynx, actresses are very rarely afflicted in that way. But if the present craze of women for aping men even in their weaknesses continues, it cannot be expected that they will escape the consequences. The fair creatures whom I have seen smoke, however, did not seem likely to do themselves much harm, for they either toyed with the cigarette in a Platonic sort of way, or smoked with their lips, "puffing out innocuous blasts of dry smoke," to use the words of Charles Lamb, but taking care that very little passed inwards beyond the "barrier of the teeth." I cannot imagine, however, that any lady who cares about her voice would expose it even to that slight risk.

I have entered somewhat minutely into the various forms

of harm which a smoker may inflict upon himself, but unfortunately it is not necessary to smoke in order to be a victim of tobacco. Even seasoned vessels often find their neighbours' pipes or cigars very trying, and, for a person with a delicate throat, exposure to an atmosphere laden with the fumes of tobacco is even worse than smoking. Dr. Ramon de la Sota, a Spanish physician who has given much attention to the subject, states that he is very frequently called upon to treat Spanish ladies who do not themselves smoke, for irritation of the throat, caused, according to him, by the ungallant habits of their male relatives "who do not deny themselves the cigar either at table or in the drawing-room or even in the bedroom." The same gentleman has seen some of the worst effects of tobacco in the throats of women (non-smokers) employed in the large cigar factory at Seville. "Smoking concerts" should be *anathema maranatha* to the vocalist who has a proper regard for his instrument; he should also scrupulously avoid smoking-carriages on the Underground Railway, especially at the time of the evening exodus from the City, and all other places where smokers most do congregate.

The effects of over-smoking on the throat, when the habit has not been too long indulged in, can as a rule be easily cured by the simple remedy of discontinuing the practice which engenders them. In considering the evils produced by smoking it should be borne in mind that there are two bad qualities contained in the fumes of tobacco. The one is the poisonous nicotine, and the other is the high temperature of the burning tobacco. The Oriental hookah, in which the smoke is cooled by being passed through water before reaching the mouth, is probably the least harmful form of indulgence in tobacco, and the cigarette which is so much in vogue nowadays is most certainly the worst. It owes this "bad eminence" to the very mildness of its action, people being tempted to smoke all day long, and easily accustoming themselves to inhale the fumes into their lungs and thus saturating their blood with the poison.

To sum up, I believe that most people can smoke in moderation without injury, and that to many tobacco acts as a useful nerve sedative. On the other hand, if indulged in to excess the habit is always injurious, and I am sure that a great many persons either cannot see or wilfully shut their eyes to the "scientific frontier" which separates moderation from abuse. It must also be borne in mind that the condition of the throat, as well as that of the general health, varies greatly at different times, and that an amount of smoking which at one time would be attended with no bad effect might at another produce serious harm. Every smoker knows that when the stomach is out of order the pipe or cigar loses its charm, but it is not so generally known that at such times the tongue (which to the experienced eye is a mirror of the invisible stomach) and the throat are more vulnerable than usual to tobacco. If nature's warnings on these points are disregarded, as they generally are, the smoker will bring on himself much unnecessary discomfort and even suffering. In connection with the variation in susceptibility just referred to, it may be mentioned that persons leading an outdoor life can, as a rule, smoke with much greater impunity than those who spend most of their time indoors. It is, further, worthy of remark that the inhabitants of warm climates suffer less than the dwellers in what is, probably on the *a non lucendo* principle, called the *temperate* climate of England. This is doubtless due to the greater resisting power of throats less harassed by fogs and east winds, and partly perhaps to the use of milder tobacco.

To conclude with a little practical advice, I would say to any one who finds total abstinence too heroic a stretch of virtue, let him smoke only after a substantial meal; and if he be a singer or speaker, let him do so after and never before using the voice. Let him smoke a mild Havannah or a long-stemmed pipe charged with some cool-smoking tobacco. If the charms of the cigarette are irresistible, let it be smoked through a mouthpiece which is kept clean with ultra-Mohammedan strictness. Let him refrain from smoking pipe, cigar, or cigarette to the bitter, and it may be added, rank and oily end. Your Turk, who is very choice in his smoking and thoroughly understands the art, always throws away the *near* half of his cigarette. Let the singer who wishes to keep in the "perfect way" refrain from inhaling smoke, and let him take it as an axiom that the man in whom tobacco increases the flow of saliva to any marked degree is not intended by nature to smoke. Let him be strictly moderate in indulgence —the precise limits each man must settle for himself—and he will get all the good effect of the soothing plant without the bane which lurks in it when used to excess.

THE USE AND ABUSE OF HOSPITALS.

THERE is nothing in our social organization on which we may more legitimately pride ourselves than on the number and magnificence of our hospitals, which all owe their existence to private charity, or, it may be, to private enterprise, and fulfil their mission of healing and relieving human suffering without assistance from the State. How well managed these institutions on the whole are is proved by the comparative rarity of any complaints against them, even in these days when the New Journalism flashes its bull's-eye into every nook and cranny of the social fabric, and welcomes every real or imaginary backsliding as an opportunity for truculent posters and sensational headlines. The very eagerness with which the most trumpery "scandal" connected with a hospital is seized upon by penny-a-line philanthropists is the strongest possible testimony to the admirable manner in which these institutions are as a rule conducted. And indeed one may apply Carlyle's saying about doctors to hospitals: whatever else may be wrong, they are in the right, and can await judgment without fear. True it is that there are no human institutions which are not to some extent open to abuse, but there are few which do more real tangible good than hospitals; they take no account of creed or country or personal worth, but, like Heaven, send the rain of their beneficence on the just and the unjust without distinction. Of course there are spots even on the sun of charity, and beautiful as our hospital system is in the idea, human weakness and, alas! human passion, too often act as disturbing influences to its perfect fulfilment in practice. In some cases the faults in the administration of what are called "medical charities" are merely the *défauts de leur qualités*, the excess of their virtue; but in other cases positive abuses have crept in and are allowed to flourish with such Upas-like rankness as almost to nullify the power of the hospitals for good. The hospitals themselves long resented the very notion of inquiry into the details of their management as a slur on their good name; but nothing is sacred for the reformer, and general excellence of character only makes him the more keen to discover imperfections and remedy defects. The cry for inquiry has grown stronger and stronger, and now our whole hospital system may be said to be on its trial.

The evils of indiscriminate medical relief were first pointed out by Mr. Hare, in an article * of considerable merit published many years ago. Up to that date, so far as I am aware, there had never been the slightest complaint on the subject, but since then an agitation has been kept up, mainly by members of the medical profession, which has at last led to the appointment of a Special Committee of the House of Lords to inquire into the whole matter. The opposition has been chiefly directed against the out-patient departments of hospitals; and several of our medical charities, in view of the undesirable publicity which they felt to be impending, made hasty efforts to set their houses in order by limiting in some degree the baneful prodigality of their method of administering relief.

Before considering in detail the various means which at present exist for affording medical relief, it may be well to call attention to the large number of sufferers who have to be provided for. The population of London since the various out-lying suburbs have been included amounts to not less than 5,000,000; and in addition to this all the hospitals—but more particularly the special hospitals—draw a large number of cases from the country. Amongst the 5,000,000 a very large number of course belong to those classes who are entirely unable, or who are barely able, to provide themselves with medical attend-

---

* "London Charities." By Thomas Hare. The *Times*, March 29 and April 1, 1862.

ance. Some writers who have given attention to the subject affirm that no fewer than 1,500,000 persons are relieved annually by the hospitals and dispensaries of London, but this number is probably much exaggerated. Not only do a large number of patients treated in the London hospitals come from the provinces, but in many cases statisticians have mistaken the number of visits for the number of individual patients, and, like stage soldiers, the patients have thus been counted over and over again. Making allowance, however, for these various sources of fallacy, there is no doubt that there is an enormous number of sufferers in London and its suburbs who cannot afford to provide themselves with medical treatment.

The actual machinery for their relief at present consists: First, of the Poor Law infirmaries, which only receive paupers; secondly, of the hospitals and free dispensaries which provide gratuitous medical treatment for the necessitous poor—that is to say, those who are just able to support themselves and their families, but cannot provide themselves with medical treatment when ill; and, thirdly, of the provident dispensaries and clubs which afford help in sickness to those who earn good wages. These various agencies no doubt all do a considerable amount of good, though, as in the case of many other organizations, the good is unfortunately not unalloyed. It will be desirable to consider each kind of institution separately, and to show, as far as the limits of this article will permit, the proportion of good and evil which each possesses.

The Poor Law infirmaries, having been so recently established, are well constructed from a sanitary point of view, and the defects in these institutions are mostly due to the economic difficulty. The number of medical officers is quite insufficient, and the economy which is exercised, as regards medical comforts, and probably even medical remedies, impairs, and often, to a greater or less extent, destroys, their efficiency. The few medical men attached to these institutions are barely able to attend to their routine duties, and it is impossible for them to advance medical science. Thus, comparing the London Hospital, which has 780 beds, with the Marylebone Poor Law Infirmary, and its 740 beds, we find that the hospital has on its medical staff thirty-five legally qualified practitioners, whilst the infirmary has only three! The immense amount of clinical material which the Poor Law infirmaries might afford is thus entirely lost to the medical profession, and there can be little doubt that, if the infirmaries were properly utilized, the cry for a large out-patient department kept up by hospital physicians would at once cease.

With regard to general hospitals of large size, there is a growing feeling both within the medical profession and among practical sanitarians and administrators that they are open to many objections. In the first place, they are an unscientific anachronism, the crowding together of such a vast number of diseased persons being as much out of place in cities as intramural burial of the dead. Indeed, it is extremely likely that the germs derived from such accumulations of every form of disease are more dangerous to the community than those which after several years may emanate from dead bodies. Sir James Simpson, many years ago, called attention to the dangers of what he called "hospitalism"—that is to say, the peculiar unhealthiness caused by large aggregations of persons suffering from different kinds of disease who poison the air with their exhalations; and there is no doubt that in many cases they exchange microbes till recovery often becomes difficult even for the strongest. The condition of these large hospitals may not inaptly be compared to the moral atmosphere of a prison; it is well known that though a lad may go in ethically sound, except for the single lapse from righteousness for which he is condemned, he often comes out utterly depraved by the mass of moral foulness in which he has had to live. It has been shown that the death-rate in large hospitals, after surgical operations, is very much higher than in small ones, though the operator in the former case may have been a man of the highest skill, and in the latter a raw beginner; indeed, I know of one instance, and I dare say there are many others, in which patients taken out of a general hospital, and placed in tents, in inclement weather, rapidly recovered, whilst previously the mortality had been excessive. I understand that a distinguished German surgeon, Professor Thiersch, of Leipzig, is so penetrated with the conviction that the crowding of numbers of patients in one building is a fatal mistake, that he now treats all his cases in open tents. The more satisfactory results obtained in the smaller charities can be accounted for only by their superior healthiness. The old Hôtel Dieu, of Paris, which had sheltered persons suffering from every form of disease for many centuries, became at last so soaked with infection that it was necessary to pull it down. Our large London hospitals should follow the example of the large schools like Charterhouse, St. Paul's, and Christ's Hospital, and remove themselves into the country. The ground on which they stand might, as in the case of St. Bartholomew's, St. George's, St. Mary's, or the Westminster Hospital, be sold for an enormous sum, which might be much more profitably applied for the benefit of the sick poor if used to build little villages of one-storey cottage hospitals in the pure country air. These small hospitals might be built of iron, and taken down from time to time, thus giving them a fresh lease of sanitary life every few years at a relatively slight cost. Of course a small building should be left at the original site in town, for the reception of cases of accident, and there should also be accommodation for an out-patient department, reduced to its proper dimensions. The latter would then serve as a receiving-house for the main hospital in the country, as in the case of the Hampstead Consumption Hospital, which has its out-patient department in Tottenham Court Road. If sentiment demanded some artistic memorial of the ancient pile swept away by the broom of sanitary reform, the site, as I recently pointed out to the Lords' Committee, might be marked for the veneration of posterity by a griffin or some other appropriate emblem. There would be no difficulty about the medical staff. The assistant-physicians and surgeons would attend, as at present, to the cases of accident and to the out-patients in London; the senior officers could run out to the hospital by train at least as easily as a physician living in Cavendish Square can go to the London Hospital; and as for the students, the change would no doubt be welcomed by parents and guardians as beneficial both to health and morals.

The second objection to large hospitals is, that for practical purposes the relief which they afford may be said to be indiscriminate. This feature, from its inevitable tendency to engender and foster habits of improvidence in the poorer classes, makes it stink in the nostrils of economists. I do not hesitate to say that the out-patient department in hospitals where the patients contribute nothing towards the expense of their treatment is the greatest pauperizing agency at present existing in this country. It is quite hopeless to expect that ignorant people will make any provision against a possible day of sickness, as long as they can without payment command what they believe to be the best medical skill in the country, for anything that may happen to them from a cut finger to a tumour in the brain. So far from thinking it any disgrace to accept medical charity, they come to look upon treatment at a hospital as something altogether different from outdoor relief, something, in fact, to which they have a natural right, and which blesseth both him that gives and him that takes. This spirit is too often encouraged by subscribers who give "letters" without regard to the patient's circumstances. Large firms subscribe with the avowed object of having medical assistance on the cheapest terms for those in their employment, and rich people in the same way seek to rid themselves of trouble and expense in case of illness among their servants. This shows that the wealthy are provident if the poor are not; but the practical outcome of it is that the out-patient department is flooded with persons who are not proper objects of charity, and who, in accepting medical relief, are diverting funds contributed on the understanding that they were to be applied for the benefit of those who could not afford to pay. Viewed in this light, the system is nothing less than a misappropriation of money and a fraud on the whole body of subscribers, and nothing more clearly shows its demoralizing effect than the fact that persons, not otherwise dishonest or devoid of self-respect, should feel no scruple about taking advantage of it for themselves or for others.

The third objection to the general hospitals, as at present organized, is the cruel hardship which their indiscriminate charity inflicts on the medical practitioners in their neighbourhood. These men find the competition of the hospitals simply ruinous, for, however they may lower their fees, they must still be in the same position relatively to those institutions as the gentleman who stole the raw material for his baskets was to his rival who "conveyed" his baskets ready made. Complaints on this subject are loud and bitter amongst those members of the medical profession whose lot is chiefly cast among the lower middle classes, and, in fact, it is the instinct of self-preservation in the general practitioners of the large towns throughout the country that is the real motive power in the present agitation. The "struggle for life" on the part of the medical practitioner may at first sight appear to concern only himself, and the public may be disposed to think that it could bear his suppression with tolerable fortitude; but there is another side to the question. If the treatment in the out-patient departments of hospitals is cheap, it is also too often nasty; it is impossible that in such a crowd of patients every one should receive much individual attention. Moreover, the care of a large proportion of the cases is necessarily delegated by the staff to subordinates, who are often not only inexperienced, but positively ignorant. That of course is not their fault; they are there to learn, and they must begin on somebody. I have no doubt whatever that in all ordinary ailments a patient is pretty certain to get more attention and better treatment from the outside practitioner, who charges a moderate fee, than from the overworked physician at a general hospital, or the third year's student, into whose hands he is just as likely to fall. The crushing out of the general practitioner, therefore, would be a very real misfortune to the lower middle class and the social strata immediately below it.

The out-patient department is defended by the hospital authorities on the ground that a large selection of cases is necessary for the training of medical students. "A case is a case," they say, "whether the patient earns five shillings a week or fifty. It would not do for us to be too scrupulous as to the reception of patients, or we should lose a considerable part of our educational material." This sounds very plausible, but it will not bear examination. It is on the medical, as distinguished from the surgical, side that the great overcrowding takes place, and students, as a rule, know as little of the inside of the medical out-patient room as Falstaff said he did of the inside of a church. "It is not in the bond;" they are not obliged to attend, and as the proceedings in the medical out-patient room are usually dull and very unedifying, they naturally set foot in it as little as possible. In some hospitals, where there are elementary classes on the examination of patients, there may on certain days be a fair attendance, but as a rule the proportion of those who put in an appearance is very small, as compared with the number of those who inscribe their names as pupils. Thus in one of the best general hospitals, where the average number of pupils is from 150 to 200, not more than from three to six students attend daily. Even these are not volunteers; most of them only attend in order that they may subsequently secure the minor resident appointments open to students. A considerable proportion of those pupils who occasionally visit the out-patient department do not stay out the performance, but slink away as soon as they think they can safely do so. If, therefore, these overcrowded rooms are, as the hospital authorities contend, essential for teaching purposes, the wonderful unanimity shown by the students in refusing to profit by the opportunities of instruction there provided for them seems to call for explanation. The answer is easy. Students do not go there, because they do not find it "pay" to do so; from the mass of patients there is little or nothing to be learnt, and in order to see one or two instructive cases the whole afternoon must be practically wasted. The truth is that the out-patient department would be vastly more useful to every one if it were reduced to manageable dimensions, by the free elimination of the cases which are of no use for teaching, and which either do not require treatment, or should get it elsewhere. Professor Stromeyer, the inventor of the operation for club-foot, used to say that, for the purpose both of learning and teaching, twenty beds were not only sufficient, but that better work could be done with a few cases than with a much larger number. Indeed, a few cases thoroughly studied are of infinitely more value than a large number hurried through as if the doctor was trying to "break a record."

The educational plea is, however, only a pretext. The real reason of the laxity in admitting out-patients is the desire to make a goodly show of work in the eyes of the public, with the object—perfectly legitimate in itself—of attracting subscriptions. The vast number of sufferers treated looks very imposing in the Annual Report, and charitable persons are thereby moved to unloose their purse-strings for the support of so deserving an institution. The hospitals, in fact, compete against each other exactly like rival shops, and strive to "increase their business" by the usual statistical and other devices. There is something vulgar and degrading in this hospital drumbeating and touting, but "charity covers a multitude of sins," and the excellence of the object might well make offences against taste be condoned if the good done were not almost counterbalanced by the evils inseparable from the system. As it is, those that profit most by the whole thing are the contractors who supply the provisions and the medicine made use of by the patients. The patients are pauperised, the doctors victimised, the subscribers imposed upon. The whole system cries aloud for reform, and the present scandalous waste of charity cannot be too quickly "mended or ended."

The fourth objection to the general hospitals lies in the absurd restrictions which exclude from the hospital staffs many of the men best fitted to hold these appointments. At present only Members or Fellows of the London College of Physicians and Fellows of the English College of Surgeons are at most London hospitals eligible for the staff. The Membership of the College of Physicians represents little more than the ability to construe a passage of Celsus (it must be acknowledged with shame that this apparently simple requirement often proves a sad stumbling-block to our latter-day doctors) and the possession of the thirty guineas which must be paid for the diploma. Yet this scientifically worthless qualification is the Open Sesame to the doors of hospitals which are sternly closed against the holders of medical degrees like those of the Universities of London, Cambridge, Oxford, Dublin, and Edinburgh, which represent the high-water mark of professional knowledge.

The Fellowship of the College of Surgeons, which hospital surgeons are now generally required to hold, is an excellent diploma, but in all important particulars it is not a more severe test than that of the Master in Surgery * of the London University, or of several examinations in Edinburgh and in Dublin. The monopoly claimed by the Colleges is a survival of the period when these bodies held absolute sway over things medical in this country, to the great detriment both of scientific progress and the public well-being; the whole thing is now obsolete and dead, and should be decently buried.

The objections that have been raised to special hospitals are numerous, though careful consideration will show that in the main they are unfounded. The superior persons who advance them ground their opposition on the alleged fact that the special institutions draw many cases away from the general hospitals, and thus often leave insufficient material for the teaching of students. It may, however, be asked how it is that the special hospitals attract from the older charities persons suffering from particular diseases. The obvious answer is that the patients find that they are more quickly cured in the special hospitals. The only question, therefore, to be decided is whether the interests of the patient or those of the teachers of the healing art are to be considered as the more weighty. I have little doubt myself that, in the opinion of the public generally, and of the subscribers to the hospitals, the welfare of the patients will take the first place. It may be added that the staff of the general hospitals would, owing to want of special skill and experience, be unable, in many cases, to use the opportunities of practice the loss of which they profess to deplore.

A more practical objection to special hospitals is that they

---

* This diploma is now accepted at the London Hospital in lieu of the Fellowship, but I am not aware that it is so at any other of the general hospitals in the metropolis.

THE USE AND ABUSE OF HOSPITALS.

are supposed by some people to divert subscriptions from the general hospitals. I do not believe, however, that this objection is well founded. As a matter of fact, it may be stated broadly that amongst the wealthy there are two classes—those who subscribe to several hospitals, both general and special, and those who give nothing to either. I believe it will be found that the greater number of the subscribers are persons who have themselves suffered from the disease which the hospital they subscribe to is specially intended to treat, or that such subscribers know of servants or dependants who have been relieved by these institutions. That a subscription has been withdrawn from a general hospital, and given to a special hospital, is a circumstance which has certainly never come to my notice. The real objection in the minds of the medical profession to special hospitals is that they are supposed to be largely instrumental in promoting the success of specialists, who are disliked, for sufficiently obvious reasons, by those for whose services there is a decreasing demand. Ordinary practitioners look upon specialists with much the same jealousy as the labourer regards the skilled artisan, and this feeling has been assiduously fostered by consulting physicians and surgeons, who, with the exception of those who practise as what I have elsewhere called "veiled specialists," have begun to find their occupation gone and their professional existence imperilled.

Attempts have been made to discount the utility of special hospitals by pointing out that these institutions are frequently, if not always, established by medical men. In this, however, they are by no means singular. The days of Rahere, who is supposed to have founded St. Bartholomew's Hospital, and even of Guy, who left a sum of money to establish the large hospital in the Borough, have long passed by. Donations are indeed sometimes made to hospitals by rich philanthropists who, like Polycrates, seek to propitiate fortune by voluntary sacrifice, and legacies are left by others, who try to lighten their ghostly ship for its passage over the Styx by throwing cargo overboard; but the benevolent generally devise their wealth to many different institutions, and we find that the initiative in establishing general hospitals is taken quite as often by medical men as it is in the case of special hospitals. Thus the London Hospital was established in the year 1740 by Mr. John Harrison, a celebrated surgeon of that day. Charing Cross Hospital was founded by Dr. Golding, who had built up a lucrative *clientèle* on the basis of an extensive gratuitous practice.* St. Mary's Hospital was founded entirely by medical men, the late Mr. Samuel Lane, an eminent surgeon, being a moving spirit in the enterprise. Even in the case of St. George's Hospital we find that, though the institution originated in a quarrel among certain managers of the Westminster Hospital, medical men were very ready to promote the undertaking. In the same way it could easily be shown that the smaller general hospitals established in recent years have been founded either by a medical man, or by a combination of physicians and surgeons. Are we to believe that the founders of special hospitals were only influenced by sordid motives, whilst those who established general hospitals were all actuated by the purest spirit of benevolence? The fact, I believe, is that in the establishment of hospitals, whether general or special, the object has usually been of a mixed character. Whatever the motive, however, the benefit to the community has been the same.

Dispensaries are of two kinds—those of the older type, which are supported by subscribers who give letters of recommendation, and the modern provident institutions, which receive payment from the patients themselves. The co-existence of the two institutions is impossible. The free dispensaries destroy those which demand payment. For this reason—*i.e.* on account of the existence of free dispensaries and general hospitals which admit patients without payment—the provident

* "Origin of Charing Cross Hospital," by Benjamin Golding, M.D., 1867. W. H. Allen & Co., Waterloo Place, Pall Mall. The author ingenuously remarks that the time of the young practitioner "cannot be employed more beneficially either to himself or others, etc., etc.," than in extending "his opportunities of seeing diseases," and he therefore recommends the young medical man to devote some hours daily to "prescribing gratuitously for sick persons who are too poor to pay a fee."

system has been a failure in London. But the fact of its success in Manchester seems to justify the hope that it might be successfully introduced in London.

The sick clubs in this country have, on the whole, proved a success. Some have, no doubt, failed through fraudulent conduct on the part of the managers, and others through not being based on strict actuarial principles; but several, like the Oddfellows and the Foresters, have been completely successful, and have shown the capacity of the working classes in managing their own affairs.

The bad effects of gratuitous medical relief have been abundantly shown, and it is not denied that they exist to a very large extent, not only in London, but practically everywhere throughout the country. The time has come when the abuse must be abolished. But how is this to be done? The evil is "gross as a mountain, open, palpable," but during the many years that acute minds have been grappling with the problem, no satisfactory solution has been suggested. The difficulty is to devise a scheme that shall be at once adequate to cope with the enormous mass of human suffering which is always with us, and yet be in harmony with sound economic principles. No hindrance must be placed in the way of the development of medical science, nor must the facilities for the training of doctors be in any way curtailed or trammelled; both these things are of the most vital importance to the common weal, and any scheme of hospital reform which interfered with them would on that ground alone be foredoomed to failure. Lastly, in the interest of the public itself, that most useful member of society, the general medical practitioner, must, as far as is consistent with the "greatest good of the greatest number," be considered. How to combine mercy for the sick with some amount of justice to those who minister to their needs—that is the question. I am not prepared with a panacea for the evils that have been described; I merely venture to throw out a few suggestions for their abatement.

Aggrieved practitioners, who have had the bread taken out of their mouths by the hospitals, have sometimes said in their haste that the out-patient department should be reformed altogether out of existence. This drastic remedy, however, would probably defeat its own object. Men aiming at the higher spheres of practice must somehow get material out of which to construct a reputation. If the hospitals closed their doors to out-patients, numerous private consulting-rooms would be opened, where bread, in the form of gratuitous medical advice, would be thrown on the running waters in the hope that it might return again after many days in the shape of fees. Under such a dispensation the last state of the general practitioner would be worse than the first. In Berlin a large number of such private out-patient departments exist under the name of "Polikliniks," and it need hardly be said that hosts of people avail themselves of the gratuitous advice and treatment there offered who could well afford to pay for it. Naturally, under these circumstances, hundreds of struggling middle-class practitioners find it impossible to make a living.

The real remedy for the congestion of the out-patient department is depletion. All cases in which a genuine claim to the receipt of hospital relief cannot be established should be eliminated. For this purpose two things are necessary—viz. a definite water-line of poverty, above which charity is not permitted to extend, and an adequate system of inquiry to prevent imposture. Such inquiries, though necessarily very imperfectly carried out, reduced the number of out-patients at the London Hospital in one year by 6900, and at St. Bartholomew's by 25,349 in five years. At the Royal Free Hospital such inquiries showed 61½ per cent. of the applicants for treatment to be in circumstances not fairly entitling them to relief; at the Children's Hospital, in Great Ormond Street, 57 per cent. were found to be ineligible for the same reason. At Manchester, in the course of a few years, a well-organized system of inquiry has reduced the proportion of cases in which hospital charity is abused from 42·32 to about 6 per cent.

The difficulties of such a system of investigation are great, but the facts just mentioned show that they are not insuperable. However slight the actual diminution effected may be, it is always a saving of money to the hospital, as well as of time and energy to the medical staff. The average cost of an out-patient at the London Hospital has been estimated by Mr. Nixon, the house governor, at 4s., so that the reduction in numbers above-mentioned was equivalent to a saving of £1466 in one year. Mr. Burdett* has shown that the total cost of an out-patient varies at different hospitals from 2s. to 11s. A comparison of these figures with those showing the proportion of cases in which hospital relief is abused will serve to give some idea as to the terrible waste of charity that takes place in London alone. Inquiry into the circumstances of applicants to be effectual must be universal, and a necessary preliminary to the carrying out of any plan of the kind is an agreement among all hospitals as to the conditions under which relief is to be given, and an engagement on the part of each of them to adhere strictly to the rules established by common consent. What is wanted, in short, may be briefly described as a trades-unionism of public charities.

The first thing required as the basis of this agreement is a definition of the degree of the poverty which shall entitle a man to relief for himself and his family. It is obvious that this is not an easy matter, for no hard-and-fast limit of income can be laid down without risk of exemplifying the Roman maxim that the strictest legality may involve the most grievous injustice.

An income which may be comparative wealth for a single man, or a married couple without encumbrances, may, in the case of people burdened with a large family, be only barely sufficient to keep body and soul together. The cases most needing relief are not always the very poor, but are often found in that social stratum, which was happily described by Mr. Goschen, in introducing a recent Budget, as the one in which a black coat begins to be worn. It would be a gross violation of the spirit, if not of the letter, of charity to exclude, by an arbitrary "wage limit," clerks and other small *employés*, curates, widows of officers living on the pittance doled out by a grateful country, unsuccessful artists, musicians out of employment, and many others who by courtesy are not generally classed among the poor. People of this kind are often more

* "Hospitals and the State."

really destitute, besides feeling the miseries of want far more keenly, than those to the manner born, whose poverty is naked and not ashamed. The proposed inquiry must therefore include not only the bare figure of the applicant's income, but all the circumstances of his position; and the restrictive regulations should not be harshly enforced, but should be interpreted in the most merciful spirit, and if there be any doubt as to the merits of the case the applicant should always have the benefit of it.

The following is a sketch of the plan which has been found to work well at Manchester, and which has been accepted as fairly satisfactory by many of the most ardent reforming spirits in the medical profession. All patients applying at a hospital for treatment are subjected to a preliminary interrogatory by the clerk as to their circumstances; they are then admitted to the out-patient room, where they are treated by the assistant physician or surgeon on duty. Strict inquiry is then made as to their fitness to receive gratuitous relief, and in a few days they are visited at their own homes by an inspector of the Provident Society. The "wage limit" is as follows:—For a single man or woman, 12s. a week; for a man and his wife, 18s. a week, 1s. 6d. extra per week being allowed for each child. If the family resources are found to exceed these limits, the hospital's ticket is withdrawn, and the patient advised to join one of the provident dispensaries, of which there is a well-organized system at Manchester. Each hospital subscribes a small sum annually to the Provident Society to defray the cost of these inspections. Under this system it seems to be generally admitted by those who know the facts that there is very little abuse of hospital charity at Manchester. The wage limit appears to me a trifle low, and indeed it has recently been proposed to raise it to 15s. weekly for single persons, and 20s. for a married couple. Cases of accident, of course, always receive treatment at once, and no inquiry seems to be made about them by the Provident Society. If, however, such persons be found to be possessed of means, the hospital which gives relief should undoubtedly have the first right to recover payments. The plan is undoubtedly a step in the right direction, but to make it completely successful it is obvious that the system of provident dispensaries requires to be developed to a far larger extent than that at present existing in London. The provident dispensary should be able to provide effective assistance, not only for the ordinary run of human ailments, but for special cases of all kinds ; and persons in a position to subscribe to a provident system, but who, through want of thrift, have not taken the precaution to do so, should not be allowed to receive relief except at the Poor Law or pauper hospitals. Patients who make use of such institutions should forfeit for a time their political rights—that is to say, the right of voting for members of Parliament, for seven years.* Although I would not compel anybody to subscribe under the provident system, it certainly seems right that those who do not make some sacrifice to insure medical attendance when they are ill should forfeit some privilege in return for the gratuitous relief which they receive.

Much as I object to the bureaucratic despotism which governs everything in Prussia, I must confess that the system of insurance against sickness which is there in force is not without its merits, and if it could be established in this country as a voluntary measure it would effect a vast amount of good. By the Prussian law of June 15, 1883, all workmen are compelled to insure against sickness. They can do so either through the general office of their town or district, through the local office of the parish in which they live, through the private society organized by the firm or factory where they are employed, through a guild or public society, or through a private office registered under the Act. All these offices are under the immediate control of the local authorities, who act for the State. Private offices may make rules for themselves in matters of detail, but in all essential points they must conform to the provisions of the law in question. The amount of insurance is 1½ per cent. of the wages earned. Of this one-third is defrayed by the employer, the remaining two-thirds being deducted by him from the workman's wages before they are paid. When a

* The object of this term of years is to insure the unthrifty a loss of political privilege on at least one occasion.

workman falls ill, he is entitled from the beginning of his illness to free medical attendance with medicine, an allowance of money, and, if necessary, spectacles and various surgical appliances. If he has no one to look after him, or if he cannot be properly nursed at home, he is admitted to the hospital, and while he is there, if he has a family dependent on him, part of the money allowance is handed over to them. If he is out of work, he is assisted for a certain time with money from the insurance fund. If he dies, burial money is paid to his relatives. All these regulations apply to women as well as to men. Discretionary powers are vested in the local authorities to increase or diminish, under certain circumstances, the amount of insurance paid, the amount of assistance allowed, and the length of time during which it is given. Contractors who employ a large number of men, whether temporarily or permanently, in making railways, canals, and roads, in river or dike works, in building fortresses, etc., are obliged to established an insurance fund. If they fail to do so, they are compelled to pay out of their own pockets to such of their workmen as fall ill the amount of assistance prescribed by law, and burial money to the families of those who die. Employers who do not carry out the obligations imposed on them by the law, or who use their private insurance offices to exact from their workmen more than is due, or put pressure on them, are liable to fines. Between 8,000,000 and 9,000,000 male and female workers are insured under the law of June 15, 1883. It will be seen that in its main features the German plan resembles the system of benefit clubs by which so many English working-men provide against the day of misfortune, with the radical difference that the latter is optional, and the former compulsory and therefore universal. The German system is open to the objection that it amounts to "State Socialism," but many who have witnessed the misery caused by improvidence would be glad to see it prevented even at the cost of a slight infringement of the Briton's hereditary privilege to "do as he likes."

My own plan, which I can only sketch out here in the barest outline, would be a comprehensive arrangement in which every patient needing assistance would have it provided for him—at his own expense if possible, but, if not, by private benevolence or out of the public money—and in which every medical practitioner would find a place. The present machinery could with comparatively little modification be adapted to the purpose. What is chiefly wanted, it seems to me, is that the Poor Law infirmaries, the hospitals, and the provident dispensaries should be combined so as to form one large system of eleemosynary medical relief, somewhat on the lines of the French *Assistance Publique*. That is to say, the whole machinery should be controlled by a central authority, with more or less independent local sub-centres, or *ganglia*, if I may use a physiological expression, in every large town and district.

In France all the hospitals and dispensaries are under the control of the *Assistance Publique*. In Paris, patients seeking hospital relief apply in the first instance at the Bureau Central, where there is a staff of physicians and surgeons whose sole duty it is to examine all who present themselves, and pass them on to the various hospitals for treatment. In London there should be a Medical Relief Office in every parish, where patients could be sorted by experienced officials into their proper classes, and could be at once provided with a ticket of admission to the nearest Poor Law infirmary, hospital, or dispensary, according to circumstances. The Poor Law infirmary would, of course, be absolutely free; for the hospital a trifling fee—say from one shilling to three shillings a week during attendance—should be payable; for the dispensary the payment would be on a definite actuarial scale. The great point is that these three parts of the machinery should be co-ordinated together, not only for the administration of medical relief, but for purposes of medical education. The Poor Law infirmaries and the dispensaries should be open to medical students just as the hospitals are, and the students should assist in the treatment of patients under the supervision of the medical officers. In this way, an enormous amount of valuable material, which, as things are at present, is utterly wasted so far as clinical instruction is concerned, could be utilized, with results to the progress of medicine which can hardly be estimated. Each hospital should be, as it were, the sun of a system of satellite provident dispensaries, the medical officers of the hospital acting as consulting physicians and surgeons to the dispensaries, and acute or serious cases amongst the dispensary patients being received into the hospital. The special hospitals would fit into the frame just as they are. As pauperizing agencies these institutions have always done much less harm than the general hospitals. The plan of having special departments at the general hospitals would, I think, be inadequate, as the best specialists will not consent to work in a position "a little lower than the angels" of the general staff. The special departments have not hitherto been provided with the necessary equipment, and though this defect may be remedied in the future, they will remain under the control of the governing body of the whole hospital, and between the zeal for economy with which these gentlemen are eaten up, and the jealousy of the other members of the staff, the special department is too likely to pine away in the cold shade of neglect. That the special hospitals, as a matter of fact, meet the wants of the patients better than special departments at the general hospitals is obvious from the far larger numbers which attend the former, in spite of the small payment which they have in most cases to make. The so-called provident principle could not be directly applied to special hospitals, but there is no reason why they should not be incorporated in the general system which I have described. The rate for insurance against particular diseases would, however, have to be made higher than the ordinary rate, as none but persons actually suffering from them would join. But the difficulty is purely actuarial, and could no doubt be equitably adjusted with a little ingenuity.

I have suggested that a small charge should be made to out-patients at hospitals, and I am strongly of opinion that such a system of payment, carefully graduated according to the patient's means, would of itself do much to diminish the evils now existing. At the Hospital for Diseases of the Throat, which I founded in 1863, and which has served as the model for many similar institutions at home and abroad, all patients, except such as are out of work, or otherwise unable to pay, contribute in proportion to their means. Between five thousand

and six thousand patients attend in the course of the year, and of these about three-fourths pay something towards the cost of their treatment. The patient is questioned as to his circumstances by a clerk, but there is no systematic inquiry by any outside organisation. The guiding principle has always been rather to allow the hospital to be a little imposed upon than to screw payment out of those unable to afford it. The plan has worked admirably in every way; whilst there has always been an abundance of patients, the time of the medical officers has not been frittered away by crowds of trivial cases, no real case of necessity, so far as I know, has been excluded from the benefits of the hospital, and injury has not been done to society by enforced pauperisation. It has not been found that the plan prevents charitable persons from subscribing; on the contrary, it seems to be generally approved of. The experience of other special hospitals where payment is made by patients is equally favourable. The extension of the system to all hospitals, general as well as special, appears to me eminently desirable, but it cannot be denied that at present the majority of hospital physicians and surgeons are opposed to it. They think that it would interfere with teaching, as patients who paid would not care to be examined by the "'prentice hands" of the students. There has been no difficulty of this kind at the Throat Hospital; so far from this being the case, patients seem to be flattered by the interest they excite, probably accepting it as a tribute to the obscurity of their cases.

In the Prussian hospitals payment is universal. All sorts and conditions of persons are freely admitted, and patients are divided into three classes, according to the rate of payment. In Class I., which is popularly designated the "luxurious" one, they pay from six to nine shillings a day; in Class II., from four to six shillings; and in Class III., about one shilling and ninepence a day. Children pay one shilling and threepence a day. People who cannot pay for themselves are paid for by the Poor Law Board at third-class rates, but those who can pay generally do so, as persons who receive relief from the Poor Law Board forfeit their political rights. Patients who are paid for by the Poor Law Board have to refund the money by small instalments if they can. Those who are too poor to give anything are treated in the hospitals at the expense of the parish to which they belong. Of course this system, inasmuch as it does not apply to out-patients, is not strictly comparable to that which exists at the hospitals in London which now require some payments. Out-patients in the Prussian capital are provided for by the various public "Polikliniks" in connection with the *Berliner Verein für häusliche Gesundheitspflege*, where they receive gratuitous advice, and frequently also medicine. Besides these there are the numerous private "Polikliniks" already referred to, so that, on the whole, Berlin, in proportion to its population, is probably not far behind London in point of the abuse of medical relief.

To return to the plan of an organised system of medical assistance for the poorer classes which I have suggested, it may be well to point out that I am not proposing to revolutionise present arrangements, or to hand over the control of hospitals to the State. Mr. Herbert Spencer has ably pointed out the many evils of State control, and these evils would certainly make themselves felt if the State were to interfere in hospital matters. The Central Board, on which all hospitals, asylums, and public dispensaries would be represented, would merely supervise the work of the hospitals as the General Medical Council does the examinations of the various medical licensing bodies. Each hospital would preserve its administrative autonomy, but its accounts and other details of management should be open to inspection. Moreover, accounts should be kept on a uniform system, instead of the present more or less intentional chaos, which prevents any proper comparison between different institutions in respect of economic efficiency. Some of the general hospitals prevent the inspection of the accounts in a manner which, in the present day, can only be regarded as a public scandal. A few years ago, when I was endeavouring to make some comparison of the expenditure per patient in the different hospitals of London, I wrote to the medical superintendent of Guy's Hospital for the balance-sheet of that institution. I received a reply to the effect that only a limited number of Reports were published for the Governors of the Hospital (I believe between thirty and forty), and that the Governors were not permitted to allow any person to see these Reports. It is to be hoped that the Select Committee of the House of Lords, now sitting, will let a little daylight into the dark financial places of these highly exclusive organisations.

The Poor Law infirmaries would remain as they are, except that visiting physicians and surgeons would be appointed as in the case of hospitals, and there would be resident and non-resident pupils, who should take an active part in the work. As regards provident dispensaries the case is different. They should be better organised, and should be extended so as to cover the whole area of London and other towns, and also of the rural districts.

One necessary result of the unification of medical relief would be a better distribution of hospitals. At present there are quarters where several are massed together, to the great detriment of their individual usefulness, and others in which one hospital has to serve for an extensive and thickly populated district. Thus in London we have an overcrowding of hospitals on the north side of the Thames, and practically only two for the vast area south of the river. I am speaking only of general hospitals; special hospitals do not exist for the supply of local needs alone, but draw their patients from all over London, and largely also from the country.

But whilst the necessity for the thorough organisation of medical relief is loudly called for, an analogous reform might be effected with great advantage in the machinery of medical education in London. At present there are in the metropolis no fewer than eleven fully equipped schools of medicine, besides one for women only. This unnecessary multiplication of schools implies a grievous waste of teaching power, and consequent inferiority in the quality of the instruction given, that is all the more deplorable inasmuch as it could so easily be remedied. The cure is, in one word, unification. How this is to be brought about it would be out of place to discuss here; but I cannot refrain from saying that our legislators will be ill-advised if they show too nice a regard for vested interests and paltry jealousies in dealing with this matter. The process must be carried out by the hand of iron in the velvet glove. There was much wailing and gnashing of teeth among the Grand Dukelings of Pumpernickel and Saurkrautstadt, and other Serene Transparencies, at their forcible absorption into the mighty German Empire that has grown up before our eyes; but most of them acknowledge by this time, like Candide, that all is for the best in the best of all possible worlds. This is what I should like to see done with the collection of educational molecules which at present supply all the medical training that can be got in London. The largest city in the world would then have a school of medicine worthy of it.

A necessary condition of the scheme of medical relief which has been suggested would be that all hospital appointments should be thrown open to legally qualified medical practitioners, regardless of the source or nature of their diplomas. Napoleon's motto, "La carrière ouverte aux talents," would be the fundamental principle of the new arrangement. The dispensary appointments would be open to all the practitioners in any given district who cared to take them, and the dispensary would be the first rung of the ladder leading to the highest hospital posts.

I have not thought it worth while to attempt to fill in the details of the plan of medical relief which has been sketched out in this essay. I have only, as it were, marked out the lines on which the foundation should be laid; the architectural elaboration of the design must be left to more competent hands. I think it has been shown that only very comprehensive measures of reform can make a cosmos out of the present utter confusion; perhaps, indeed, under existing circumstances, a perfect system of hospital administration is impossible. When the socialistic millennium so confidently looked for by increasing numbers of believers has come upon the earth, there will perhaps be no more abuse of hospitals; but till then, there must always be some. After all, it is better that charity should be abused to a certain extent, than that it should be chained up and trammelled about with all sorts of restraints as if it were a dangerous animal. The

THE USE AND ABUSE OF HOSPITALS.

gentle dew droppeth from heaven upon the place beneath without waiting to be satisfied as to the strict necessity of the operation. I would rather that charity should be bestowed unnecessarily on two or three unworthy recipients than that one case of genuine suffering should go unrelieved.

EXERCISE AND TRAINING.

Exercise.

ALTHOUGH every form of exercise is in its degree training, and, on the other hand, the larger part of training is exercise, it will tend to "lucidity" to deal with the two subjects separately. As exercise is the physical duty of every man, woman, and child, while training is necessary only in the case of candidates for Olympic crowns, or rather, the cups which are their modern equivalents, it will be convenient to begin with the former.

That a certain amount of exercise is needful for health is one of the few things about which all doctors are agreed, and one of the still fewer things as to which medical teaching is submissively accepted by the non-professional public. Unfortunately, intellectual assent no more implies practical performance in the domain of hygiene than in that of morals. It is by those "in populous cities pent," by professional and business men chained to the desk or the consulting-room, and by women, that exercise is most apt to be neglected. With regard to young ladies, indeed, it is not so very long since nearly all exercise worthy of the name was tabooed by Mrs. Grundy as only fit for tomboys and as tending to give an appearance of robust health which was thought to be incompatible with refinement. More rational notions are now beginning to prevail, however, and the limp anæmic maiden with uncomfortable prominences is rapidly giving place to a type more like the Greek ideal of healthy womanhood. The ruddy-

EXERCISE AND TRAINING.

cheeked, full-limbed girl of to-day, who climbs mountains, rides, swims, rows, and is not afraid of the health-giving kisses of the god of day, is a living illustration of the value of exercise. She is healthier, stronger, more lissom, and withal more intellectual, more energetic and self-reliant, as well as more amiable and better tempered, than her wasp-waisted beringleted great-grandmother, with her languid elegance and her Draconian code of feminine decorum. In the physical "betterment" which is so conspicuous in the girls of the period lies the best hope for the future of our race.

A belief appears to be widely entertained that there is a certain antagonism between brain power and muscular development, and it is inferred that we are as inferior to our forefathers in bodily prowess as we are superior to them in intellectual activity. The moral is supposed to be pointed by the example of the "noble savage;" and the lithe, sinewy frames of the Zulus and Hadendowas are contrasted with the less powerful physique of our men. So far, however, from physical deterioration being a necessary consequence or accompaniment of intellectual progress, there can be little doubt that we are, on the whole, better men than our predecessors in body as well as in mind. Your antique Roman was a fine specimen of the human animal, as is still visible to us in his big bones and the rough imprint left thereon by the mighty thews and sinews which once moved them. Modern Englishmen, however, need fear no comparison in this respect with the noblest Roman of them all. As regards our own ancestors, we have a sure proof that they were inferior to us in physique in the fact that the armour in the Tower is much too small for the Guardsmen of the present day. Of course, so many stunted inheritors of generations of physical and moral disease people the slums of our great cities, and so many "unfit" persons are now kept alive by improved medical art, who in the good old times would not have survived infancy, that I dare say, if the whole population is taken into account, our average height and chest girth might make a poor show beside those of certain nations of antiquity and some savage races of the present day. The case would, however, be different if our large stock of weaklings which modern benevolence and science save from premature "elimination" were first deducted from the total.

Though "muscular Christianity"—that curious cult of the biceps as a divinely appointed instrument for the regeneration of sinners—may be said to have died with its prophet, the principle that the mental faculties require for their fullest exercise a basis of bodily health remains as a solid residue of Charles Kingsley's teaching. Other things being equal, the race that is strongest in muscle will also be most powerful in brain. The intellectual predominance of the Greeks was, I am convinced, largely due to their almost religious care of the body. The Germans were mere Dryasdust pedants and unprofitable dreamers till the institution of compulsory military service by Stein, after the crushing defeat of the Prussians at Jena, wrought a physical regeneration which speedily enabled them to take their place in the forefront of intellectual progress. In like manner, under the energising influence of the drill sergeant, a physical renaissance has within our own memory taken place in Italy, whereby the subtle brains of her sons are being rapidly weaned from *concetti* and dilettante trifling to manlier objects.

That proper exercise of the body is a powerful factor in the development of the mind is no paradox, but a plain physiological truth. Without a sufficient supply of pure blood the brain can no more do its work efficiently than a steam engine without coal; and without muscular exercise purification of the blood is incomplete and inadequate for the needs of the intellectual machine when it is subjected to any extraordinary strain. A nation of laggards in the flesh will also be sluggish in spirit, and brains half asphyxiated by imperfectly aërated blood will breed nothing but unwholesome mysticism, criticism of life in Count Tolstoi's later style, and schemes for the regeneration of society akin to that by which Medea tried to renew the youth of her father. The "long-haired men and the short-haired women," whose chief notion of social reform seems to be the abolition of self-restraint, would be healthier in mind as well as in body if they would ventilate the close chambers of their brains by regular outdoor exercise. If, amidst the hysterical sentimentalism which is one of the "notes" of these *fin de siècle* days, the English mind yet retains a good deal of its old robust virility, this is principally due to the healthy love of field sports which is still the "badge of all our tribe."

Our zeal for physical culture is not, however, always according to knowledge, and while our enthusiasm for exercise is often at fever heat when we are "juvenile and curly," it is apt to fall to zero when the waist has become simply a "geographical expression." From excess as well as from insufficiency of bodily movement much harm may result, and it may therefore be of some use to explain in ordinary language the general principles which should govern the exercise of the muscles at different periods of life. The application of these principles in particular cases must be left to each individual's own judgment, but I hope to be able to furnish some hints for guidance. The reader need hardly be reminded that I speak from the medical rather than the athletic point of view.

Before going further, a few words must be said as to the physiology of exercise—that is to say, its effects on the body generally, and on its various parts and organs individually. There is a natural craving in the muscles for movement, as there is in the stomach for food and in the lungs for air. This feeling is the expression of a physiological need which can only be disregarded at the expense of health. Want of exercise means disuse of the muscles, and disuse is inevitably followed by wasting. Any one who has seen a broken limb that has been kept motionless in splints even for a few weeks must have noticed how lean and shrivelled it appears—how "fall'n its muscles' brawny vaunt" by the side of its fellow-member.

The effects of exercise are twofold—first, local, on the muscles themselves; and secondly, general, on the body as a whole. The former produces muscular strength, the latter the state of functional perfection of the vital organs and harmonious co-operation of their several activities which constitutes health. Muscular strength and vigour of constitution are not at all the same thing, though they are often confounded by ignorant athletes and their trainers. A first-rate athlete may have within him the germs of consumption or be otherwise unsound, and muscular power may even be developed at the expense of the rest of the system, as the memory may be cultivated to the detriment of the other mental faculties.

The *local* effects of exercise consist in an increase in bulk and a hardening of the substance of the muscles brought directly or indirectly into play by the movements executed. These effects are well exemplified in persons whose occupation involves the constant use of one set of muscles, and the experienced eye can often read a man's trade in the peculiarities of his muscular development. Muscular specialism, in fact, leaves its mark on the body as clearly as intellectual specialism, when not corrected by general culture, does on the mind. It is the frequent contraction of the muscles, even more than the force employed, that produces such remarkable effects; the musical conductor's biceps is developed by the light rod he wields as certainly as the blacksmith's by his hammer, and the late Sir Michael Costa had a right arm which many a brawny son of Vulcan might have envied. The overgrown calves of *premières danseuses* may also be cited as instances in point. Balzac, in " La Dernière Incarnation de Vautrin," mentions "the formidable breadth and thickness of the hands" which was the only thing about Sanson, the son of the executioner of Louis XVI., that betrayed his descent from an unbroken line of public headsmen extending over six centuries. In most persons the right hand is bigger than the left, because it is more used, and a friend who, like Cato, has begun to play the violoncello in mature age, has just shown me that the fingers of his left hand are already about an eighth of an inch broader than those of his right from manipulation of the strings. In the lame the sound leg is disproportionately large, owing to its having to do double work. I have often been struck when abroad by the relatively enormous development of the arms and shoulders in beggars whose lower limbs were disabled and who had therefore to drag themselves along with their hands.

EXERCISE AND TRAINING.

Exercise not only causes an increase in the size of the muscles but betters the quality of their tissue. The fibres gain in elasticity as well as in strength, and become at once freer and more accurate in their action ; they are less easily fatigued, and recover their tone more quickly. In a word, the functional efficiency as well as the structure of muscle is improved by exercise, and, as Helmholtz has pointed out, practice creates *a habit* whereby in any given act only the muscles necessary for the required movements contract. The maximum of work is done with the minimum expenditure of energy.

The *general* effects of exercise are produced mainly through the agency of the heart and lungs. The stress of violent exertion, as every one knows, makes the breathing more rapid, and the beat of the heart quicker and stronger, than under ordinary conditions. The greater rapidity of respiration means that more oxygen is taken into the lungs, and therefore more blood is cleansed of the physiological sewage thrown into it by the tissues through which it has passed in its circulation through the body ; while by the increased activity of the heart this purified blood is distributed in greater abundance to every part of the economy. The lungs and the heart themselves share in the good effects of exercise, and thus become still more able to do their appointed work ; the chest grows more capacious, the lungs larger and more elastic, the heart firmer in structure and more vigorous in action. The little muscles which encircle the stomach and the intestinal tube are quickened into greater activity, while their contractile power is increased, a matter which, trifling as it may seem, is of incalculable importance for the health of the mind as well as of the body. The other internal organs, those secret laboratories where Nature performs feats of chemical transmutation beyond the dreams of alchemy, and the glands of various kinds, any derangement of whose functions may give rise to seas of trouble against which medicine takes arms in vain, are enabled to work to better advantage by being supplied with better raw material in the shape of more generous blood. The body is at once better nourished and kept more free from the burdensome accumulation of superfluous tissue by the more rapid and complete removal of waste matters. The nerves, too, and the brain, which is, as it were, the sun of the nervous system, are maintained in the highest state of functional efficiency in the same way as the other organs. The general effects of exercise are therefore, briefly, a more abundant supply of better blood to all tissues and organs; hence all the component elements of the body are better nourished, so that each is able to play its allotted part to the best possible advantage. In fact, the effects of exercise may be summed up in half a dozen words: Better fuel, and more of it, for the vital engine.

It must not be supposed that all forms of exercise produce exactly the same effects. Some develop particular groups of muscles, while the others, together with the great physiological centres—the heart, the lungs, and the brain—have, as it were, to "stand out." Thus, in lifting weights or executing movements of any kind with one arm, though the limb may become tired out, one does not become hot or "blown;" the exercise is almost purely local. If all the limbs, however, are thrown into rapid and violent movement, as in running, boxing, or swimming, the heart and the lungs join in the dance, and the whole stream of life is for the moment quickened, and broadened and deepened. Local exercise, though of course beneficial to the muscles involved, has little or no influence on the health, because its effects are merely local. For hygienic purposes it is not so much the muscles as the internal organs that need to be exercised; but this can only be done by movements which bring them into rapid play. Hence chamber gymnastics and the highly elaborate acrobatic movements which require complicated arrangements of ropes and bars and pulleys (though I am far from wishing to deny their value) can never take the place of old-fashioned games for the young, and riding and walking for those declined into the vale of years.

The manifold evils arising from deficient exercise need not be dwelt upon here. I need only say that if a proper amount of exercise is not taken, not only do the muscles become weak and flabby, but the functions of every organ and the soundness of every tissue must suffer. There is imperfect elimination of waste matters, the muscles and the internal organs become encumbered with superfluous fat, the heart becomes weak, the lungs are never thoroughly emptied and gradually lose their elasticity, appetite dwindles to vanishing point, digestion becomes a burden only to be borne with wailing and gnashing of teeth, and the joy and brightness of health give place to incapacity for either work or pleasure, irritability and "leaden-eyed despair." In the young particularly exercise is necessary for moral as well as for physical health; in violent movement in the open air their superabundant nervous energy finds free vent; if pent up it is too likely to force a way out in wrong directions.

In the following essay I shall apply the principles now laid down, and shall explain the amount and kind of exercise required at different ages.

EXERCISE AND TRAINING.

EXERCISE—(*continued*).

COMING now to what preachers call the application of the text, the practical bearing of what has been said about exercise in the previous essay may be briefly pointed out. For this purpose it will be convenient to follow man in the "order of his going" through childhood, adolescence, maturity, and old age—the four principal stages of his journey from the cradle to the grave.

In the child the physiological craving for movement shows itself with the unrestrained freedom of the natural animal. If a healthy baby is allowed to have free play for its limbs it will go through a series of improvised acrobatic performances, twisting its limbs and turning them into knots that might excite the envy of a professional "contortionist." It is an excellent plan to give an infant perfect muscular freedom for some time every day; it should be disencumbered of any superfluous clothing and laid on a rug or some soft material on the floor and allowed to kick and throw itself about to its heart's content. On the general principle, apparently, that every natural tendency is a prompting of the evil spirit, it used to be the universal custom to restrain the movements of infants by swathing them in innumerable bandages, as if they were diminutive mummies. With the eager life within them thus "cabin'd, cribbed, confined," the poor little things must have been mere bundles of helpless misery, and in many cases must have been dwarfed in their growth, if not deformed. The more enlightened among the doctors fulminated against the practice for centuries, but in that, as in most other things, medical wisdom cried out in the streets and no man regarded it. It needed the genius of Rousseau to persuade the more civilised part of the world of the senseless cruelty of tight swaddling clothes, and even at this day his teaching has not entirely prevailed. Any traveller in Italy, Spain, and some parts of France can see for himself that infantile hygiene is still in the semi-barbarous stage. One effect of the "trussing" of the limbs in infancy may be observed in the crowds of cripples and misshapen creatures that one sees round the doors of churches in the South. Nothing strikes the "intelligent foreigner" in England more than the high standard of physical development and the comparative rarity of deformity in the bulk of our population. When staying at hotels abroad, I have often noticed the admiration aroused among the natives by the superior size and strength of my juvenile countrymen. One reason of this excellence of physique undoubtedly is that the British baby is from the first allowed an amount of liberty in the use of his limbs befitting the future citizen of a free country.

As the child grows older the boisterousness with which it romps may be taken as a pretty sure index of its state of health. Mr. Herbert Spencer speaks with a sympathetic insight which was hardly to be expected from a philosopher—and moreover, I believe I may add, a bachelor—of the torture which it is to a healthy child to "sit still." Wordsworth is a physiologist as well as a poet when he says that a child "feels its life in every limb." But by long continued confinement and restraint—that is, by being made to live under totally unnatural conditions—this wholesome exuberance of vitality may be lost and give place to listlessness and even positive dislike of play. Dr. Fernand Lagrange, who has written a valuable work on exercise in childhood,* says that for years past alarm has been felt by those charged with the education of the young in France, "because children have lost the taste for exercise." This he

* "L'Hygiène de l'Exercise chez les Enfants et les jeunes Gens." (Félix Alcan. Paris: 1890.)

attributes entirely to the sinister predominance of the schoolmaster in modern child life. The denial of Nature's rights in respect of play is followed by an unfailing Nemesis in the form of ill-health, or what is perhaps still worse, by gradual adaptation to circumstances, leading to a joyless childhood, a flabby, languid youth, a stunted, stagnant maturity, and a premature old age. In the French *lycées* the bad effects, moral and physical, of insufficient exercise are writ so large as to strike the most indifferent eye. It would be wonderful if it were otherwise, seeing that the only playground the poor boys have to disport themselves in is an enclosure about as cheerful as the yard of a prison, and in this for a few minutes in the day they toil through a set gymnastic task as enlivening as the treadmill.

In English schools of a corresponding class things are very different; but, as regards the lower *couches sociales*, is not the schoolmaster too much with us also? In our devouring zeal for the gospel of the three R's we are apt to forget that, as Mr. Herbert Spencer puts it, "The first requisite for success in life is to be a good animal." This is a much more important matter both for the present rising generation and for the future of our race than the precocious passing of "standards" and the earning of capitation grants for teachers. To my mind, the physical education of our children is one of the most urgent questions of the day, and it is one which might well engage the attention of our legislature if they could spare a little time from their exciting game of "I'm the King of the Castle." If a small fraction of the attention that is given to the rearing of cattle were given to the bringing up of children, Walt Whitman's prophetic vision of a nation of "forty millions of magnificent persons" would be in a fair way of being realized. We have a Minister of Agriculture whose duty it is to see that the four-footed commonwealth sustains no detriment; why should there not be a Minister of Hominiculture, charged with the development of the national resources in respect of that not altogether valueless product, man? The "perfectibility" of the human race depends much more on physical than on mental culture; for intellect, energy of will, and strength of moral fibre are largely dependent on sound bodily health.

How, then, are children to be made "good animals"? By the fullest possible development of their bodily powers. How is this development to be compassed? Adapting Danton's famous saying, I answer, By exercise, by exercise, and yet again by exercise. There can be no dispute about this; the only question is as to the form and amount of the exercise. The period of childhood may be taken as extending from the age of two or three years up to puberty. Now, what is wanted at this stage is not so much the acquisition of muscular strength or skill as a solid foundation of general health. In childhood exercise should be almost exclusively general or *hygienic*; indeed, I am inclined to think that the less purely local or *athletic* exercise a growing child has the better it will be, not only for its constitution, but for its future muscular development. Very young children should be encouraged to run about, to trundle hoops, or, if at the seaside, to build castles, etc., on the sand—in short, to play and romp instead of dawdling. Walking about with a nursemaid, who possibly takes more interest in infantry than in infants, can hardly be amusing, and may be extremely fatiguing to her little charges. In the way of systematic exercise for young children there is nothing better than the Kindergarten movements; the fact that they are done in company with other children, and often to the accompaniment of song, assimilates these little drills to games and lessens the danger of their being looked upon as tasks. For older children no methodical exercise, however scientifically arranged, can compare with the boisterous outdoor games which bring every muscle into play, lash the heart into a gallop, and make the vital bellows—the lungs—blow the fire of life into a glow. The excitement of the game is what doctors would call its "active principle," for gladness is the best of all tonics. Even the shouting, however it may vex the ears of "tough seniors," is in itself an important element in the exercise, as it brings the lungs and the muscles of the chest and throat into vigorous action.

It is a melancholy fact, however, that, as Mr. Walter Besant

pointed out some years ago, neither the children nor the young
people of the lower classes—in London, at any rate—really
know how to play; and I am afraid that neither the People's
Palace nor the teaching of Toynbee Hall philanthropists has
done much to remedy this state of things. It is to be hoped
that the London Playing-fields Committee, which was formed
for the purpose of providing facilities for cricket and other
games for shopmen and other toilers, may do something also
for the children of the slums, who in their crowded courts
have nothing better than "tip-cat" or "hop-scotch" to
amuse themselves with. In France, as M. Lagrange tells us,
games have almost fallen into oblivion, even among the
children of the well-to-do. In Belgium some years ago open-
air games had become a lost art, and a movement was set
on foot by some enlightened educational reformers to teach
children to play! So well have the games answered that
gymnastic apparatus, trapezes, etc., have now all but disappeared from Belgian schools. The result is that "the children
are straighter, stronger, and more gay," the last point being,
even as regards health, just as important as the others. In
the United States physical culture is also beginning to be made
a part of the ordinary school curriculum. At Boston Dr.
Edward M. Hartwell has just been appointed Doctor of Physical
Training in the public schools at a salary of 3,000 dol. a year,
and the Ling or Swedish system of exercises is being introduced into many American schools. Muscular drill is not
quite the same thing as games; but, as Sir Thomas More said,
"Marry, it is somewhat." I believe it would add immensely
to the usefulness of Board schools as nurseries of efficient
citizens if, as is the case in the public schools of Belgium, their
teaching staff included a *Professeur de Jeux*. It would be no
loss to the community if a few of the 'ologies with which the
brains of poor little starvelings are at present forced into premature exhaustion were sacrificed to make room for the sound
physical and moral training supplied by well-ordered play.

Among the upper classes, thanks to the somewhat excessive
precautions against "over-pressure" taken in our public schools
and universities, the *studiosa juventus* of this country gives at

least as much time and attention to the cultivation of its muscles as to that of its brain. It is this early physical training that makes the members of that class of society politely termed "barbarians" by Matthew Arnold as superior in body as they are often inferior in mind to those who have to bear the yoke of life from their childhood. Parents are sometimes unwilling to allow their children to share in the games of their companions—especially football—from fear of accidents. On this subject I cannot do better than quote the words of Dr. Clement Dukes, whose medical experience of schoolboys, as physician to Rugby for many years, is probably unrivalled. "If," he says, with regard to football, "twenty years' experience at the very birthplace of this much-abused game, played three or four times every week in winter—and very warm games sometimes, owing to the rivalry between houses for the glory of being 'cock-house'—counts for anything, it ought to make parents and doctors consider the matter more thoughtfully. I have never yet had one serious accident from football —no accident more severe than I have had from cricket, house runs, steeplechases, swimming baths, gymnasiums, and above all, by-play. If the game were always played by boys the outcry against football must cease." Dr. Dukes, however, while insisting that no boy should be admitted into a public school who cannot take his part in games, and severely blaming the too complaisant doctors who sign certificates of unfitness simply to please timid mothers, lays stress on the necessity of separating the small boys from the big ones, and letting them play by themselves. Much of the danger of outdoor games, and much of the dislike felt for them by many boys, arises from the custom which is or used to be prevalent at certain public schools of making the smaller boys of nine or ten join in football or cricket with young sons of Anak of eighteen or nineteen. With regard to girls, I agree with Mrs. Garrett Anderson that a Winchester, a Charterhouse, and a Rugby are wanted for them as well as for their brothers. With one or two exceptions (among which I should certainly number football and cricket) girls can play at the same games as boys, and they should be encouraged and, unless physically unfit, compelled to do so. Gymnastics should not, I think, be attempted by girls before the age of twelve or thereabouts, and then they should be carefully adapted to the child's powers and should be pursued under the supervision of an experienced medical adviser. Marching and wheeling, practice with light dumb-bells and staves, etc., especially if the manœuvres are gone through to the accompaniment of music, are particularly suited to young girls. They give grace and precision to the movements, while developing the strength.

Adolescence extends from puberty (about fourteen) to twenty-three or thereabouts; strictly speaking, it reaches to twenty-five, as the growth cannot be considered complete till then. There are two easily distinguishable periods in adolescence, the first of which may be called the maturity of boyhood, while the second is the dawn of manhood. In the former the conditions and limitations of exercise are much the same as for the pre-puberty period. They resolve themselves into this: Plenty of exercise, no training. While the body is in active growth all the vital energy seems concentrated on the process of development. There is no storing up of reserve force, as in adult life; every atom of material is immediately used up in meeting the wants of the growing organism. Exercise, whether in games or in gymnastic manœuvres, is useful as helping the due performance of the vital functions, but anything like fatigue is most injurious.

In estimating the dangers of any particular kind of exercise it is not the Heraclidæ but the ordinary sons of men who must form the basis of any general formula. The weaker lads are often tall, growth having outrun general development, and in their case violent and prolonged muscular exercise should not be permitted till the frame is sufficiently consolidated to bear the expenditure of nervous and vital energy which it entails. From twenty to thirty it matters little what kind of exercise is taken so long as it is sufficient without being excessive. For men who live in towns it is often very important to obtain the maximum amount of exercise in a relatively short time, and in such cases a gallop for an hour or even three-quarters of an hour answers the purpose well. Fencing, however, is perhaps the most effective form of concentrated exercise; but it has the disadvantage of exercising the right side of the body much more than the left, and thus in some cases producing a slight deviation from perfect symmetry. Rowing, or rather sculling, is perhaps the most perfect form of exercise for young men and girls, for nearly all the muscles of the body are brought into play with the exception of those passing from the front of the chest to the arm. In young persons with a tendency to phthisis or asthma I have many times seen sculling effect a complete cure. During the period of adolescence gymnastics under a competent instructor are often of the most signal service, especially to young people who are naturally awkward or otherwise physically backward.

I need not dwell upon the necessity of exercise for women further than to say that competent authorities look upon it as the best safeguard against certain diseases peculiar to their sex, the enormous prevalence of which at the present day is no doubt in great measure due to the physical indolence which many of them have been taught to consider as a grace rather than a defect—I had almost said a vice. In view of this it is satisfactory to learn that the Ladies' Berkely Athletic Club, founded little more than a year ago in New York, should already have become a flourishing "institution." I may say here that I think it is a mistake for women to aim directly at the development of muscle; the Venus of Milo, not the half-masculine Amazon, must always be the type of physical perfection for them. Their exercise should, therefore, be chiefly *hygienic* rather than *athletic*. A great French anatomist, Cruveilhier, was ungallant enough to say that whatever women might learn to do they never could succeed in running gracefully. Candour compels me to say that I think the indictment true, but that and throwing the cricket ball are about the only things which they cannot do with twice the grace and nearly all the strength of men.

In early manhood and at that variable period which is known as the "prime of life" the object must be to keep as much as one possibly can of the stamina acquired in the days when the Blue Ribbon of the athlete seemed the only thing worth living for. A man cannot expect to maintain his "condition" under the storm and stress of active life; he must be satisfied with having laid a foundation of physical strength which will make his subsequent life happier, longer, and more useful than it would otherwise have been. His delight in, and capacity for, most forms of exercise will continue unabated for many years past the age (forty-six) fixed by the Romans as the limit of enlistment. Those requiring elasticity of the bones will be given up first; football is a dangerous anachronism after five and twenty. Those calling for swiftness of foot will be surrendered next, and the sacrifice is made easier by increasing weight of body and stiffness of limb. In the borderland between youth and middle age many men are apt to exceed in the matter of exercise, possibly from unwillingness to acknowledge that cruel Time is beginning to claw them in his clutch; for them, therefore, a little of what Dr. Johnson would have called "sufflamination" will often be required. On the other hand, those on whom middle age has stamped its mark, whose "wind" is like woman's love (according to Hamlet), and whose waistcoat is beginning to yield to circumstances, have, as it were, to be driven to the stake of physical exertion.

The amount and kind of exercise required by people between forty and fifty depend largely on individual peculiarities. There are, however, certain definite standards by which the amount of physical work done in different kinds of exercise can be accurately estimated. It is calculated that an ordinary labourer does work which is the equivalent of lifting from 300 to 400 tons one foot in a working day, and Professor Haughton reckons that a man walking on a nearly level surface at the rate of about three miles an hour, expends as much force as would raise one-twentieth part of the weight of his body through the distance walked. Now, supposing a man weighs 11 st. 6 lb., or 160 lbs., in his clothes, in walking a mile he would raise 8 lb. one mile, or 18·86 tons one foot; if he walked six miles at the same rate he would have raised 113 tons one foot. This would represent a fair standard of exercise for a healthy man of fifty years of age; if younger he should do rather more, if older he might do less.

I have already pointed out that riding is an excellent "pemmican," or concentrated essence of exercise; but it is especially in middle life that Sydenham's aphorism holds, that the outside of a horse is the best thing for the inside of a man. Steady going, however, ought to be the rule, and a Bishop's cob is the ideal mount after fifty, except in the case of hunting-men who are as much at home in the saddle as other folks are in a bath-chair. Oliver Wendell Holmes, who, it must not be forgotten, is a doctor, and even an ex-professor of anatomy, as well as a charming writer, speaks with almost Pindaric enthusiasm of riding, during which the liver "goes up and down like the dasher of a churn in the midst of the other vital arrangements," while "the brains also are shaken up like coppers in a money-box." Perhaps the mutual collision of brain cells and "higher centres" may be as stimulating to the intellect as the "shock of minds" in debate. For those who cannot afford horse exercise there is the tricycle, which, as the means of exercise for the middle-aged, has a great future before it. Dr. Oscar Jennings, an English physician practising in Paris, has written a book, "La Santé par le Tricycle," in which he tells how he diminished his circumference, which was beginning to give signs of Falstaffian possibilities, and evicted a host of infirmities by cycling alone without any other forms of exercise. Then there is golf, an ideal game for those whose names are no longer in the scroll of youth; but with writers like Mr. Arthur Balfour and Mr. Andrew Lang to hymn its praises it needs no additional *vates sacer*. To sum up, middle-aged people between, say, thirty-five and fifty-five or sixty, should ride or cycle one hour or walk two hours every day. These exercises may be varied if the opportunity offers by rowing or fencing, but I do not as a rule recommend men over fifty to swim long distances, or, indeed, in these latitudes, to remain for more than a few minutes in the water. I cannot conclude my remarks on middle age without an emphatic word of warning as to the dangerous mistake that is often made by men who rush off to Wales or Switzerland after a year of exhausting brainwork, insufficient exercise, and too probably overfeeding, and straightway proceed to climb the first hillside they come to, or take long fatiguing walks, thus passing at once from a long period of repose to violent exertion with muscles flabby from disuse and a heart utterly unprepared for any sudden call. Can we wonder at the result that often follows ? For those over forty-five there can be no doubt that the best view of a mountain is from its foot. Of course a practised mountaineer like Professor Tyndall, whose muscles have been hardened by many years of climbing, may continue the exercise with impunity up to a comparatively advanced age, but such cases cannot safely be taken as examples by mere "men of mould."

We pass next to old age, and the first question that meets us is : When does old age begin ? Some men are old at forty, whilst others may almost be said to be young at eighty. A man is just as old as his tissues, particularly those of his heart and brain, and there are octogenarians who for mental and even physical volatility might be their own grandsons.

The secret of such perpetual youth lies mostly in regular exercise, whether in felling trees or in the humbler form of the daily "constitutional." Even when life has at last fallen into the sere and yellow leaf, exercise of a kind and amount suited to the "shrunk shanks," stiff joints, brittle bones, and other evidences of senility will keep the furnace of the vital locomotive aglow long after others less carefully stoked have paled their ineffectual fires. But this can only be done (to continue the metaphor) by slackening speed and reducing pressure. If old men will jump hedges as in their salad days they will not improbably do so to a musical accompaniment of snapping thigh bones. If they run to catch trains, their hearts are extremely likely to mark their sense of such an outrage by stopping work ; Dr. Hammond, a distinguished American physician, has collected seventy cases which have occurred in one city during the last ten years of men dying suddenly from running after street cars.

If a man has ridden all his life, he may continue to do so as long as he can sit a horse, otherwise this exercise is too violent for the aged. The "constitutional" is unquestionably the sheet anchor of old age so far as exercise is concerned. I need say nothing more about it than that each walk should be taken with a definite purpose, if it is only to set one's watch by a particular clock. To have an object of some kind makes all the difference between wholesome exercise and the listless dragging about of the dead weight of one's own body which makes walking one of the most fatiguing as well as the dreariest of all forms of motion.

To sum up the whole subject, the golden rule for exercise, through all the seven chapters of man's strange eventful history, is to use it so that the stream of life shall flow swift and clear, never stagnating like a muddy pond, and, on the other hand, never dashing itself to pieces in mere foam and fury.

In the next essay I shall deal with "Training," to which these papers on exercise have been introductory.

EXERCISE AND TRAINING.

Training: Its Bearing on Health.

I.

From Exercise we pass naturally to Training. If the former keeps the physiological instrument in tune, the latter raises it to the athletic concert-pitch. Training is, in fact, the higher education of the body, whereby not only the muscles (which supply the movements) but the great vital motors which govern them—especially the heart and the lungs—are developed to the highest attainable perfection, and drilled to harmonious co-operation with each other.

As there are two kinds of intellectual education — the general, which aims at developing the mental powers all round; and the technical, which fits them for exercise in a special direction—so the body may be trained for general efficiency, or for the performance of a particular feat. In the former case the object aimed at is to increase the working power of the muscles, and to make the lungs and heart capable of adapting themselves readily to conditions of sudden and prolonged strain to which, under ordinary circumstances, they are not subjected —in short, to improve "muscle," "wind," and "staying power." These are the elements which make up what is known in sporting language as "condition," the essential feature of which is not so much mere strength as the power of resisting fatigue. When a man is out of condition his muscles are flabby and overgrown with fat (a physiological weed which flourishes rankly when the garden of the body is left uncultivated), his lungs do not expand to their full capacity, and the nervous centres which control the locomotive apparatus are dull in perception and sluggish in response. The machinery, in fact, is rusty and out of gear from want of use. A man out of training may be able to meet any sudden call on his muscular resources, but he will not be equal to any prolonged exertion. Even in short efforts he has to expend a disproportionate amount of energy in accomplishing what a man in training can do "without turning a hair."

While general training makes the body capable of bearing severe and protracted exercise, special training aims at developing particular groups of muscles, or at giving the power to use the whole strength and weight of the body to the best advantage for a definite purpose, as, for instance, in running, wrestling, rowing; or, again, in fencing and various gymnastic feats, which may be called the fine arts of muscular exercise. General training, in short, supplies a basis of "condition" on which special training rears its superstructure of "form," or whatever else the wise call it; in a word, the former gives strength, the latter skill. That special training by itself does not suffice to fit a man for the performance of a particular feat is shown by experience, which is the only trustworthy guide in such matters. It is generally acknowledged by oarsmen that constant practice in rowing, without any other kind of exercise, is about the worst possible preparation for a boat-race. Frequent handling of the oars will give finish of style, but it will not give the stamina required for the excitement and struggle of a race.

In discussing the details of training, I must again remind the reader that I speak as a doctor and not as an athletic oracle; it is, therefore, their bearing on the maintenance of the health that I am chiefly concerned with. From this point of view it will be convenient, in the first place, to consider the general effects of training. A complete system of training must include not only appropriate muscular exercise, but the regulation of the diet and a strictly disciplined manner of living. The rules of the art, however they may differ in particular points, are all framed with the view of attaining the following objects: First, the removal of superfluous "flesh," or, in plain language, fat; secondly, increase in size and "betterment" in the quality of the muscles; and thirdly, increase of resistance to fatigue, or "staying power." The ground has first of all to be cleared of rubbish, then muscle must be built up, and, lastly, stability must be given to the structure.

The first effect of training is, therefore, to reduce the weight. Sometimes this takes place very rapidly. Dr. R. J. Lee, who has written a valuable little book on the subject,[*] states that a friend of his who was suddenly called upon to take an oar in the Cambridge University boat shortly before the crew came up to Putney, lost a stone in weight in two days—seven pounds each day. The process of reduction is carried out partly by the skin and partly by the lungs. By the increased activity of the former the "too, too solid flesh" literally melts, thaws, and resolves itself into a dew in the form of perspiration, while the ampler draughts of air taken in by the lungs, figuratively speaking, fan the flame of oxidation in which the fat is burnt up. The war against the "flesh" should not, however, be carried on too ruthlessly, or dangerous exhaustion may result. Individual differences of organisation must be taken into account, for there are men whose soundness seems to depend to a certain extent on their fat, as Samson's strength did on his hair; under intelligent training they may make serviceable athletes, but if reduced too far or too fast they "go to pieces."

Reduction in weight is effected by exercise assisted by diet —in fact, by the opposite treatment to that adopted in fattening cattle. The formation of fat is prevented by cutting off the supply of foods which tend to produce it; that is to say, those substances which contain a large proportion of sugar or starch, of which potatoes and pastry may be mentioned as typical examples. Under this *régime* those who resemble Hamlet in being "fat and scant of breath" may in a short

[*] "Exercise and Training: Their Effects upon Health," p. 35. (Smith, Elder and Co., London, 1873.)

time lose their convexity of waist and be able to rival the hero of "The Lady of the Lake," of whom we are told that

> "Right up Ben Lomond would he press,
> Yet not a sigh his toil confess."

In treating of exercise I referred to the development of muscle, which is the result of frequent and systematic use. Of course each muscle has its own limits of growth beyond which it can no more increase than a man can by thinking add a cubit to his stature. But it is not merely the size of the muscle that is augmented; the firmness of its substance, the contractility of its fibre, its freedom from the encumbrance of superfluous fat either on its surface or between the fleshy strands, its alertness and precision in answering the lightest prick of the spur or touch of the rein applied by the will, in short its whole structure and constitution are improved, and its power of effective work magnified tenfold. It is to this improved quality of the muscles that the feeling of "corkiness," which is the surest sign of good "condition," is due; and the clearness of the skin, which is another effect of training, is the result of the increased activity of the glands of the skin and other organs engaged in the removal of waste matters alluded to in a previous article.

The most important effect of training, however, is the development of "staying power." In considering the nature of this quality muscular fatigue must be distinguished from general exhaustion. The former may be experienced apart from the latter after working certain sets of muscles too long or too violently, as in holding a heavy weight out at arm's length. The fatigue in this case is purely local, and, if extreme, is expressed by more or less acute pain in the affected muscles when moved. When a muscle is highly contracted the blood vessels which convey nourishment to it are compressed by the fibres among which they lie. Carlyle quotes a passage from an old Norse Edda about Thor grasping his hammer "till the knuckles grow white." The whiteness here referred to is caused by the absence of blood, which is entirely squeezed out of the part by the strong bending of the joint. This is just what happens in a firmly contracted muscle. The little elastic tubes which convey the blood have their contents pressed out of them ; in this way after a time—greater or less according to the person's condition—the muscle is completely emptied of its blood, and as "the blood is the life" loss of vital energy naturally follows. The pain which is felt in tired-out muscles may be explained by the bloodless condition of the nerves which vitalise them ; it is, in fact, the cry of these living telegraph wires for fresh blood, to quote an old definition of neuralgia.

If local fatigue is due to deprivation of blood, general fatigue is a consequence of want of breath. When all the muscles of the body or a considerable number of them are in a state of violent contraction, as in struggling, a large mass of blood is retarded in its passage in the lungs, and an immense strain is thereby thrown on the heart in its endeavours to overcome the impediment. If the heart cannot pump the blood through the lungs fast enough these organs become overloaded, and a partial block in the circulation ensues. Under these circumstances the blood cannot be purified fast enough and distributed to the parts where it is urgently wanted. The situation is, as politicians say, one of great "tension"—a true physiological crisis which expresses itself to the sufferer's sensations as the "distress," "loss of wind," etc., familiar to athletes out of training. If the crisis were to continue in the acute stage for any length of time, the only solution would be rupture of a blood vessel or stoppage of the heart. Neither of these accidents is, I believe, unknown in human "sporting" annals, but they are much more common among horses which can only protest against being over-ridden by dying. Browning has given a vivid picture of this equine tragedy in "How they brought the Good News from Ghent to Aix." First Dirck's horse falls :—

> "One heard the quick wheeze
> Of her chest, saw the stretched neck and staggering knees,
> And sunk tail and horrible heave of the flank
> As down on her haunches she shuddered and sank."

Then it is the turn of Ioris's steed :—

> "All in a moment his roan
> Rolled neck and croup over, lay dead as a stone.

There is, however, in the organs of the human body a wonderful power of adaptation to circumstances, *if they are given a little time*, and herein lies the grand secret of successful training. *Festina lente* should be the trainer's motto. Exercise must be carefully graduated, and should never be protracted to the point of exhaustion. An interval of perfect rest should follow every exertion. I believe some trainers for foot races allow their man to run the whole course at full speed only once during his period of preparation, and they insist that this exertion shall be followed by a whole day's rest.

Rapid recovery from fatigue is a result of training hardly less valuable than staying power, and where training reaches the dignity of high art is in bringing out the whole muscular capabilities of a man, without ever allowing the circulatory crisis above described to become so severe that the organs involved have any difficulty in recovering themselves. Even the best trained athlete feels fatigue after exertion, but a very short time suffices to restore him to his former vigour. A young friend who recently rowed in the University Boat Race informs me that on reaching the winning-post he felt so utterly exhausted that he could scarcely get out of his boat ; ten minutes or a quarter of an hour later, however, after a shower bath he felt as fresh as if he had taken no part in the contest. If a man remains exhausted for some hours after violent exercise it is a sure sign that training is being pushed beyond his strength.

The general principles of training underlie the preparation for any kind of athletic exercise. In addition to this each sport has its own special code of training rules built up by the experience of shrewd and keenly interested observers. The details of these I must leave to specialists ; I can only touch on a few points in which as a doctor I am particularly interested, and for the sake of convenience I will take rowing as the text of my remarks. There can be no doubt, I think, that much of the harm which used to be laid at the door of rowing was in reality attributable to the injudicious system of training which candidates for aquatic honours had to go through not so very long ago. The rules as regards diet were needlessly Spartan, or, rather, they were more adapted for purely carnivorous animals than for human beings; they caused indigestion and loss of appetite in many cases without any compensating advantages. The boils which used to give rise to so much suffering among crews in training were the direct result of the lowered vitality induced by unsuitable diet. The great truth that in the matter of food hard and fast rules as uncompromising as the laws of the Medes and Persians are unphysiological has at last penetrated the *dura mater* of trainers, and is even beginning to find its way into the medical mind. In some recent essays on food, Sir William Roberts, one of our men of light and leading on this subject, arrives at the conclusion that, after all, the real criterion of the suitability of any particular article of food is to be found in answers to the questions, Do you like it? and Does it agree with you? In fact, the real guide is natural desire tempered by experience. The foregoing remarks refer to the nature of the food taken, but they apply equally to the quantity. As Rabelais says in speaking of Gargantua's supper, "tant en prenoit que lui estoit de besoing à soy entretenir et nourrir. Ce que est la vraye diete prescrite par l'art de bonne et seure medicine quoy qu'un tas de badaux medecins herselés en l'officine des Arabes conseillent le contraire."

As I have already said, however, there are certain things which must be used very sparingly, if at all, in training. Such things as pastry, rich soups and sauces, oily fish, like herring, mackerel, eels, or salmon,* game, pork, and fat

---

* Salmon, which is generally looked upon with suspicion by dietetic authorities, is said by some people to be easily digestible if fresh and properly cooked. Dr. Turnbull, of Coldstream, who by judicious regimen reduced himself from 22 stone to 15 stone 7lb. in about fifteen months, says that salmon is seldom properly boiled, except on the banks of the Tweed, or by those who cook in the way practised there. The fish should be "crimped" as soon as possible after being caught; that is to say, it must be split up lengthwise along the back and then cut crosswise into pieces of such a size as to form a suitable portion for each guest. "When the fish is to be cooked, the water in the fish-kettle, to which twice as much as two conjoined hands can lift of salt has previously been added, is brought to the boil, and the pieces of fish put in, arranged upon the drainer just as they are afterwards to be placed

meat generally, potatoes, beetroot, etc., which have a decided tendency to produce fat, and anything—as for example, cheese—which experience may have shown to be difficult of digestion, should be avoided.

Apart, however, from those things which are directly contra-indicated, considerable latitude may with advantage be allowed in respect both of the nature and the amount of food taken.

I am indebted to an Oxford friend for the following details as to the present system of diet adopted by the young University athletes training for the great aquatic event of the year. On getting up at 7.15 a.m., they take a biscuit and a glass of milk, then they go for a *gentle* walk for a mile. Breakfast, at 8.30, consists of tea or cocoa (two cups at the most), sole, or some other kind of fish, chop, with a poached egg on it, and some green food. No marmalade (for which Oxford men, unless they are much belied, have a weakness) is allowed till two weeks before the race. At luncheon they have cold meat with one glass of beer. At dinner, the *menu* includes fish, chicken, turkey, or joint (always some kind of fresh meat), milk pudding, and stewed fruit (rhubarb by preference); two glasses of beer are allowed, and after dinner one orange and a glass of port may be taken. At 10 p.m. they go to bed. This seems to me a very sensible dietary, with plenty of muscle-forming elements in it, but not too carnivorous. I particularly approve of the breakfast which, though of Homeric abundance, and appalling to a person of indifferent digestion, must give a healthy young man a solid basis of support to begin the day on.

Jackson, Byron's pugilistic guide, philosopher, and friend,

upon the dish. The water is again brought fully to the boiling point, and kept so assiduously by the cook for five minutes. At the termination of that period the fish-kettle is removed from the fire, and the fish taken out upon the drainer. If these details are attended to, the salmon will be boiled to perfection, and will be found not only perfectly digestible but possessing a delicacy of flavour not brought out by any other method. To boil salmon whole, as is frequently done, is simply to do an injustice both to the fish and to the person who is to partake of it."—*Edinburgh Med. and Surg. Journal.*

and a famous trainer of prize-fighters, used to begin training on a clear foundation by a little preliminary physicking. He fed his men principally on beef and mutton, the lean of fat meat being preferred; veal, lamb, and pork he rightly held to be less digestible. Fish he thought a "watery kind of diet," suitable for those who wish to sweat themselves down. Stale bread was the only vegetable food allowed. The quantity of fluid permitted was three and a-half pints a day, but fermented liquors were absolutely forbidden. Two full meals with a light supper were usually taken. The amount of exercise was very great, as indeed it had need to have been in order to work off the waste products of so much animal food. The great defect of this system is the proscription of vegetables, and it is only within comparatively recent times that this pernicious superstition has been finally got rid of. I do not, however, suppose that, with the amount of exercise Jackson made his pupils undergo, the want of vegetables did much real harm. The Guachos of South America, who almost pass their lives in the saddle, and who lead a life of constant activity resembling that of a carnivorous animal, scarcely ever taste anything but beef; it should be added, however, that, as Darwin tells us, they do not eat largely even of that. Sir Francis Head relates that for many weeks together, while riding in the Pampas, he ate nothing whatever but beef very roughly cooked, and though at the same time he endured an immense amount of fatigue he never felt exhausted. Great as are the virtues of beefsteak, however, there are many men whom a too carnivorous diet does not suit, and in such cases Nature is a better guide than all the trainers, and, I may add, than all the physicians in the world. In connection with this subject it cannot be too clearly understood that men can grow into full strength and can maintain the most vigorous physique on any diet from which the food-stuffs necessary for the proper nourishment of the body can be extracted in sufficient quantity. As Dr. Parkes says,* formerly throughout the north of England and Scotland there were successive generations of some of the finest men in the

---

* "The Personal Care of Health," p. 19.

world who lived on oatmeal and milk, and on the opposite side of the globe we find the splendid races of Northern India living on barley, wheat, millet, and rice. "The Roman gladiator trained on barley, and the Roman soldier in campaigns when meat could not be got carried corn, which he ground in handmills, and then boiled in water, and made a strong vegetable soup, something like the old English fermenty. On this food he marched and conquered as no other race has done." In spite of this, I do not think that young Englishmen, especially of the class which supplies University oarsmen, would care to train on barley; they will probably think that meat is good enough for them.

It is now, I understand, generally admitted that though it is well to limit the amount of liquid taken during training, it is quite possible for a man to get himself into excellent condition without undergoing the tortures of unsatisfied thirst. In this respect, also, the Oxford system is in harmony with the principles of physiology and the dictates of common-sense. There can be no harm in a glass or two of sound ale or a little light wine such as hock or claret at dinner. The glass of port afterwards I confess I think unnecessary as long as the training process is well borne. If, however, a man shows any sign of falling into the state known as "overtrained," that is to say, when the reducing process is too rapid or too severe, a little port or dry champagne at meals may be found beneficial. Spirits should be strictly abstained from, as they tend to prevent the elimination of carbonic acid. Excessive drinking of water, or of gaseous mineral waters, should on no account be indulged in; but I do not think that any harm can be done by drinking a moderate amount of water immediately after exercise. Although this is contrary to the general view, physicians and physiologists have for some time recognized its truth. The fallacy is still, unfortunately, acted on in dealing with horses, the poor beasts being often driven quickly in hot weather without being allowed even a mouthful of water. In India, where the natives are devoted to their horses, water without stint is allowed, and this is also true of the Cape of Good Hope, and no evil results have, so far as I know, been seen to ensue.

The solace of an occasional pipe or cigar would probably not be hurtful, but trainers are unanimous in forbidding tobacco in any form. The cause of their attitude in this matter is no doubt the fear that moderation might lead to excess; and, convinced as I am of the deplorable effects of over-indulgence in smoking on steadiness and precision of muscular movement, I cannot say that I feel surprised at the apprehensions of trainers.

With respect to clothing, there is nothing particular to say, except that belts and all supports of the kind should, if possible, be dispensed with; surgeons are almost unanimous in condemning them as having a tendency indirectly to cause rupture. The clothing should be loose, especially about the chest and abdomen, and anything that compresses the diaphragm (lower part of the ribs) is a distinct hindrance to active exercise. The American cowboy, I believe, controls his bucking horse by cording tightly with a girth the abdominal muscles over the expanding flanks, thus limiting the action of the diaphragm, and making great leaps impossible. This, I imagine, "Buck Taylor" and his comrades do by the light of nature; but if they had been professors of anatomy and riding combined, they could not have hit on a more effective device.

With regard to sleep, I thoroughly agree with Dr. Lee that the duration of it "must be left entirely to the demands of the system, and should not be interrupted, however long it may continue." There is, perhaps, no surer sign of health than the capacity of sleeping soundly for several hours on end. It is not only the ravelled sleeve of care that is knit up by sleep, but the worn tissues have time to recover themselves, and on waking the system is like a watch that has been wound up. It is not so much the quantity of sleep that is important as the quality; and if there is a certain amount of truth in the old saying that one hour before midnight is worth two after, it is because in healthy persons the first sleep is usually sounder than any that follows. An excellent sign of good "condition" is complete recuperation after short sleep, that is to say, the power of waking refreshed after six, or even five, hours of good sleep. This shows that the system easily recovers itself after fatigue ; and this is one of the physical characteristics that most help to prolong life. Among a number of centenarians mentioned by Sir George Humphry, this quality of being fully refreshed by comparatively short sleep was present in a very large proportion. On the other hand, there is no surer sign of overwork than disturbed sleep, and this symptom in a man under training should always be looked on with suspicion.

Coming next to exercise during training, though the subject is not one on which I can speak with special authority, I would, on general principles, deprecate rigid uniformity in this not less than in diet. The exercises should be as far as possible adapted to the individual, and it is very important that they should be varied in character. Thus, if running a certain distance before breakfast "takes too much out of" a man, let walking be substituted ; in no case should the exercise be at all violent or prolonged before the morning meal. The exercise during the day should consist in short spells of gymnastic practice, or games such as fives, or swimming, besides the particular exercise required by the contest for which the man is being trained ; but, as already said, in no case should exercise of any kind be pushed to the point of exhaustion. A good part of each day should be spent in physical repose (I do not mean sleep), and it is a good plan to allow a day of relaxation from time to time. One thing which I consider very important is that the mind should also be as far as possible at rest, while the body is undergoing training.

In regard to rowing in particular, the Oxford plan seems well adapted for its purpose. For the sake of variety the practice takes place in three different localities; first at Oxford, then at Cookham, or some place farther down the river than Oxford, and lastly at Putney. At Oxford the programme consists of a long row in the afternoon, six or seven miles down the river and back ; occasionally, however, a trot home is substituted for the return journey. While at Cookham the crew go out for a morning row at eleven ; this consists of a short spin and "tubbing." In the afternoon there is a long row, the crew getting back in time for dinner. They often go out for a stroll at nine, apparently more with the view of keeping themselves awake than by way of exercise. At Putney everything is much the same as at Cookham. If the men are a little stale, however, or "off their feed," instead of the afternoon row they go for a ride. The training lasts some six or seven weeks. As my Oxonian informant points out, the old ideas of absolute rigidity in training are now quite obsolete as regards exercise not less than diet, and, what is of special importance, much more attention is paid to the requirements of individual cases than formerly. The young oarsman whom I have already quoted tells me that he never felt so well in his life as during the six weeks before the race; he felt, as he expresses it, as if he had no body at all! With regard to Cambridge, I have no such details as those I have obtained from Oxford; but I had occasion a few years ago to collect a considerable amount of information on this subject from the various colleges, and I was struck by the same wholesome elasticity in their rules which is so conspicuous in those of Oxford.

To sum up, the effects of training are increased size, firmness, and contractility of muscle, a peculiar feeling of freedom and lightness of the limbs, and especially the power of enduring severe and prolonged exertion without exhaustion, and of recovering rapidly from fatigue. The skin becomes clear and does not "bruise" easily; wounds heal quickly, and the effects of injury disappear with marvellous rapidity. All this shows that the body is at its maximum of health. But the effects of training are not confined to the body; the mind shares in the general well-being of the economy, and gains in clearness and vigour. As Falstaff said of sherris-sack, training "ascends me into the brain; dries me there all the foolish and dull and crudy vapours which environ it;" the condition, in short, is an ideal one of *mens sana in corpore sano*.

EXERCISE AND TRAINING.

Training: Its Bearing on Health.

II.

The moral discipline involved in a proper system of training must not be lost sight of. It is no exaggeration to say that obedience to lawful authority, self-restraint, self-sacrifice, tenacity of purpose, and loyal co-operation with others towards a common end—in short, most of the virtues which make a good man and a public-spirited citizen — are fostered by training.

An excellent form of training is found in military drill, which, unlike the mere preparation for athletic feats, aims at bringing the body into a permanent state of physical efficiency. Dr. Parkes speaks with enthusiasm of "the results of drills and gymnasia on weedy recruits of seventeen or eighteen years of age." "I have known," he says,* "a young man grow four inches between seventeen and twenty-two, and develop into a splendid man, which would never have been the case had he not enlisted." All competent authorities agree that if the drill-sergeant has fair material to work upon, and if his zeal is occasionally tempered by the discretion of the medical officer, the increase in height, weight, and chest-girth is very marked in young recruits, especially during the first few months after enlistment. The guiding principle in the military training of recruits is the same as in purely athletic training,

* "On the Personal Care of Health," p. 13.

and is expressed in the familiar proverb which tells us that Rome was not built in a day. Everything must be done by degrees, and failure is certain to follow the attempt to hurry the slow but steady processes of nature. The recruit must be trained well within his powers of endurance at first, and the work should be very gradually increased, so that the heart and lungs may have time to adapt themselves to meet the increased strain to which they are subjected.

From time to time cries of alarm are raised as to the supposed physical decadence of Englishmen. The agricultural districts are being depleted by a constant stream of migration to the large centres of population, and the effects of town life are already clearly legible in the stunted frames of the adolescents of the labouring and lower middle classes, and they are certain to show themselves more and more in succeeding generations. To put the case somewhat roughly, muscle is dying out, and nerves are taking its place. What is the remedy for this decline and fall of English manhood, which must inevitably in time thrust our country from its pride of place among the nations? How are the undergrown young artisans and the pale, narrow-chested clerks to be rescued from the physical degeneration which is threatening not only them but their offspring? I answer, by the saving ministry of the drill-sergeant. Of course I am fully aware that the very name of compulsory military service is hateful to free-born Britons, but have we not a very fair equivalent ready to our hands? If proper encouragement were given to the Volunteer system, and if our citizen soldiers, instead of being alternately snubbed and even more offensively patronized by the military authorities, were helped and stimulated in every way to make themselves efficient, we should hear less of the decay of our national thews and sinews. A proper system of drill and such an amount of voluntary military service as need not interfere with other avocations would, I am convinced, be the means of regenerating, morally as well as physically, a large proportion of the "submerged tenth" and the scarcely less miserable social strata just above it. Of the results, both to body and character, of military training there cannot be a better proof than the far-reaching effects which have already been produced by the Volunteer movement ; and in the fullest possible extension of that movement lies our best hope of continuing to justify the words of Goldsmith :—

> "Pride in their port, defiance in their eye,
> I see the lords of humankind pass by."

Having laid so much stress in previous essays on the advantages of exercise and training, it behoves me now to utter a few words of warning as to the dangers of wrong methods of physical education, and even of right methods injudiciously applied. In connection with this subject it will also be convenient to discuss the evils of immoderate indulgence in athletic exercises. A few years ago there was a great outcry as to the injurious effects which "athleticism" was alleged to have, not only on the body, but on the mind and character of its devotees. The late Mr. Skey, a surgeon of repute in his day, made parents and guardians feel very uncomfortable by his denunciations of athletic contests generally, and of the University Boat Race in particular; and Mr. Wilkie Collins bettered the instruction by depicting (in "Man and Wife") the typical athlete as a brutal ruffian with the thews, and also the tastes, intellect, and language, of a coalheaver. That there was a certain basis of truth in Mr. Skey's statements no one competent to judge of such matters will deny ; but, as usual, the sensational writers spoilt the case by absurd exaggerations which brought the perfectly sound doctrine they were meant to enforce into contempt. The attacks of calmer and better informed critics, however, gradually led to a radical reform in the whole theory and practice of athletics. Many of the evils formerly attributed to such exercises were seen to be really due to wrong methods of training ; at the present day, as has already been said, the most successful trainers are much more ready to listen to the advice of medical men than was the case some years ago, and consequently the evil effects of athleticism are less apparent than they used to be.

Any system of bodily discipline is likely to be hurtful : first, if it is begun at too early an age ; secondly, if it is too severe or too prolonged; thirdly, if, owing to special circumstances, it is unsuitable to the person subjected to it. Under these three heads all the evils which may be caused by training are comprised; but it must of course be borne in mind that there are innumerable individual peculiarities of constitution and conformation which have to be taken into account. It can hardly be wondered at, therefore, that, even with the light of medical science to guide them, the most experienced trainers occasionally make mistakes.

Nothing like systematic training should ever be attempted before the growth of the body is nearly complete, except in the case of acrobats, where sacrifices must be made and risks run. During adolescence, while the limbs and organs are in process of active development, the whole available stock of vital energy is required to meet the immediate wants of the growing organism. There is a fundamental difference between adolescents and adults in this, that though the former may be actually the stronger men as far as muscle is concerned, they have much less staying power than the latter; growing lads, in fact, having no assets to avert physiological bankruptcy when there is any extraordinary call on their physical resources, while fully developed men in good health have always a considerable balance in their favour. The difference is well illustrated by the way in which seasoned soldiers bear the fatigues and privations of a campaign as compared with young recruits. The "gaunt men of thirty," to use the words of Sir Henry Havelock, win battles by sheer power of marching where weedy youngsters would fall fainting by the wayside. It is obvious that athletic training, which, especially at the outset, is a reducing process, cannot safely be undergone by bodies in a transition stage which of itself makes the heaviest demands on the vital powers.

If training is begun at too early an age the development of the body, so far from being promoted, is too likely to be prematurely arrested thereby. Growing lads who have to do work beyond their strength often become stunted in stature, and it has been observed in French *lycées* that boys have stopped growing at as early an age as twelve in consequence of excessive practice in the gymnasium. Not only is the growth interfered with, but deformity and even disease frequently result from premature over-use of the muscles. During adolescence the bones are soft and spongy; they are to a considerable extent composed of gristle rather than solid osseous material, and the different parts of which they consist are imperfectly welded together. They may not inaptly be compared to a wall in course of building where the mortar is not yet dry. Moreover, young bones have a relatively large amount of blood in them: they are in fact in a state of congestion which makes them prone to inflammation from comparatively slight causes, as a building containing a large quantity of combustible material is liable to be set on fire by a trifling accident. This physiological congestion of the bones is particularly marked in the neighbourhood of joints, and it is accordingly in these parts that mischief is most likely to arise. Given the conditions which I have described, it is easy to understand how curvature of the spine, bruising of delicate tissues, bleeding into the interior of joints, inflammation, abscess, and even partial disintegration of bones, with many other evils, often follow muscular efforts too severe for the imperfectly consolidated framework of a growing body.

In addition to what has been said about the damage to bones and ligaments, it must be borne in mind that in adolescents the vital organs, such as the heart and the lungs, are also in course of active growth, and often find it difficult to keep pace with the increasing demands made on them by the rapidly developing organism. If under these circumstances a lad is taken and put through a severe course of training, can it be wondered at if the overtaxed heart should become unable to meet its liabilities, or the lungs should give way under the strain (as by rupture of a blood vessel or overstretching, with consequent loss of elasticity of their air cells)?

From what has been stated it will, I think, be clear that too early training of growing lads is something worse than a physiological crime; it is a stupid and shortsighted mistake, which in ninety-nine per cent. of the cases in which it is attempted defeats its own purpose, and, even in the few instances in which the immediate object in view is attained, often leaves a legacy of mischief the effects of which make themselves felt later on.

When, then, it will be asked, is it safe to begin training? The answer is, when growth is so far complete as to make the body able to bear the extra strain put on its resources by the increased work it has to do under training. Before the eighteenth year, the shafts of the limb bones are not fully ossified, and it is not till a somewhat later period that the upper and lower portions of these bones, which develop separately, become firmly soldered to the shaft. Even after that, growth still goes on, and the bony framework of the body is not fully consolidated till between the twenty-fifth and thirtieth years. The heart, lungs, and other organs do not attain their full development till about the same period, the greatest progressive growth taking place between the eighteenth and twenty-fifth years. From these data it may be concluded that no severe course of athletic training should ever be undergone before the age of eighteen at least, and no prolonged effort requiring endurance as well as muscular strength, such as rowing in the University Boat Race, or the long marches and other fatigues of a campaign, should be undertaken before twenty. Even at that age rapid training for an athletic contest of any severity should not be undergone without a warranty of soundness having first been obtained from a medical man.

The mention of campaigning in connection with the subject under consideration naturally suggests certain reflections as to the present condition of our army. Speaking, as I do, merely as a doctor, I do not expect the military authorities to listen to me—they have disregarded the advice of far more competent counsellors,—and I touch on the subject here only because I think it a public duty to do so. Perhaps by constant "pegging away," to use General Grant's historic phrase, some impression may in time be made on the official mind, which has shown itself even more than usually unreceptive in this matter.

At present, as all medical men who are acquainted with the

condition of the army are agreed, a very large majority of recruits are too young to make really useful soldiers. There is no higher authority on all that concerns the physique of the soldier than Sir W. Aitken, the distinguished Professor of Pathology in the Army Medical School at Netley, and he assures us that the British Army is at present made up to a great extent of "boy-soldiers," a very large proportion of whom "have not, at the time of their enlistment, reached their maturity of growth nor complete development as regards the bones, the muscles, and the internal solid organs of their bodies, especially the heart, lungs, liver, and kidneys." It is demonstrable that this physical immaturity most seriously affects the efficiency of these lads as soldiers, both as regards staying power, and as regards predispositions beyond the average of civilians of the same age to certain diseases. I can only echo the words of the late Dr. Parkes, who may almost be called the father of military hygiene, when he says: "There is no doubt that to send young lads of eighteen to twenty into the field is not only a lamentable waste of material but is positive cruelty. At that age such soldiers, as Napoleon said, merely strew the roadsides and fill the hospitals. The most effective armies have been those in which the youngest soldiers have been twenty-two years of age." Fortunately we have had nothing but "little wars" on our hands for many years, or the truth of these remarks would no doubt have received some mournful illustrations.

Even in our conflict with savages, however, the *personnel* of our army has not always in these latter days shown to great advantage. I am afraid poor old Cetewayo's warriors, or the fanatical spearmen of the Soudan, would have made short work of the weedy boys—how different from the "bold yeomen whose limbs were made in England" who in old days did battle for their country's honour!—whom we sent out against them, if they had fought on anything like equal terms. I am not decrying the poor lads, who did their best, and at any rate knew how to die as heroically as the most seasoned veterans. They had plenty of pluck; it was not their fault that they were deficient in stamina. It is devoutly to be hoped, however, that

our altars and hearths may have stronger arms than these to
defend them if we are ever again engaged in a great European
war.

For the boyishness of our army I believe that Lord Wolseley
is largely responsible. "Our Only General" has always shown
himself somewhat intolerant and even contemptuous of medical
advice and of those whose business it is to offer it, though
probably no one knows better than he does that it is to the
doctors that he is indebted for most of his victories. He has
indeed found his laurels in the medicine chest rather than on
the tented field. Lord Wolseley says : "Give me young men ;
they do what they are bid, and they go where they are told."
Therein he differs from Napoleon, who said after the disastrous
battle of Leipzig : "I must have grown men." I dare say it is
true enough that "boy-soldiers" will go where they are told
when their legs are strong enough to carry them there, but
there is not a shadow of doubt that but for medical skill and
medical equipments, such as have never been available on the
battlefields at any previous period of the world's history, Lord
Wolseley's beardless warriors would have perished like flies in
the deserts of the Soudan.

The foregoing remarks refer in the main to active service,
but every word that has been said about the evils of athletic
training at too early an age applies also to military drill, which
is indeed a particularly elaborate and prolonged system of
training. It is desirable, therefore, either that recruits should
not be taken under twenty years of age, or if taken earlier they
should not be subjected to the ordinary system of drill in all
its severity till their frames are sufficiently well knit. The
Duke of Cambridge, I believe, has several times said that it is
impracticable to get recruits to enlist at twenty or twenty-one.
If that is the case let them be taken at eighteen or thereabouts,
and let them pass through a period of probation for two years,
till it can be seen whether they are likely to make efficient
soldiers. During that time let their strength be developed by
judicious training, the exercises being carefully graduated
according to their power of endurance, and the whole process
being carried out under medical supervision. I entirely agree

with Dr. Parkes, whose opinion was expressed in the following words: "If the State will recognize the immaturity of the recruit of eighteen years of age, and will proportion his training and his work to his growth, and will abstain from considering him fit for the heavy duties of peace and for the emergencies of war till he is at least twenty years of age, then it would seem that there is not only no loss but a great gain by enlisting men early."* The amount and quality of training, in short, must be strictly adapted to the bodily development of the recruit, and, above all, the process must be a *gradual* one; any attempt to hurry the work of nature can only end in failure or disaster.

* "Hygiene," sixth ed., p. 529.

EXERCISE AND TRAINING.

Training: Its Bearing on Health.

III.

THE injurious effects of premature work and training are seen in horses even more conspicuously than in men. Every horse-breeder knows that a young horse put too early to work will in all probability not grow to the size of its compeers which are left unharnessed till they are fully developed. Moreover, the bones and ligaments are very apt to yield under the strain which they are not firm enough to resist, and the result is seen in the establishment of that generally dilapidated and tumble-down appearance known as "standing over." The reason why so many of the London cab horses, especially those between the shafts of four-wheelers, look when standing on the rank as if they must inevitably fall on their knees, is not so much that they are underbred as that they are overdriven when only three or four years old. Too early training for the racecourse is even more pernicious than premature draught work. The waste of magnificent horseflesh entailed by races for two-year-olds must be a source of regret not unmixed with indignation to all those who have at heart the improvement of our breed of horses. It is hardly an exaggeration to say that these races ruin nine-tenths of our thoroughbred horses before they reach maturity, and it would be well if they were altogether abolished. The greatest amount of mischief is done when two-year-old racing commences very early in the year. An attempt was made some years ago to induce the Jockey Club to pass a rule that no two-year-old race should take place before a certain date. There was, I believe, a considerable preponderance of opinion among the members in favour of the proposal, but it was abandoned in deference to the remonstrances of the people living in the towns where the earliest races take place, who contended that the new arrangement would prevent their fixtures finding a place in the Racing Calendar.

Of course there are "infant prodigies" in the equine as in the human species, and two-year-old horses have won races as Napoleon won victories at an age when ordinary men have hardly left college. To cite only two instances which occur to me, The Bard won the earliest two-year-old race in the year at Lincoln, and won fifteen other races as a two-year-old, being only just beaten for the Derby by Ormonde. Donovan also won the earliest two-year-old race of the year, and afterwards got all the great races both as a three- and as a four-year-old. Exceptional cases like these, however, cannot be taken as disproving the teaching of experience with regard to the majority of young horses. The mischief done by too early training, and the barbarous treatment often employed to counteract its evil effects, cannot be better described than in the words of a great veterinary authority, Professor Varnell, which I need make no apology for quoting: "Many young horses are trained when not more than a year and a half old, and a large proportion of them are thereby lamed for life. Their joints become diseased, their ligaments and terdons strained, and their bones and the membranes covering them inflamed. In this condition they are placed in the hands of the veterinary surgeon, very often with a peremptory order to fire and blister the affected limbs. Instances are not unknown when only one leg is affected for a request to fire the opposite one also, on the supposition that it would be strengthened by the operation. If the suggestion is acted on, the poor animal's legs are canterised with the hot iron, and he is again handed over to the trainers. Such a horse might stand the training, but in all probability he would break down in the first race he ran."

Another source of danger in training is the exhausting nature of the process if injudiciously carried out. If the amount or kind of work prescribed is such as to cause serious and lasting fatigue, a condition of "over-pressure" is induced which is not only a real disease in itself, but a possible predisposing cause of graver ailments. Physiology teaches us that the contraction of muscle is attended with the production of various chemical substances, such as carbonic acid, lactic acid, urea, creatin, sugar, phosphates, etc. In the normal state these waste matters—the ashes of the fire of life—are easily got rid of by the kidneys, lungs, and other organs which play the part of *dustmen* to the economy. The greater the work done the larger, naturally, is the amount of waste matters produced; and if work is increased beyond a certain point the physiological dustbin becomes full faster than it can be emptied. In that case the waste matters accumulate in the muscles and give rise to the feeling of fatigue; indeed, fatigue can be artificially induced by injecting into the muscles of a perfectly fresh animal an "extract" of the muscles of another that is tired out. In healthy persons a comparatively short period of rest suffices for the removal of the waste matters, and fatigue disappears. It may be said here that this happy result is much assisted by allowing athletes a sufficient amount of sleep, as, in addition to the repose afforded to the muscles thereby, there is during sleep much less formation of the poisonous materials that cause fatigue than in the waking state. Hence sleep is a particularly favourable condition for the "working off" of the poisons generated during exercise. If, however, the work to be done is too severe, or too prolonged, the elimination of waste matters cannot keep pace with their production, the system becomes saturated with them, and "auto-intoxication" results, the man being in truth poisoned by materials of his own manufacture. The dose may be sufficient to cause death, as in the case reported by Dr. Bertherand of two native runners in Algiers, who died immediately after having run respectively 192 kilometres in 45 hours and 252 kilometres in 62 hours. On examination of the bodies nothing was found beyond the ordinary signs of excessive fatigue (intense blackness of the blood owing to deficient aëration, great softening and discoloration of the muscles, extravasation of blood in various parts of the skin and mucous membranes, with extremely rapid decomposition). It is well known that the flesh of animals which have died in a state of great exhaustion has a very disagreeable smell and taste, and putrefies very quickly ; if eaten it is likely to cause symptoms of poisoning. Instances of this, I believe, sometimes occur among the inmates of Spanish poorhouses, to whom the carcases of the bulls killed in the bullfights are sometimes handed over ; so bad, however, is the flesh of the animals after the terrible struggle they have gone through, that even the hungriest pauper will often refuse to eat it. It is now coming to be recognised that many of the cases of so-called "sun-stroke" among soldiers on the march are really due to the auto-intoxication by waste products which I have described.

I have said that fatigue, if excessive and prolonged, may sometimes rise to the dignity of a disease, and indeed so severe are the symptoms which it may induce that it has more than once been mistaken for typhoid fever. Moreover, the general prostration of the vital powers which constitutes the condition of "over-pressure" (of which fatigue is only the indicative sensation as hunger is of inanition) makes the system much less able than it normally is to resist the attacks of any microbes that may be going about seeking whom they may devour. It is thought by some experienced observers that this may possibly be a factor of some importance in the well-known liability of soldiers to typhoid fever. In the case of an outbreak of that disease in barracks, the blame is always laid on the sanitary conditions of the buildings, and no doubt generally with perfect justice. Still instances have been known in which, after the drains had undergone a solemn sanitary lustration and the whole arsenal of scientific disinfectants had been exhausted in vain, the epidemic has ceased as if by enchantment on the commanding officer being replaced by a less exacting disciplinarian. How large a part in the production of these epidemics is played by excessive drill, forced marches, etc., cannot be definitely stated, but it is certainly considerable, and it is well known that young soldiers not yet broken to fatigue are particularly prone to be attacked by typhoid fever.

The danger arising from the fatigue during training can, to a large extent, be avoided by making the process very gradual. Fatigue, as has been said, is a poison; but by judicious management tolerance can be established exactly as in the case of many other poisons, as, for example, tobacco, opium, and arsenic. Habit will make a man able to bear without the least distress an amount of fatigue which only a short time before would have utterly disabled him; but the habit can only be acquired by degrees, and at first especially by advancing from step to step very cautiously.

I can touch but very lightly on the evil effects which too severe a course of training may have on the heart. Most doctors are familiar with the "irritable heart" of young athletes and soldiers; the pulse is rapid and irregular with some amount of palpitation, showing that the circulatory apparatus has been somewhat over-strained. Another symptom often observed in athletes—notably, I believe, in the wrestlers of Cumberland—is a peculiar slowness of the heart's action. Signs of heart failure are common in over-worked recruits; they suffer from shortness of breath, with discomfort and pain about the region of the heart, even on slight exertion. They become languid and are easily tired and liable to attacks of faintness. The symptoms are due to the increase in the size of the heart not keeping pace with the greater amount of work demanded of it. "Setting up" drill, owing to the forced bulging out of the chest which it involves, is a fertile source of such troubles. Fortunately the remedy in most cases is simple and certain. The zeal of the drill-sergeant must be moderated by the discretion of the doctor; exercise must be carefully regulated so as to keep well within the limits of the man's powers of endurance, and, above all, a due amount of rest must be allowed to the over-strained heart. This rest is best obtainable by lying down and keeping perfectly quiet for a couple of hours in the middle of the day. In all young soldiers and athletes the heart should be carefully watched so that work may be discontinued or considerably lightened at the first sign of inefficiency. Another thing that must be kept under close supervision is the variation in weight that takes place under training. If a man, after the initial process of reduction has disencumbered him of his superfluous tissue, continues progressively to lose weight in spite of adequate feeding and careful regulation of the work which he has to do, it is probable that he will never make an efficient soldier or athlete.

With regard to the danger of training arising from peculiarities of constitution or conformation in the person subjected to it, all that need be said here is that the very first thing to be aimed at by the trainer or the drill-sergeant is the elimination of the unfit. No one, as has already been said, should be allowed to go into training until he has been examined by an experienced medical man and found to be free, not only from actual disease, but from recognizable seeds of future mischief. Persons with disease or notable weakness of the heart; or with marked delicacy of the lungs, or even a distinct tuberculous inheritance; or with rupture or any tendency thereto; or who are so fat that the reducing process will have to be exceptionally severe; or who are suffering or ever have suffered from chronic disease of any bone or joint— all, in short, who have any "weak spot" in their bodily equipment, should be uncompromisingly rejected.

On the whole, however, while it would be unwise to shut one's eyes to dangers of premature training and excessive exercise, it would be still more foolish to exaggerate them. By weeding out the weaklings in the first place, and by carefully tempering the wind to the shorn lamb, so to speak, in the case of those actually under training, there is practically little danger of any real harm being done. The best rule of conduct for both trainer and those undergoing training is embodied in Talleyrand's counsel to young diplomatists: "Surtout, messieurs, pas trop de zèle." Obedience to this golden maxim will, with the help of medical advice as a controlling or at least a sanctioning agency, effectually prevent most of the evils which have been mentioned.

Sensible trainers and athletes can afford to laugh at the sweeping statements that are still made from time to time as to the ruinous effects of exercise and training on the majority of those who find pleasure in the use and development of the strength with which Nature has endowed them. To read such denunciations, one would think man was made to spend the days of his youth in a bath-chair, with a maiden aunt at his elbow to keep the wind of heaven from visiting his cheek too roughly. When one reads in an American newspaper that "of the thirty-two all-round athletes in a New York club of five years ago, three are dead of consumption, five have to wear trusses, four or five are lop-shouldered, and three have catarrh and partial deafness," or sees Dr. Patton, chief surgeon of the National Soldiers' Home at Dayton, Ohio, quoted as saying that of the 5,000 soldiers in that institution "fully 80 per cent. are suffering from heart disease in one form or another, due to the forced physical exertions of the campaigns," one can only suppose, either that the statements go considerably beyond the strict limit of truth, or that our Anglo-Saxon race has lost some of its native toughness by transplantation to the other side of the Atlantic. Even if the 5,000 soldiers are all invalids, and the proportion of heart disease among them is really as large as it is said to be, it would, I imagine, be as difficult to prove as it is easy to assert that this was altogether due to campaigning. Before admitting this, one would like to know a good deal more about the ages and personal habits of these afflicted veterans.

From vague statements of the kind referred to one need only appeal to accurate statistics collected by competent authorities. No form of athletic exercise has been more fiercely condemned as the source of all kinds of physical evil than the University Boat Race, and yet on dispassionate examination the greater part of the indictment fades away in the light of truth like the baseless fabric of a vision. Some years ago Dr. J. E. Morgan, of Manchester, himself formerly captain of his College boat, instituted a series of painstaking inquiries among all the oarsmen who had rowed in the University Boat Race between 1829 and 1869, extending his inquiries among their relatives and friends, with the view of determining what effect that contest and the training preparatory thereto had had on their health and longevity. He found that out of a total of 294 only seventeen either described themselves or were spoken of by their friends—in some instances with very considerable reservation—as having suffered more or less from their labours. By careful analysis of these cases, however, Dr. Morgan found that in several of them the evil was in all probability unconnected with rowing, whilst in others it was directly traceable to the fact that the men had rowed when "stale" from over-training, or when unfit for such an exertion owing to illness. A few seemed to have suffered not so much from rowing as from discontinuance of the exercise, and more or less sudden subsidence into a sedentary life. It is worthy of note that in only two or three cases was the heart the organ that was supposed to have been damaged, and in one of these cases the heart was known to have been affected before rowing had been much indulged in, while in another the patient himself attributed his condition to his having trained and rowed too young. Several of the men were consumptive, and it was not likely rowing shortened their lives. That the alleged baneful effects of the great boat race are absurdly exaggerated is proved by some elaborate actuarial calculations by which Dr. Morgan demonstrates that, judging from past experience, University oarsmen have in point of fact a longer expectation of life than other people. It is interesting to note that of a total of thirty-nine deaths which occurred in the period of forty years over which his inquiry extends, only 7·4 per cent. were due to heart affections, whilst the mortality from lung disease was also greatly below the average. Among the whole number of oarsmen there was no single example of any of those rapidly fatal forms of heart disease (rupture of valves, aneurism, etc.) which every hospital physician meets with from time to time in men whose occupation involves much muscular effort. In only two cases was rupture of a blood-vessel caused by rowing in the boat race. Dr. Morgan sums up the results of his inquiry as follows : *

* "University Oars," p. 41. Macmillan and Co., London, 1873.

"From these statistics it appears that 115 (or 39 per cent. of the whole) were benefited by their exertions, 162 (or 55 per cent.) were in no way injured, while seventeen (or about 6 per cent.) refer to themselves, or are spoken of by their friends, as having sustained that amount of injury" which, as already said, on close analysis turns out to be open to considerable doubt.

The results of Dr. Morgan's accurate investigation ought to settle this question once for all. It establishes the very thesis for which I have been contending, viz. that whilst training and exercise pursued with reasonable precautions are beneficial to the great majority of men, they are undoubtedly injurious in a few exceptional cases. The mistake made by the thorough-going opponents of athleticism is in mourning over the candidate for muscular fame who breaks down under training, and refusing to be comforted by the thought of the ninety-nine who flourish under it. So blinded are these well-meaning people by prejudice that I have actually seen Dr. Morgan's figures quoted in several quarters as a striking proof of the disastrous effect of the University Boat Race. The seventeen "victims" are cited, but not a word is said about the remaining two hundred and seventy-seven! This is an abuse of statistics similar to that which we are so well accustomed to in the case of fanatical temperance advocates, anti-vaccinators, "et hoc genus omne."

The truth, as usual, lies between the two extremes, but if I were compelled to choose between rampant athleticism and what I may call the bath-chair theory of muscular life, I should unhesitatingly prefer the former as being on the whole less hurtful to the individual and to the race.

INFLUENZA.

When influenza once more appeared among us towards the close of 1889 it was at first looked upon by most people rather as a convenient means of escape from troublesome engagements or a decent pretext for a few days' rest—tempered perhaps by French novels—than as a serious disease. Amid the number of new maladies which medical science has in recent years added to the catalogue of human ills, influenza had been almost forgotten, and the present generation knew little about it, except by tradition. Now that its power for mischief has been unpleasantly brought home to most of us, there is some risk of the danger being unduly magnified. Influenza at its worst hardly reaches the dignity of a pestilence, and I confess it does not seem to me to be worthy of the spiritual steel of the Bishop of Lincoln. Like Mistress Quickly, I hope there is no need to trouble ourselves with any such thoughts yet. It would, however, be a grievous error to despise influenza too much, for, if the disorder is comparatively trifling in itself, it is serious, and even formidable, in its possible consequences. All past experience shows that epidemics of influenza have been accompanied by a great increase of the ordinary death-rate; the disease, though killing few with its own hand, seems to sharpen the dart of other ailments. In persons weakened by chronic disease or unsound in constitution—especially when the flaw is in the lungs or the heart—an attack of influenza often quickens the smouldering embers of their complaint into a flame in which the feeble remnants of life are speedily consumed. In those previously healthy it not infrequently sows the seeds of other diseases more deadly than itself, and even when no definite organic damage appears to remain, it sometimes leaves its mark in lasting impairment of vitality. In these various ways the effects of influenza on the public health may be more far-reaching than those of cholera and other scourges, which work greater immediate havoc, and on this ground it deserves the earnest attention of all governments which consider it to be the first duty of a civilized power to provide for the safety of its own citizens, rather than for the scientific extermination of its neighbours.

Influenza is not like some other diseases, a product of advanced civilization; it is referred to by Hippocrates and other ancient medical writers, and a formidable list of epidemics in various parts of the world between the years 1173 and 1875 is given by Hirsch.* It is obvious, however, that no list of this kind can be exhaustive, either as to the actual number of epidemics, or the area of prevalence of the several outbreaks. It is not till the sixteenth century that we meet with anything like detailed records on the subject, and it is tolerably safe to assume that, till long after that time, only the more serious outbreaks were chronicled. Even at the present day, when the machinery for the collection of statistics is so much nearer perfection than it has ever been, it is difficult and indeed impossible to obtain trustworthy information as to the prevalence and diffusion of diseases over a very large part of the earth's surface. Even as to China, which lies under some suspicion of being the natural home of influenza, as India is of cholera, we have nothing but rumours of the vaguest kind.

With regard to our own country, we have a fairly complete history of epidemics of influenza which occurred in 1510, 1557, 1580, 1658, 1675, 1710, 1729, 1732–3, 1737–8, 1743, 1758, 1762, 1767, 1775, 1782, 1803, 1831, 1833, and 1837.† Further

* "Handbook of Geographical and Historical Pathology," vol. i. chap. i.
† The original records of these various outbreaks were collected and edited by the late Dr. Theophilus Thompson, and published by the Sydenham Society in 1852. A new edition of this valuable work was brought out not long ago by his son, Dr. Symes Thompson.

visitations took place in 1843 and 1847–8, besides limited outbreaks in 1841, 1842, 1844, 1846-7, and 1866. That there were other intermediate epidemics which found no medical pen to chronicle them is shown by such accidental references as the following, which occurs in Miss Strickland's " Life of Mary Stuart." In a letter, dated November, 1562, Randolph, the English Resident at the Scottish Court, says : " Immediately upon the Queen's arrival here (Holyrood) she fell acquainted with a new disease that is common in this town, called here the ' New Acquaintance,' which also passed through her whole household, sparing neither lord, lady, nor damoiselle—not so much as either French or English. It is a pain in their heads that have it, and a soreness in their stomach, with a great cough ; it remaineth with some longer, with other shorter time as it findeth apt bodies for the nature of the disease. The Queen kept her bed six days ; there was no appearance of danger, nor many that die of the disease except some old folk." The "New Acquaintance" is a very old acquaintance now, and much has been written on it by learned doctors, but I do not know that the prominent features of the disease have ever been more accurately hit off than in these few lines of Elizabeth's clear-sighted envoy.

In the records of all these epidemics, through the mist of obsolete pathological theory, the characteristics of the disease as we know it from present experience can be distinctly recognized. Thus Willis, in his " Description of a Catarrhal Feaver Epidemical in the Middle of the Spring in the Year 1658," mentions the "troublesome cough, with great spitting, also a Cartarrh falling down on the palat, throat, and nostrils," and the " feaverish distemper, Joyned with heat and thirst, want of appetite, a spontaneous weariness and a grievous pain in the back and limbs," and he also speaks of the " want of strength and languishing." Our English Hippocrates, Sydenham, in his " Epidemic Coughs of the Year 1675," says the disease, which he clearly discriminates from ordinary catarrh, " attacked with pains in the head, back and limbs," afterwards " falling upon the lungs." Later we find Huxham of Plymouth—a medical worthy in whom I take a particular interest, as to him we owe one of the best descriptions of diphtheria—giving a really excellent account of the epidemic of 1729: "The disorder began at first with a slight shivering; this was presently followed by a transient *erratic* heat, an headache, and a violent and troublesome sneezing; then the back and lungs were seized with flying pains, which sometimes attacked the breast likewise, and though they did not long remain there, yet were very troublesome, being greatly irritated by the violent cough which accompanied the disorder. . . . These complaints were like those arising from what is called *catching cold*, but presently a slight fever came on, which afterwards grew more violent. . . . Several likewise were seized with a most racking pain in the head, often accompanied with a slight delirium. Many were troubled with a singing in the ears, and numbers suffered from violent ear aches, which in some turned to an abscess; exulcerations and swellings of the fauces were likewise very common. . . . It generally went off about the fourth day, leaving behind a troublesome cough, which was very often of long duration; and such a dejection of strength as one would hardly have suspected from the shortness of the time. . . . On the whole this disorder was rarely mortal, unless by some very great error arising in the treatment of it; however, this very circumstance proved fatal to some, who making too slight of it, either on account of its being so common, or not thinking it very dangerous, often found asthmas, hectics, or even consumptions themselves the forfeitures of their inconsiderate rashness." The last words contain pretty well the substance of the matter. John Arbuthnot (Pope's "Friend to my Life"), speaking of the epidemic of 1732, mentions that "the fever left a debility and defection of appetite and spirits much more than in proportion to its strength or duration." Again, with regard to 1737, we learn from Huxham that the epidemic in that year was "not unlike in its attack to the epidemic catarrhal fever of the year 1733, but much more violent." He adds, "Numbers were now miserably tortured with the toothache who had never had a bad tooth in their head . . . in some, one half of the head was affected as if by an exquisite hemicrania." Further on, speaking of 1743, Huxham speaks of the disease as a "feveret," and he says, "This fever seemed to have been exactly the same with that which, in the spring, was rife all over Europe, termed the 'Influenza.'"* He adds that "in London it increased very greatly the number of burials, rising them in one week only to at least a thousand." In the epidemic of 1762 we are told by Sir George Baker that "those persons suffered most severely who could not obtain a respite from labour; more especially those who worked daily in the open air. Among this class the pestilence was so violent that it destroyed many of them within four days, in spite of remedies."

It is needless to multiply quotations from eye-witnesses of the various epidemics; it is sufficient to state that there is a chain of medical evidence which conclusively proves the essential identity of the disease throughout. In all, mention is made of the rapidity of its spread, the universality of its prevalence, whole cities being struck down as at a blow, the suddenness of onset, the shivering, the agonizing headache, the pain in the muscles, the catarrhal symptoms accompanied or replaced by intestinal troubles, the speedy subsidence of the primary disease with the pronounced liability to inflammation of the lungs and air-passages, the excessive prostration caused by an affection apparently so insignificant, and the not infrequent legacy of organic mischief or damaged constitution. Just as no two sufferers from influenza present exactly the same symptoms, so no epidemics are precisely alike in all their details; there are variations in type due no doubt to differences in the severity of the outbreak and to changes in the habits and constitution of the people. Thus in 1510, in addition to the ordinary symptoms of catarrh, particular mention is made of violent pain over the eye, pain in the abdomen, delirium, and, from the seventh to the eleventh day, syncope and "starting" of the tendons; in 1580, of bleeding at the nose, insomnia, giddiness, swelling of the glands beside the ear, and bilious vomiting; in 1658, spitting of blood, and great pain in the head; in 1675, bilious derangement; in 1729, rheumatic pains; in 1732-3,

* John Huxham, "Observations on the Air and Epidemical Diseases," vol. ii. London, 1758.

discharge of blood from the nose, lungs, and bowels; in 1737, sickness, salivation, toothache, and rheumatic pains; in 1743, skin eruptions, inflamed eyes, and dysentery; in 1758, a feeling of rawness in the throat and windpipe; in 1782, loss of smell and taste, a sensation of contusion of the limbs, and soreness of the cheek-bones; in 1831, loss of taste, and soreness behind the breast-bone; and in 1837, a feeling of weight and pain in the forehead, sometimes also at the top and back of the head, soreness over the breast-bone, severe pain in the back, acrid discharge from the eyes and nostrils, and diarrhœa.

In all these epidemics, in spite of minor variations, the catarrhal phenomena seem to have overshadowed every other element in the disease to such an extent as to mask its real nature. Inflammation of the respiratory mucous membrane, with consequent flux from the nose, windpipe, and lungs, was thought to be the essential feature of the malady, and the error has become crystallized in the expression "influenza cold," often used, not only by the public, but by medical men, to denote a cold of more than ordinary severity. I am inclined to think that this misconception is, at least in some measure, responsible for the very high rate of mortality which has been attributed to the present epidemic in Sheffield and other places in Yorkshire and also in London. After a winter of extraordinary duration and severity, and a spring of exceptional malignity, it is not wonderful that the old and the weakly should go down with bronchitis and pneumonia like grass before the mower's scythe. Even without the influenza these two diseases would, under the circumstances, have claimed hecatombs of victims; and to a man already sore smitten by the east wind a very small dose of influenza "will serve,' as Mercutio says. It is hardly fair, however, to set down all these deaths to the account of the influenza; that may be the immediate cause, but the "efficient cause," as the scholastics would say, is the previous sapping of the foundation which makes it easy for the most insignificant enemy to batter down the citadel of life.

There is another point which I can only touch on lightly

here. Influenza is the very Proteus of diseases, a malady which assumes so many different forms that it seems to be not one, but all diseases' epitome, and its symptomatology includes almost everything, from running at the nose to inflammation of the brain. In times of epidemic such as the present, illness of every kind is likely to be laid at the door of influenza; every cold, every headache, every bilious attack is ascribed to the same ubiquitous—or, as we say, "pandemic"—morbic agency, as in the Middle Ages all the motley brood of skin diseases were impartially classified and treated as leprosy. Statistics both of the prevalence and the mortality of influenza are therefore apt to be vitiated by more than the usual fallacies which beset all such censuses of disease, and a corresponding liberal allowance for error should be made when dealing with it.

The first step towards a right understanding of the nature of influenza is to get rid of the notion that catarrh is an inseparable adjunct of the disease. It is really an acute specific fever running a definite course like measles or scarlatina. It would be tedious and unprofitable to describe in detail the symptoms and complications of a disorder which is no doubt painfully familiar to many of my readers. It may, however, be stated that numerous and diverse as are its manifestations, they may all be grouped under three heads, viz. catarrhal, abdominal, and nervous. We have thus three well-marked types, each of which includes several varieties; all three may be intermingled or may succeed each other in the same case. It is this series of pathological combinations and permutations which gives the disease that superficial complexity of aspect which made Mrs. Carlyle playfully suggest that the doctors had agreed to call half a dozen different diseases by one name in order to simplify treatment. I have used the words "superficial complexity," because under all its disguises I believe the disease to be at bottom perfectly simple.

The bewildering diversity of symptoms becomes intelligible if we regard them as the results of disordered nervous actions. The extraordinary disturbance in our telegraphic systems sometimes caused by a thunderstorm is as nothing compared with the freaks played by the living conductors in the human body if anything throws the governing centres out of gear. In my opinion, then, the answer to the riddle of influenza is poisoned nerves. The cause of the disease I take to be a specific poison of some kind which gains access to the body, and having an elective affinity for the nervous system wreaks its spite principally or entirely thereon. In some cases it seizes on that part of it which governs the machinery of respiration; in others on that which presides over the digestive functions; in others again it seems, as it were, to run up and down the nervous keyboard, jarring the delicate mechanism and stirring up disorder and pain in different parts of the body with what almost seems malicious caprice. It is this that explains the almost infinite variety of neuralgic pains—head ache, ear ache, face ache, lumbago, cramp in the stomach, etc.—which forms so distressing a feature of the malady. It also explains the absolute loss of smell and taste which makes the taking of food the most wearisome of tasks; and it gives us the key to disorders of the sight and hearing, and the severe, though happily transient, affections of the eye and ear, which so frequently accompany influenza, and the lethargic stupor which occasionally follows it. It is the profound impression made on the nervous system by the poison, that explains nearly all the after effects of the malady, and especially that prolonged and sometimes even permanent loss of vital energy which is perhaps its worst legacy. The same deterioration of nerve force is seen in the slow and unsatisfactory healing of wounds which nearly all surgeons have observed in patients who have suffered from influenza. Even spontaneous gangrene of the extremities has taken place in several cases as if the disease induced premature old age. As the nourishment of every tissue and organ in the body is under the direct control of the nervous system, it follows that anything which affects the latter has a prejudicial effect on the former; hence it is not surprising that influenza in many cases leaves its mark in damaged structure. Not only the lungs, but the kidneys, the heart, and other internal organs and the nervous matter itself may suffer in this way. No wonder that so many persons never "feel the same" after an attack; that some develop consumption, that a few become paralyzed, and that there are even instances in which insanity has followed the malady.

What, then, is the nature of this insidious poison that has so baleful an effect on the nerves? On that point the doctors of the end of the nineteenth century are as much in the dark as their predecessors at the beginning of the sixteenth. We have not got beyond the "something subtle and occult" of Molineux. It is needless to say that microbes have been sought for, and several have been found, but not, so far, the one that is "wanted." Those that have been arrested on suspicion by Cornil and Babes of Paris, Jolles of Vienna, Kelbs of Zurich, and others have all failed to satisfy the crucial test of inoculation; "colonies" of them have been carefully bred to a proper degree of virulence and have then been injected into rabbits and other martyrs of scientific research. The unfortunate animals have died with symptoms indicative of blood-poisoning; but not of influenza. That the cause of the disease, however, is a living germ of some kind can hardly be doubted; this is the only hypothesis which explains all the facts. The sky, the sea, the earth, and the waters under the earth have been searched in vain for something that would furnish a solution of the riddle. The weather has been tried and found wanting; one has only to glance through the list of epidemics to see that influenza has been rife in every possible variety of weather and at every season of the year. It has prevailed in different places at the same time under exactly opposite meteorological conditions. We may therefore say with Sydenham, "Concerning the nature and quality of that disposition of the air on which the disease depends, as well as of many other things on which the doting and arrogant crowd of philosophers trifle, we are totally ignorant." Plagues of insects such as the *Bostrichus typographus*, which abounded in 1665, 1757, 1763, and 1783; the *Arctia phæorrhœa*, which committed great ravages in 1731 and 1732; the brown-tail moth, which had a price put upon its head in 1782; and the aphis, vast flights of which darkened the air in the northern counties of England in 1836, have been thought to be in some way connected with the influenza which prevailed in these years; but though the possibility of insects conveying infection cannot be gainsaid, it has not been shown that there is any relation between them and the epidemic.

Ozone in the atmosphere, "seleniureted hydrogen," and other telluric emanations have been conjectured to have something to do with its causation, but it occurs with equal intensity in places differing as widely as possible in climate and soil. At present the living germ holds the field, but as to the exact nature of the organism we must wait for enlightenment at the hands of some of the patient workers who seek for the sources of disease in the realm of the infinitely little.

As to the mode of diffusion of influenza, all the evidence seems to me to point to its being air-borne. "Horsed upon the sightless couriers of the air," it is conveyed from its secret birthplace and drops from beneath the clouds—not exactly like mercy—upon the place beneath. If this should happen to be a thickly populated district, the germ no doubt multiplies itself as it passes from house to house and from town to town; whether it becomes more virulent in the process I am not aware that there is any evidence to show. Influenza thus spreads both by aërial transportation and by contagion; the latter alone is inadequate to explain the sudden outbreak of the disease in widely distant countries at the same time, and the curious way in which it has been known to attack the crews of ships at sea, where communication with infected places or persons was out of the question. Thus Admiral Kempenfeldt (the hero of Cowper's poem, "The *Royal George*") sailed on May 2, 1782, with the intention of cruising between Brest and the Lizard. On the 27th, although there had been no communication with the shore, the crew of one of the ships were attacked with influenza, and soon the whole squadron was so severely affected that it had to return to port in the second week in June. Again, to quote Sir Thomas Watson, on April 3, 1833, the *Stag* frigate was coming up the Channel, and arrived at two o'clock off Berry Head on the Devonshire coast, all on board being at that time well. In half an hour afterwards, the breeze being easterly and blowing off the land, forty men were down with the influenza; by six o'clock the number was increased to sixty, and by two o'clock the next day to one hundred and sixty.* On the same day, Sir Thomas Watson saw the first two cases in London, the whole town being smitten with it on that and the following day. On the same day, also, a regiment at Portsmouth was seized, so that next morning so many men were ill that garrison duty could not be performed by it. Many similar occurrences have been recorded in other epidemics. It is impossible to explain such cases by contagion; the victims can only have succumbed to a cause acting on them all at the same instant of time, as they would all have got wet if exposed to a shower of rain. In the case of these sudden visitations of influenza we must suppose that there is something like a shower of germs.

On the other hand, the evidence as to contagion is not less conclusive. Cullen relates that on a little island, fifteen or twenty leagues off the west coast of Scotland, there lived in his day twenty or thirty poverty-stricken families who had no other communication with the mainland than through the rent collector, who visited them once a year. On the occasion of one of these visits the collector's men, who were ill with influenza, introduced it into the island, and on the following day the whole population was coughing. In many instances during the last epidemic there was tolerably clear proof that the disease had been introduced into towns or villages previously free by persons coming from infected places. The fact that it was, during the present epidemic, brought to the House of Commons by witnesses from Sheffield is, I believe, generally accepted by those in a position to judge; it appears certain that the members of the committee before whom the witnesses

* "Principles and Practice of Physic," 4th ed., vol. ii., p. 41. London, 1857.

appeared were attacked first, and they subsequently spread it through the House. That the disease can be conveyed by dead bodies—as is known to be the case in other contagious diseases, such as diphtheria, etc.—seems to be shown by the following narrative, which I take from a paper by Dr. Guiteras in the Philadelphia *Medical Times* of April 10, 1880 :—An American gentleman in bad health contracted influenza in London, and died of a relapse in Paris in December, 1879. His body was embalmed and sent to Philadelphia, where it was exposed to the view of his family. This was immediately followed by an outbreak of influenza, which first affected the members of the family, next friends in close intercourse with them, next the medical attendant of some of them, next the housekeeper and one or two of the doctor's patients, the whole number affected being eighteen.

Regarding the treatment of influenza, there is not much to be said. As in all fevers which run a definite course, the doctor's duty is practically confined to keeping up the patient's strength, and warding off complications. The best way to do this is to insist on his going to bed as soon as the enemy is upon him, and remaining there as long as it is necessary. If this were done as a matter of routine in every case of influenza, however trivial it may seem to be, there would be fewer deaths from relapses and complications. In very mild cases it may be sufficient to confine the patient to his room ; but if allowed to be up he will be almost sure to take liberties with himself and catch cold by some trifling exposure. It is the mild attacks that often lead to the worst consequences, simply because they are neglected. The great prostration, which is usually one of the most marked features of the disease, should be combated by the judicious use of stimulants and by a diet as generous as the patient can be induced to take. Elimination of poisonous products should be promoted in the usual way, but anything like "lowering" treatment should be religiously avoided. It is a fatal mistake to treat influenza as an acute inflammatory disease ; support, not depletion, is the secret of success. This truth was sometimes even borne in on the minds of the older physicians by witnessing the disastrous effects of bleeding in influenza; and I need not say that the evidence must indeed have been overwhelmingly strong to make these champions of the lancet believe that their favourite panacea was worse than useless. How convincing the evidence was we may learn from an example. In the epidemic of 1557, in a small town near Madrid, some 2000 persons contracted the disease; they were all bled, and—all died. Mr. Rider Haggard's blood-thirsty imagination could not conceive a more wholesale butchery! Most modern authors attribute the enormous mortality in the older epidemics not so much to the influenza itself as to the treatment: "Seignare, seignare, ensuita purgare," was the general rule, with the result that the patient was deprived of his life as well as cured of his disease.

There is one point to which I think it well to call special attention. There are, of course, fashions in medicine as in other things, and at present what are called "antipyretics," that is to say, remedies which reduce the temperature, are much in vogue. The clinical thermometer is a most valuable instrument, but it should not be made a fetish. In certain fevers, as, for instance, in rheumatism, where the mere excess of heat-production may kill the patient, reduction of the temperature is a matter of vital importance, and almost any means may justifiably be used to that end. In a "feveret" like influenza, however, a temperature of 103 degrees or even 104 degrees, has no serious significance; it will speedily subside of itself, and requires no aid from medical art. It should never be forgotten that some drugs which reduce temperature also reduce the patient, and experienced physicians could tell of many deaths due solely to the unwise use of these agents by practitioners who take the thermometer as a guide to be followed with unreasoning obedience.

After recovery the really dangerous time may be said to have come. The busy man will not be restrained, but will rush back to his work, and in a week or two he is in the deadly grip of pneumonia. For some little time after the most trivial attack of influenza the greatest care is necessary to prevent relapse, and it will be well if extra precautions are taken against catching cold for a considerable period afterwards. Of the consequences of influenza it may be said with the most literal truth that he that loveth the danger shall perish in it.

THE NEW YACHTING.

In the middle of August last year (1890), after an exceptionally fatiguing season, I was still busy in my consulting-room, though sighing for release, and half inclined to say to my servant, "Tie up the knocker, say I'm sick, I'm dead." Suddenly a well-known and much-travelled member of Parliament, whom I had advised to go to Mont Dore, appeared on the scene with the announcement that he had just heard of what promised to be a very pleasant cruise to the Crimea. He wished to know whether that would not suit him as well as the French health resort. I was obliged to tell him that it would not, but it struck me at once that it would probably suit *me*. I therefore sent without delay to the offices of the Orient line and secured two berths, for my son and myself, on board the *Chimborazo*, which was announced to start from Tilbury on August 30th. On the morning of Sunday, August 31st, we reached Plymouth, and, after a splendid passage through the Bay of Biscay, found ourselves at 10 a.m. on Tuesday, September 2nd, opposite Cape Finisterre, some fifty or sixty miles from the Boy Rock off Cape Vilano, where the ill-starred *Serpent* was destined to meet her tragic fate a few months later. Steaming along the coast of Portugal, we were able to admire the picturesque mountain ranges behind Vigo, and gazed with interest on Torres Vedras, where Wellington constructed his famous lines in 1810. We had a good view of Cintra, and in the distance could be seen on the hillside, the old castle where Dom Manuel watched for the return of Vasco de Gama from his fateful voyage.

By this time most of us had fairly settled down amidst our new surroundings, and I may here take the opportunity of saying a few words as to these. With respect to the accommodation and the arrangements made for the comfort of the passengers, all that need be remarked is that everybody on board, with so far as I know only one exception, was satisfied. This is saying a good deal, for John Bull on his travels is not always easy to please. One great element of comfort was that we were not overcrowded, for there were not more than eighty passengers, and the steamer could easily have carried from a hundred and fifty to two hundred. There was a capital saloon with seven separate tables, where we chose and kept our places. Each of these tables soon had a name of its own; thus, the one presided over by the captain was "the high and mighty;" another was known as "the select;" another, which was graced by the presence of two live C.B.'s, "the superior persons," and so on. The people who sat at the same tables naturally formed little coteries, but there was never anything like cliquism or exclusiveness.

As regards the vital question of food, I can only say that, though I have travelled by the great transatlantic steamers, by the "P. and O.," and by the South African and Australian lines, I have never seen anywhere on board ship such a well-appointed table as on the *Chimborazo*. As a philanthropist, I was pleased to observe that most of the passengers did full justice to the excellent fare provided for them. The wines were good and by no means dear, but it will comfort Sir Wilfrid Lawson to hear that the wants of total abstainers were amply provided for with ginger ale, soda water, and the other exhilarating fluids in which they are wont to drown their sorrow for the sins of their less temperate fellow-men. Whilst we were in a hot climate, I noticed that the favourite drink in the smoking-room was "John Collins," an effervescing beverage of very slight alcoholic strength. Many learned discussions took place as to the inventor of this popular refresher, and the general idea was that we were indebted to

America for its discovery; patriotism compels me, however, to claim it for my own country, and the following lines clearly settle the vexed question :—

> "My name is John Collins, head waiter at Limmer's,
> The corner of Conduit Street, Hanover Square;
> My chief occupation is pouring out brimmers
> For many young gentlemen, bothered with care."

The ship was commanded by Captain Ruthven, who, I believe, is the commodore of the Orient line, and is certainly a first-rate sailor; I found him a most obliging, courteous gentleman, but some of the passengers thought he might have been a little more "diffusive," and that it would have been an advantage if his social attentions had been rather more catholic and less concentrated. But in the management of his ship he left nothing to be desired. He always took his vessel as near the shore as was consistent with safety, and went slow enough to allow us full enjoyment of whatever there was to be seen, even stopping for a few minutes when the scenery was particularly beautiful or interesting. The first officer, Mr. Scott, and the three junior officers, vied with each other in their attention to the passengers. Our doctor was unfortunately unwell during nearly the whole of the voyage; but Mr. Burgess, of Streatham, who happened to be on board, took his duties on himself, and most kindly and skilfully looked after those requiring medical help. Our purser was a man in whom dignity of appearance was tempered with affability of manner in a way which seemed to show that he had formed himself after the most approved royal models. His urbane condescension in answering silly questions was only equalled by his inexhaustible patience in ministering to the wants and even the whims of those who sought his help. Another functionary who largely contributed to the greatest happiness of the greatest number was Commander Hull, whom I can only describe as a sort of "delicate Ariel" benevolently placed at our disposal by the Company to execute our behests and generally make our paths smooth. This gentleman was the guide, philosopher, and friend of every passenger; a walking encyclopædia of information regarding the places to be visited, how to get to them, and how to see them to the best advantage. Like the great ancestor of the President of the French Republic, Commander Hull "organized victory" over all the difficulties of travel—routes, transport, hotel accommodation, and even backsheesh!

The passengers formed a microcosm on the whole fairly representative of the upper middle strata of English society. There was nobody of oppressive elevation of rank among us, though we narrowly missed the honour of having the bombarder of Alexandria on board. There were two C.B.s, the "superior persons" already alluded to; a well-known Member of Parliament; six or seven barristers, including a Q.C., with about an equal number of "gentlemen by Act of Parliament;" two owners of yachts well known at Cowes and other places where yachtsmen most do congregate; an architect familiar with the masterpieces of his art in Greece and elsewhere; a distinguished novelist noted for his vivid word-painting of landscapes and seascapes; an artist, known to gods, men, and dealers as Mr. Tristram Ellis, but to us, in our holiday trip, as the "lightning artist of the *Chimborazo;*" the English professor of the dismal science at the University of Edinburgh and the author of the beautiful prose-poem—"Thoth;" several warriors belonging to the reserve forces; a couple of doctors and a dentist. The Church was not represented, a circumstance regarded as of good omen by the sailors. We had over thirty ladies on board, some young and others of a "certain age," but none that could justly be called old. Among them was one who had earned celebrity as an Alpine explorer; a young poetess who recited her own verses in the gloaming to an appreciative circle; and a lady whose wanderings in many lands rivalled those of Odysseus. So great was the effect which the mingled dignity and suavity of this fair pilgrim's manner produced on the natives wherever we landed, in the way of obtaining admission to otherwise inaccessible public buildings, that we gave her the name of the *Grande Dame.* When the frost of suspicion, with which every free-born Briton at first regards those of his compatriots with whom he does not happen to be acquainted, had melted under the genial influence of personal companionship, the travellers on board the *Chimborazo* proved to be as agreeable a set of people as one could wish to meet.

Macaulay says somewhere that people on a sea voyage have three principal resources for passing the time, viz. eating twice as many meals as they do on shore, quarrelling, and lovemaking. Of the last-named of these devices I must leave some of the younger members of the party to speak. As for quarrelling, my fellow-travellers in the *Chimborazo* were too well bred to indulge in that pastime in public, though, as there were several married couples on board, I cannot answer for what may have occurred "behind the veil." In the matter of eating it must be admitted that many of our companions laid in supplies of "provant" whenever the opportunity offered, which would have satisfied even that experienced campaigner, Dugald Dalgetty; but at sea there is always a possibility of complications occurring at any moment which may make the taking of sustenance difficult, if not impossible, and it is well therefore to be prepared for emergencies. There was, however, no lack of other amusements on the *Chimborazo*. We had a band which played every day on deck between 12 and 1 o'clock, and again either during or after dinner, and there was plenty of amateur music besides. Two of the ladies played the violin very well, and one of the young men was a charming singer. There was also a gentleman from Glasgow who witched our ears with the ballads of his native land. There was dancing for the younger folk, while the elders took their pleasure sadly with chess and backgammon. A rubber of whist was always played for an hour in the morning and again in the afternoon, and a mild game of poker was often indulged in in the smoking-room. On deck cricket and amateur photography were the chief amusements. Of the latter fine art there were some fifteen or twenty active votaries, besides numerous candid friends and self-appointed *amici curiæ* always ready to offer criticism and advice. Portraits, groups, and innumerable views were thus taken, and if I possessed all the sun pictures which were promised me by my fair fellow-travellers I should be able to open an exhibition of amateur photography. Nor was the cultivation of the tourist mind neglected. There was much poring over guide-books, and, in one or two cases, over works of heavier metal like those of Kinglake and Gibbon.

Sometimes when we were approaching a new place Commander Hull would give a little lecture in the evening on the objects of interest to be looked for, and point out the best way to see the various sights. As he had been a great traveller his knowledge was extensive, and his observations were always valuable and usually entertaining, except when they were drawn from a certain recondite authority, whom he comprehensively alluded to as "Old John Murray," instead of from his own experience. Mr. Tristram Ellis also gave a couple of very instructive lectures on the places of interest which lay in our line of route, illustrating his remarks with his own charming pictures.

It is time, however, to return to our cruise, and it may be well to state here that I do not propose to give a log of the ship's course or a description of scenes which are, no doubt, familiar to many of my readers, and can be read in any guide-book. I will content myself with a rapid sketch of the principal places which we saw, dwelling only on one or two in which, for one reason or another, I was myself particularly interested.

We passed Cape St. Vincent on the evening of September 3rd, and at one o'clock on the next day we were off "Trafalgar's Bay." Being unable to land at Tangiers on account of a heavy ground swell, which would have made landing in small boats very dangerous, Captain Ruthven decided to alter his course and take us to Algiers by way of compensation. The disappointment was not so keenly felt by me as by many of my fellow-passengers, as I had visited Tangiers some years before. Here I venture to make a little digression in order to mention that I do not consider the climate of Tangiers a good one in winter. It is not sufficiently protected from winds, and it is not warm enough to be a good place for invalids; moreover there is often a good deal of rain. I can, however, strongly advise people who want a change in April, and who like being on the sea, to run down to Gibraltar on a Peninsular and Oriental steamer, cross over to Tangiers, spend a week or two there, and return the same way as they went. For Members of Parliament, barristers, and others, who require a change before the season commences, or for those who wish to avoid the cold winds of our English spring (modern style), a short stay at Tangiers will be found just what is wanted.

We reached Algiers on September 6th. Here we felt the comfort of the arrangements made for us by the Company, when, instead of having to do battle with the native boatmen, we were quickly landed by our own smart sailors, and a regular service of boats was established between the ship and the shore. I need not describe Algiers; a description of Regent Street would have as much novelty at this time of day. I noticed a great falling off in the way the public buildings and the beautiful Jardin d'Essai, the Kew of Algiers, are kept, as compared with their condition during the reign of Napoleon III. The development of Algiers, both as a town and as a province, was, like the Hausmannisation of Paris, a hobby of the late Emperor, and I suppose it is a sign of loyalty to the Republic to show disrespect to his memory in this way. The principal French street leading up to the old town, which is occupied by Arabs, reminded me very much of the Chinese quarter of San Francisco; the resemblance may have been due to the contrast noticeable in each case between the Orientalism of the denizens, their manners, customs, food, wares, etc., and the comfortable European appearance of the houses they live in.

During a previous visit to Algiers I had made what doctors call a clinical experiment on myself by smoking hasheesh, or "kif," as they call it in Algiers, in a native coffee-house. I did not repeat the experiment, but it may be interesting to recall some of its details. The pipe used for the purpose has a long tube and a large bowl, though the actual cavity into which the drug is put is not much bigger than the tiny opium pipe of the Chinese. The pipe is lighted by a youth, who heats a small piece of charcoal to a white heat, and puts it in the pipe. The smoker takes one deep whiff and passes the pipe on to his neighbour, and in this way the kif circulates like the wine-bottle, but in more silent fashion. Your turn soon comes round again, and in about ten minutes you are under the influence of the drug. I cannot say that in my case the effect in any way resembled the *paradis artificiel* described by Théophile Gautier, but then I am not a poet. I found the effect pleasant and exhilarating, and both I and a friend who accompanied me noticed that our power of ascending the somewhat precipitous streets of the old town of Algiers without fatigue was greatly increased. We got through a large amount of sight-seeing, and returned to our hotel, feeling buoyant and not at all exhausted; nor did the next morning bring headache or repentance. How it might have fared with us, however, had we taken a sufficient quantity of the drug to cause sleep, as the practised smokers do, I am unable to say.

Heading next for Sicily, we reached Palermo on September 8th, but I cannot linger over the familiar beauties of the bay, nor the noble cathedral, nor the Saracenic architecture of some of the buildings, nor the ultra-Zoalesque horrors of the Capucin catacombs. We weighed anchor again on the evening of the 10th, and rose betimes on the following morning in order to see the Lipari Islands, and try to recall a little classical emotion in passing between Scylla and Charybdis. The rock was easily made out, but the famous whirlpool was voted a very insignificant affair. Small craft, however, still sometimes come to grief there when the wind is in a certain quarter. Steaming along the picturesquely mountainous coast of Sicily, we in due course arrived at Syracuse, where we stayed twenty-four hours. One of the most interesting things to me here was the fountain of Arethusa, which springs from a little pool some twenty feet below the level of the ground. Growing in the pool was a quantity of beautiful papyrus, a fine species of sedge, which attains to a height of twelve to fifteen feet. The papyrus is jealously guarded, but the *Grande Dame* was able to procure some fine specimens, and amused herself the next day by showing us how the ancients made their papyrus rolls.

Leaving Syracuse, with its wonderful amphitheatres, its Street of Tombs, its fabled "Ear of Dionysius," its catacombs (which are said to be more extensive than those of Rome), and

its genial and hospitable inhabitants, we steamed on to Athens.
For two or three hours before arriving there we had a splendid
view of the wondrous city which was so long the sun of civili-
sation to the rest of Europe. The white pile of the Acropolis,
perched upon the bold brown crag, made a picture which can
never be forgotten. As we came nearer we thought we could
make out Lycabettus and Hymettus, and there was a vast display of æsthetic enthusiasm mingled with cheap erudition fresh
culled from the guide-books. It had been arranged that we
should go into the Piræus, but our "lightning artist" induced
the captain to enter the Bay of Phalerum instead. This was
a distinct improvement, as the Piræus, though redolent of the
classics, has an ancient and fish-like smell which is distressing
to modern noses, whereas Phalerum is a bright little seaside
resort much frequented by the present inhabitants of the Grecian
capital. On arriving at Athens most of the passengers at once
went on shore, and took up their residence in a hotel.

My first visit was, of course, to the Acropolis, where I went
in the company of Mr. Tristram Ellis, whose familiarity with
Athens—as "extensive and peculiar" as Sam Weller's knowledge of London—made him an excellent *cicerone*. On reaching the Acropolis, we had the good fortune to fall in with two
gentlemen, Messrs. Schultz and Barnsley, who were in Greece
on an artistic mission, studying the Byzantine churches. It is
hardly an exaggeration to say that both these gentlemen knew
every stone of the Acropolis, and they were most obliging in
showing us everything of special interest in the shortest possible
time. After seeing the Propylæa, the Parthenon, the Erech-
theum, and the Nikeapteros, and spending some time in the
museum where the antiquities are derived exclusively from the
Acropolis, we passed on to the Areopagus, the seat of the famous
tribunal which sat at night so as to be free from the disturbing
influence of popular feeling. Among the high crimes and mis-
demeanours with which it was competent to deal, it is somewhat startling to find idleness grouped with murder, treason,
and irreligion, and punishable with heavy penalties. It is
obvious, however, that in a community where there is no leisured
class, idleness is an offence against the State; and this is how

it will have to be dealt with if Socialism ever becomes established as the ruling principle of civilized life. We next visited the theatre of Dionysius, where the plays of the great Greek dramatists were performed before audiences as cultured and as critical as those present on first nights at the Lyceum. But what a difference there is between a "new and original" play by Æschylus, Sophocles, or Aristophanes, and one by any of the "eminent hands" of our own day! On the following day I had intended to go up Pentelicus, from which a very extensive view may be obtained—it is one of the mountains which "look on Marathon,"—but I was prevented from making the excursion by a message which I received from that most gracious lady, the Duchess of Sparta, intimating that she would drive into Athens from her country house at Tatoi, and receive me in her palace. Her Royal Highness looked, I thought, rather delicate, but she said she found the climate of Greece delightful. Though a note of sadness naturally ran through the conversation, the Duchess was most kind and sympathetic, as I had always found her. She brightened up in speaking of the future heir to the throne of Greece, whose photograph she showed me with all the pride of a young mother. I agreed with her that he is a very prince of babies, and for the sake of his royal mother and his imperial grandparents, I hope his career will be a glorious one. I next proceeded to pay my respects to Miss Tricoupis, the sister of the Prime Minister. Her father represented Greece at the Court of St. James's, when she was a child, and she speaks English with the perfection of pronunciation which in my experience is more often met with in Greeks than in other foreigners. Miss Tricoupis is a most charming lady whose hospitality to English people is proverbial. I subsequently had the honour of an interview with Mr. Tricoupis, whose personality made a great impression on me. He is a dark man, of middle height, with a strikingly fine head. He struck me as a man of penetrating intellect and great vigour of character, with a large stock of reserved power. On leaving Mr. Tricoupis, I went again to the Acropolis to see the remains of the sanctuary of Asclepius and Hygieia, which, strange to say, had escaped me at the time of my first visit.

The sacred fountain of Asclepius remains as a spring of brackish water which, I dare say, would cure as many diseases as it did in the old days, if only *faith*, which is the "active principle" of all such healing agencies, could be restored. The treatment seems to have been a mixture of devotion and hydropathy. After washing in the fountain and offering up prayers at the altar of the god—the usual honorarium in the form of sacrifices and gifts not being forgotten—the patients wrapped in blankets were laid on the floor to "await developments," if I may borrow a phrase from our cousins over the water. A proper frame of mind was induced by putting out all lights and enjoining strict silence, and, if possible, sleep, so as to give the remedy the best chance of doing its beneficent work undisturbed by external influences. The conditions were certainly well calculated to bring about that mental state in which the sufferer's faith makes him whole, and they equally served the purpose of the priests, to whom the darkness and general atmosphere of mystery afforded a convenient opportunity of "accepting" the offerings placed on the altar by the patients or their friends.

The prescriptions which were supposed to be revealed by Asclepius in dreams varied more or less according to circumstances; but, so far as can be made out at this distance of time, they, to a great extent, consisted in simple hygienic measures as to diet, exercise, baths, etc., and religious observances, in which it may readily be supposed that offerings of what Mr. Wemmick would call "portable property," in one form or another, to the presiding deity, formed a prominent feature. So largely did water figure in the pharmacopœia of the Temple of Asclepius, that it may be gathered that the divinity agreed with Pindar that "water is the best," and indeed he might justly be termed the founder of the hydropathic system. Besides the sacrifices of animals—prototypes of those still made on the altar of medical science by vivisectors—and the various "unconsidered trifles" presented to the god by way of fee, persons who had been eased of their sufferings had votive inscriptions and reliefs put up in the temple in commemoration of the event. If they could not afford this method of recording their gratitude, they had small tablets put up on which the limb or other part which had been freed from pain or disease was rudely carved. This shows that the custom which still prevails in some parts of the south of Europe of decorating the wall of churches or shrines with arms, legs, etc., in gold, silver, or wax (according to the patient's circumstances), is a relic of a heathen observance at least two thousand five hundred years old.

A circumstance which added greatly to the interest of my visit to Athens on this occasion was that I was fortunate enough to make the acquaintance of Dr. Schliemann, whom I met in the Polytechnic School, where the wonderful collection of antiquarian treasures unearthed by him at Mycenæ was exhibited. The famous archæologist—whose explorations underground almost rival those of Stanley above it—invited several of our party to his house, where he received us with the greatest courtesy, and interested us with remarks which showed a remarkable combination of Yankee 'cuteness and German philosophy.

The National Museum at Athens is well worth a visit, being particularly rich in archaic statues and in early *steles* or sepulchral reliefs, the old Grecian equivalents of our own less artistic tombstones. These relics of antiquity are of the highest interest not only to lovers of art, but to all who think nothing that is human foreign to themselves. On these memorial tablets is depicted much of the domestic life of ancient Greece ; the mode of death is often portrayed, or the occupation of the person commemorated is indicated by appropriate symbolism. The conception of death as a journey to an undiscovered country, from whose bourne no traveller returns, finds expression in the representation of the departed person taking leave of his wife or children. There is clear evidence on many of these sepulchral reliefs that the Greeks believed in a future state. After seeing the *steles* in the Museum, we visited the ancient cemetery or Ceramicus, where the tombs which once contained them are still standing. Some of these interesting memorials have been left where they were placed by the sorrowing relatives, and some were dug up while we were looking on. I observed that they looked as fresh as if they had just left the sculptor's hands.

Before leaving Athens I was anxious to pay a visit to Eleusis, and the excursion promised to be all the more interesting that the *Grande Dame* and her charming niece volunteered to accompany me. Driving through the Pass of Daphne I enjoyed that superb view of Athens which Chateaubriand describes in his "Itinéraire." It would be presumptuous in me to attempt any word-painting of the scene after so great a master, and the reader will probably be grateful for my self-restraint. On arriving at the summit of the pass we got out to visit the monastery. The church is of Byzantine origin, but was greatly modified—shall I say Becketted?—in the eighteenth century. While we were examining it I was surprised to hear myself called by name, and on looking up I became aware of a gentleman perched up close to the roof and busy copying a mosaic. It was Mr. Barnsley, whose acquaintance I had made a day or two before in the Parthenon. Driving down the other side of the pass we saw before us the beautiful Bay of Eleusis, landlocked by Salamis. As we approached the straggling village of Eleusis large drops of rain began to fall, and we had scarcely time to hurry over the excavations of the temple before a tremendous thunderstorm broke over our heads, as though the old gods were even at this late day displeased that profane intruders should venture on the scene of the Eleusinian mysteries. Our horses got frightened, and we had to take refuge in a peasant's cottage, where we were most hospitably received. I noticed that though the floor was only hardened mud the women were comfortably dressed and looked clean and tidy, and there was no sign of the squalor and destitution that one sees in many parts of Ireland. In the evening some of us had the pleasure of dining with Mr. Haggard, *chargé d'affaires* in the absence of the British Minister, Sir Edmund Monson, and Mr. Rennell Rodd. We spent a most agreeable evening with these gentlemen, and from Mr. Haggard I learnt more about Athens and Greece generally in a couple of hours, than I could have done in as many months by my own unassisted efforts. The next day, while some members of our party went over the Arsakiou, a normal school, where fifteen hundred girls between five and eighteen years of age received an excellent education, I took the opportunity of doing a little of that shopping which is looked upon by a traveller's family at home as the most important feature of the trip. Among other things, I became the proud possessor of some light wraps and scarves, made of silk grenadine interwoven with gold, which excited the envy of many of my fair fellow-passengers. I dare say if I had been willing to "trade" I could have made a fair profit out of my purchases, as there is nothing of the kind to be got in Constantinople or Asia Minor.

Leaving Athens with regret, and I dare say with hopes of seeing it again "some day," which for most of us will fall in the Greek kalends, we steamed along the Dardanelles, scanning the shore during the hours of daylight, guide-book in hand, so as to miss nothing of interest. Vague recollections of our distant school days and of certain unpleasant episodes of that "happy time" came back to most of the male contingent, and seeing Tenedos, the plains of Troy, with the so-called tomb of Ajax, the mouth of the Skamander, and Mount Ida in the distance, I have no doubt some of us registered a secret vow to "get up" all that sort of thing again, and perhaps to attempt to grope our way through Homer in the original. These valiant resolutions generally only serve to repair the pavement of a place over which the London County Council holds no sway, but it is difficult for any one who has had the least tincture of a classical education to avoid indulging in some dreams of the kind when surrounded by places where every hill, rock, and rivulet has had its name enshrined in immortal verse and consecrated by association with heroic deeds and beautiful legends and burning thoughts that can never die. As we passed between Sestos and Abydos there was of course much quoting from Byron, who, though scorned by Mr. Swinburne and the superfine critics generally, still lives in the great heart of the people, and will continue to be read when the Lycophrons of the day are consigned to a limbo of oblivion as obscure as their own verses. I dare say Byron was more proud of having swum the Hellespont than of having written the "Bride of Abydos," and yet Captain Webb (who, like Chatterton, may truly be said to have "perished in his pride,") would probably not have thought much of the feat, which, as the noble poet boasts—

"Leander, Mr. Ekenhead, and I, did."

On approaching Constantinople the captain considerately slackened speed, so that we might come in sight of the famous city in the morning when the sun would be striking "the Sultan's turret with a shaft of light."

But, alas! it was raining when we arrived, and the city of the Golden Horn looked almost as dismal as London on a wet day. It almost seemed as though the "Clerk of the weather" was playing us a spiteful trick, for this was the first rainfall we had experienced whilst at sea. In spite of the murky atmosphere, however, Seraglio Point looked very beautiful, having behind it the large castellated buildings with massive walls, and the dome of St. Sophia with its four minarets, the whole relieved by numerous trees scattered among the buildings and mosques. Landing close by the Arsenal, we found ourselves among a host of dogs who were sprawling about and disdained to make way for, or even to notice the existence of the Giaour. They can hardly bring themselves to move even for carriages, and they are not infrequently run over, when not only the victim but all his friends within hearing give their sorrow vent in lugubrious howls. These curs form a characteristic feature of the Turkish capital, and their "points" are too well known to need description here. In Pera and Galata, where they pick up a scanty living in the gutters and dust heaps, they have, like Cassius, a lean and hungry look, but at Stamboul the Turks feed them regularly, though they look upon them as unclean animals and would on no account admit them into their houses; in that quarter they also have the benefit of legacies left for their support by "pious founders."

On landing, my son and myself with a friend found quarters at Le Club de Constantinople, where, thanks to the

T

courtesy of the obliging secretary, Mr. Mavrogordato, we were made very comfortable. The first "lion" we visited was, of course, St. Sophia. I must confess I was as much disappointed with the outside of that historic edifice as Mr. Oscar Wilde was with the Atlantic ocean. It had a naked and faded look, which acted like a wet blanket on my somewhat enthusiastic anticipations. I was still more disappointed with the inside. From my boyhood I had looked forward to visiting St. Sophia "as the terrestrial paradise, the second firmament, the car of the cherubim, the throne of the glory of God, the marvel of the earth," and so forth. Standing in St. Mark's, I have often thought, recalling the descriptions I had read, "This is gorgeous, but how much grander and more beautiful must St. Sophia be!" It was a cruel disenchantment. In St. Mark's everything is rich almost to excess, yet the magnificence of the detail is everywhere made to contribute to the general effect so as to form one harmonious whole. On the other hand, what strikes one most about St. Sophia is the tawdry character of the ornaments, the ill-assorted colours, and the wretched way in which the ancient mosaics have been patched up with stucco. The whole thing has that indescribable "shabby-genteel" look which Oriental magnificence so often has when seen near. In short, one might suppose that the Turks had of malice aforethought done their utmost by tasteless defacement and barbaric ornament to destroy the original beauty of this famous temple, as if to show their contempt for Christian architecture. One would be almost content to see Constantinople in the hands of the Russians if they would make St. Sophia once more what it was thirteen centuries ago, when the Emperor Justinian exclaimed, "Solomon, I have surpassed thee!"

On leaving St. Sophia we went to the Mosque of Sulciman the Magnificent, which was begun in 1550 and finished five years later. Its grand simplicity is in strong contrast with the meretricious and discordant splendours of St. Sophia. The weather having by this time cleared up, we made an excursion to Therapia, steaming along the European side of the Bosphorus. On the way we passed the splendid palace of the Sultan, Dolma

Bagtche, which from the water presents an appearance of great magnificence and richness. Marble steps descend from the palace to the sea, and the numerous balconies and terraces with their delicate tracery give a lightness to the structure which, in spite of its immense size, made it look more like the abode of the fairy monarch Oberon than of the "thunder-bolt, the bone-crusher, the shedder of blood," to quote only a few of the decorative epithets which figure among the titles of the Commander of the Faithful. Just beyond the palace are the beautiful gardens of Beshiktash, and a little beyond them is the palace of Yildiz, with a small mosque near it. On reaching Therapia we went to pay our respects to the British Ambassador; but, finding that Sir William White was taking his siesta, we passed on to the residence of the secretaries of the Embassy. The new Embassy is a very handsome building, but the old house was more interesting to me. In this wooden structure, which looks like a handsome bungalow, Lord Stratford de Redclyffe used to spend the summer months. Notwithstanding the high talents and great diplomatic experience of our present representative, it is not now as it was in the days of the "Great Elchi," when the British Ambassador had only to say, "Do this," and the Sultan did it. It is the influence of the representative of the big battalions of Germany which is now preponderant at the Turkish Court. The gentlemen of the Embassy received us very kindly, and after we had drunk one of the twelve cups of coffee which are supposed to be consumed daily by every one living in Constantinople, they took us for a walk in the beautiful woods at the back of the residence. In several places the trees are cut away and stone seats are put so that good views of the Bosphorus and the opposite shore may be obtained.

The next day, after visiting the mosques of Sultan Ahmed and Mahomed II. at Stamboul, I drove to the Tophane suburb, some three or four miles from the city, to present myself to the Grand Vizier, to whom his Excellency Rustem Pasha, the well-known and much-esteemed representative of the Porte at the Court of St. James's, had kindly given me a letter of introduction. Kiamil Pasha is a very handsome man, between fifty and sixty years of age, of medium height and dark complexion, with regular features, and a remarkably thoughtful expression. His manner was very gentle and refined, and he gave me the impression of being a man of great intelligence. I believe that Friday, the day on which I called, is supposed to be a day of rest, but I found the Grand Vizier engaged with a gentleman on business. I remarked to him that he worked very hard, and he said, "Yes, I do; and I have been doing so for five years without any rest. I am not so fortunate as Lord Salisbury or Mr. Gladstone, who go away to their country houses. I can never leave my post for a day." I ventured to remark that his Majesty the Sultan was himself a very hard-working man and looked into every detail. "Yes," replied the Pasha, "it is quite true, and that, of course, gives a great deal of additional work to me and my colleagues." After conversing with his Highness for a little time I took my leave in order to be present at the ceremony of the Salaamlik, that is, the State visit of the Sultan to the mosque. There is a pavilion in the grounds of the palace adjoining the mosque, from which infidels are allowed to see the procession. Cards of admission have to be obtained from an ambassador, and those who hold them are supposed to be the Sultan's guests, and are therefore under his special protection. When at Therapia, the day before, I had got some cards, but on arriving at the pavilion I found all the best windows occupied by passengers from the *Chimborazo*, who had found backsheesh, judiciously administered in the right quarters by Commander Hull, as effectual an "open sesame" as the more orthodox tickets. There was a strong guard of soldiers on each side of the mosque. As the clock chimed the hour, the muezzin appeared on one of the minarets, and in a high, tremulous voice called out—"God is great. There is but one God. Mahomet is God's prophet. Come to prayer. Come and be saved. God is great. There is but one God. Come to prayer." After repeating these words four times, to the north, south, east, and west, the muezzin retired, and soon afterwards, the road leading to the gates of the mosque having first been carefully covered with sand, the procession appeared.

First came a motley host of distinguished officials—pashas, generals, military attachés of foreign embassies—who stood not on the order of their going but apparently went as they pleased, the Sultan himself bringing up the rear in an open carriage. As he approached, some of the *Chimborazo* visitors cheered, at which his Majesty seemed rather pleased. He has an anxious, but not disagreeable expression of countenance, and looks the student rather than the soldier. As soon as he had entered the mosque we hurried away to see the dancing dervishes, who only perform, if I may use the word, on Fridays at two o'clock, in a large room of their Tekkeh, or convent, which is open to the public on these occasions. The area in which they dance is circular in form, and the dervishes were arranged in an outer and an inner circle in the enclosure. Each one revolved gently on his toes to a curious Oriental tune played on a flute in waltz time. Their eyes were fixed or closed, their arms extended, and their robes inflated; and an individual dressed somewhat in the European style and wearing a remarkable hat which to the profane mind recalled the grotesque headpiece of Ally Sloper, acted as conductor, or, I suppose I should say, ballet-master. The pace gradually quickened till the dervishes looked like animated teetotums.

We next visited the great bazaar, which is of Byzantine structure, and is really a city within a city. The area which it covers must be very extensive. The bazaar has been so often described that I will not attempt to inflict another sketch of it on the reader. I can only say that it did not nearly come up to my expectations, and the ventilation was so bad, we were not sorry to get out of it. We next visited some of the Turkish cemeteries at Galata and Pera; nearly every inch of ground is covered with little columns surmounted with turbans for men and sprigs of myrtle for women. At present, however, I believe the Turks are all buried at Scutari, as they have a firm conviction that sooner or later they will be driven out of Europe. We also visited the great cemetery at Scutari, in which so many thousands of our fellow-countrymen lie buried. Close by, at the back of the cemetery, is a large building now used as barracks, which was once the great

English hospital in which Florence Nightingale created the science of nursing. From Scutari we took a caïque to Moda, with the intention of seeing a regatta. We arrived, however, too late to see anything but the defeat of our fellow-countrymen in a rowing match between the crews of an English and a French gunboat. Sir William White having kindly invited us to take tea on board the English gunboat *Cockatrice*, we were hospitably entertained by Commander Fritze H. E. Crowe, the officer in command, who afterwards put us on board the *Chimborazo*, which was to start the next morning. I then learnt that the Sultan had expressed a wish to see me, and that a Court official had come to the Pavilion for me ; but I had already left to go and see the dancing dervishes. I had also missed the opportunity of seeing the Old Seraglio, the Treasury, and the palaces of Beylerbey and Dolma Bagtche, to which his Majesty had graciously invited the passengers, sending six of the Imperial caïques for them. As if these disappointments were not sufficient, I next made the pleasing discovery that my luggage, which had somehow been brought on board without the formality of passing through the Custom House, had been impounded by a vigilant official. I sent my son to the Custom House to recapture our baggage, but he was too late, and neither persuasive French nor vigorous English, nor even the name of the Grand Vizier, made any impression on the stolid *non possumus* attitude of the Turkish officials. My luggage was finally rescued from durance vile by the personal intervention of the Grand Vizier, whose courtesy to me in this "eightpenny matter" makes the episode one of the most remarkable of all my travels. One tries in vain to imagine what would happen if a Turkish citizen were to call at the house of an English Prime Minister during the sacred hour of dinner, and ask him to make the Custom House authorities give up his portmanteau.

The next morning we left Constantinople, and after a pleasant passage over the ill-famed waters of the Euxine, arrived opposite Sebastopol on the morning of September 21st. The sun was shining and the town looked very bright, the white buildings and the domed churches producing a fine effect. After having a good view of the town we steamed north, and between twelve and one were within a few miles of Eupatoria. We now turned round, and this time steering south and keeping near the coast, we came in about an hour to the ruins of the old fort, where the Allies landed on the 14th of September, 1854. Keeping quite near the cliffs, in a little more than half an hour we were at the river Bulganak, which the Allies crossed on the afternoon of the 19th of September. Half an hour more brought us to the mouth of the Alma, and from the deck of the steamer, with good glasses, we had an admirable view of the battle-field. It was quite easy to make out the two villages of Bourliouk and Tarkantav. The white houses could be seen in each village, and the green trees between them looked very pretty on the plain. The Kourgané Hill, on the other side of the river, where the Russian cavalry were posted, was plainly visible, and it was easy to understand what terrible destruction the heavy battery placed on the lower slope of the hill must have caused to Codrington's division, as it advanced after crossing the river. We fancied we could make out the pathway, on the steep left bank of the river very near to the sea, where Bosquet's brigade climbed up, unfortunately placing itself entirely out of the range of the battle-field.

As, for reasons intelligible only to the Russian official mind, we could not get permission to land at the Alma, we steamed to Sebastopol, where, after prolonged inspection by representatives of both the civil and military powers, it was decided that we might be allowed to set foot on Russian soil without risk of the immediate disruption of the Empire. The town itself is very uninteresting, but it still bears numerous marks of the siege. We drove out to the Malakoff, where nothing remained of the famous fort but a grassy hill planted with bushes and ornamental trees. A winding path leads to the top. We picked up a number of relics, such as bullets, pieces of canister-cases, fragments of shot, broken bayonets, rusty sword-handles, and even sardine-boxes. We next visited the great Redan, walking from the English rifle-pits right up to the mound. It was really a distinct dale, first gradually down and then gradually up again to the mound, and the distance from the pits by our measurements was at least two hundred and fifty yards. We examined some of the most advanced rifle-pits, and found that about a foot to a foot and a half below the ground there was no soil whatever but simply rock. It was this circumstance which made it impossible for the British to push their rifle-pits close up to the forts, and rendered the storming of the Redan so much more formidable an undertaking than that of the Malakoff, where the soft ground permitted the French to carry their rifle-pits close up to the Russian guns. Whilst the British troops were being slaughtered in masses for *several minutes* by a heavy fire of grape-shot, the French in a *few seconds* were in the Malakoff. From where we were standing we had a very extensive view out to sea, whilst across the harbour the Star Fort and the great pyramid which marks the situation of the Russian cemetery were conspicuous objects. We then drove to Cathcart Hill to see the English cemetery, which is well kept and picturesquely planted with shrubs. I noticed on the tombs many names that "grace their country's story," and on my return to England I was able to tell several of my friends that the graves of their relatives were well looked after. In the afternoon some of us got small boats from the natives, and rowed past the ironclads, at a little distance from which we saw that great fiasco, the *Popoffka*, now discharging the useful, but humble, function of an asylum and hospital. We rowed some little distance up the mouth of the Tchernaya, and after disembarking and crossing the river we went up a steep path to visit a very interesting Byzantine church hewn out of the cliffs near their summit. Some of our party afterwards descended into the valley, and, recrossing the river, climbed the heights on the other side, passing over the very ground that General Pauloff, with his huge body of infantry and nearly one hundred guns, had traversed on that dull grey morning when the Allies were to have been hurled into the sea.

On the following day, after a somewhat hurried inspection of Todleben's museum, which is a dismal collection of old models, weapons, and prints, we drove to Balaclava. The sun was shining and a gentle breeze blowing, but it did not need much imagination to conceive how different the bleak, barren upland would be when covered with several inches of snow, the thermometer below zero, and a howling wind playing at ninepins with the tents; or perhaps, worse still, when the cold rain fell pitilessly, and the ground was a mere sea of mud, that "fifth element" which Napoleon said he had discovered in Russia. Turning aside to see the French cemetery we found it kept in excellent order by a Frenchman. We visited the house in which Lord Raglan lived; his portrait hangs in the room on the ground floor in which he died. One can recognize in the face the noble disposition and the kind and generous nature, but did he possess that "peculiar and intuitive faculty for the reading of a battle-field" attributed to him by Kinglake? On raising the picture we found behind it a marble tablet with the following inscription: "In this room died Field Marshal Lord Raglan, G.C.B., Commander-in-chief of the British Army in the Crimea, 28th June, 1855." Continuing our drive we found ourselves overlooking the ground where General Scarlett, with a squadron of the Inniskillings and two squadrons of the Greys, the celebrated three hundred of the heavy brigade, charged up hill a mass of three thousand Russian cavalry. We could see where the General, accompanied by his young Aide-de-Camp, Alec Elliot, and closely followed by two horsemen, his orderly, the celebrated swordsman with the curious name of Shegog, and his trumpeter, full fifty yards in advance of his own three squadrons, broke into the mighty masses of the Russians. Soon after we passed the village of Kadekoi, and then the sea, and the little harbour of Balaclava, so landlocked that it looks like a lake, came into view. Whilst we were waiting for lunch we walked through the village and noticed the picturesque ruins of the old Genoese castle, and the cross put up as a memorial of the great work of Florence Nightingale. Having partaken of a frugal meal, we drove back to the field of Balaclava, and were put down within half a mile of Canrobert's Hill. After walking to this point and staying there a few minutes we passed on to the third Redoubt or Aratabia, from which we had a good view of the famous "valley of death." It strikes me as an ideal ground for a mimic cavalry duel, the spectators standing on the Causeway Heights or the Fiorkine Hills; but it certainly is not a well-chosen place for six hundred horsemen to charge into the mouth of a strong battery of artillery, whilst the hills on each side are occupied by huge masses of infantry. A monument stands where the Russian battery was posted. A good number of our party descended into the valley, and our young poetess recited, with much feeling but in admirable taste, "The Charge of the Light Brigade," on the very spot over which the gallant horsemen had ridden to death! In looking at the scene of so much heroism one could not help thinking with bitterness how it has in many cases been rewarded by an ungrateful country. These poor fellows did not haggle as to the amount of blood they were prepared to shed, and it is to my mind nothing less than a national disgrace that red tape should tie up the public purse in such a case. However, Mr. Stanhope has recently announced that, at last, some provision is to be made for the survivors of those who fought so bravely in our last great war.

After a drive of a couple of hours, we arrived at the base of the heights of Inkerman; some of the party got down and climbed the hill, but the learned and discreet, of whom I was one, made a slight *détour*, and finally ascended by a new road which passes close to the spot where General Cathcart, in making a flank movement, was, in his turn, outflanked and killed in fighting his way back. We finally arrived on The Heights close to The Barrier, around which so many of our gallant soldiers fell on the 5th of November, 1854. We left our carriage and walked on to Shell Hill, from which there is a capital view all over the country. With the battle-field under one's eyes it is easy to see how cramped the space is, and how lucky it was for our troops that the Russians could not bring their enormous masses of men into play. We next proceeded to the Sandbag Battery, where a mass of stones, and what looked like a fragment of wall, still remain. It is now surrounded by scrub oaks and other trees fifteen or twenty feet in height. On returning to our ship we wiped out the memory of these ancient feuds with a dance on board, to which the

Admiral in command at Sebastobol and the principal officials, with their wives and daughters, were invited. A visit to the ruins of Khersonesus next morning brought our stay at Sebastopol to a close.

On leaving that city we steamed round Cape Kherson, passing Balaclava and running along the grand mountainous cliffs of the southern coast of the Crimea. The hills, which are for the most part of a red colour, are very bold, precipitous, and angular, while the beautiful trees which have been planted round the palaces and villas along the coast make an agreeable contrast to the rockbound shore. The scenery seemed to me on the whole more magnificent than that of the Italian Riviera, principally because the coast mountains are higher and nearer to the sea. In the afternoon we reached the pretty town of Yalta. The mountains at the back are closer to the town than anywhere along the Franco-Italian Riviera, except at Mentone. The next day we explored the town and its neighbourhood, seeing the Imperial Palace at Livadia, the palace of Prince Woronzoff at Aloupka, with its superb gardens in which their are two Wellingtonias planted by the Prince and Princess of Wales in 1869.

I consider that Yalta is an admirable health resort for persons whose lungs are delicate. English people would find it an agreeable change after having spent several winters on the Riviera. Of course it would not be advisable for those suffering from active disease to take so long a journey, but persons threatened with consumption, or those whose lungs contain healed cavities—extinct volcanoes of disease—and who still find it necessary to winter abroad, would, I have no doubt, benefit greatly by the change of environment they would experience by living some months in this little oasis of civilization in the desert of Tartar barbarism.

From Yalta we returned to Constantinople, and, after receiving our letters and newspapers and dropping two passengers, we steamed on to Mudania. Immediately on landing we drove to Broussa, the ancient capital of the Turks in Asia before they obtained a foothold in Europe. Here are the tombs of the first Ottoman sultans. There are eight of them—

miserable domed buildings, mostly octagonal or hexagonal in shape, and containing the bodies of the sultans' wives as well as their own. The tombs of the sultans look like long wooden coffins, which, instead of being flat on the top, are angular, like the stone tombs often seen in English churchyards. Over the coffins are large pieces of green silk, finely embroidered with gold and silver thread; but the metal is tarnished, the silk worm-eaten or worn away, and these funereal adornments now present a very forlorn appearance. The coffins of the wives are generally about half the size of those of the sultans, and are covered with very simple green silk trappings. Some of the mosques at Broussa are exquisitely beautiful, and the Grand Bazaar is much more interesting than that of Constantinople. The silks and embroideries of Broussa are renowned throughout the world, and both the merchants and their wares are much more purely Asiatic in character than in European Turkey, the Jewish element in particular being much less visible. Broussa, which has repeatedly suffered from earthquakes and teems with hot springs, is famous for its baths, and several of our party went through the ordeal—or enjoyed the luxury, whichever expression may be preferred—of a genuine Turkish bath, the thoroughgoing character of which might have satisfied the late Mr. Urquhart. Whilst "doing" Broussa our headquarters were at Chekirje, a health resort near it, where a whole hotel had been chartered for us. Some Armenian visitors who were spending the summer there were very courteous and hospitable to our party. After a most agreeable stay amidst surroundings which gave us a very fair idea of Asiatic life, we returned to Mudania and re-embarked for Malta, homeward bound. Early in the morning of October 30th we passed into the circular gulf of Santorin from the north, that is, between the islands of Thera and Therasia. Here the captain delayed the ship for half an hour to give Mr. Tristram Ellis an opportunity of making some sketches. In the afternoon we had a good view of Crete, and in the evening we passed Serigo, losing sight of land after that till we arrived at Malta on October 4th.

Malta has been recommended as a health resort, although I cannot understand on what grounds. It is the most windy place I have ever been in, and it is extremely dusty, whilst the glare of the sun is most disagreeable. It is further afflicted with one of the most disgusting harbours in the world, and has the questionable privilege of possessing a special fever of its own production. On October 9th we reached Gibraltar, and on the 13th we arrived at Plymouth in a dense fog, as if to prevent our having any doubt of the fact that we were really home again in "Old England."

Thus ended one of the most interesting and delightful trips it has ever been my lot to enjoy. I think every one was pleased, most were benefited, and those who cared to take advantage of the abundant opportunities offered to them were instructed.

When we were nearing the shores of England I made a careful medical inspection of my fellow-passengers, and came to the conclusion that, with one or two exceptions, they had all greatly benefited in health by the excursion. Those who on setting out looked well, now looked better; and those who had looked "sicklied o'er with the pale cast of thought" or worry or illness, now had the glow of health on their faces. On myself the effect of the trip was almost like that of the fabled elixir of life; I felt, comparatively speaking, like Faust after his "great transformation scene" from age to youth.

This, my first experience of the "new yachting" leads me to think that it has a great future before it, for it has many advantages compared with the ordinary form of that amusement. Of course, there are some exclusive persons who do not care to mingle with the common herd, and who prefer to take their pleasure in a craft which makes one feel that there is some truth in Johnson's definition of a ship as "a prison, with the chance of being drowned." Even sailing in a large and well-fitted yacht, with a select party of one's "inner circle" of acquaintances on board, does not always come up to the ideal of human felicity. A friend of mine, who has had a yacht for many years, tells me that people are more selfish on board a yacht than under any other circumstances. There are many other worries attending the possession of a yacht, apart from the expense which it entails.

In the new yachting there is no unpleasantness as to the choice of places to be visited, nor are carefully arranged plans liable to be disarranged at the last moment by the thoughtlessness or unpunctuality of friends. You have the pleasures of companionship without any of the responsibilities of a host or the obligations of a guest. You can enjoy the sea and the air —charged with ozone, which is the champagne of the lungs, and free from any taint of vegetable or animal corruption— just as fully as if you were an Alexander Selkirk on a floating island; and you have many comforts which cannot be had even on the largest and best appointed yachts. I can strongly recommend what I may call the "omnibus yacht," if not exactly as a "pentacle of rejuvenescence," still as one of the best remedies I know for the effects of overwork or prolonged illness. Only, in order to get the full benefit of it, the traveller must change his mind as well as his sky. He must leave all his professional and other worries behind him, and give strict orders that no business letters or telegrams shall be forwarded to him. Let him say with Tibullus, "Carry me through remotest peoples, carry me over the waves, where no woman [read "client," "patient," or "constituent," according to circumstances] shall know my way." Then let him allow himself to be borne along, seeing many men and cities, and throwing himself completely into the life of the moment, absorbing new impressions and new experiences, as a plant draws nourishment from the surrounding air. Let him be content that the thing does him good, without troubling himself why it should do so, or insisting on having his sensations translated into scientific phraseology. The great benefit of such a trip is repose in a pure atmosphere with constant change of scene. Further, there is the important circumstance that in a voyage in a well-appointed ship, a man is amid ideal sanitary surroundings, where the bacilli (or a large proportion of them) cease from troubling, and the drain-afflicted householder is, or ought to be, at rest. Many people to whom ordinary yachting would be intolerable on account of sea-sickness, could defy the enemy on a large ship, and in case of accidental illness of any kind, the latter has advantages too obvious to need mention. On the whole, I can echo the sentiments expressed in the following classical lines which I had the pleasure of hearing recited by the author himself, the Honourable Member for the *Chimborazo*, as the Greek poets used to read their own verses at public festivals :—

"If you're sick of seeing patients, or of interviewing clients,
Or have lectured quite sufficiently on politics and science;
If your legislative powers are in want of reparation,
And you've spent a tedious session in the service of the nation;
.   .   .   .
Then I stake my word upon it that the best thing you can do, sir,
Is to take an ocean voyage in an Orient Company's cruiser."

THE RELATION OF GENERAL CULTURE TO PROFESSIONAL SUCCESS.

THE advantages of general culture are denied only by those too ignorant to appreciate them; but its influence on professional success is not, I am disposed to think, so fully or so universally recognised by professional men as it ought to be. Indeed, some appear to imagine that there is a kind of incompatibility or mutual antagonism between wide culture and professional knowledge or skill. This view appears to be particularly entertained with respect to what I may term the more *technical* professions, as, for example, medicine and engineering; and hence one hears it constantly asserted, even by persons themselves not altogether destitute of culture, that the sooner a lad intended for such a career is set to acquire the knowledge and skill directly fitting him for the exercise of his calling the better. They do not, perhaps, go so far as to say that the less such a youth is encumbered "with mere literary instruction and education," as the severely practical founder of the Mason Science College at Birmingham somewhat contemptuously called it, the greater are his chances of achieving success in the business of his life, but it comes to much the same thing in reality. Of course, in many cases a lad has to be put with the least possible delay to the study of a profession by which he can earn his bread, for the all-sufficient reason that his family cannot afford the time or the money necessary for a complete preliminary education. Even among those, however, who cannot plead narrowness of means as an excuse, and who do not; like the late Sir Josiah Mason, regard "mere literary instruction and education" as a positive hindrance to the acquisition of more profitable knowledge, it is too often the case that general culture is neglected simply because it is looked upon as ornamental rather than useful. They are men who, like Mr. Gradgrind in *Hard Times*, pin their faith on what they call "solid facts," and have a healthy contempt for "elegant trifling." Milton, as a Cambridge mathematician is said to have complained, "proves nothing." Plato does not tell us how to build a bridge, nor Cervantes how to draw a deed of conveyance.

Therefore, argues our "practical" man, though literature is all very well in its way, especially when money can be made by it, a man who has to prepare himself for a profession has no time for such things; they are pretty toys which must be thrown aside when the real work of life has to be faced. At best they may perhaps be allowed occasionally, like a visit to the theatre, for the amusement of an hour of leisure. I propose to attempt to show that what I may call the Gradgrind view of general culture is shortsighted and mischievous, even from the standpoint of mere utility, as it tends to make men neglect what can hardly fail to prove a most powerful help in whatever profession they adopt. In other words, I maintain that general culture, in addition to its higher claims on our respect, has a practical value for professional men which can scarcely be over-estimated.

In obedience to the precept of Locke, I will clear the ground by a definition of terms. What is general culture? Many use the expression as the antithesis to technical knowledge, and they are right as far as they go, but the definition is very inadequate. Some think culture synonymous with classical learning, others with a sort of superficial smattering of miscellaneous literature and art. Matthew Arnold, the great apostle who preached his gospel of culture in season and out of season to the Philistines, defined it as "the knowledge of the best that has been thought and said in the world." Professor Huxley objects to this definition as onesided, inasmuch as it does not recognise science as an element of culture, whereas, he contends, science affords a "criticism of life" as valuable as literature, but of a different kind, appealing as it does, not to authority or to what anybody may have thought or said, but to fact. Huxley admits, however, that an exclusively scientific training will bring about a mental twist as surely as an exclusively literary training. Newman speaks of the cultivation of the mind as meaning "the force, the steadiness, the comprehensiveness, and the versatility of intellect, the command over our own powers, the just estimate of things as they pass before us, which sometimes, indeed, is a natural gift, but commonly is not gained without much effort and the exercise of years." These luminous words give the essence of the matter in a nutshell. Culture is not the possession of a stock of facts or ideas, literary, scientific, artistic, or philosophical; it is a *condition* of the intellect, or rather of the whole microcosm, analogous to that state of physical perfection which athletes strive to attain to by training. Culture implies strength, sureness, and flexibility of mind, and the development of all its faculties to the highest possible degree, so that they can be concentrated without difficulty on any subject that may present itself. A man of culture is not necessarily a giant in any particular sphere of intellectual effort, but he is a *potential* giant in many; he has the world of human activity at his feet, so to speak, and can bring the whole force of his trained mind to bear on any province thereof which he may select.

If this be the nature of culture, surely it is the very height of folly for any one, however intolerant of anything which is not "practical," to decry it as useless. It is, on the contrary, the most distinctly *useful* attainment which a man can have, for it makes him master of himself and of all his intellectual resources; it teaches him to distinguish accurately what he knows from what he does not know; what he can do from what he cannot; it gives him powers and pleasures and sympathies which those who have not gone through a similar discipline know nothing of; it makes him a complete man, not a mere bread-winning machine. General culture, therefore, although not directly imparting the special knowledge required for the exercise of any profession, makes a man in the highest degree fit to receive it. He acquires it, too, at once more easily and quickly and more thoroughly than those whose faculties are, as it were, in a state of nature. Culture, in short, prepares the soil for any kind of seed that may be sown in it, and supplies the fructifying influence which makes it grow and ripen. To use the noble words of Milton, it fits a man "to perform justly, skilfully, and magnanimously all the offices, both private and public, of peace and war."

Culture, therefore, being a condition of intellectual efficiency of mental health comparable to the state of bodily well-being when all the organs work harmoniously together, the practical question arises, how is this most desirable object to be attained? Culture is not an innate quality or a heaven-born gift; every man has to acquire it for himself by laborious and protracted effort. There is only one way of bringing the mind to full functional perfection, and that is by cultivation. Its different faculties must be disciplined and increased in power by exercise: in one word, they must be carefully *trained*. The two chief objects to be attained in intellectual training are *accuracy* and *breadth*. As for the *instruments* of culture, by which I mean the special studies which serve best for the acquisition of it, I confess I am strongly in favour of the older discipline by means of which so many generations of men of the highest eminence, both in the world of thought and that of action, have been made what they were, namely, classical and mathematical studies. The mind that will not be made accurate by conscientious study of the close-linked chains of mathematical reasoning, and by minute analysis of the grammatical structure of the ancient languages, will hardly have its congenial deficiency remedied by any other means. It is this which makes classical studies so extraordinarily valuable, even though "small Latin and less Greek" remain as a permanent possession in after life. The *facts* themselves may be forgotten, but the mental vigour gained by striving to master them will not be lost. It is a vulgar error to despise the study of Greek and Latin as being nothing but a matter of *words*; language is very near akin to thought, and dissection of the one is an immense help towards the analysis of the other, which no one

will deny to be an important element in mental training.
Further, the study of words leads to an exact appreciation of
their meaning and force, hence to scrupulous accuracy in the
use of them. This is a very important matter indeed : care in
the selection of words is a virtue closely connected with intellectual veracity ; and the opposite defect has caused an infinite
loss of time, vexation of spirit, and misunderstanding of all
kinds, probably ever since "this foolish compounded clay man"
could, with any approach to correctness, define himself as
animal rationale. There is no surer mark of culture than a
clear perception of the meaning of words with logical precision
in using them.

Priceless, however, as classical literature is as an instrument
of culture, it is neither all-sufficient nor indispensable. A man
whose whole attention has been given to the ancient writers,
however much he may appreciate their artistic beauty, is little
better than a pedant—a condition which is absolutely incompatible with culture, as I understand it, that is to say, as a
habit of mind the reverse of exclusive. If culture is a "criticism
of life," it should include a knowledge of the "very form and
pressure" of the age in which one lives ; it is obvious that this
cannot be got from the classics. Neither is ancient literature
indispensable for culture, especially to those whose birthright
gives them access to the writings of the many master minds in
every order of thought and imagination who have expressed
themselves in our own tongue. A man who cannot extract
culture from Shakespeare, Milton, Swift, Hume, Gibbon, Burns,
Scott, Shelley, John Henry Newman, Carlyle, Ruskin, Tennyson,
Browning, and innumerable others, will certainly not profit
any more by the profoundest study of the classical writers.
Classical culture must always remain the privilege of the few
who happen to have time or special opportunity, but the
treasures of English literature are open to all Englishmen, and
the possibilities of culture which they contain may compensate
for exclusion from any other source.

While thus laying stress on literature as an instrument of
culture, I would not have it supposed that I agree with those
who deny that science may be advantageously used with the

same object. On the contrary, I think it essential that scientific instruction shall form an integral part of every scheme of education. A culture that is purely literary or purely scientific is not worthy of the name. Culture is before everything catholic, and narrowness of any kind is incompatible with it. If it is important to know "the best that is thought and said in the world," it is just as necessary to realise, in the words of Huxley, "that Nature is the expression of a definite order with which nothing interferes, and that the chief business of mankind is to learn order and govern themselves accordingly."

A certain amount of artistic culture is within the reach of most persons, and should on no account be neglected. I believe that a much larger number of persons would possess real executive talent in art if in childhood preliminary instruction were given in technical matters, especially in drawing. The mere criticism of art is not sufficient, it tends to make a man *dilettante*. For those, however, who do not possess any artistic faculty I would strongly recommend the learning of a handicraft. Artistic training develops the emotional side of a man's nature, which is sometimes weakened by the too exclusive cultivation of the intellectual powers, whilst the practice of a handicraft not only affords manual discipline, but it teaches habits of close observation, and the necessity for the greatest precision ; it also makes a cultivated man more able to enter into sympathy with those whose hard lot necessitates unceasing manual toil. Goethe uttered a great truth when he said that no side of man's complex nature can be safely neglected ; every faculty of the soul, the mind, and the body should be developed to the greatest possible extent, so that each man may attain the full power and dignity of his nature, realising the Greek ideal of the καλοκαγαθος—the beautiful and good man, or "gentleman," as Coleridge translates it.

Culture, however, is not to be got from books alone, nor, indeed, from solitary study of any kind. Books are, of course, indispensable : they are the quarries from which the stones for the intellectual edifice are obtained. But the shaping and polishing are more effectively done by contact with other minds. There can be no doubt that a well-appointed university is the best place for acquiring culture. Not merely because instruction in every branch of knowledge may be got there, but because it is given by the voice of a living teacher, and sifted and refined by the criticism of many minds. A University education above all prepares a man for the business of life, by fitting him to deal with his fellow-men. To quote Newman once more, "It gives a man a clear conscious view of his own opinions and judgments, a truth in developing them, and eloquence in expressing them. It teaches him to see things as they are, to go right to the point, to disentangle a skein of thought, to detect what is sophistical, and to discard what is irrelevant." It is the contact with many minds of various structure, but all in the exuberant activity of growth, which is the most valuable element in a University education; the course of study and the examinations are in my opinion of quite secondary importance. With regard to our present highly developed system of examination, which forms so marked—I may even say, so aggressive—a feature in our modern life, I venture to think that so far from helping culture it is altogether opposed to it. It leads a man to work, not for the sake of learning or for the training of his mind, but in order that he may out-manœuvre his examiners, or that he may win prizes. That is the height of his ambition: worse still, the capacity of accomplishing these feats becomes his sole test of intellectual merit. Culture establishes a harmonious balance of power among the mental faculties, each being developed to its utmost limits and none being crushed out or withered for want of use. The examination system, on the contrary, develops the memory altogether in excess of the higher powers of the mind, and substitutes for the lofty ideal of knowledge that which will *pay* in the examination room; the one is a joy and "possession for ever," the other a mere *tool* which is thrown aside when it has served its purpose. The Chinese have, I understand, a system of examination which is so complete and perfect as to be a subject of envy to the "coaches" and "crammers" and other educational vampires who suck the intellectual life-blood of the ingenious youth in these islands; yet, in spite of its advantages in this respect, that country has made scarcely any appreciable progress for many centuries. Are we tending towards a similar petrifaction of our civilization and national life?

But what, it may be asked, has all this to do with the acquisition of professional knowledge? A little reflection will show that it has a very real and practical bearing. Culture prepares the soil; if the seed of knowledge falls on a rock it withers away, if among thorns they grow up and choke it. An untrained mind acquires knowledge with infinitely more difficulty than a disciplined intelligence, and masters it less thoroughly. There is a want of insight, of grasp, of the sense of proportion, and of intellectual tact in those whose minds have not been developed by the mental gymnastics of general culture, which puts them at an enormous disadvantage in the acquisition of new ideas. Even if they succeed in learning more facts than their better-trained rivals, they lack the power of weighing and estimating, discriminating and co-ordinating them. They are the slaves of minutiæ, incapable alike of generalisation or distinction; intellectually they "cannot see the forest for the trees." Matthew Arnold was particularly struck by this in the competitive examinations for admission to the Indian Civil Service; he noticed that while candidates who had been prepared by "crammers" usually knew more than those who came straight from a public school, the latter knew incomparably better what they had learned.

The notion that culture, so far from being a help to the acquisition of professional knowledge, is really an obstacle thereto, is founded on a confusion of thought which it may be worth while to clear up. It would be just as reasonable to suppose that training could be a disqualification for an athlete in the performance of his feats. It is true, however, that culture, though not directly an impediment to the acquisition of professional knowledge, may indirectly produce an almost equivalent effect by creating a distaste for it. There is no doubt that a cultured man may at first take less kindly to technical study than one whose mind is more or less a *tabula rasa*, waiting for something to be written on it. Sir Benjamin

Brodie tells us that he found it difficult at first to concentrate his mind, which had been fed on the classical writers, on the dreary minutiæ of anatomy. In like manner the barbarous jargon and tedious technicalities of law may not unnaturally revolt a man sensitive to literary beauty on his first introduction to them. Another thing which has led to the notion that mental cultivation is antagonistic to the acquisition of technical knowledge is the fact that dilettanteism, which is a smattering of literary and artistic commonplaces, is often confounded with true culture. Dilettanteism certainly does disqualify the mind for grappling with difficulties, and is a bar to the attainment of solid knowledge of any kind; but dilettanteism is not culture, though it may bear superficial resemblance to it.

I am willing, however, to admit that as all minds are not cast in the same mould, the same kind of cultivation is not universally applicable. Doctors, in dealing with their patients, have to take into account what they call *idiosyncrasies*, that is to say, peculiarities of constitution, which exemplify the literal truth of the old saw, "What is one man's meat is another man's poison." Thus we find that in certain persons opium causes excitement instead of sleep; in others such generally harmless things as eggs, various kinds of fish, and even mutton act as violent poisons. There are mental as well as bodily idiosyncrasies, and training which is beneficial to most will be useless or even injurious to some. I am strongly of opinion that there are certain minds which can be over-cultivated, that is to say, educated beyond their faculties. Athletes tell us that a man may be *overtrained*; then instead of becoming more and more master of his muscles he breaks down—"goes stale," I believe, is the technical expression—and becomes unequal to the task for which he was being prepared. Now, although Mr. Arthur Balfour has ridiculed the idea that a man could be over-educated, I must confess that his arguments seemed to me more ingenious than convincing. I am not speaking of too much learning; there can, I imagine, be no question that a man may be overwhelmed by the dead weight of mere amorphous erudition to such an extent that his reasoning powers lie buried beneath it. The man's mind becomes unwieldy, like the body of one of those "armadillo wights" of the days of chivalry, who were so oppressed by the weight of their armour that when unhorsed they could not rise from the ground without assistance. In disease it often happens that overgrowth of one tissue element is associated with wasting of others; a mass is formed, the pressure of which generally cuts off the nutrition of the neighbouring parts: it crushes them out of existence in fact, and if it is of what we call *malignant* nature it actually devours them, and takes their place. Something of the same sort occurs in a mind afflicted with an overgrowth of book learning; the powers of observation, reflection, and judgment are impaired or altogether destroyed; only receptiveness is left, a receptiveness of opinions rather than of facts and ideas. Culture of this kind—if such it can be called—is absolutely inimical to professional knowledge. Genuine culture promotes and preserves the *health* of the mind, and makes it alert, inventive, and self-sustaining; it enables us to see things as they are, and is therefore of the very highest value in helping us not merely to receive but to digest and assimilate knowledge of all kinds. Excessive book learning, on the other hand, leads to *disease* of the mind, makes it sluggish and inert as regards independent effort, and, worst fault of all, as far as the acquisition of professional knowledge is concerned, it tends to substitute a blind, indiscriminating, mechanical regard for authority, an idolatrous worship of books, for the accurate perception of facts and their mutual relations, which is the very essence of knowledge which has to be used for the guidance of men.

The direct bearing which general culture has on professional success is therefore obvious. But what is "professional success"? It is not merely making a living, still less the accumulation of wealth, though, of course, if a man cannot support himself by his profession he can hardly be said to "succeed" in it. Real success implies adding to the stock of professional knowledge which has been gathered by his predecessors; it implies raising or at least maintaining the credit and influence of his profession; it implies giving the benefit of one's technical skill to the greatest possible number of persons who stand in need of it; it implies developing one's sphere of usefulness to the utmost extent, and being an efficient piece of the machinery of society and advancing the welfare of mankind in every direction as far as lies in one. A man who looks on his profession as nothing better than a means of extracting as much money as he can from his fellow-creatures cannot be said to achieve success, however rich he may become; he lives altogether for the lowest part of his nature, and hardly deserves to rank higher in the hierarchy of creation than a successful beast of prey.

Having explained what is the nature of professional success, let me briefly allude to the qualities which enable a man to achieve it, with especial reference to the bearing of general culture on each of them. What I may call the personal factors of professional success, that is to say, the factors which belong solely to the man himself, are (1) an adequate amount of the technical knowledge and skill which are his stock-in-trade; (2) the power of using that knowledge and skill with the best possible effect, and of applying them swiftly and surely to individual cases as they come before him; (3) a knowledge of human nature, and of the wants, feelings, necessities, prejudices, and motives of action of men and women in different spheres of life, so that he may know how to deal with them and how to be most useful to them; (4) the power of influencing others, that is to say, the power of winning their confidence, convincing their intellects, and directing their will.

With regard to the first of these points, I have endeavoured to prove that culture is of the greatest possible service as an aid to the acquisition of professional knowledge. A man destitute of culture may, indeed, "know his work," but other things being equal he will not know it so well as one whose intellect has been thoroughly trained. In particular, he will not know his own weak points so clearly—and a knowledge of the exact limits of our own powers is essential for the successful use of them. Almost without exception our leading men in Parliament, in the Church, and at the Bar are men of undoubted culture. Journalism, which thirty years ago was mainly in the hands of semi-literate penny-a-liners, is now largely recruited from the Universities; even the Stage (if that can be called a profession) now recognises the importance of general culture in addition to special training. In my own profession a like change is in progress; the Apothecary, the "College and Hall man," who knew his trade by rule of thumb, and was in respect of general culture on a level with other small shopkeepers, has almost disappeared, and it is difficult to recognise his lineal descendant in the refined gentleman, who has a soul above gallipots and can cultivate thriving colonies of the most recently caught microbe and talk about "Shakespeare and the musical glasses" besides. To what is the great improvement both in the efficiency and in the social position of the medical profession in this country due but to the more generally diffused intellectual culture within its ranks? This, so far from making men worse doctors, has made the profession, as a whole, so much more proficient in their art that the old traditional sneers about us have become almost obsolete. I do not say we are more learned than our predecessors—on the contrary, we are, as a class, less erudite than the Diafoiruses so justly ridiculed by Molière; but there can be no doubt we are more cultured, that is to say, we have a clearer insight into things as they are, and *therefore* we are more practical and more efficient.

That culture gives us the power of using technical knowledge with the best effect is a truth so obvious that I need not dwell upon it. Compare what Moltke (in speaking of the American Civil War, I believe) called the "scrambling of armed mobs" with the calm resistless advance of a Macedonian phalanx, or an army corps of "thinking bayonets"; each man in the mob may be bigger, stronger, and better armed than the disciplined soldiers, yet the crowd is scattered by the troops like chaff by the wind. It is the discipline, the training, and the intelligent direction to a definite end that make the difference. It is the same thing with a disciplined mind as compared with an untrained one. The precise object to be aimed at is clearly perceived, and the whole faculties of the mind are then brought to bear upon it. The secret of Napoleon's magnificent generalship consisted, it appears, in swiftly concentrating his attack on one point of the enemy's position and crushing resistance by superior numbers. This he did successfully even when his force as a whole was inferior to that of his opponents. This exactly illustrates the effect of culture on the intellect; it enables it to mass its powers on the particular matter before it, and in this way it will succeed where a mind naturally more powerful but without the advantage of training will fail.

With regard to the knowledge of human nature and the consequent power of dealing with men and women, which I have mentioned as an important element of professional success, I have no doubt many would say that this cannot be got from books, but only from actual contact with living fellow-creatures. This is unquestionably true to a certain extent, but it is equally true that here also culture is of great assistance. No one will deny that a knowledge of history, "philosophy teaching by example," as Bolingbroke called it, is of the highest use to the politician; familiarity with the past enables him to understand the present and, to some extent, predict the future. Just as the inspection of a dead body enables a physician to interpret the signs and forecast the issue of a disease, literature "holds the mirror up to nature"; it is the reflection of human life and the expression of human character and human passion. This being so, can there be a doubt that if it is not actually the key which unlocks the souls of our fellow-creatures to us it at least teaches us how to use it? Here, as in everything else, the mind trained to analysis, to accuracy of observation, to caution in deduction, must see more clearly and see further than one which is guided purely by the light of nature. Culture, which is essentially familiarity with many minds and their workings, gives a power of sympathetic insight—a delicate perception of the effect of words and facts on different persons—which is hardly ever a natural gift. Without this the clergyman fails to understand the spiritual needs of his flock; he preaches over their heads, or quite wide of the mark; his ministrations, however well meant, leave those to whom they are offered cold and unmoved, perhaps even repel them. Frequently a new member, even if able, well-informed, and an effective speaker to other audiences, fails to catch the tone of the House of Commons. This may, of course, happen to any one at first, as it happened to Disraeli and many others, from a variety of causes. If, however, the ill-success is permanent, I think it will always be found to depend on want of culture of one kind or another, which makes the orator incapable of that intuitive perception of the effect of his words on his audience, which is the direct outcome of sympathy with their average intellectual constitution. He is unable, in the words of Goethe, to "imitate their manner of conceiving."

A barrister cannot plead his client's cause without understanding not only the facts of the case, but the character and mind of the man he has to defend, and of his opponents. A physician who would treat his patients as machines which get out of order, without knowing or caring for the working of the subtler part of their economy, and without taking into account not merely the particular bodily ill with which they happen to be afflicted, but their character and their relations to those around them, would do little good, even as far as immediate physical necessities are concerned. If you know a man's strength and his weakness you know how to deal with him. This gives you that confidence in yourself which begets confidence in others. A large part of the secret of professional success is the power not merely of giving good advice, but of inducing those who consult you to follow it. To this end different persons will be influenced in different ways, and it is the intuitive sympathetic perception of how each of them can be most effectually led to submit his will to yours that will enable you to guide them in the way they should go. A man may have a thorough knowledge of his profession and great skill in applying it, but unless he can *manage* his clients, patients, parishioners, or whatever they may be, he will fail in attaining the highest success. Nothing so fits a man for this delicate duty as culture, which will make a man useful and effective, where a man of greater professional learning and skill may be powerless for good.

SWIMMING.

It has often been thought curious that man should be the only animal that cannot swim naturally, but it would be much more curious if man *could* swim. Various causes have been put forward as the reason why man cannot swim. Thevenot, in his "Art of Swimming," published in the year 1711, maintained that it was the fear of drowning that prevented people swimming; but this cannot be the case, as adults standing in water of only four feet in depth, in which they could not drown, nevertheless cannot swim. Whilst very young animals can swim enough to keep themselves afloat for a short time, the human infant, if placed in water before it is old enough to understand the danger, is quickly drowned. Some physiologists maintain that the cause of a human being not being able to swim is, that the centre of gravity in man is in the head when the body is thrown forward; hence the head tends to sink deeper than the rest of the body, and in this way the mouth goes under water and the respiratory tract is closed. I do not, however, believe that this is the cause of man being unable to swim, as in the case of the lion and the ox the centre of gravity is certainly in the head and neck, and both these animals are good swimmers. The fact is that the specific gravity of an animal is less than that of salt water and only a little above that of fresh water, and very slight regular movement is sufficient to keep an animal or human being above water. Every swimmer knows that when resting vertically in the water, either by "treading water" or slightly moving the hands laterally, he can maintain himself in a safe position; but when four-footed animals find themselves in water the movement they make with their extremities is only a very slight variation of their ordinary mode of progression on land, and hence the youngest animal can generally swim easily. It is very improbable that man has been able to swim naturally since he exclusively assumed the upright position in walking. That our remote ancestors could not swim appears probable from other evidence. Thus, it is scarcely likely that people would have sought safety by dwelling in the so-called "lake habitations" on small islands near to the margin of lakes, but surrounded by deep water, if man of that period had been able to swim. It appears also from the experience of Mr. Ashe, as recorded in "Two Kings of Uganda," that the natives on the borders of the Victoria Nyanza lakes are unable to swim, and Mr. Ashe gave immense satisfaction by swimming in a pond for the amusement of one of their sable majesties. It is true that the natives of the Sandwich Islands at the present day swim with extraordinary grace and agility, but there is no evidence to prove that this art has not been acquired in quite recent times. The bas-reliefs of Nineveh represent men swimming across rivers supported by inflated skins. In the Greek age, besides the case of Ulysses and Diomed swimming in the sea after the capture of the horses of Rhesus, we have the well-known nightly feat of Leander swimming from Abydos to Sestos to visit his sweetheart Hero. Lord Byron performed the same feat in 1810, and with Lieutenant Echenhead swam over the same course somewhat later in seventy minutes. The Romans looked upon swimming as a rudiment of education, and if they wished to speak of a man who was thoroughly illiterate they would say he could *neither read nor swim*. Does not Shakespeare tell us how Cassius saved the life of Cæsar, when the great man cried out in the troubled waters of the Tiber, "Help me, Cassius, or I sink"? Then Cassius bore him "from the waves," and he was saved. If Cassius had not saved Cæsar Britain might never have been conquered. The fine old Roman roads in England would never have been made, and we should not have enjoyed the advantage of four hundred years of Roman rule had not Cassius been a good swimmer.

SWIMMING.

In the French army swimming is now compulsory, and as every man is obliged to be a soldier, in a few years every Frenchman will be able to swim. Mr. P. H. Hamerton, in his recent work on England, notices how many more people swim in France than in England; but at any rate we have produced better swimmers than France. In the English army every encouragement is given to the men to learn swimming, though it is not compulsory. In places where there is any provision for natation, lists are kept of all who can swim, in order that they may act as pickets and look after the men who are unable to swim.

The value of swimming as a hygienic exercise can be shown in many ways. In the first place the act requires the inhalation of a very large quantity of air. Taking 1 as the standard of the amount of air inhaled when lying down, the following table, taken from Dr. Edward Smith's work, shows the amount inspired in other positions and movements:—

In lying	1
In sitting	1·18
In standing	1·33
In walking 1 mile an hour	1·90
„ 2 miles an hour	2·76
„ 3 „ „	3·23
In carrying 34 lbs.	3·50
„ 63 lbs.	3·84
In *swimming*	4·33

In inhaling so much air a large amount of carbonic acid is exhaled. In addition to this effect, there is no exercise except rowing which calls into play so many muscles at the same time. From these facts two lessons may be deduced: 1st, in order to permit of the inhalation of large quantities of air, the stomach ought to be empty, or in other words swimming should generally be done before a meal; the employment of so many muscles also indicates the necessity of taking food soon after swimming. The best time for swimming in the summer is probably early in the morning and between five and seven in the afternoon. The principal precautions to be taken with regard to swimming are two: first, not to stay too long in the water; and secondly, not to stay too long *under* water. With regard to the first proposition it is difficult to fix an exact time, but everything depends on the temperature of the water. If the water is really warm, as in a swimming bath, a person may stay in as long as half an hour without injury; but in swimming in rivers and in the sea from seven to fifteen minutes is generally as much as can be endured with advantage. There are, however, so many variations in different constitutions that it is impossible to lay down absolute laws. Everything depends on the bather's own sensations. If he has a good reaction and feels well, warm, and hungry after swimming, it matters little how long he remains in the water. If, on the other hand, he feels cold when he comes out, if his teeth chatter, the fingers being very white and the nails blue, it shows that the swimmer has stayed too long in the water, and that he ought not to remain so long another time. With regard to diving, I have seen many cases of deafness which had arisen from swimmers remaining too long beneath the surface. A neat dive is no doubt very pretty and quite harmless, though repeated "headers" are likely to prove injurious; but swimming under water for a long time is extremely likely to set up disease. Dogs living at the water-side and constantly going into the water nearly always become deaf, and frequently suffer from a disease of the auditory passage, which is called by veterinary surgeons the canker.

While the preceding remarks might seem to apply principally to men and boys, in my opinion girls ought to be instructed to swim quite as much as boys. We have lately had illustrations of what ladies can do in the way of saving life by swimming. The coolness and courage of Miss Hackett was an exploit worthy of the greatest admiration. After all, swimming is not difficult to learn. The fool in the Greek fable has often been laughed at for saying that he would not go into the water until he could swim, but he was not such a very stupid person as he at first sight appeared to be. The movements of swimming could easily be acquired out of water if a person were put on a chair, or still better on a small ottoman, on his stomach. In going through these evolutions the important matter is to continue the practice for two or

three minutes without stopping, then practise again in the
same way for two or three minutes, and so on repeatedly, until
all the muscles required in swimming become strengthened.
Although young swimmers take great pains with their arms
and hands, they often forget about their legs. This is a
great mistake, as the legs are at least four times as powerful
as the arms in swimming. When we desire to speak of a clever
and experienced parliamentary tactician, we speak of him as
an "old parliamentary hand," but if we wish to praise an experienced swimmer, he ought to be described as an "old
natatory leg." The lower extremities are so often made use of
to describe undesirable persons, that it is satisfactory at least
to know, in connection with swimming, that it is not an oppro-
brious epithet. It is to be hoped the time will come when the
Board schools will unite together in the large towns, and
establish gymnasiums and swimming baths in every district.
The expense of building such establishments would not be very
great, and they could be maintained at a very low cost. Of
their practical usefulness there could be no doubt.

In the press, and will shortly be published.

LIFE OF SIR MORELL MACKENZIE

BY

REV. H. R. HAWEIS, M.A.

LONDON: W. H. ALLEN & CO., WATERLOO PLACE, S.W.

St. Dunstan's House, Fetter Lane,
London, E.C. 1892.

Select List of Books in all Departments of Literature

PUBLISHED BY

Sampson Low, Marston & Company, Ld.

ABBEY and PARSONS, *Quiet Life*, from drawings; motive by Austin Dobson, 31s. 6d.
ABBOTT, CHARLES C., *Waste Land Wanderings*, 10s. 6d.
ABERDEEN, EARL OF. See Prime Ministers.
ABNEY, CAPT., *Thebes and its Greater Temples*, 40 photos. 63s.
—— and CUNNINGHAM, *Pioneers of the Alps*, new ed. 21s.
About in the World. See Gentle Life Series.
—— *Some Fellows*, from my note-book, by "an Eton boy," 2s. 6d.; new edit. 1s.
ADAMS, CHARLES K., *Historical Literature*, 12s. 6d.
ADDISON, *Sir Roger de Coverley*, from the "Spectator," 6s.
AGASSIZ, ALEX., *Three Cruises of the "Blake,"* illust. 2 vols. 42s.
ALBERT, PRINCE. See Bayard Series.
ALCOTT, L. M. *Jo's Boys*, a sequel to "Little Men," 5s.
—— *Life, Letters and Journals*, by Ednah D. Cheney, 6s.
—— *Lulu's Library*, a story for girls, 3s. 6d.
—— *Old-fashioned Thanksgiving Day*, 3s. 6d.
—— *Proverb Stories*, 3s. 6d.

ALCOTT, L. M., *Recollections of my Childhood's Days*, 3s. 6d.
—— *Silver Pitchers*, 3s. 6d.
—— *Spinning-wheel Stories*, 5s.
—— See also Low's Standard Series and Rose Library.
ALDAM, W. H., *Flies and Fly-making*, with actual specimens on cardboard, 63s.
ALDEN, W. L. See Low's Standard Series.
ALFORD, LADY MARIAN, *Needlework as Art*, 21s.; l. p. 84s.
ALGER, J. G., *Englishmen in the French Revolution*, 7s. 6d.
Amateur Angler in Dove Dale, a three weeks' holiday, by E. M. 1s. 6d., 1s. and 5s.
ANDERSEN, H. C., *Fairy Tales*, illust. in colour by E. V. B. 25s., new edit. 5s.
—— *Fairy Tales*, illust. by Scandinavian artists, 6s.
ANDERSON, W., *Pictorial Arts of Japan*, 4 parts, 168s.; artist's proofs, 252s.
ANDRES, *Varnishes, Lacquers, Siccatives, & Sealing-wax*, 12s. 6d.
Angler's strange Experiences, by Cotswold Isys, new edit., 3s. 6d.
ANNESLEY, C., *Standard Opera Glass*, the plots of eighty operas, 3rd edit., 2s. 6d.

A Select List of Books

Annual American Catalogue of Books, 1886-69, each 10s. 6d., half morocco, 14s.
—— 1890, cloth, 15s., half morocco, cloth sides, 18s.
Antipodean Notes; a nine months' tour, by Wanderer, 7s. 6d.
APPLETON, *European Guide*, new edit., 2 parts, 10s. each.
ARCHER, W., *English Dramatists of To-day*, 8s. 6d.
ARLOT'S *Coach Painting*, from the French by A. A. Fesquet, 6s.
ARMYTAGE, HON. MRS., *Wars of Queen Victoria's Reign*, 5s.
ARNOLD, E., *Birthday Book;* by Kath. L. and Constance Arnold, 4s. 6d.
—— E. L. L., *Summer Holiday in Scandinavia*, 10s. 6d.
—— *On the Indian Hills, Coffee Planting, &c.*, 2 vols. 24s.
—— R., *Ammonia and Ammonium Compounds*, illust. 5s.
Artistic Japan, text, woodcuts, and coloured plates, vols. I.-VI. 15s. each.
ASBJÖRNSEN, P. C., *Round the Yule Log*, 7s. 6d.; new edit. 5s.
ASHE, R. P., *Two Kings of Uganda;* six years in Eastern Equatorial Africa, 6s.; new edit. 3s. 6d.
—— *Uganda, England's latest Charge*, stiff cover, 1s.
ASHTON, F. T., *Designing fancy Cotton and Woollen Cloths*, illust. 50s.
ATCHISON, C. C., *Winter Cruise in Summer Seas;* "how I found" health, 16s.
ATKINSON, J. B. *Overbeck*. See Great Artists.
ATTWELL, *Italian Masters*, especially in the National Gallery, 3s. 6d.

AUDSLEY, G. A., *Chromolithography*, 44 coloured plates and text, 63s.
—— *Ornamental Arts of Japan*, 2 vols. morocco, 23l. 2s.; four parts, 15l. 15s.
—— W. and G. A., *Ornament in all Styles*, 31s. 6d.
AUERBACH, B., *Brigitta* (B. Tauchnitz), 2s.; sewed, 1s. 6d.
—— *On the Height* (B. Tauchnitz), 3 vols. 6s.; sewed, 4s. 6d.
—— *Spinoza* (B. Tauchnitz), 2 vols. 4s.
AUSTRALIA. See F. Countries.
AUSTRIA. See F. Countries.
Autumn Cruise in the Ægean, by one of the party. See "Fitzpatrick."
BACH. See Great Musicians.
BACON. See English Philosophers.
—— DELIA, *Biography*, 10s. 6d.
BADDELEY, W. ST. CLAIR, *Love's Vintage;* sonnets and lyrics, 5s.
—— *Tchay and Chianti*, a short visit to Russia and Finland, 5s.
—— *Travel-tide*, 7s. 6d.
BAKER, JAMES, *John Westacott*, new edit. 6s. and 3s. 6d.
BALDWIN, J., *Story of Siegfried*, illust. 6s.
—— *Story of Roland*, illust. 6s.
—— *Story of the Golden Age*, illust. 6s.
—— J. D., *Ancient America*, illust. 10s. 6d.
Ballad Stories. See Bayard Series.
Ballads of the Cid, edited by Rev. Gerrard Lewis, 3s. 6d.
BALLANTYNE, T., *Essays*. See Bayard Series.

In all Departments of Literature.

BALLIN, ADA S., *Science of Dress*, illust. 6s.
BAMFORD, A. J., *Turbans and Tails*, 7s. 6d.
BANCROFT, G., *History of America*, new edit. 6 vols. 73s. 6d.
Barbizon Painters, by J. W. Mollett—I. Millet, T. Rousseau, and Diaz, 3s. 6d. II. Corot, Daubigny and Dupré, 3s. 6d.; the two in one vol. 7s. 6d.
BARING-GOULD. See Foreign Countries.
BARLOW, A., *Weaving*, new edit. 25s.
—— P. W., *Kaipara, New Z.*, 6s.
—— W., *Matter and Force*, 12s.
BARRETT. See Gr. Musicians.
BARROW, J., *Mountain Ascents*, new edit. 5s.
BASSETT, *Legends of the Sea*, 7s. 6d.
BATHGATE, A., *Waitaruna, New Zealand*, 5s.
Bayard Series, edited by the late J. Hain Friswell; flexible cloth extra, 2s. 6d. each.
Chevalier Bayard, by Berville.
De Joinville, St. Louis.
Essays of Cowley.
Abdallah, by Laboullaye.
Table-Talk of Napoleon.
Vathek, by Beckford.
Cavalier and Puritan Songs.
Words of Wellington.
Johnson's Rasselas.
Hazlitt's Round Table.
Browne's Religio Medici.
Ballad Stories of the Affections, by Robert Buchanan.
Coleridge's Christabel, &c.
Chesterfield's Letters.
Essays in Mosaic, by T. Ballantyne.
My Uncle Toby.
Rochefoucauld, Reflections.
Socrates, Memoirs from Xenophon.
Prince Albert's Precepts.

BEACONSFIELD, *Public Life*, 3s. 6d.
—— See also Prime Ministers.
BEAUGRAND, *Young Naturalists*, new edit. 5s.
BECKER, A.L., *First German Book*, 1s.; *Exercises*, 1s.; *Key* to both, 2s. 6d.; *German Idioms*, 1s. 6d.
BECKFORD. See Bayard Series.
BEECHER, H. W., *Biography*, new edit. 10s. 6d.
BEETHOVEN. See Great Musicians.
BEHNKE, E., *Child's Voice*, 3s. 6d.
BELL, *Obeah, Witchcraft in the West Indies*, 2s. 6d.
BELLENGER & WITCOMB'S *French and English Conversations*, new edit. Paris, bds. 2s.
BENJAMIN, *Atlantic Islands as health, &c., resorts*. 16s.
BERLIOZ. See Gr. Musicians.
BERVILLE. See Bayard Series.
BIART, *Young Naturalist*, new edit. 7s. 6d.
—— *Involuntary Voyage*, 7s. 6d. and 5s.
—— *Two Friends*, translated by Mary de Hauteville, 7s. 6d.
See also Low's Standard Books.
BICKERSTETH, ASHLEY, B.A., *Outlines of Roman History*, 2s. 6d.
—— E. H., Exon., *Clergyman in his Home*, 1s.
—— *From Year to Year*, original poetical pieces, morocco or calf, 10s. 6d.; padded roan, 6s.; roan, 5s.; cloth, 3s. 6d.
—— *Hymnal Companion*, full lists post free.
—— *Master's Home Call*, new edit. 1s.
—— *Octave of Hymns*, sewn, 3d., with music, 1s.

A Select List of Books

BICKERSTETH, E. H., Exon., *Reef, Parables, &c.*, illust. 7s. 6d. and 2s. 6d.
—— *Shadowed Home*, n. ed. 5s.
BIGELOW, JOHN, *France and the Confederate Navy*, an international episode, 7s. 6d.
BILBROUGH, *'Twixt France and Spain*, 7s. 6d.
BILLROTH, *Care of the Sick*, 6s.
BIRD, F. J., *Dyer's Companion*, 42s.
—— F. S., *Land of Dykes and Windmills*, 12s. 6d.
—— H. E., *Chess Practice*, 2s. 6d.
BISHOP. See Nursing Record Series.
BLACK, ROBERT, *Horse Racing in France*, 14s.
—— W., *Donald Ross of Heimra*, 3 vols. 31s. 6d.
—— *Novels, new and uniform edition in monthly vols.* 2s. 6d. ea.
—— See Low's Standard Novels.
BLACKBURN, C. F., *Catalogue Titles, Index Entries, &c.* 14s.
—— H., *Art in the Mountains*, new edit. 5s.
—— *Artists and Arabs*, 7s. 6d.
—— *Breton Folk*, new issue, 10s. 6d.
—— *Harz Mountains*, 12s.
—— *Normandy Picturesque*, 16s.
—— *Pyrenees*, illust. by Gustave Doré, new edit. 7s. 6d.
BLACKMORE, R.D., *Georgics*, 4s. 6d.; cheap edit. 1s.
—— *Lorna Doone, édit. de luxe*, 35s., 31s. 6d. & 21s.
—— *Lorna Doone*, illust. by W. Small, 7s. 6d.
—— *Springhaven*, illust. 12s.; new edit. 7s. 6d. & 6s.
—— See also Low's Standard Novels.

BLAIKIE, *How to get Strong*, new edit. 5s.
—— *Sound Bodies for our Boys and Girls*, 2s. 6d.
BLOOMFIELD. See Choice Editions.
Bobby, a Story, by Vesper, 1s.
BOCK, *Head Hunters of Borneo*, 36s.
—— *Temples & Elephants*, 21s.
BONAPARTE, MAD. PATTERSON, *Life*, 10s. 6d.
BONWICK, JAMES, *Colonial Days*, 2s. 6d.
—— *Colonies*, 1s. ea.; 1 vol. 5s.
—— *Daily Life of the Tasmanians*, 12s. 6d.
—— *First Twenty Years of Australia*, 5s.
—— *Last of the Tasmanians*, 16s.
—— *Port Philip*, 21s.
—— *Lost Tasmanian Race*, 4s.
BOSANQUET, C., *Blossoms from the King's Garden*, 6s.
—— *Jehoshaphat*, 1s.
—— *Lenten Meditations*, I. 1s. 6d.; II. 2s.
—— *Tender Grass for Lambs*, 2s. 6d.
BOULTON, N. W. *Rebellions, Canadian life*, 9s.
BOURKE, *On the Border with Crook*, illust., roy. 8vo, 21s.
—— *Snake Dance of Arizona*, 21s.
BOUSSENARD. See Low's Standard Books.
BOWEN, F., *Modern Philosophy*, new ed. 16s.
BOWER. See English Philosophers.
—— *Law of Electric Lighting*, 12s. 6d.
BOYESEN, H. H., *Against Heavy Odds*, 5s.
—— *History of Norway*, 7s. 6d.

In all Departments of Literature. 5

BOYESEN, *Modern Vikings*, 6s.
Boy's *Froissart, King Arthur, Mabinogian, Percy,* see "Lanier."
BRADSHAW, *New Zealand as it is*, 12s. 6d.
—— *New Zealand of To-day*, 14s.
BRANNT, *Fats and Oils*, 35s.
—— *Soap and Candles*, 35s.
—— *Vinegar, Acetates*, 25s.
—— *Distillation of Alcohol*, 12s. 6d.
—— *Metal Worker's Receipts*, 12s. 6d.
—— *Metallic Alloys*, 12s. 6d.
—— and WAHL, *Techno-Chemical Receipt Book*, 10s. 6d.
BRASSEY, LADY, *Tahiti*, 21s.
BRÉMONT. See Low's Standard Novels.
BRETON, JULES, *Life of an Artist*, an autobiography, 7s. 6d.
BRISSE, *Menus and Recipes*, new edit. 5s.
Britons in Brittany, by G. H. F. 2s. 6d.
BROCK-ARNOLD. See Great Artists.
BROOKS, NOAH, *Boy Settlers*, 6s.
BROWN, A. J., *Rejected of Men*, 3s. 6d.
—— A. S. *Madeira and Canary Islands for Invalids*, 2s. 6d.
—— *Northern Atlantic*, for travellers, 4s. 6d.
—— ROBERT. See Low's Standard Novels.
BROWNE, LENNOX, and BEHNKE, *Voice, Song, & Speech*, 15s.; new edit. 5s.
—— *Voice Use*, 3s. 6d.
—— SIR T. See Bayard Series.
BRYCE, G., *Manitoba*, 7s. 6d.
—— *Short History of the Canadian People*, 7s. 6d.

BUCHANAN, R. See Bayard Series.
BULKELEY, OWEN T., *Lesser Antilles*, 2s. 6d.
BUNYAN. See Low's Standard Series.
BURDETT-COUTTS, *Brookfield Stud*, 5s.
BURGOYNE, *Operations in Egypt*, 5s.
BURNABY, F. See Low's Standard Library.
—— Mrs., *High Alps in Winter*, 14s.
BURNLEY, JAMES, *History of Wool*, 21s.
BUTLER, COL. SIR W. F., *Campaign of the Cataracts*, 18s.
—— *Red Cloud*, 7s. 6d. & 5s.
—— See also Low's Standard Books.
BUXTON, ETHEL M. WILMOT, *Wee Folk*, 5s.
—— See also Illust Text Books.
BYNNER. See Low's Standard Novels.
CABLE, G. W., *Bonaventure*, 5s.
CADOGAN, LADY A., *Drawing-room Comedies*, illust. 10s. 6d., acting edit. 6d.
—— *Illustrated Games of Patience*, col. diagrams, 12s. 6d.
—— *New Games of Patience*, with coloured diagrams, 12s. 6d.
CAHUN. See Low's Standard Books.
CALDECOTT, RANDOLPH, *Memoir*, by H. Blackburn, new edit. 7s. 6d. and 5s.
—— *Sketches*, pict. bds. 2s. 6d.
CALL, ANNIE PAYSON, *Power through Repose*, 3s. 6d.
CALLAN, H., M.A., *Wanderings on Wheel and Foot through Europe*, 1s. 6d.
Cambridge Trifles, 2s. 6d.

Cambridge Staircase, 2s. 6d.
CAMPBELL, LADY COLIN, *Book of the Running Brook*, 5s.
—— T. See Choice Editions.
CANTERBURY, ARCHBISHOP. See Preachers.
CARLETON, WILL, *City Ballads*, illust. 12s. 6d.
—— *City Legends*, ill. 12s. 6d.
—— *Farm Festivals*, ill. 12s. 6d.
—— See also Rose Library.
CARLYLE, *Irish Journey in 1819*, 7s. 6d.
CARNEGIE, ANDREW, *American Four-in-hand in Britain*, 10s. 6d.; also 1s.
—— *Round the World*, 10s. 6d.
—— *Triumphant Democracy*, 6s.; new edit. 1s. 6d.; paper, 1s.
CAROVÉ, *Story without an End*, illust. by E. V. B., 7s. 6d.
Celebrated Racehorses, 4 vols. 126s.
CÉLIÈRE. See Low's Standard Books.
Changed Cross, &c., poems, 2s. 6d.
Chant-book Companion to the Common Prayer, 2s.; organ ed. 4s.
CHAPIN, *Mountaineering in Colorado*, 10s. 6d.
CHAPLIN, J. G., *Bookkeeping*, 2s. 6d.
CHATTOCK, *Notes on Etching* new edit. 10s. 6d.
CHERUBINI. See Great Musicians.
CHESTERFIELD. See Bayard Series.
Choice Editions of choice books, illustrated by C. W. Cope, R.A., T. Creswick, R.A., E. Duncan, Birket Foster, J. C. Horsley, A.R.A., G. Hicks, R. Redgrave, R.A., C. Stonehouse, F. Tayler, G. Thomas, H. G. Townsend,

Choice Editions—continued.
E. H. Wehnert, Harrison Weir, &c., cloth extra gilt, gilt edges, 2s. 6d. each; re-issue, 1s. each.
Bloomfield's Farmer's Boy.
Campbell's Pleasures of Hope.
Coleridge's Ancient Mariner.
Goldsmith's Deserted Village.
Goldsmith's Vicar of Wakefield.
Gray's Elegy in a Churchyard.
Keats' Eve of St. Agnes.
Milton's Allegro.
Poetry of Nature, by H. Weir.
Rogers' Pleasures of Memory.
Shakespeare's Songs and Sonnets.
Elizabethan Songs and Sonnets.
Tennyson's May Queen.
Wordsworth's Pastoral Poems.
CHREIMAN, *Physical Culture of Women*, 1s.
CLARK, A., *A Dark Place of the Earth*, 6s.
—— Mrs. K. M., *Southern Cross Fairy Tale*, 5s.
CLARKE, C. C., *Writers, and Letters*, 10s. 6d.
—— PERCY, *Three Diggers*, 6s.
—— *Valley Council;* from T. Bateman's Journal, 6s.
Classified Catalogue of English-printed Educational Works, 3rd edit. 6s.
Claude le Lorrain. See Great Artists.
CLOUGH, A. H., *Plutarch's Lives*, one vol. 18s.
COLERIDGE, C. R., *English Squire*, 6s.
—— S. T. See Choice Editions and Bayard Series.
COLLINGWOOD, H. See Low's Standard Books.
COLLINSON, Adm. SIR R., *H.M.S. Enterprise in Search of Franklin*, 14s.
CONDER, J., *Flowers of Japan; Decoration*, coloured Japanese Plates, 42s. nett.

CORREGGIO. See Great Artists.
COWLEY. See Bayard Series.
COX, DAVID. See Great Artists.
COZZENS, F., *American Yachts*, pfs. 21*l*.; art. pfs. 31*l*. 10*s*.
—— See also Low's Standard Books.
CRADDOCK. See Low's Standard Novels.
CREW, B. J., *Petroleum*, 21*s*.
CRISTIANI, R. S., *Soap and Candles*, 42*s*.
—— *Perfumery*, 25*s*.
CROKER, MRS. B. M. See Low's Standard Novels.
CROUCH, A. P., *Glimpses of Feverland* (West Africa), 6*s*.
—— *On a Surf-bound Coast*, 7*s*. 6*d*.; new edit. 5*s*.
CRUIKSHANK G. See Great Artists.
CUDWORTH, W., *Abraham Sharp*, 26*s*.
CUMBERLAND, STUART, *Thought-reader's Thoughts*, 10*s*. 6*d*.
—— See also Low's Standard Novels.
CUNDALL, F. See Great Artists.
—— J., *Shakespeare*, 3*s*. 6*d*., 5*s*. and 2*s*.
CURTIN, J., *Myths of the Russians*, 10*s*. 6*d*.
CURTIS, C. B., *Velazquez and Murillo*, with etchings, 31*s*. 6*d*. and 63*s*.
CUSHING, W., *Anonyms*, 2 vols. 52*s*. 6*d*.
—— *Initials and Pseudonyms*, 25*s*; ser. II., 21*s*.
CUTCLIFFE, H. C., *Trout Fishing*, new edit. 3*s*. 6*d*.
DALY, MRS. D., *Digging, Squatting, &c., in N. S. Australia*, 12*s*.

D'ANVERS, N., *Architecture and Sculpture*, new edit. 5*s*.
—— *Elementary Art, Architecture, Sculpture, Painting*, new edit. 10*s*. 6*d*.
—— *Elementary History of Music*, 2*s*. 6*d*.
—— *Painting*, by F. Cundall, 6*s*.
DAUDET, A., *My Brother Jack*, 7*s*. 6*d*.; also 5*s*.
—— *Port Tarascon*, by H. James, 7*s*. 6*d*.; new edit. 5*s*.
DAVIES, C., *Modern Whist*, 4*s*.
DAVIS, C. T., *Bricks, Tiles, &c.*, now edit. 25*s*.
—— *Manufacture of Leather*, 52*s*. 6*d*.
—— *Manufacture of Paper*, 28*s*.
—— *Steam Boiler Incrustation*, 8*s*. 6*d*.
—— G. B., *International Law*, 10*s*. 6*d*.
DAWIDOWSKY, *Glue, Gelatine, &c.*, 12*s*. 6*d*.
Day of my Life, by an Eton boy, new edit. 2*s*. 6*d*.; also 1*s*
DE JOINVILLE. See Bayard Series.
DE LEON, EDWIN, *Under the Stars and Under the Crescent*, 2 vols. 12*s*.; new edit. 6*s*.
DELLA ROBBIA. See Great Artists.
Denmark and Iceland. See Foreign Countries.
DENNETT, R. E., *Seven Years among the Fjort*, 7*s*. 6*d*.
DERRY (Bishop of). See Preachers.
DE WINT. See Great Artists.
DIGGLE, J. W., *Bishop Fraser's Lancashire Life*, new edit. 12*s*. 6*d*.; popular ed. 3*s*. 6*d*.
—— *Sermons for Daily Life*, 5*s*

DOBSON, AUSTIN, *Hogarth*, with a bibliography, &c., of prints, illust. 24s.; l. paper 52s. 6d.
—— See also Great Artists.
DODGE, MRS., *Hans Brinker, the Silver Skates*, new edit. 5s., 3s. 6d., 2s. 6d.; text only, 1s.
DONKIN, J. G., *Trooper and Redskin; N. W. mounted police, Canada*, 8s. 6d.
DONNELLY, IGNATIUS, *Atlantis, the Antediluvian World*, new edit. 12s. 6d.
—— *Cæsar's Column*, authorized edition, 3s. 6d.
—— *Doctor Huguet*, 3s. 6d.
—— *Great Cryptogram*, Bacon's Cipher in Shakespeare, 2 vols. 30s.
—— *Ragnarok: the Age of Fire and Gravel*, 12s. 6d.
DORE, GUSTAVE, *Life and Reminiscences*, by Blanche Roosevelt, fully illust. 24s.
DOS PASSOS, J. R., *Law of Stockbrokers and Stock Exchanges*, 35s.
DOUDNEY, SARAH, *Godiva Durleigh*, 3 vols. 31s. 6d.
DOUGALL, J. D., *Shooting Appliances, Practice, &c.*, 10s. 6d.; new edit. 7s. 6d.
DOUGHTY, H. M., *Friesland Meres and the Netherlands*, new edit. illust. 10s. 6d.
DOVETON, F. B., *Poems and Snatches of Songs*, 5s.; new edit. 3s. 6d.
DU CHAILLU, PAUL. See Low's Standard Books.
DUNCKLEY ("Verax.") See Prime Ministers.
DUNDERDALE, GEORGE, *Prairie and Bush*, 6s.
Dürer. See Great Artists.
DYKES, J. OSWALD. See Preachers.

Echoes from the Heart, 3s. 6d.
EDEN, C. H. See Foreign Countries.
EDMONDS, C., *Poetry of the Anti-Jacobin*, new edit. 7s. 6d. and 21s.
Educational Catalogue. See Classified Catalogue.
EDWARDS, *American Steam Engineer*, 12s. 6d.
—— *Modern Locomotive Engines*, 12s. 6d.
—— *Steam Engineer's Guide*, 12s. 6d.
—— H. SUTHERLAND. See Great Musicians.
—— M. B., *Dream of Millions, &c.*, 1s.
—— See Low's Standard Novels.
EGGLESTON, G. CARY, *Juggernaut*, 6s.
Egypt. See Foreign Countries.
Elizabethan Songs. See Choice Editions.
EMERSON, DR. P. H., *East Coast Yarns*, 1s.
—— *English Idylls*, new ed. 2s.
—— *Naturalistic Photography*, new edit. 5s.
—— *Pictures of East Anglian Life*; plates and vignettes, 105s. and 147s.
—— and GOODALL, *Life on the Norfolk Broads*, plates, 126s. and 210s.
—— *Wild Life on a Tidal Water*, copper plates, ord. edit. 25s.; édit. de luxe, 63s.
—— R. W., by G. W. COOKE, 8s. 6d.
—— *Birthday Book*, 3s. 6d.
—— *In Concord*, a memoir, 7s. 6d.
English Catalogue, 1863-71, 42s.; 1872-80, 42s.; 1881-9, 52s. 6d.; 5s. yearly.

English Catalogue, Index vol. 1837-56, 26s.; 1856-76, 42s.; 1874-80, 18s.
—— Etchings, vol. v. 45s. ; vi., 25s.; vii., 25s.; viii., 42s.
English Philosophers, edited by E. B. Ivan Müller, M.A., 3s. 6d. each.
Bacon, by Fowler.
Hamilton, by Monck.
Hartley and James Mill, by Bower.
Shaftesbury & Hutcheson; Fowler.
Adam Smith, by J. A. Farrer.
ERCKMANN-CHATRIAN. See Low's Standard Books.
ERICHSON, Life, by W. C. Church, 2 vols. 24s.
ESMARCH, F., Handbook of Surgery, 24s.
Essays on English Writers. See Gentle Life Series.
EVANS, G. E., Repentance of Magdalene Despar, &c., poems, 5s.
—— S. & F., Upper Ten, a story, 1s.
—— W. E., Songs of the Birds, n. ed. 6s.
EVELYN, J., An Inca Queen, 5s.
—— John, Life of Mrs. Godolphin, 7s. 6d.
EVES, C. W., West Indies, n. ed. 7s. 6d.
FAIRBAIRN, A. M. See Preachers.
Familiar Words. See Gentle Life Series.
FARINI, G. A., Kalahari Desert, 21s.
FARRAR, C. S., History of Sculpture, &c., 6s.
—— Maurice, Minnesota, 6s.
FAURIEL, Last Days of the Consulate, 10s. 6d.
FAY, T., Three Germanys, 2 vols. 35s.

FEILDEN, H. St. J., Some Public Schools, 2s. 6d.
—— Mrs., My African Home, 7s. 6d.
FENN, G. Manville. See Low's Standard Books.
FENNELL, J. G., Book of the Roach, n. ed. 2s.
FFORDE, B., Subaltern, Policeman, and the Little Girl. 1s.
—— Trotter, a Poona Mystery, 1s.
FIELD, Maunsell B., Memories, 10s. 6d.
FIELDS, James T., Memoirs, 12s. 6d.
—— Yesterdays with Authors, 16s.; also 10s. 6d.
Figure Painters of Holland. See Great Artists.
FINCK, Henry T., Pacific Coast Scenic Tour, 10s. 6d.
FITCH, Lucy. See Nursing Record Series, 1s.
FITZGERALD. See Foreign Countries.
—— Percy, Book Fancier, 5s. and 12s. 6d.
FITZPATRICK, T., Autumn Cruise in the Ægean, 10s. 6d
—— Transatlantic Holiday, 10s. 6d.
FLEMING, S., England and Canada, 6s.
Foreign Countries and British Colonies, descriptive handbooks edited by F. S. Pulling, M.A. Each volume is the work of a writer who has special acquaintance with the subject, 3s. 6d.
Australia. by Fitzgerald.
Austria-Hungary, by Kay.
Denmark and Iceland, by E. C. Otté.
Egypt, by S. L. Poole.
France, by Miss Roberts.
Germany, by L. Sergeant.
Greece, by S. Baring Gould.

Foreign Countries, &c.—*cont.*
Japan, by Mossman.
Peru, by R. Markham.
Russia, by Morfill.
Spain, by Webster.
Sweden and Norway, by Woods.
West Indies, by C. H. Eden.
FOREMAN, J., *Philippine Islands*, 21s.
FOTHERINGHAM, L. M., *Nyassaland*, 7s. 6d.
FOWLER, *Japan, China, and India*, 10s. 6d.
FRA ANGELICO. See Great Artists.
FRA BARTOLOMMEO, ALBERTINELLI, and ANDREA DEL SARTO. See Great Artists.
FRANC, Maud Jeanne, *Beatrice Melton*, 4s.
—— *Emily's Choice*, n. ed. 5s.
—— *Golden Gifts*, 4s.
—— *Hall's Vineyard*, 4s.
—— *Into the Light*, 4s.
—— *John's Wife*, 4s.
—— *Little Mercy; for better, for worse*, 4s.
—— *Marian, a Tale*, n. ed. 5s.
—— *Master of Ralston*, 4s.
—— *Minnie's Mission, a Temperance Tale*, 4s.
—— *No longer a Child*, 4s.
—— *Silken Cords and Iron Fetters, a Tale*, 4s.
—— *Two Sides to Every Question*, 4s.
—— *Vermont Vale*, 5s.
A plainer edition *is published at* 2s. 6d.
France. See Foreign Countries.
FRANCIS, F., *War, Waves, and Wanderings*, 2 vols. 24s.
—— See also Low's Standard Series.
Frank's Ranche; or, My Holiday in the Rockies, n. ed. 5s.

FRANKEL, Julius, *Starch Glucose, &c.*, 18s.
FRASER, Bishop, *Lancashire Life*, n. ed. 12s. 6d.; popular ed. 3s. 6d.
FREEMAN, J., *Melbourne Life, lights and shadows*, 6s.
FRENCH, F., *Home Fairies and Heart Flowers*, illust. 24s.
French and English Birthday Book, by Kate D. Clark, 7s. 6d.
French Revolution, Letters from Paris, translated, 10s. 6d.
Fresh Woods and Pastures New, by the Author of "An Angler's Days." 5s., 1s. 6d., 1s.
FRIEZE, Dupré, *Florentine Sculptor*, 7s. 6d.
FRISWELL, J. H. See Gentle Life Series.
Froissart for Boys, by Lanier, new ed. 7s. 6d.
FROUDE, J. A. See Prime Ministers.
Gainsborough and Constable. See Great Artists.
GASPARIN, *Sunny Fields and Shady Woods*, 6s.
GEFFCKEN, *British Empire*, 7s. 6d.
Generation of Judges, n. e. 7s. 6d.
Gentle Life Series, edited by J. Hain Friswell, sm. 8vo. 6s. per vol.; calf extra, 10s. 6d. ea.; 16mo, 2s. 6d., except when price is given.
Gentle Life.
About in the World.
Like unto Christ.
Familiar Words, 6s.; also 3s. 6d.
Montaigne's Essays.
Sidney's Arcadia, 6s.
Gentle Life, second series.
Varia; readings, 10s. 6d.
Silent hour; essays.
Half-length Portraits
Essays on English Writers.
Other People's Windows, 6s. & 2s. 6d.
A Man's Thoughts.

In all Departments of Literature.

George Eliot, by G. W. Cooke, 10s. 6d.
Germany. See Foreign Countries.
GESSI, ROMOLO PASHA, *Seven Years in the Soudan*, 18s.
GHIBERTI & DONATELLO. See Great Artists.
GILES, E., *Australia Twice Traversed*, 1872-76, 2 vols. 30s.
GILL, J. See Low's Readers.
GILLESPIE, W. M., *Surveying*, n. ed. 21s.
Giotto, by Harry Quilter, illust. 15s.
—— See also Great Artists.
GIRDLESTONE, C., *Private Devotions*, 2s.
GLADSTONE. See Prime Ministers.
GLENELG, P., *Devil and the Doctor*, 1s.
GLOVER, R., *Light of the World*, n. ed., 2s. 6d.
GLÜCK. See Great Musicians.
Goethe's Faustus, in orig. rhyme, by Huth, 5s.
—— *Prosa*, by C. A. Buchheim (Low's German Series), 3s. 6d.
GOLDSMITH, O., *She Stoops to Conquer*, by Austin Dobson, illust by E. A. Abbey, 8ls.
—— See also Choice Editions.
GOOCH, FANNY C., *Mexicans*, 16s.
GOODALL, *Life and Landscape on the Norfolk Broads*, 126s. and 210s.
—— &EMERSON, *Pictures of East Anglian Life*, £5 5s. and £7 7s.
GOODMAN, E. J., *The Best Tour in Norway*, 6s.
—— N. & A., *Fen Skating*, 5s.
GOODYEAR, W. H., *Grammar of the Lotus, Ornament and Sun Worship*, 63s. nett.

GORDON, J. E. H., *Physical Treatise on Electricity and Magnetism*. 3rd ed. 2 vols. 42s.
—— *Electric Lighting*, 18s.
—— *School Electricity*, 5s.
—— Mrs. J. E. H., *Decorative Electricity*, illust. 12s.
GOWER, LORD RONALD, *Handbook to the Art Galleries of Belgium and Holland*, 5s.
—— *Northbrook Gallery*, 63s. and 105s.
—— *Portraits at Castle Howard*. 2 vols. 126s.
—— See also Great Artists.
GRAESSI, *Italian Dictionary*, 3s. 6d.; roan, 5s.
GRAY, T. See Choice Eds.
Great Artists, Biographies, illustrated, emblematical binding, 3s. 6d. per vol. except where the price is given.
Barbizon School, 2 vols.
Claude le Lorrain.
Correggio, 2s. 6d.
Cox and De Wint.
George Cruikshank.
Della Robbia and Cellini, 2s. 6d.
Albrecht Dürer.
Figure Paintings of Holland.
Fra Angelico, Masaccio, &c.
Fra Bartolommeo, &c.
Gainsborough and Constable.
Ghiberti and Donatello, 2s. 6d.
Giotto, by H. Quilter, 15s.
Hogarth, by A. Dobson.
Hans Holbein.
Landscape Painters of Holland.
Landseer.
Leonardo da Vinci.
Little Masters of Germany, by Scott; éd. de luxe, 10s. 6d.
Mantegna and Francia.
Meissonier, 2s. 6d.
Michelangelo.
Mulready.
Murillo, by Minor, 2s. 6d.
Overbeck.
Raphael.

Great Artists—continued.
Rembrandt.
Reynolds.
Romney and Lawrence, 2s. 6d.
Rubens, by Kett.
Tintoretto, by Osler.
Titian, by Heath.
Turner, by Monkhouse.
Vandyck and Hals.
Velasquez.
Vernet & Delaroche.
Watteau, by Mollett, 2s. 6d.
Wilkie, by Mollett.
Great Musicians, edited by F. Hueffer. A series of biographies, 3s. each :—
Bach, by Poole.
Beethoven.
*Berlioz.
Cherubini.
English Church Composers.
*Glück.
Handel.
Haydn.
*Marcello.
Mendelssohn.
Mozart.
* Palestrina and the Roman School.
Purcell.
Rossini and Modern Italian School.
Schubert.
Schumann.
Richard Wagner.
Weber.
 * *Are not yet published.*
Greece. See Foreign Countries.
GRIEB, *German Dictionary*, n. ed. 2 vols. 21s.
GRIMM, H., *Literature*, 8s. 6d.
GROHMANN, *Camps in the Rockies*, 12s. 6d.
GROVES, J. PERCY. See Low's Standard Books.
GUIZOT, *History of England*, illust. 3 vols. re-issue at 10s. 6d. per vol.
—— *History of France*, illust. re-issue, 8 vols. 10s. 6d. each.
—— Abridged by G. Masson, 5s.
GUYON, MADAME, *Life*, 6s.

HADLEY, J., *Roman Law*, 7s. 6d.
Half-length Portraits. See Gentle Life Series.
HALFORD, F. M., *Dry Fly-fishing*, n. ed. 25s.
—— *Floating Flies*, 15s. & 30s.
HALL, *How to Live Long*, 2s.
HALSEY, F. A., *Slide Valve Gears*, 8s. 6d.
HAMILTON. See English Philosophers.
—— E. *Fly-fishing*, 6s. and 10s. 6d.
—— *Riverside Naturalist*, 14s.
HAMILTON'S *Mexican Handbook*, 8s. 6d.
HANDEL. See Great Musicians.
HANDS, T., *Numerical Exercises in Chemistry*, 2s. 6d.; without ans. 2s.; ans. sep. 6d.
Handy Guide to Dry-fly Fishing, by Cotswold Isys, 1s.
Handy Guide Book to Japanese Islands, 6s. 6d.
HARDY, A. S., *Passe-rose*, 6s.
—— THOS. See Low's Standard Novels.
HARKUT, F., *Conspirator*, 6s.
HARLAND, MARION, *Home Kitchen*, 5s.
Harper's Young People, vols. I.—VII. 7s. 6d. each; gilt 8s.
HARRIES, A. See Nursing Record Series.
HARRIS, W. B., *Land of the African Sultan*, 10s. 6d.; l. p. 31s. 6d.
HARRISON, MARY, *Modern Cookery*, 6s.
—— *Skilful Cook*, n. ed. 5s.
—— MRS. B. *Old-fashioned Fairy Book*, 6s.
—— W., *London Houses*, Illust. n. edit. 1s. 6d., 6s. net; & 2s. 6d.

HARTLEY and MILL. See English Philosophers.
HATTON, Joseph, *Journalistic London*, 12s. 6d.
—— See also Low's Standard Novels.
HAWEIS, H.R., *Broad Church*, 6s.
—— *Poets in the Pulpit*, 10s. 6d. new edit. 6s.; also 3s. 6d.
—— Mrs., *Housekeeping*, 2s. 6d.
—— *Beautiful Houses*, 4s., new edit. 1s.
HAYDN. See Great Musicians.
HAZLITT, W., *Round Table*, 2s 6d.
HEAD, Percy R. See Illus. Text Books and Great Artists.
HEARD, A.F., *Russian Church*, 16s.
HEARN, L., *Youma*, 5s.
HEATH, F. G., *Fern World*, 12s. 6d., new edit. 6s.
—— Gertrude, *Tell us Why*, 2s. 6d.
HELDMANN, B., *Mutiny of the "Leander,"* 7s. 6d. and 5s.
—— See also Low's Standard Books for Boys.
HENTY, G. A., *Hidden Foe*, 2 vols. 21s.
—— See also Low's Standard Books for Boys.
—— Richmond, *Australiana*, 5s.
HERBERT, T., *Salads and Sandwiches*, 6d.
HICKS, C. S., *Our Boys, and what to do with Them; Merchant Service*, 5s.
—— *Yachts, Boats, and Canoes*, 10s. 6d.
HIGGINSON, T. W., *Atlantic Essays*, 6s.
—— *History of the U.S.*, illust. 14s.

HILL, A. Staveley, *From Home to Home in N.-W. Canada*, 21s., new edit. 7s. 6d.
—— G. B., *Footsteps of Johnson*, 63s.,; édition de luxe, 147s.
HINMAN, R., *Eclectic Physical Geography*, 5s.
Hints on proving Wills without Professional Assistance, n. ed. 1s.
HOEY, Mrs. Cashel. See Low's Standard Novels.
HOFFER, *Caoutchouc & Gutta Percha*, 12s. 6d.
HOGARTH. See Gr. Artists.
HOLBEIN. See Great Artists.
HOLDER, Charles F., *Ivory King*, 8s. 6d.
—— *Living Lights*, 8s. 6d.
—— *Marvels of Animal Life*, 8s. 6d.
HOLM, Saxe, *Draxy Miller*, 2s. 6d. and 2s.
HOLMES, O. Wendell, *Before the Curfew*, 5s.
—— *Over the Tea Cups*, 6s.
—— *Iron Gate, &c., Poems*, 6s.
—— *Last Leaf*, 42s.
—— *Mechanism in Thought and Morals*, 1s. 6d.
—— *Mortal Antipathy*, 8s. 6d., 2s. and 1s.
—— *Our Hundred Days in Europe*, new edit. 6s.; l. paper 15s.
—— *Poetical Works*, new edit., 2 vols. 10s. 6d.
—— *Works*, prose, 10 vols.; poetry, 4 vols.; 14 vols. 84s. Limited large paper edit., 14 vols. 294s. nett.
—— See also Low's Standard Novels and Rose Library.
HOLUB, E., *South Africa*, 2 vols. 42s.
HOPKINS, Manley, *Treatise on the Cardinal Numbers*, 2s. 6d.

Horace in Latin, with Smart's literal translation, 2s. 6d.; translation only, 1s. 6d.
HORETZKY, C., *Canada on the Pacific*, 5s.
How and where to Fish in Ireland, by H. Regan, 3s. 6d.
HOWARD, BLANCHE W., *Tony the Maid*, 3s. 6d.
—— See also Low's Standard Novels.
HOWELLS, W. D., *Suburban Sketches*, 7s. 6d.
—— *Undiscovered Country*, 3s. 6d. and 1s.
HOWORTH, H. H., *Glacial Nightmare*, 18s.
—— *Mammoth and the Flood*, 18s.
HUDSON, N. H., *Purple Land that England Lost;* Banda Oriental 2 vols. 21s.: 1 vol. 6s.
HUEFFER, E. See Great Musicians.
HUGHES, HUGH PRICE. See Preachers.
HUME, F., *Creature of the Night*, 1s.
Humorous Art at the Naval Exhibition, 1s.
HUMPHREYS, JENNET, *Some Little Britons in Brittany*, 2s. 6d.
Hundred Greatest Men, new edit. one vol. 21s.
HUNTINGDON, *The Squire's Nieces*, 2s. 6d. (Playtime Library.)
HYDE, *Hundred Years by Post*, 1s.
Hymnal Companion to the Book of Common Prayer, separate lists gratis.
Iceland. See Foreign Countries.
Illustrated Text-Books of Art-Education, edit. by E. J. Poynter, R.A., illust. 5s. each.
Architecture, Classic and Early Christian.

Illust. Text-Books—continued.
Architecture, Gothic and Renaissance.
German, Flemish, and Dutch Painting.
Painting, Classic and Italian.
Painting, English and American.
Sculpture, modern.
Sculpture, by G. Redford.
Spanish and French artists.
INDERWICK, F. A., *Interregnum*, 10s. 6d.
—— *Sidelights on the Stuarts*, new edit. 7s. 6d.
INGELOW, JEAN. See Low's Standard Novels.
INGLIS, *Our New Zealand Cousins*, 6s.
—— *Sport and Work on the Nepaul Frontier*, 21s.
—— *Tent Life in Tiger Land*, 18s.
IRVING, W., *Little Britain*, 10s. 6d. and 6s.
—— *Works*, " Geoffrey Crayon " edit. 27 vols. 16l. 16s.
JACKSON, J., *Handwriting in Relation to Hygiene*, 3d.
—— *New Style Vertical Writing Copy-Books*, Series I. 1—8, 2d. and 1d. each.
—— *New Code Copy-Books*, 22 Nos. 2d. each.
—— *Shorthand of Arithmetic*, Companion to all Arithmetics, 1s. 6d.
—— L., *Ten Centuries of European Progress*, with maps, 12s. 6d.
JAMES, CROAKE, *Law and Lawyers*, new edit. 7s. 6d.
—— HENRY. See Daudet, A.
JAMES and MOLÉ'S *French Dictionary*, 3s. 6d. cloth; roan, 5s.
JAMES, *German Dictionary*, 3s. 6d. cloth; roan 5s.
JANVIER, *Aztec Treasure House*, 7s. 6d.; new edit. 5s.

Japan. See Foreign Countries.
JEFFERIES, RICHARD, *Amaryllis at the Fair*, 7s. 6d.
—— *Bevis*, new edit. 5s.
JEPHSON, A. J. M., *Emin Pasha relief expedition*, 21s.
JERDON. See Low's Standard Series.
JOHNSTON, H. H., *The Congo*, 21s.
JOHNSTON-LAVIS, H. J., *South Italian Volcanoes*, 15s.
JOHNSTONE, D. L., *Land of the Mountain Kingdom*, now edit. 3s. 6d. and 2s. 6d.
JONES, MRS. HERBERT, *Sandringham, Past and Present*, illust., new edit. 8s. 6d.
JULIEN, F., *Conversational French Reader*, 2s. 6d.
—— *English Student's French Examiner*, 2s.
—— *First Lessons in Conversational French Grammar*, n. ed. 1s.
—— *French at Home and at School*, Book I. accidence, 2s.; key, 3s.
—— *Petites Leçons de Conversation et de Grammaire*, n. ed. 3s.
—— *Petites Leçons*, with phrases, 3s. 6d.
—— *Phrases of Daily Use*, separately, 6d.
KARR, H. W. SETON, *Shores and Alps of Alaska*, 16s.
KARSLAND, VEVA, *Women and their Work*, 1s.
KAY. See Foreign Countries.
KENNEDY, E. B., *Blacks and Bushrangers*, now edit. 5s., 3s. 6d. and 2s. 6d.
KERR, W. M., *Far Interior, the Cape, Zambesi, &c.*, 2 vols. 32s.
KERSHAW, S. W., *Protestants from France in their English Home*, 6s.
KETT, C. W., *Rubens*, 3s. 6d.

Khedives and Pashas, 7s. 6d.
KILNER, E. A., *Four Welsh Counties*, 5s.
King and Commons. See Cavalier in Bayard Series.
KINGSLEY, R. G., *Children of Westminster Abbey*, 5s.
KINGSTON. See Low's Standard Books.
KIPLING, RUDYARD, *Soldiers Three, &c.*, stories, 1s.
—— *Story of the Gadsbys*, new edit. 1s.
—— *In Black and White, &c.*, stories, 1s.
—— *Wee Willie Winkie, &c.*, stories, 1s.
—— *Under the Deodars, &c.*, stories, 1s.
—— *Phantom Rickshaw, &c.*, stories, 1s.
*** The six collections of stories may also be had in 2 vols. 3s. 6d. each.
—— *Stories*, Library Edition, 2 vols. 6s. each.
KIRKALDY, W. G., *David Kirkaldy's Mechanical Testing*, 84s.
KNIGHT, A. L., *In the Web of Destiny*, 7s. 6d.
—— E. F., *Cruise of the Falcon*, new edit. 3s. 6d.
—— E. J., *Albania and Montenegro*, 12s. 6d.
—— V. C., *Church Unity*, 5s.
KNOX, T. W., *Boy Travellers*, new edit. 5s.
KNOX-LITTLE, W. J., *Sermons*, 3s. 6d.
KUNHARDT, C. P., *Small Yachts*, new edit. 50s.
—— *Steam Yachts*, 16s.
KWONG, *English Phrases*, 21s.
LABOULLAYE, E., *Abdallah*, 2s. 6d.
LALANNE, *Etching*, 12s. 6d.

LAMB, Chas., *Essays of Elia*, with designs by C. O. Murray, 6s.
LAMBERT, *Angling Literature*, 3s. 6d.
Landscape Painters of Holland. See Great Artists.
LANDSEER. See Great Artists.
LANGLEY, S. P., *New Astronomy*, 10s. 6d.
LANIER, S., *Boy's Froissart*, 7s. 6d.; *King Arthur*, 7s. 6d.; *Mabinogion*, 7s. 6d.; *Percy*, 7s. 6d.
LANSDELL, Henry, *Through Siberia*, 1 v. 15s. and 10s. 6d.
—— *Russia in Central Asia*, 2 vols. 42s.
—— *Through Central Asia*, 12s.
LARDEN, W., *School Course on Heat*, n. ed. 5s.
LAURIE, A., *Secret of the Magian, the Mystery of Ecbatana*, illus. 6s. See also Low's Standard Books.
LAWRENCE, Sergeant, *Autobiography*, 6s.
—— and ROMNEY. See Great Artists.
LAYARD, Mrs., *West Indies*, 2s. 6d.
LEA, H. C., *Inquisition*, 3 vols. 42s.
LEARED, A., *Marocco*, n. ed. 16s.
LEAVITT, *New World Tragedies*, 7s. 6d.
LEFFINGWELL, W. B., *Shooting*, 18s.
—— *Wild Fowl Shooting*, 10s. 6d.
LEFROY, W., Dean. See Preachers.
LELAND, C. G., *Algonquin Legends*, 8s.
LEMON, M., *Small House over the Water*, 6s.

Leo XIII. Life, 18s.
Leonardo da Vinci. See Great Artists.
—— *Literary Works*, by J. P. Richter, 2 vols. 232s.
LIEBER, *Telegraphic Cipher*, 42s. nett.
Like unto Christ. See Gentle Life Series.
LITTLE, Arch. J., *Yang-tse Gorges*, n. ed., 10s. 6d.
Little Masters of Germany. See Great Artists.
LONGFELLOW, *Miles Standish*, illus. 21s.
—— *Maidenhood*, with col. pl. 2s. 6d.; gilt edges, 3s. 6d.
—— *Nuremberg*, photogr. illu. 31s. 6d.
—— *Song of Hiawatha*, illust. 21s.
LOOMIS, E., *Astronomy*, n. ed. 8s. 6d.
LORNE, Marquis of, *Canada and Scotland*, 7s. 6d.
—— *Palmerston.* See Prime Ministers.
Louis, St. See Bayard Series.
Low's French Readers, edit. by C. F. Clifton, I. 3d., II. 3d., III. 6d.
—— *German Series.* See Goethe, Meissner, Sandars, and Schiller.
—— *London Charities*, annually, 1s. 6d.; sewed, 1s.
—— *Illustrated Germ. Primer*, 1s.
—— *Infant Primers*, I. illus. 3d.; II. illus. 6d. and 7d.
—— *Pocket Encyclopædia*, with plates, 3s. 6d.; roan, 4s. 6d.
—— *Readers*, I., 9d.; II., 10d.; III., 1s.; IV., 1s. 3d.; V., 1s. 4d.; VI., 1s. 6d.

Low's Select Parchment Series.
Aldrich (T. B.) Friar Jerome's Beautiful Book, 3s. 6d.
Lewis (Rev. Gerrard), Ballads of the Cid, 2s. 6d.
Whittier (J. G.) The King's Missive. 3s. 6d.

Low's Stand. Library of Travel (except where price is stated), per volume, 7s. 6d.
1. Butler, Great Lone Land; also 3s. 6d.
2. —— Wild North Land.
3. Stanley (H. M.) Coomassie, 3s. 6d.
4. —— How I Found Livingstone; also 3s. 6d.
5. —— Through the Dark Continent, 1 vol. illust., 12s. 6d.; also 3s. 6d.
8. MacGahan (J. A.) Oxus.
9. Spry, voyage, *Challenger*.
10. Burnaby's Asia Minor, 10s. 6d.
11. Schweinfurth's Heart of Africa, 2 vols. 15s.; also 3s. 6d. each.
12. Marshall (W.) Through America.
13. Lansdell (H). Through Siberia, 10s. 6d.
14. Coote, South by East, 10s. 6d.
15. Knight, Cruise of the *Falcon*, also 3s. 6d.
16. Thomson (Joseph) Through Masai Land.
19. Ashe (R. P.) Two Kings of Uganda, 3s. 6d.

Low's Standard Novels (except where price is stated), 6s.
Baker, John Westacott.
Black (W.) Craig Royston.
—— Daughter of Heth.
—— House Boat.
—— In Far Lochaber.
—— In Silk Attire.
—— Kilmeny.
—— Lady Siverdale's Sweetheart.
—— New Prince Fortunatus.
—— Penance of John Logan.
—— Stand Fast, Craig Royston!
—— Sunrise.
—— Three Feathers.

Low's Stand. Novels—continued
Blackmore (R. D.) Alice Lorraine.
—— Christowell.
—— Clara Vaughan.
—— Cradock Nowell.
—— Cripps the Carrier.
—— Ereme, or My Father's Sins.
—— Kit and Kitty.
—— Lorna Doone.
—— Mary Anerley.
—— Sir Thomas Upmore.
—— Springhaven.
Brémont, Gentleman Digger.
Brown (Robert) Jack Abbott's Log.
Bynner, Agnes Surriage.
—— Begum's Daughter.
Cable (G. W.) Bonaventure, 5s.
Coleridge (C. R.) English Squire.
Craddock, Despot of Broomsedgo.
Croker (Mrs. B. M.) Some One Else.
Cumberland (Stuart) Vasty Deep.
De Leon, Under the Stars and Crescent.
Edwards (Miss Betham) Half-way.
Eggleston, Juggernaut.
French Heiress in her own Chateau.
Gilliat (E.) Story of the Dragonnades.
Hardy (A. S.) Passe-rose.
—— (Thos.) Far from the Madding.
—— Hand of Ethelberta.
—— Laodicean.
—— Mayor of Casterbridge.
—— Pair of Blue Eyes.
—— Return of the Native.
—— Trumpet-Major.
—— Two on a Tower.
Harkut, Conspirator.
Hutton (J.) Old House at Sandwich.
—— Three Recruits.
Hoey (Mrs. Cashel) Golden Sorrow.
—— Out of Court.
—— Stern Chase.
Howard (Blanche W.) Open Door.
Ingelow (Jean) Don John.
—— John Jerome, 5s.
—— Sarah de Berenger.
Lathrop, Newport, 5s.
Mac Donald (Geo.) Adela Cathcart.
—— Guild Court.

Low's Stand. Novels—continued.
Mac Donald (Geo.) Mary Marston.
—— Orts.
—— Stephen Archer, &c.
—— The Vicar's Daughter.
—— Weighed and Wanting.
Macmaster, Our Pleasant Vices.
Macquoid (Mrs.) Diane.
Musgrave (Mrs.) Miriam.
Osborn, Spell of Ashtaroth, 5s.
Prince Maskiloff.
Riddell (Mrs.) Alaric Spenceley.
—— Daisies and Buttercups.
—— Senior Partner.
—— Struggle for Fame.
Russell (W. Clark) Betwixt the Forelands.
—— Frozen Pirate.
—— Jack's Courtship.
—— John Holdsworth.
—— Little Loo.
—— My Watch Below.
—— Ocean Free Lance.
—— Sailor's Sweetheart.
—— Sea Queen.
—— Strange Voyage.
—— The Lady Maud.
—— Wreck of the *Grosvenor*.
Stenart, Kilgroom.
Stockton (F. R.) Ardis Claverden.
—— Bee-man of Orn, 5s.
—— Hundredth Man.
—— The late Mrs. Null.
Stoker, Snake's Pass.
Stowe (Mrs.) Old Town Folk.
—— Poganuc People.
Thomas, House on the Scar.
Thomson, Ulu, an African Romance.
Tourgee, Murvale Eastman.
Tytler (S.) Duchess Frances.
Vane, From the Dead.
Wallace (Lew.) Ben Hur.
Warner, Little Journey in the World.
Woolson (Constance Fenimore) Anne.
—— East Angles.
—— For the Major, 5s.
—— Jupiter Lights.
  See also Sea Stories.

Low's Stand. Novels, new issue at short intervals, 2s. 6d. and 2s.
Blackmore, Alice Lorraine.
—— Christowell.
—— Clara Vaughan.
—— Cripps the Carrier.
—— Kit and Kitty.
—— Lorna Doone.
—— Mary Anerley.
—— Tommy Upmore.
Cable, Bonaventure.
Croker, Some One Else.
Cumberland, Vasty Deep.
De Leon, Under the Stars.
Edwards, Half-way.
Hardy, Laodicean.
—— Madding Crowd.
—— Mayor of Casterbridge.
—— Trumpet-Major.
—— Two on a Tower.
Hatton, Old House at Sandwich.
—— Three Recruits.
Hooy, Golden Sorrow.
—— Out of Court.
—— Stern Chase.
Holmes, Guardian Angel.
Ingelow, John Jerome.
—— Sarah de Berenger.
Mac Donald, Adela Cathcart.
—— Guild Court.
—— Stephen Archer.
—— Vicar's Daughter.
Oliphant, Innocent.
Riddell, Daisies and Buttercups.
—— Senior Partner.
Stockton, Bee-man of Orn, 5s.
—— Dusantes.
—— Mrs. Lecks and Mrs. Aleshine.
Stowe, Dred.
—— Old Town Folk.
—— Poganuc People.
Thomson, Ulu.
Walford, Her Great Idea, &c., Stories.
Low's German Series, a graduated course. See "German."
Low's Readers. See English Reader and French Reader.
Low's Standard Books for Boys, with numerous illustrations, 2s. 6d. each; gilt edges, 3s. 6d.

Low's Stand. Books for Boys—continued.

Adventures in New Guinea: the Narrative of Louis Tregance.
Biart (Lucien) Adventures of a Young Naturalist.
—— My Rambles in the New World.
Boussenard, Crusoes of Guiana.
—— Gold Seekers, a sequel to the above.
Butler (Col. Sir Wm., K.C.B.) Red Cloud, the Solitary Sioux: a Tale of the Great Prairie.
Cahun (Leon) Adventures of Captain Mago.
—— Blue Banner.
Célière, Startling Exploits of the Doctor.
Chaillu (Paul du) Wild Life under the Equator.
Collingwood (Harry) Under the Meteor Flag.
—— Voyage of the *Aurora*.
Cozzens (S. W.) Marvellous Country.
Dodge (Mrs.) Hans Brinker; or, The Silver Skates.
Du Chaillu (Paul) Stories of the Gorilla Country.
Erckmann - Chatrian, Brothers Rantzau.
Fenn (G. Manville) Off to the Wilds.
—— Silver Cañon.
Groves (Percy) Charmouth Grange; a Tale of the 17th Century.
Heldmann (B.) Mutiny on Board the Ship *Leander*.
Henty (G. A.) Cornet of Horse: a Tale of Marlborough's Wars.
—— Jack Archer; a Tale of the Crimea.
—— Winning his Spurs: a Tale of the Crusades.
Johnstone (D. Lawson) Mountain Kingdom.
Kennedy (E. B.) Blacks and Bushrangers in Queensland.
Kingston (W. H. G.) Ben Burton; or, Born and Bred at Sea.
—— Captain Mugford; or, Our Salt and Fresh Water Tutors.
—— Dick Cheveley.
—— Heir of Kilfinnan.

Low's Stand. Books for Boys—continued.

Kingston (W. H. G.) Snowshoes and Canoes.
—— Two Supercargoes.
—— With Axe and Rifle on the Western Prairies.
Laurie (A.) Conquest of the Moon.
—— New York to Brest in Seven Hours.
MacGregor (John) A Thousand Miles in the *Rob Roy* Canoe on Rivers and Lakes of Europe.
Maclean (H. E.) Maid of the Ship *Golden Age*.
Meunier, Great Hunting Grounds of the World.
Muller, Noble Words and Deeds.
Perelaer, The Three Deserters; or, Ran Away from the Dutch.
Reed (Talbot Baines) Sir Ludar: a Tale of the Days of the Good Queen Bess.
Rousselet (Louis) Drummer-boy: a Story of the Time of Washington.
—— King of the Tigers.
—— Serpent Charmer.
—— Son of the Constable of France.
Russell (W. Clark) Frozen Pirates.
Stanley, My Kalulu—Prince, King and Slave.
Winder (F. H.) Lost in Africa.

Low's Standard Series of Books by popular writers, cloth gilt, 2s.; gilt edges, 2s. 6d. each.

Alcott (L. M.) A Rose in Bloom.
—— An Old-Fashioned Girl.
—— Aunt Jo's Scrap Bag.
—— Eight Cousins, illust.
—— Jack and Jill.
—— Jimmy's Cruise.
—— Little Men.
—— Little Women and Little Women Wedded.
—— Lulu's Library, illust.
—— Shawl Straps.
—— Silver Pitchers.
—— Spinning-Wheel Stories.
—— Under the Lilacs, illust.
—— Work and Beginning Again, ill.

Low's Stand. Series—continued.
Alden (W. L.) Jimmy Brown, illust.
—— Trying to Find Europe.
Bunyan (John) Pilgrim's Progress, (extra volume), gilt, 2s.
De Witt (Madame) An Only Sister.
Francis (Francis) Eric and Ethel, illust.
Holm (Saxe) Draxy Miller's Dowry.
Jerdon (Gert.) Keyhole Country, illust.
Robinson (Phil) In My Indian Garden.
—— Under the Punkah.
Roe (E. P.) Nature's Serial Story.
Saintine, Picciola.
Samuels, Forecastle to Cabin, illust.
Sandeau (Jules) Seagull Rock.
Stowe (Mrs.) Dred.
—— Ghost in the Mill, &c.
—— My Wife and I.
—— We and our Neighbours.
See also Low's Standard Series.
Tooley (Mrs.) Life of Harriet Beecher Stowe.
Warner (C. Dudley) In the Wilderness.
—— My Summer in a Garden.
Whitney (Mrs.) A Summer in Leslie Goldthwaite's Life.
—— Faith Gartney's Girlhood.
—— Hitherto.
—— Real Folks.
—— The Gayworthys.
—— We Girls.
—— The Other Girls: a Sequel.
⁎ *A new illustrated list of books for boys and girls, with portraits of celebrated authors, sent post free on application.*
LOWELL, J. R., *Among my Books*, Series I. and II., 7s. 6d. each.
—— *My Study Windows*, n. ed. 1s.
—— *Vision of Sir Launfal*, illus. 63d.
MACDONALD, A., *Our Sceptred Isle*, 3s. 6d.
—— D., *Oceania*, 6s.

MACDONALD, GEO., *Castle Warlock, a Homely Romance*, 3 vols. 31s. 6d.
—— See also Low's Standard Novels.
—— SIR JOHN A., *Life*.
MACDOWALL, ALEX. B., *Curve Pictures of London*, 1s.
MACGAHAN, J. A., *Oxus*, 7s. 6d.
MACGOUN, *Commercial Correspondence*, 5s.
MACGREGOR, J., *Rob Roy in the Baltic*, n. ed. 3s. 6d. and 2s. 6d.
—— *Rob Roy Canoe*, new edit., 3s. 6d. and 2s. 6d.
—— *Yawl Rob Roy*, new edit., 3s. 6d. and 2s. 6d.
MACKENNA, *Brave Men in Action*, 10s. 6d.
MACKENZIE, SIR MORELL, *Fatal Illness of Frederick the Noble*, 2s. 6d.
MACKINNON and SHADBOLT, *South African Campaign*, 50s.
MACLAREN, A. See Preachers.
MACLEAN, H. E. See Low's Standard Books.
MACMASTER. See Low's Standard Novels.
MACMURDO, E., *History of Portugal*, 21s.; II. 21s.; III. 21s.
MAHAN, A. T., *Influence of Sea Power on History*, 18s.
Maid of Florence, 10s. 6d.
MAIN, MRS., *High Life*, 10s. 6d.
—— See also Burnaby, Mrs.
MALAN, A. N., *Cobbler of Cornikeranium*, 5s.
—— C. F. DE M., *Eric and Connie's Cruise*, 5s.
Man's Thoughts. See Gentle Life Series.
MANLEY, J. J., *Fish and Fishing*, 6s.

MANTEGNA and FRANCIA. See Great Artists.
MARCH, F. A., *Comparative Anglo-Saxon Grammar*, 12s.
—— *Anglo-Saxon Reader*, 7s. 6d.
MARKHAM, ADM., *Naval Career*, 14s.
—— *Whaling Cruise*, new edit. 7s. 6d.
—— C. R., *Peru.* See Foreign Countries.
—— *Fighting Veres*, 18s.
—— *War Between Peru and Chili*, 10s. 6d.
MARSH, G. P., *Lectures on the English Language*, 16s.
—— *Origin and History of the English Language*, 18s.
MARSHALL, W. G., *Through America*, new edit. 7s. 6d.
MARSTON, E., *How Stanley wrote " In Darkest Africa,"* 1s.
—— See also Amateur Angler, Frank's Ranche, and Fresh Woods.
—— W., *Eminent Actors*, n. ed. 6s.
MARTIN, J. W., *Float Fishing and Spinning*, new edit. 2s.
Massage. See Nursing Record Series.
MATTHEWS, J. W., *Incwadi Yami*, 14s.
MAURY, M. F., *Life*, 12s. 6d.
—— *Physical Geography and Meteorology of the Sea*, new ed. 6s.
MEISSNER, A. L., *Children's Own German Book* (Low's Series), 1s. 6d.
—— *First German Reader* (Low's Series), 1s. 6d.
—— *Second German Reader* (Low's Series), 1s. 6d.
MEISSONIER. See Great Artists.

MELBOURNE, LORD. See Prime Ministers.
MELIO, G. L., *Swedish Drill*, 1s. 6d.
MENDELSSOHN *Family*, 1729-1847, Letters and Journals, 2 vols. 30s.; new edit. 30s.
—— See also Great Musicians.
MERRIFIELD, J., *Nautical Astronomy*, 7s. 6d.
MERRYLEES, J., *Carlsbad*, 7s. 6d. and 9s.
MESNEY,W., *Tungking*,3s. 6d.
Metal Workers' Recipes and Processes, by W. T. Brannt,12s.6d.
MEUNIER, V. See Low's Standard Books.
Michelangelo. See Great Artists.
MILFORD, P. *Ned Stafford's Experiences*, 5s.
MILL, JAMES. See English Philosophers.
MILLS, J., *Alternative Elementary Chemistry*, 1s. 6d.
—— *Chemistry Based on the Science and Art Syllabus*, 2s. 6d.
—— *Elementary Chemistry*, answers, 2 vols. 1s. each.
MILTON'S *Allegro*. See Choice Editions.
MITCHELL, D.G.(Ik. Marvel) *English Lands, Letters and Kings*, 2 vols. 6s. each.
—— *Writings*, new edit. per vol. 5s.
MITFORD, J., *Letters*, 3s. 6d.
—— MISS, *Our Village*, illust. 5s.
Modern Etchings, 63s. & 31s.6d.
MOLLETT, J. W., *Dictionary of Words in Art and Archæology*, illust. 15s.
—— *Etched Examples*, 31s. 6d. and 63s.
—— See also Great Artists.

MONCK. See English Philosophers.
MONEY, E., *The Truth About America*, 5s.; now edit. 2s. 6d.
MONKHOUSE. See G. Artists.
Montaigne's Essays, revised by J. Hain Friswell, 2s. 6d.
—— See Gentle Life Series.
MOORE, J. M., *New Zealand for Emigrant, Invalid, and Tourist*, 5s.
MORFILL, W. R., *Russia*, 3s. 6d.
MORLEY, HENRY, *English Literature in the Reign of Victoria*, 2s. 6d.
—— *Five Centuries of English Literature*, 2s.
MORSE, E. S., *Japanese Homes*, new edit. 10s. 6d.
MORTEN, *Hospital Life*, 1s.
MORTIMER, J., *Chess Player's Pocket-Book*, new edit. 1s.
MORWOOD, V. S., *Our Gipsies*, 18s.
MOSS, F. J., *Great South Sea*, 8s. 6d.
MOSSMAN, S., *Japan*, 3s. 6d.
MOTTI, PIETRO, *Elementary Russian Grammar*, 2s. 6d.
—— *Russian Conversation Grammar*, 5s.; Key, 2s.
MOULE, H. C. G., *Sermons*, 3s. 6d.
MOXLEY, *West India Sanatorium. and Barbados*, 3s. 6d.
MOXON, W., *Pilocereus Senilis*, 3s. 6d.
MOZART, 3s. Gr. Musicians.
MULLER, E. See Low's Standard Books.
MULLIN, J. P., *Moulding and Pattern Making*, 12s. 6d.
MULREADY, 3s. 6d. Great Artists.
MURILLO. See Great Artists.

MUSGRAVE, MRS. See Low's Standard Novels.
—— *SavageLondon*, n. e. 3s. 6d.
My Comforter, &c., Religious Poems, 2s. 6d.
Napoleon I. See Bayard Series.
Napoleon I. and Marie Louise, 7s. 6d.
NELSON, WOLFRED, *Panama*, 6s.
Nelson's Words and Deeds, 3s. 6d.
NETHERCOTE, *Pytchley Hunt*, 8s. 6d.
New Democracy, 1s.
New Zealand, chromos, by Barraud, 168s.
NICHOLSON, *British Association Work and Workers*, 1s.
Nineteenth Century, a Monthly Review, 2s. 6d. per No.
NISBET, HUME, *Life and Nature Studies*, 6s.
NIXON, *Story of the Transvaal*, 12s. 6d.
Nordenskiöld's Voyage, trans. 21s.
NORDHOFF, C., *California*, new edit. 12s. 6d.
NORRIS, RACHEL, *Nursing Notes*, 2s.
NORTH, W., *Roman Fever*, 25s.
Northern Fairy Tales, 5s.
NORTON, C. L., *Florida*, 5s.
NORWAY, G., *How Martin Drake Found his Father* illus. 5s.
NUGENT'S *French Dictionary*, new edit. 3s.
Nuggets of the Gouph, 3s.
Nursing Record Series, text books and manuals. Edited by Charles F. Rideal.
1. Lectures to Nurses on Antiseptics in Surgery. By E. Stanmore Bishop. With coloured plates, 2s.

Nursing Record Series—contin.
2. Nursing Notes. Medical and Surgical information. For Hospital Nurses, &c. With illustrations and a glossary of terms. By Rachel Norris (née Williams), late Acting Superintendent of Royal Victoria Military Hospital at Suez, 2s.
3. Practical Electro-Therapeutics. By Arthur Harries, M.D., and H. Newman Lawrence. With photographs and diagrams, 1s. 6d.
4. Massage for Beginners. Simple and easy directions for learning and remembering the different movements. By Lucy Fitch, 1s.

O'BRIEN, *Fifty Years of Concession to Ireland*, vol. i. 16s.; vol. ii. 16s.
—— *Irish Land Question*, 2s.
OGDEN, JAMES, *Fly-tying*, 2s. 6d.
O'GRADY, *Bardic Literature of Ireland*, 1s.
—— *History of Ireland*, vol. i. 7s. 6d.; ii. 7s. 6d.
Old Masters in Photo. 73s. 6d.
Orient Line Guide, new edit. 2s. 6d.
ORLEBAR, *Sancta Christina*, 5s.
Other People's Windows. See Gentle Life Series.
OTTÉ, *Denmark and Iceland*, 3s. 6d. Foreign Countries.
Our Little Ones in Heaven, 5s.
Out of School at Eton, 2s. 6d.
OVERBECK. See Great Artists.
OWEN, DOUGLAS, *Marine Insurance*, 15s.
Oxford Days, by a M.A., 2s. 6d.
PALGRAVE, *Chairman's Handbook*, new edit. 2s.
—— *Oliver Cromwell*, 10s. 6d.

PALLISER, *China Collector's Companion*, 5s.
—— *History of Lace*, n. ed. 21s.
PANTON, *Homes of Taste*, 2s. 6d.
PARKE, *Emin Pasha Relief Expedition*, 21s.
PARKER, E. H., *Chinese Account of the Opium War*, 1s. 6d.
PARSONS, J., *Principles of Partnership*, 31s. 6d.
—— T. P., *Marine Insurance*, 2 vols. 63s.
PEACH, *Annals of Swainswick*, 10s. 6d.
Peel. See Prime Ministers.
PELLESCHI, G., *Gran Chaco*, 8s. 6d.
PENNELL, H. C., *Fishing Tackle*, 2s.
—— *Sporting Fish*, 15s. & 30s.
Penny Postage Jubilee, 1s.
PERRY, NORA, *Another Flock of Girls*, illus. by Birch & Copeland, 7s. 6d.
Peru, 3s. 6d. Foreign Countries.
PHELPS, E. S., *Struggle for Immortality*, 5s.
—— SAMUEL, *Life*, by W. M. Phelps and Forbes-Robertson, 12s.
PHILLIMORE, C. M., *Italian Literature*, new. edit. 3s. 6d.
PHILLIPPS, W. M., *English Elegies*, 5s.
PHILLIPS, L. P., *Dictionary of Biographical Reference*, new. edit. 25s.
—— W., *Law of Insurance*, 2 vols. 73s. 6d.
PHILPOT, H. J., *Diabetes Mellitus*, 5s.
—— *Diet Tables*, 1s. each.
Picture Gallery of British Art. I. to VI. 18s. each.
—— *Modern Art*, 3 vols. 31s. 6d. each.

PINTO, *How I Crossed Africa,* 2 vols. 42s.
Playtime Library. See Humphrey and Huntingdon.
Pleasant History of Reynard the Fox, trans. by T. Roscoe, illus. 7s. 6d.
POCOCK, R., *Gravesend Historian,* 5s.
POE, by E. C. Stedman, 3s. 6d.
—— *Raven,* ill. by G. Doré, 63s.
Poems of the Inner Life, 5s.
Poetry of Nature. See Choice Editions.
Poetry of the Anti-Jacobin, 7s. 6d. and 21s.
POOLE, *Somerset Customs and Legends,* 5s.
—— S. LANE, *Egypt,* 3s. 6d. Foreign Countries.
POPE, *Select Poetical Works,* (Bernhard Tauchnitz Collection), 2s.
PORCHER, A., *Juvenile French Plays,* 1s.
Portraits of Racehorses, 4 vols. 126s.
POSSELT, *Structure of Fibres,* 63s.
—— *Textile Design,* illust. 28s.
POYNTER. See Illustrated Text Books.
Preachers of the Age, 3s. 6d. ea.
Living Theology, by His Grace the Archbishop of Canterbury.
The Conquering Christ, by Rev. A. Maclaren.
Verbum Crucis, by the Bishop of Derry.
Ethical Christianity, by H. P. Hughes.
Sermons, by Canon W. J. Knox-Little.
Light and Peace, by H. R. Reynolds.
Faith and Duty, by A. M. Fairbairn.
Plain Words on Great Themes, by J. O. Dykes.
Sermons, by the Bishop of Ripon.

Preachers of the Age—continued.
Sermons, by Rev. C. H. Spurgeon.
Agoniæ Christi, by Dean Lefroy, of Norwich.
Sermons, by H. C. G. Moule, M.A.
Volumes will follow in quick succession by other well-known men.
Prime Ministers, a series of political biographies, edited by Stuart J. Reid, 3s. 6d. each.
1. Earl of Beaconsfield, by J. Anthony Froude.
2. Viscount Melbourne, by Henry Dunckley ("*Verax*").
3. Sir Robert Peel, by Justin McCarthy.
4. Viscount Palmerston, by the Marquis of Lorne.
5. Earl Russell, by Stuart J. Reid.
6. Right Hon. W. E. Gladstone, by G. W. E. Russell.
7. Earl of Aberdeen, by Sir Arthur Gordon.
8. Marquis of Salisbury, by H. D. Traill.
9. Earl of Derby, by George Saintsbury.
** *An edition, limited to 250 copies, is issued on hand-made paper, medium 8vo, bound in half vellum, cloth sides, gilt top. Price for the 9 vols. 4l. 4s. nett.*
Prince Maskiloff. See Low's Standard Novels.
Prince of Nursery Playmates, new edit. 2s. 6d.
PRITT, T. N., *Country Trout Flies,* 10s. 6d.
Reynolds. See Great Artists.
Purcell. See Great Musicians.
QUILTER, H., *Giotto, Life, &c.* 15s.
RAMBAUD, *History of Russia,* new edit., 3 vols. 21s.
RAPHAEL. See Great Artists.
REDFORD, *Sculpture.* See Illustrated Text-books.
REDGRAVE, *Engl. Painters,* 10s. 6d. and 12s.

In all Departments of Literature. 25

REED, Sir E. J., *Modern Ships of War*, 10s. 6d.
—— T. B., *Roger Ingleton, Minor*, 5s.
—— *Sir Ludar*. See Low's Standard Books.
REID, Mayne, Capt., *Stories of Strange Adventures*, illust. 5s.
—— Stuart J. See Prime Ministers.
—— T. Wemyss, *Land of the Bey*, 10s. 6d.
Remarkable Bindings in British Museum, 168s.; 94s. 6d.; 73s. 6d. and 63s.
REMBRANDT. See Great Artists.
Reminiscences of a Boyhood, 6s.
REMUSAT, *Memoirs*, Vols. I. and II. new ed. 16s. each.
—— *Select Letters*, 16s.
REYNOLDS. See Gr. Artists.
—— Henry R., *Light & Peace, &c. Sermons*, 3s. 6d.
RICHARDS, J. W., *Aluminium*, new edit. 21s.
RICHARDSON, *Choice of Books*, 3s. 6d.
RICHTER, J. P., *Italian Art*, 42s.
—— See also Great Artists.
RIDDELL. See Low's Standard Novels.
RIDEAL, *Women of the Time*, 14s.
RIFFAULT, *Colours for Painting*, 31s. 6d.
RIIS, *How the Other Half Lives*, 10s. 6d.
RIPON, Bp. of. See Preachers.
ROBERTS, Miss, *France*. See Foreign Countries.
—— W., *English Bookselling*, earlier history, 7s. 6d.
ROBIDA, A., *Toilette*, coloured, 7s. 6d.

ROBINSON, "*Romeo*" *Coates*, 7s. 6d.
—— *Noah's Ark*, n. ed. 3s. 6d.
—— *Sinners & Saints*, 10s. 6d.
—— See also Low's Standard Series.
—— *Wealth and its Sources*, 5s.
—— W. C., *Law of Patents*, 3 vols. 105s.
ROCHEFOUCAULD. See Bayard Series.
ROCKSTRO, *History of Music*, new ed. 14s.
RODRIGUES, *Panama Canal*, 5s.
ROE, E. P. See Low's Standard Series.
ROGERS, S. See Choice Editions.
ROLFE, *Pompeii*, 7s. 6d.
Romantic Stories of the Legal Profession, 7s. 6d.
ROMNEY. See Great Artists.
ROOSEVELT, Blanche R. *Home Life of Longfellow*, 7s. 6d.
ROSE, J., *Mechanical Drawing*, 16s.
—— *Practical Machinist*, new ed. 12s. 6d.
—— *Key to Engines*, 8s. 6d.
—— *Modern Steam Engines*, 31s. 6d.
—— *Steam Boilers*, 12s. 6d.
Rose Library. Popular Literature of all countries, per vol. 1s., unless the price is given.
Alcott (L. M.) Eight Cousins, 2s.; cloth, 3s. 6d.
—— Jack and Jill, 2s.; cloth, 5s.
—— Jimmy's cruise in the *Pinafore*, 2s.; cloth, 3s. 6d.
—— Little Women.
—— Little Women Wedded; Nos. 4 and 5 in 1 vol. cloth, 3s. 6d.
—— Little Men, 2s.; cloth gilt, 3s. 6d.

Rose Library—continued.
Alcott (L. M.) Old-fashioned Girls, 2s.; cloth, 3s. 6d.
—— Rose in Bloom, 2s.; cl. 3s. 6d.
—— Silver Pitchers.
—— Under the Lilacs, 2s.; cloth, 3s. 6d.
—— Work, A Story of Experience, 2 vols. in 1, cloth, 3s. 6d.
Stowe (Mrs.) Pearl of Orr's Island.
—— Minister's Wooing.
—— We and Our Neighbours, 2s.
—— My Wife and I, 2s.
Dodge (Mrs.) Hans Brinker, or, The Silver Skates, 1s.; cloth, 5s.; 3s. 6d.; 2s. 6d.
Lowell (J. R.) My Study Windows.
Holmes (Oliver Wendell) Guardian Angel, cloth, 2s.
Warner (C. D.) My Summer in a Garden, cloth, 2s.
Stowe (Mrs.) Dred, 2s.; cloth gilt, 3s. 6d.
Carleton (W.) City Ballads, 2 vols. in 1, cloth gilt, 2s. 6d.
—— Legends, 2 vols. in 1, cloth gilt, 2s. 6d.
—— Farm Ballads, 6d. and 9d.; 3 vols. in 1, cloth gilt, 3s. 6d.
—— Farm Festivals, 3 vols. in 1, cloth gilt, 3s. 6d.
—— Farm Legends, 3 vols. in 1, cloth gilt, 3s. 6d.
Clients of Dr. Bernagius, 2 vols.
Howells (W. D.) Undiscovered Country.
Clay (C. M.) Baby Rue.
—— Story of Helen Troy.
Whitney (Mrs.) Hitherto, 2 vols. cloth, 3s. 6d.
Fawcett (E.) Gentleman of Leisure.
Butler, Nothing to Wear.
ROSS, Mars, *Cantabria*, 21s.
ROSSINI, &c., See Great Musicians.
Rothschilds, by J. Reeves, 7s. 6d.
Roughing it after Gold, by Rux, new edit. 1s.
ROUSSELET. See Low's Standard Books.

ROWBOTHAM, F. J., *Prairie Land*, 5s.
Royal Naval Exhibition, a souvenir, illus. 1s.
RUBENS. See Great Artists.
RUGGLES, H. J., *Shakespeare's Method*, 7s. 6d.
RUSSELL, G.W. E., *Gladstone*. See Prime Ministers.
—— W. Clark, *Mrs. Dines' Jewels*, 2s. 6d.
—— *Nelson's Words and Deeds*, 3s. 6d.
—— *Sailor's Language*, illus. 3s. 6d.
—— See also Low's Standard Novels and Sea Stories.
—— W. Howard, *Prince of Wales' Tour*, illust. 52s. 6d. and 84s.
Russia. See Foreign Countries.
Saints and their Symbols, 3s. 6d.
SAINTSBURY, G., *Earl of Derby*. See Prime Ministers.
SAINTINE, *Picciola*, 2s. 6d. and 2s. See Low's Standard Series.
SALISBURY, Lord. See Prime Ministers.
SAMUELS. See Low's Standard Series.
SANDARS, *German Primer*, 1s.
SANDEAU, *Seagull Rock*, 2s. and 2s. 6d. Low's Standard Series.
SANDLANDS, *How to Develop Vocal Power*, 1s.
SAUER, *European Commerce*, 5s.
—— *Italian Grammar* (Key, 2s.), 5s.
—— *Spanish Dialogues*, 2s. 6d.
—— *Spanish Grammar* (Key, 2s.), 5s.
—— *Spanish Reader*, new edit. 3s. 6d.
SAUNDERS, J., *Jaspar Deane*, 10s. 6d.

SCHAACK, M. J., *Anarchy*, 16s.
SCHAUERMANN, *Ornament for technical schools*, 10s. 6d.
SCHERER, *Essays in English Literature*, by G. Saintsbury, 6s.
SCHERR, *English Literature*, history, 8s. 6d.
SCHILLER'S *Prosa*, selections by Buchheim. Low's Series 2s. 6d.
SCHUBERT. See Great Musicians.
SCHUMANN. See Great Musicians.
SCHWEINFURTH. See Low's Standard Library.
Scientific Education of Dogs, 6s.
SCOTT, LEADER, *Renaissance of Art in Italy*, 31s. 6d.
—— See also Illust. Text-books.
—— SIR GILBERT, *Autobiography*, 18s.
—— W. B. See Great Artists.
SELMA, ROBERT, *Poems*, 5s.
SERGEANT, L. See Foreign Countries.
Shadow of the Rock, 2s. 6d.
SHAFTESBURY. See English Philosophers.
SHAKESPEARE, ed. by R. G. White, 3 vols. 36s.; édit. de luxe, 63s.
—— *Annals; Life & Work*, 2s.
—— *Hamlet*, 1603, also 1604, 7s. 6d.
—— *Hamlet*, by Karl Elze, 12s. 6d.
—— *Heroines*, by living painters, 105s.; artists' proofs, 630s.
—— *Macbeth*, with etchings, 105s. and 52s. 6d.
—— *Songs and Sonnets*. See Choice Editions.
—— *Taming of the Shrew*, adapted for drawing-room, paper wrapper, 1s.

SHEPHERD, *British School of Painting*, 2nd edit. 5s.; 3rd edit. sewed, 1s.
SHERIDAN, *Rivals*, col. plates, 52s. 6d. nett; art. pr. 105s. nett.
SHIELDS, G. O., *Big Game of North America*, 21s.
—— *Cruisings in the Cascades*, 10s. 6d.
SHOCK, W. H., *Steam Boilers*, 73s. 6d.
SIDNEY. See Gentle Life Series.
Silent Hour. See Gentle Life Series.
SIMKIN, *Our Armies*, plates in imitation of water-colour (5 parts at 1s), 6s.
SIMSON, *Ecuador and the Putumayor*, 8s. 6d.
SKOTTOWE, *Hanoverian Kings*, new edit. 3s. 6d.
SLOANE, T. O., *Home Experiments*, 6s.
SMITH, HAMILTON, and LEGROS' *French Dictionary*, 2 vols. 16s., 21s., and 22s.
SMITH, EDWARD, *Cobbett*, 2 vols. 24s.
—— G., *Assyria*, 18s.
—— *Chaldean Account of Genesis*, new edit. by Sayce, 18s.
—— GERARD. See Illustrated Text Books.
—— T. ROGER. See Illustrated Text Books.
Socrates. See Bayard Series.
SOMERSET, *Our Village Life*, 5s.
Spain. See Foreign Countries.
SPAYTH, *Draught Player*, new edit. 12s. 6d.
SPIERS, *French Dictionary*, 2 vols. 18s., half bound, 2 vols., 21s.
SPRY. See Low's Stand. Library.

SPURGEON, C. H. See Preachers.
STANLEY, H. M., *Congo*, 2 vols. 42s. and 21s.
―― *In Darkest Africa*, 2 vols., 42s.
―― *Emin's Rescue*, 1s.
―― See also Low's Standard Library and Low's Standard Books.
START, *Exercises in Mensuration*, 8d.
STEPHENS, F. G., *Celebrated Flemish and French Pictures*, with notes, 28s.
―― See also Great Artists.
STERNE. See Bayard Series.
STERRY, J. Ashby, *Cucumber Chronicles*, 5s.
STEUART, J. A., *Letters to Living Authors*, new edit. 2s. 6d.; édit. de luxe, 10s. 6d.
―― See also Low's Standard Novels.
STEVENS, J. W., *Practical Workings of the Leather Manufacture*, illust. 18s.
―― T., *Around the World on a Bicycle*, over 100 illust. 16s.; part II. 16s.
STEWART, Dugald, *Outlines of Moral Philosophy*, 3s. 6d.
STOCKTON, F. R., *Casting Away of Mrs. Leck*, 1s.
―― *The Dusantes*, a sequel, 1s.
―― *Merry Chanter*, 2s. 6d.
―― *Personally Conducted*, illust. by Joseph Pennell, 7s. 6d.
―― *Rudder Grangers Abroad*, 2s. 6d.
―― *Squirrel Inn*, illust. 6s.
―― *Story of Viteau*, illust. 5s. new edit. 3s. 6d.
―― *Three Burglars*, 1s. & 2s.
―― See also Low's Standard Novels.

STORER, F. H., *Agriculture*, 2 vols., 25s.
STOWE, Edwin. See Great Artists.
―― Mrs., *Flowers and Fruit from Her Writings*, 3s. 6d.
―― *Life . . . her own Words . . . Letters and Original Composition*, 15s.
―― *Life*, told for boys and girls, by S. A. Tooley, 5s., new edit. 2s. 6d. and 2s.
―― *Little Foxes*, cheap edit. 1s.; 4s. 6d.
―― *Minister's Wooing*, 1s.
―― *Pearl of Orr's Island*, 3s. 6d. and 1s.
―― *Uncle Tom's Cabin*, with 126 new illust. 2 vols. 18s.
―― See also Low's Standard Novels and Low's Standard Series.
STRACHAN, J., *New Guinea*, 12s.
STRANAHAN, *French Painting*, 21s.
STRICKLAND, F., *Engadine*, new edit. 5s.
STUTFIELD, *El Maghreb*, ride through Morocco, 8s. 6d.
SUMNER, C., *Memoir*, new edit. 2 vols. 36s.
Sweden and Norway. See Foreign Countries.
Sylvanus Redivivus, 10s. 6d.
SZCZEPANSKI, *Technical Literature*, a directory, 2s
TAINE, H. A., *Origines*, I. Ancient Régime, French Revolution, 3 vols.; Modern Régime, vol. I. 16s.
TAYLOR, H., *English Constitution*, 18s.
―― R. L., *Analysis Tables*, 1s.
―― *Chemistry*, 1s. 6d.
Techno-Chemical Receipt Book, 10s. 6d.

TENNYSON. See Choice Editions.
Ten Years of a Sailor's Life, 7s. 6d.
THAUSING, Malt and Beer, 45s.
THEAKSTON, British Angling Flies, 5s.
Thomas à Kempis Birthday-Book, 3s. 6d.
—— Daily Text-Book, 2s. 6d.
—— See also Gentle Life Series.
THOMAS, BERTHA, House on the Scar, Tale of South Devon, 6s.
THOMSON, JOSEPH. See Low's Standard Library and Low's Standard Novels.
—— W., Algebra, 5s.; without Answers, 4s. 6d.; Key, 1s. 6d.
THORNTON, W. PUGIN, Heads. and what they tell us, 1s.
THORODSEN, J. P., Lad and Lass, 6s.
TICKNOR, G., Memoir, new edit., 2 vols. 21s.
TILESTON, MARY W., Daily Strength, 4s. 6d.
TINTORETTO. See Great Artists.
TITIAN. See Great Artists.
TODD, Life, by J. E. Todd, 12s.
TOURGÉE. See Low's Standard Novels.
TOY, C. H., Judaism, 14s.
Tracks in Norway, 2s., n. ed. 1s.
TRAILL. See Prime Ministers.
Transactions of the Hong Kong Medical Society, vol. I. 12s. 6d.
TROMHOLT, Aurora Borealis, 2 vols., 30s.
TUCKER, Eastern Europe, 15s.
TUCKERMAN, B., English Fiction, 8s. 6d.
—— Lafayette, 2 vols. 12s.
TURNER, J. M. W. See Gr. Artists.

TYSON, Arctic Adventures, 25s.
TYTLER, SARAH. See Low's Standard Novels.
—— M. C., American Literature, vols. I. and II. 24s.
UPTON, H., Dairy Farming, 2s.
Valley Council, by P. Clarke, 6s.
VANDYCK and HALS. See Great Artists.
VANE, DENZIL, Lynn's Court Mystery, 1s.
—— See also Low's Standard Novels.
Vane, Young Sir Harry, 18s.
VELAZQUEZ. See Gr. Artists.
—— and MURILLO, by C. B. Curtis, with etchings, 31s. 6d. and 63s.
VERE, SIR F., Fighting Veres, 18s.
VERNE, J., Works by. See page 31.
Vernet and Delaroche. See Great Artists.
VERSCHUUR, G., At the Antipodes, 7s. 6d.
VIGNY, Cinq Mars, with etchings, 2 vols. 30s.
VINCENT, F., Through and through the Tropics, 10s. 6d.
—— Mrs. H., 40,000 Miles over Land and Water, 2 vols. 21s.; also 3s. 6d.
VIOLLET-LE-DUC, Architecture, 2 vols. 31s. 6d. each.
WAGNER. See Gr. Musicians.
WALERY, Our Celebrities, vol. II. part i., 30s.
WALFORD, MRS. L. B. See Low's Standard Novels.
WALL, Tombs of the Kings of England, 21s.
WALLACE, L., Ben Hur, 2s. 6d.
—— Boyhood of Christ, 15s.
—— See also Low's Stand. Novs.

WALLACE, R., *Rural Economy of Australia and New Zealand*, illust. 21s. nett.

WALLER, C. H., *Names on the Gates of Pearl*, 3s. 6d.

—— *Silver Sockets*, 6s.

WALTON, *Angler*, Lea and Dove edit. by R. B. Marston, with photos., 210s. and 105s.

—— *Wallet-book*, 21s. & 42s.

—— T. H., *Coal-mining*, 25s.

WARNER, C. D., *Their Pilgrimage*, illust. by C. S. Reinhard, 7s. 6d.

—— See also Low's Standard Novels and Low's Standard Series.

WARREN, W. F., *Paradise Found, Cradle of the Human Race*, illust. 12s. 6d.

WASHBURNE, *Recollections (Siege of Paris, &c.)*, 2 vols. 36s.

WATTEAU. See Great Artists.

WEBER. See Great Musicians.

WEBSTER, *Spain*. See Foreign Countries and British Colonies.

WELLINGTON. See Bayard Series.

WELLS, H. P., *Salmon Fisherman*, 6s.

—— *Fly-rods and Tackle*, 10s. 6d.

—— J. W., *Brazil*, 2 vols. 32s.

WENZEL, *Chemical Products of the German Empire*, 25s.

West Indies. See Foreign Countries.

WESTGARTH, *Australasian Progress*, 12s.

WESTOBY, *Postage Stamps; a descriptive Catalogue*, 6s.

WHITE, RHODA E., *From Infancy to Womanhood*, 10s. 6d.

—— R. GRANT, *England without and within*, new ed. 10s. 6d.

—— *Every-day English*, 10s. 6d.

WHITE, R. GRANT, *Studies in Shakespeare*, 10s. 6d.

—— *Words and their Uses*, new edit. 5s.

—— W., *Our English Homer, Shakespeare and his Plays*, 6s.

WHITNEY, MRS. See Low's Standard Series.

WHITTIER, *St. Gregory's Guest*, 5s.

—— *Text and Verse for Every Day in the Year*, selections, 1s. 6d.

WHYTE, *Asia to Europe*, 12s.

WIKOFF, *Four Civilizations*, 6s.

WILKES, G., *Shakespeare*, 16s.

WILKIE. See Great Artists.

WILLS, *Persia as it is*, 8s. 6d.

WILSON, *Health for the People*, 7s. 6d.

WINDER, *Lost in Africa*. See Low's Standard Books.

WINSOR, J., *Columbus*, 21s.

—— *History of America*, 8 vols. per vol. 30s. and 63s.

WITTHAUS, *Chemistry*, 16s.

WOOD, *Sweden and Norway*. See Foreign Countries.

WOLLYS, *Vegetable Kingdom*, 5s.

WOOLSEY, *Communism and Socialism*, 7s. 6d.

—— *International Law*, 6th ed. 18s.

—— *Political Science*, 2 vols. 30s.

WOOLSON, C. FENIMORE. See Low's Standard Novels.

WORDSWORTH. See Choice Editions.

Wreck of the "Grosvenor," 6d.

WRIGHT, H., *Friendship of God*, 6s.

—— T., *Town of Cowper*, 6s.

WRIGLEY, *Algiers Illust.* 45s

Written to Order, 6s.

BOOKS BY JULES VERNE.

WORKS.	Large Crown 8vo. Containing 350 to 600 pp. and from 50 to 100 full-page illustrations.		Containing the whole of the text with some illustrations.	
	Handsome cloth binding, gilt edges.	Plainer binding, plain edges.	Cloth binding, gilt edges, smaller type.	Limp cloth.
	s. d.	s. d.	s. d.	s. d.
20,000 Leagues under the Sea. Parts I. and II.	10 6	5 0	3 6	2 0
Hector Servadac	10 6	5 0	3 6	2 0
The Fur Country	10 6	5 0	3 6	2 0
The Earth to the Moon and a Trip round it	10 6	5 0	2 vols., 2s. en.	2 vols., 1s. ea.
Michael Strogoff	10 6	5 0	3 6	2 0
Dick Sands, the Boy Captain	10 6	5 0	3 6	2 0
Five Weeks in a Balloon	7 6	3 6	2 0	1 0
Adventures of Three Englishmen and Three Russians	7 6	3 6	2 0	1 0
Round the World in Eighty Days	7 6	3 6	2 0	1 0
A Floating City	7 6	3 6	2 0	1 0
The Blockade Runners			2 0	1 0
Dr. Ox's Experiment	—	—	2 0	1 0
A Winter amid the Ice	—	—	2 0	1 0
Survivors of the "Chancellor".	7 6	3 6	3 6	2 0
Martin Paz			2 0	1 0
The Mysterious Island, 3 vols.:—	22 6	10 6	6 0	3 0
I. Dropped from the Clouds	7 6	3 6	2 0	1 0
II. Abandoned	7 6	3 6	2 0	1 0
III. Secret of the Island	7 6	3 6	2 0	1 0
The Child of the Cavern	7 6	3 6	2 0	1 0
The Begum's Fortune	7 6	3 6	2 0	1 0
The Tribulations of a Chinaman	7 6	3 6	2 0	1 0
The Steam House, 2 vols.:—				
I. Demon of Cawnpore	7 6	3 6	2 0	1 0
II. Tigers and Traitors	7 6	3 6	2 0	1 0
The Giant Raft, 2 vols.:—				
I. 800 Leagues on the Amazon	7 6	3 6	2 0	1 0
II. The Cryptogram	7 6	3 6	2 0	1 0
The Green Ray	5 0	3 6	2 0	1 0
Godfrey Morgan	7 6	3 6	2 0	1 0
Kéraban the Inflexible:—				
I. Captain of the "Guidara"	7 6	3 6	2 0	1 0
II. Scarpante the Spy	7 6	3 6	2 0	1 0
The Archipelago on Fire	7 6	3 6	2 0	1 0
The Vanished Diamond	7 6	3 6	2 0	1 0
Mathias Sandorf	10 6	5 0	3 6	2 vols 1 0 each
Lottery Ticket	7 6	3 6	2 0	1 0
The Clipper of the Clouds	7 6	3 6	2 0	1 0
North against South	7 6	3 6		
Adrift in the Pacific	6 0	3 6		
The Flight to France	7 6	3 6		
The Purchase of the North Pole	6 0			
A Family without a Name	6 0			
César Cascabel	6 0			

Celebrated Travels and Travellers. 3 vols. 8vo, 600 pp., 100 full-page illustrations, 7s. 6d., gilt edges, 0s. each:—(1) The Exploration of the World. (2) The Great Navigators of the Eighteenth Century. (3) The Great Explorers of the Nineteenth Century.

PERIODICAL PUBLICATIONS

OF

Sampson Low, Marston & Company, Ld.

SCRIBNER'S MAGAZINE.

A Superb Illustrated Monthly. Price One Shilling.

Containing Contributions from the pens of many well-known Authors, among whom may be mentioned Thomas Bailey Aldrich, Sir Edwin Arnold, Andrew Lang, Sarah Orne Jewett, H. M. Stanley, Robert Louis Stevenson, R. H. Stoddard, Frank R. Stockton.

THE NINETEENTH CENTURY.

A MONTHLY REVIEW. Edited by JAMES KNOWLES.

Price Half-a-Crown.

Amongst the contributors the following representative names may be mentioned:—Lord Tennyson, the Right Hon. W. E. Gladstone, Cardinal Manning, Mr. J. A. Froude, Mr. Ruskin, Mr. G. A. Watts, R.A., Earl Grey, the Earl of Derby, Lord Acton, Mr. Herbert Spencer, Mr. Frederick Harrison, Mr. Algernon C. Swinburne, Mr. Leslie Stephen, Professor Huxley, Sir Theodore Martin, Sir Edward Hamley, Professor Goldwin Smith, and Sir Samuel Baker.

THE PUBLISHERS' CIRCULAR,

AND

BOOKSELLERS' RECORD OF BRITISH & FOREIGN LITERATURE.
WEEKLY. Every Saturday. Price Three-Halfpence.

SUBSCRIPTION.

Inland ... ... Twelve Months (post free) 8s. 6d.
Countries in the Postal Union ... ,, ,, ,, 11s. 0d.

THE FISHING GAZETTE.

A Journal for Anglers.

Edited by R. B. MARSTON, Hon. Treas. of the Fly Fishers' Club.
Published Weekly, price 2d. Subscription, 10s. 6d. per annum.

The *Gazette* contains every week Twenty folio pages of Original Articles on Angling of every kind. The paper has recently been much enlarged and improved.

"Under the editorship of Mr. R. B. Marston the *Gazette* has attained a high standing."—*Daily News*. "An excellent paper."—*The World*.

LONDON: SAMPSON LOW, MARSTON & COMPANY, LIMITED,
ST. DUNSTAN'S HOUSE, FETTER LANE, FLEET STREET, E.C.

www.ingramcontent.com/pod-product-compliance
Lightning Source LLC
Chambersburg PA
CBHW031850220426
43663CB00006B/571